Sex and Gender

REVIEW OF PERSONALITY AND SOCIAL PSYCHOLOGY

Sex and Gender

Editors
PHILLIP SHAVER and CLYDE HENDRICK

7

REVIEW of PERSONALITY and SOCIAL PSYCHOLOGY

Published in cooperation with
the Society for Personality and Social Psychology, Inc.

SAGE PUBLICATIONS
The Publishers of Professional Social Science
Newbury Park   London   New Delhi

For information address:

SAGE Publications, Inc.
2111 West Hillcrest Drive
Newbury Park, California 91320

SAGE Publications Ltd.
28 Banner Street
London EC1Y 8QE
England

SAGE Publications India Pvt. Ltd.
M-32 Market
Greater Kailash I
New Delhi 110 048 India

Printed in the United States of America

International Standard Book Number 0-8039-2929-3
0-8039-2930-7 (pbk.)

International Standard Series Number 0270-1987

THIRD PRINTING

CONTENTS

Editors' Introduction
Phillip Shaver and Clyde Hendrick   7

1. Gender, Genes, and the Social Environment:
   A Biosocial Interactionist Perspective
   Douglas T. Kenrick   14

2. The Troubled Quest for Masculinity,
   Femininity, and Androgyny
   J. G. Morawski   44

3. Social Constructionism and the Study
   of Human Sexuality
   Leonore Tiefer   70

4. Sexual Violence in the Mass Media:
   Social Psychological Implications
   **Daniel Linz, Edward Donnerstein, and
   Steven Penrod**   95

5. Gender, Justice, and the Psychology
   of Entitlement
   Brenda Major   124

6. Gender and Communication
   Elizabeth Aries   149

7. On Explaining Gender Differences:
   The Case of Nonverbal Communication
   Judith A. Hall   177

8. Women's Ways of Knowing: On Gaining a Voice
   **Nancy Rule Goldberger, Blythe McVicker Clinchy,
   Mary Field Belenky, and Jill Mattuck Tarule**   201

9. Women, Men, and the
   Dilemma of Emotion
   Stephanie A. Shields   229

10. Gender Schema Theory and the
    Romantic Tradition
    Sandra Lipsitz Bem   251

11. Children's Sex-Role Stereotypes:
    A Cross-Cultural Analysis
    Vanda Lucia Zammuner   272

12. Parents' Beliefs and Values About
    Sex Roles, Sex Differences, and
    Sexuality: Their Sources and Implications
    John K. Antill   294

EDITORS' INTRODUCTION

When the current wave of feminism began to break 25 years ago, few people anticipated one of its notable effects: the revitalization of academic disciplines as diverse as literature, history, biology, and psychology. Anticipated or not, that is surely what happened.

In the arts, women's neglected contributions have been discovered, displayed, and discussed; in history, women's role in everything from the family, to religion, to the national economy has been reconsidered, and a new emphasis on "real" people's lives (as opposed to the lives of politicians and military leaders) has changed the focus of the discipline. In biology, female researchers have begun to study animal social life and have already proposed new topics and emphases (e.g., infanticide, the importance of friendship and kindness in females' selection of sexual partners). In psychology, hardly a subfield has remained untouched. Sex differences in intelligence, aggressiveness, and sociability, among other traits, have been debated; and in the social-personality subfield, sexuality and what used to be called masculinity-femininity (a hyphenated, bipolar dimension now usually viewed as two orthogonal dimensions) have been reconceptualized. Some psychologists, ourselves included, suspect that psychology's shifting center of gravity, from high-tech experiments on machine-like cognitive processes to naturalistic studies of emotions and close relationships, is due in part to an increased number of female researchers.

Signs of change are also evident in the prevailing philosophies of science. Where once there were only empiricism, operationism, and logical positivism, we now have several competing epistemologies, including social constructionism. Feminist scholars, unhappy with the constraints imposed by existing methodologies and conceptual frameworks, have persistently asked, first, "Why does it have to be this way?"

and, then, "Where did this philosophical straitjacket come from?" Male researchers tend to think that the dominant philosophies and methodologies are inherently correct; female challengers see more readily that conceptual approaches are invented or constructed—and never in a social vacuum.

The results of the feminist challenge, although not always pleasant for scholars who enjoyed the prefeminist status quo, include controversy, rejuvenation, and new directions for research. Because the process of redirection is far from finished, and in fact shows no signs of settling down, it is impossible to provide a simple summing up. What we offer instead is a close look at some of the intellectual action, including an occasional peek backstage, where the struggle with ideas becomes more personal and less tidy. We have gathered together 12 chapters by personality-social psychologists whose work spans the range of current thinking about sex and gender. Each chapter presents new ideas, new problems, and either new data or novel ways of thinking about existing data. The *Review* is an annual book series, not a journal, but it is meant to be as fresh and up-to-date as a monthly or bimonthly periodical. In fact, the authors, editors, and publisher operate on such a tight schedule that our publication lag is considerably shorter than that of most journals. And, in comparison with most journals, we allow authors greater freedom to speculate, to integrate large pieces of intellectual puzzles, and to ask questions and propose new directions. Because authors' goals differ, the format and flavor of the chapters vary. We demand clear prose but otherwise do not dictate terminological or stylistic uniformity.

In the first chapter, Douglas Kenrick asks for trouble, you might say, by advocating a sociobiological approach to some of the sex differences documented by personality and social psychologists, including those found in his own work. As he says in his first paragraph, if you think the nature-nurture controversy is dead, just try slipping the term "sociobiology" into a mixed-sex conversation among psychologists. Kenrick presents a more complex version of sociobiology than most personality-social psychologists are familiar with—a "biosocial interactionist perspective." An advantage of the sociobiological approach is that it offers "distal" explanations of phenomena more usually explained "proximally" by social psychologists. Kenrick provokes rebuttal by saying that the usual kinds of explanation rely on "historical accidents." We placed this chapter first in the volume because it provides a theoretical counterweight to most of the others, which do not consider biological explanations at all.

Chapters 2 and 3 illustrate the social constructionist approach. In Chapter 2, Jill Morawski reviews the ways in which masculinity and femininity have been defined and measured by psychologists over the decades. It is easy for contemporary investigators to laugh at early attempts to measure M-F as a bipolar dimension (with items referring to such masculine activities as spitting on sidewalks!), but it isn't so funny to contemplate the eagerness with which psychologists embraced the idea of androgyny in the 1970s, a reaction suggesting motives more personal than cool pursuit of truth. Says Morawski, "The androgynous image is a mirror of the ideals of contemporary professional life, reflecting a historical moment when women professionals, in particular, required a model that promoted conventionally masculine (instru-mental) actions without compromising the feminine self." She analyzes values and pitfalls implicit in the androgyny construct, and shows why, in terms of metatheory, the "troubled quest for masculinity, femininity, and androgyny" is unlikely to reach a happy ending. Chapter 3 is related, in that Leonore Tiefer adopts a historical and social construc-tionist approach to the question of how human sexuality—which one would certainly expect to be of interest to personality-social psychol-ogists—has become almost the exclusive province of medical profes-sionals. This example illustrates nicely the social and economic processes involved in divvying up topics to distinct scientific disciplines. Before fully abandoning sex to the biologists and medicos, members of our profession might want to take Tiefer's provocative essay to heart.

Chapters 4 and 5 renew one's faith in the potential of experimental social psychology to contribute to the solution of social problems. In Chapter 4, Daniel Linz, Edward Donnerstein, and Steven Penrod summarize recent research concerning the effects on men of watching various kinds of sexually explicit and violent films. They find, in line with an essay by *Ms.* editor Gloria Steinem, that there are important differences between erotica ("mutually pleasurable sexual expression between people who have enough power to be there by positive choice," according to Steinem) and pornography ("violence, dominance, and conquest"). Social psychologists, with good and liberal intentions, contributed in 1970 to a Presidential Commission's conclusion that pornography might not be socially harmful; Linz et al. are prepared to overturn that judgment. Certain kinds of pornography seem to make rape and dehumanization of women more likely—effects obviously worth protesting—and, fortunately, research suggests effective counter-measures. In Chapter 5, Brenda Major summarizes several careful studies of the ways in which men and women pay themselves and others. She and her colleagues have ferreted out explanations for the troubling but well-established fact that women often seem satisfied with what, by male standards, is underpayment. It has been common to attribute such findings to sex differences in values—that is, to women valuing relationships more than money—which has the convenient effect of excusing or explaining away economic injustice. Major argues convincingly against the "different values" approach, and shows how women's conceptions of self-worth in work settings might be enhanced.

Chapters 6 through 9 address various aspects of communication and expression. In Chapter 6, Elizabeth Aries summarizes the large literature on sex differences in verbal and nonverbal communication. Besides presenting many interesting findings, she reveals that no single or simple explanation is likely to work for all situations. Some of the sex differences seem related to men's tendency to dominate groups, for example, but others are not. Some of women's distinctive behaviors in domestic conversations with men seem to be due to the difficulty women have in capturing men's undivided attention. Other differences fail to fit explanations based on assumptions about cross-sex communication: They are greatest when men talk with men and women talk with women, suggesting that they were not designed to maintain particular kinds of relations between the sexes. In Chapter 7, Judith Hall takes up some of the same issues in a more methods-oriented discussion. She shows how far the field of nonverbal communication is from having indisputable explanations, and she suggests ways of combining and evaluating hypotheses and theories. Taken together, these two chapters offer a fascinating overview of a substantial body of data and suggest new directions for future research.

In Chapter 8, Nancy Goldberger, Blythe Clinchy, Mary Belenky, and Jill Tarule provide an overview of their intensive study of women's ways of knowing. Not surprisingly, given Aries's review of women's difficulties in gaining the attention of the men with whom they live, Goldberger et al. find that "in private and professional life, as well as in the classroom, women often feel unheard even when they believe that they have something important to say." Women often talk about intellectual communication and development in terms of "hearing" things, getting in touch with things, having things to say, and gaining a voice. (Men more often talk about "seeing" things and gaining distance from them, or perspective on them.) Goldberger et al. identify five epistemological "positions" occupied by women at different points in intellectual development, ranging from "silence" to "constructed knowledge."

Gender differences in "emotionality" is the topic of Chapter 9, written by Stephanie Shields. She identifies several oddities related to emotions and emotionality—for example, the fact that although women are often viewed as valuing emotion, feminist psychologists have generally steered clear of the topic, perhaps fearing a kind of guilt by association. Another example: Women are generally seen as more emotional than men, but men are the ones known for expressing anger, aggression, and violence. Shields and her coworkers have recently conducted several studies to determine what people mean by emotionality, what kinds of emotion socialization practices have been recommended to parents down through the decades, and how the emotionality of male and female political candidates is evaluated by partisan observers.

The final three chapters form a set. In Chapter 10, Sandra Bem, one of the originators of the androgyny concept and, more recently, of gender schema theory, talks about kinds of schema theories: enlightenment versus romantic. Most of social-personality psychology adheres to an enlightenment (rational, realistic) conception of schemas and schema development; mental structures are viewed as reasonably accurate representations of reality, and cognitive development involves increasingly accurate modeling of stable characteristics of the world. Bem argues that, in contrast, her conception of gender schemas, including the processes by which such schemas are learned, falls within the romantic tradition, according to which mental and cultural creations are "nonrational" (not necessarily irrational) and "arbitrary." The romantic view has much in common with what Morawski and Tiefer call "social constructionism," and so indirectly argues against the dominant theme in Kenrick's sociobiological approach.

In Chapter 11, Vanda Zammuner, an Italian social developmentalist, presents data from several studies comparing gender stereotypes and gender-related preferences for toys and activities in Italy and Holland, two countries with differing systems of gender roles. She finds contrasts in children's beliefs and preferences between the two countries— differences that parallel parents' views—and also differences due to children's ages and to the kinds of schools they attend (traditional versus progressive). In general, her findings support Bem's idea that gender schemas are cultural creations, although there are still enough similarities across cultures to cause sociobiologists to stick to their guns. Zammuner's analysis includes concepts from social psychology and cognitive developmental psychology, and also acknowledges the role of self-enhancing motivation: Children define gender-appropriate behavior in ways related to age, social setting, and each sex's desire for greater fun and freedom. In the final chapter, John Antill, an Australian social psychologist, presents pioneering ideas and research on the nature of parents' beliefs and values concerning the gender socialization of children. His data fit well with Zammuner's, each investigator revealing part of a complex interplay of forces in which family members influence each other's definition of appropriate behavior for males and females. A novel feature of Antill's studies is his inclusion of questions about the causes and desirability of homosexuality. One of his findings, that fathers of boys are especially concerned about guarding against homosexuality in their sons, helps explain Zammuner's several results indicating that boys have more restrictive conceptions of gender than do girls. These last two chapters, by Zammuner and Antill, are more data-oriented than the previous 10, because these researchers' work is not so readily available to American readers.

All in all, although no book of a few hundred pages can possibly capture everything that is happening in the study of sex and gender— around the world and in many different disciplines—this one, ranging from sociobiology through social constructionism to detailed studies of pornography, entitlement, communication, epistemology, emotionality, and sex-role socialization, offers an exciting and diverse sampling. Surely there are enough ideas and challenges here to keep professionals and students busy for quite some time. The chapters illustrate the kinds of contributions that feminism, and recent changes in women's circumstances and roles (hence in men's circumstances and roles), have made to social-personality psychology. The purpose of feminism was certainly not "academic" in any sense, but because social science is part of the process by which people in industrialized societies come to define and understand themselves, disciplines such as personality and social psychology change in step with culture.

This volume marks an editorial transition from Phillip Shaver to Clyde Hendrick. We have benefited greatly from each other's help and from the generous contributions of associate editors, editorial board members, and other friends of the discipline who agreed to write reviews under tight time pressure. Especially helpful in preparing the present volume were Ellen Berscheid, Bill Ickes, Harry Reis, Alan Elms, Ken Gergen, Karen Kitchener, Judy Schwartz, Paul Secord, Carol Tavris, and Rhoda Unger. Phil Shaver would like to thank all of the people who helped carry out an editorial experiment with Volumes 5, 6, and 7 of the *Review*. Our mission, handed us by the Publications Committee of

APA's Division 8 and Sage Publications, was to explore the feasibility and attractiveness of theme-oriented volumes. (Before 1984, the *Review* was an annual series without topical constraint, something like a combination *Psychological Bulletin* and *Psychological Review* for personality and social psychologists.) We have now experimented with volumes on "Emotions, Relationships, and Health" (1984), "Self, Situations, and Social Behavior" (1985), and "Sex and Gender" (1986). Volume 8, edited by Clyde Hendrick, will deal with group processes and intergroup relations. It will take time and objectivity to assess the results of the experiment, but the available volumes are already being consulted and cited at a gratifying rate.

It has been a pleasure for the outgoing editor to work with a talented and cooperative group of authors, associate editors, reviewers, and production specialists. He wishes all the best to the new editor and his staff. It will be a pleasure to sit back and read the *Review* without having to worry about it!

—Phillip Shaver
Clyde Hendrick

1

Gender, Genes, and the Social Environment

A BIOSOCIAL INTERACTIONIST PERSPECTIVE

DOUGLAS T. KENRICK

Douglas T. Kenrick is an Associate Professor in the Social and Environmental Psychology Programs at Arizona State University. His main research interests are in the areas of personality and sexual attraction. His main theoretical interests involve the integration of sociobiological approaches with social learning and social cognition models.

As Plomin (1983) noted, it is fashionable to claim that the "nature-nurture debate" is dead, but it is also quite wrong. If you doubt Plomin, you might find it interesting to wonder aloud about the etiology of sex differences while in a mixed-sex group of psychologists. In short order, you are likely to see the corpse of this dead issue come alive with the fury of Dr. Frankenstein's monster. If you really want to run a jolt of lightning through the cadaver, slip the term "sociobiology" into the conversation.

In scholarly circles, there seem to be two major strategies for dealing with the literature on biological bases of sex differences. One might be called the *denial* strategy. In a book titled *Biological Woman: The Convenient Myth*, Hubbard (1982) suggests that modern biological ideas about sex differences are at least partly the result of the feminist political movement, and she argues for a parallel with the original development of evolutionary theory:

> Darwin's theory of sexual selection was put forward in the midst of the first wave of feminism. It seems that when women threaten to enter as equals into the world of affairs, androcentric scientists rally to point out that our *natural* place is in the home. (p. 36)

AUTHOR'S NOTE: I thank Nancy Eisenberg, Robert Hogan, William Ickes, Michael McCall, Heather McCrath, Daniel Montello, Phillip Shaver, and Melanie Trost for their helpful comments on an earlier draft of this chapter.

Hubbard's position is that there is no good evidence of differential biological influences on the behavior of men and women, and that biological theories are constructions projected from defensive political attitudes. However, the denial strategy does not come to terms with some data that are hard to deny, whatever one's scientific "constructions." Although men and women overlap on virtually every behavioral trait, there are, nonetheless, distinct mean differences in certain traits (Anastasi, 1985). Regarding violent aggressiveness, for instance, men are, compared with women, about six times more likely to commit murder. Regarding social dominance, even a totally unbiased count would find that male leaders in the military, political, and business arenas outnumber females by a tremendous ratio in our society. Men in our society seem to be more sexually driven, as judged by various criteria, such as sexual deviations, interest in promiscuous affairs, and so on (Daly & Wilson, 1979; Davison & Neale, 1982).

Psychologists frequently presume that these gender differences are due to socialization into a culture that is "macho" as a function of some sort of historical accident (e.g., Bem, 1985). This viewpoint must further presume a good deal of coincidence between the historical accidents that shaped the wide diversity of human cultures. For every society that has ever kept crime records, for instance, males are the more violent. Males have virtually always held the positions of social dominance in other societies, and have always been the primary combatants (Frieze, Parsons, Johnson, Ruble, & Zellman, 1978). Likewise, males are generally believed to be more sexually driven, across a wide spectrum of societies, from the sexually repressed Inis Beag (Messenger, 1972) to the sexually open Mangaians (Marshall, 1971). The historical accident viewpoint must be stretched thin to explain these convergences across human groups, but it becomes even thinner when one considers coincidences in sex-linked behaviors across species. For instance, where sex differences in violent aggression are found in other mammals, they virtually always indict males as the crueler (Daly & Wilson, 1979). Further, the male hormone testosterone has been found to have effects on dominance, aggressiveness, and sexual drive across a wide range of species (e.g., Bancroft, 1978; Rose, Gordon, & Bernstein, 1972; Rose, Holaday, & Bernstein, 1971). Daly and Wilson (1979) review many other findings that embarrass the denial strategy.

The other strategy might be called *compartmentalization*. Here some acknowledgment is given to the role of biological factors in sex differences, but these biological "main effects" are either left unconsidered, or are considered separately from the "main effects" of environment or cognition with which psychologists are more accustomed to dealing. There seems to be a recent shift from denial to compartmentalization, with more and more psychological researchers acknowledging that innate factors probably "interact" with the socialization environment in some way (e.g., Bem, 1985; Cook, 1985; Gilligan, 1982). Unfortunately, this acknowledgment virtually always stops at lip service, and the question "how" is left unaddressed.

Although some amount of compartmentalization is probably adaptive among researchers, who must specialize in a manageably small part of the universe, there are good reasons for us to venture into the uncertain and controversial territory between psychology and biology. For one, it seems likely that genetic differences between individuals interact in nonadditive ways with factors in the social environment. To the extent that such interactions occur, the outcomes of socialization experiences will be only poorly understood by considering genetic effects or environmental effects separately (Kenrick, Montello, & MacFarlane, 1985). If we wish to understand behavior fully, we must explicitly understand how those two realms interact. Another reason for us to be involved in research in this area is that biologists interested in these issues are often as unsophisticated about the research on learning and cognition as psychologists are about biological research, and there is no compelling reason to leave the study of interactions in their hands, by default. Biological approaches tend to be biased in ways that underplay the role of learning and cognition, factors with which we are much more familiar. Very exciting discoveries may be made in understanding gene-environment interactions in the next decade, and they will not be made by social or biological researchers working in isolation.

In this chapter I will consider the question of how genetic differences between the sexes might interact with the social environment at several levels. Developmental behavior geneticists and psychobiologists have considered the *ontogenetic* processes by which the individual genotype interacts with the environment it encounters after birth. Ethologists and comparative psychologists have studied the more immediate *proximate* mechanisms that come into play between specific features of the organism and specific features of the environment. Finally, sociobiologists have considered how these proximate mechanisms might be related to the organism's *phylogenetic* history. After briefly describing each of these areas, I will return to an explicit consideration of how social biology, social cognition, and social learning may operate in concert.

SOCIOBIOLOGY: SEX DIFFERENCES AND
THE PHYLOGENETIC ENVIRONMENT

Darwin's theory of evolution assumed (1) *variations* within species that can be inherited, and (2) *competition* for scarce resources such that only a very small fraction of offspring survive. These combine to produce *natural selection* of variations that have even a slight advantage in terms of environmental adaptations (that will produce more surviving offspring). Sociobiologists presume that the principles of natural selection apply to behaviors as well. Behavioral tendencies are assumed to be inherited along with an animal's body type. Some behavioral programs are better suited to an animal's body type and to the demands of its ecological surrounds; obviously a giraffe's body wouldn't fit well with a brain that was programmed for climbing trees or flapping forelimbs to fly.

Division of Labor, Parental Investment,
and Sexual Selection

Within a given social species, it is often adaptive to divide up the tasks. There is often a morphological differentiation that goes along with the different tasks. That is, the animals in the group may differ in size and structure in ways that make their jobs easier. For instance, the ants that guard the colony have gigantic heads and mandibles with which to block the entrance or maim alien ants that try to invade the nest.

Probably the most common division of labor and physical structure within species occurs along sex lines. The Ugandan kob, an antelope found on the plains of Africa, demonstrates, in exaggerated form, some of the differences between mammalian males and females. Males are arranged into a very steep dominance hierarchy, and they compete vigorously for a small number of "stamping grounds" (territories associated with mating). They are larger and more aggressive than females—as an adaptation for this task. Females will mate only with a male who has such a stamping ground. Courtship is brief, and the female cares for the young with no help from the male. Males will mate with any female who enters their stamping ground. In sum, males are more dominance-oriented, and are correspondingly larger and more aggressive. Females care for the offspring, and are more selective in choosing a mate.

Although the kob is an extreme case, such gender differences are the general rule among mammals (Barash, 1977; Daly & Wilson, 1979), and are seen to follow from inherent sex differences in *parental investment* (Trivers, 1972). The parental investment theory is based on the fact that females are less variable in the number of offspring they can have (usually one, two, or three a year). A given male could potentially have a very large number. (Some kob males could have over 100 offspring in a season; others have none.)

In mammalian species, the young are carried in the female's body, and then suckle at the female's breast. Therefore, the male is often unnecessary after fertilization. For these reasons, the females are in a position to be choosy about the males with whom they mate. If all that a male contributes is his genes, then the female is well served to be very picky about which genes she is going to mix with hers. It is not in the best interests of the male to be as picky because the consequences of an ill-chosen mating are less drastic for him (only the loss of the energy used in copulating, but no embryo growing in his body, and no offspring demanding milk later on).

If females are going to be picky, then the males need to demonstrate that their genes are better than those of their competitors. They do this by competing with other males in dominance hierarchies. The Ugandan kob male who manages to win a stamping ground shows that he is stronger, healthier, and more coordinated than the other males he beat out to get there. Darwin used the term *sexual selection* to refer to this process, wherein the preferences of one sex exert a selection pressure on the other sex.

What About Humans?

Sociobiologists assume that our species, like all others, has been subject to evolutionary pressures, and that some of our characteristics are shared with our mammalian relatives. In particular, human females carry the young within their bodies, and are equipped to nurse them in ways males are not. Like the kob, we are a physically dimorphic species. Females have breasts, for instance, and males are, on the average, slightly taller, and have larger muscles in their upper bodies. However, not all mammalian species are the same as the Ugandan kob. In our species, for instance, males contribute more than just genes to the offspring, and therefore all human societies have some form of marriage (Daly & Wilson, 1979).

Many peculiarities of the human species are believed to be adaptations to life as hunter-gatherers, with offspring that are helpless for a very prolonged period (see Wilson, 1978). Humans are unique in our group-living arrangements and consequent development of complex cultures. This is not to say that human culture has erased the slate of our mammalian heritage. General mammalian and specific primate characteristics are presumed to show themselves in the very cultures we construct (Lumsden & Wilson, 1981, 1983).

Thus mammalian sex differences are believed to manifest themselves against the background of human culture. Intergroup warfare has been largely the province of the larger, more aggressive male, for instance. Regarding sexuality, sociobiologists assume that male humans, like male kobs, have more potential variance in number of offspring than females do. Therefore, polygyny should be a more common cultural practice than polyandry. Daly and Wilson (1979) note that of 849 human societies studied, 708 have allowed for polygyny, whereas only 4 have also allowed polyandry (no society allows just polyandry, and not polygyny). Consistent with the Ugandan kob, females seem to be more selective in taking advantage of a casual mating opportunity, and thus only high-status males have multiple wives (Daly & Wilson, 1979). Whereas the maharajah Bhudaper Singh was simultaneously married to 350 women, most human males have no more than one wife.

The tendency to form *mating bonds* is another unique feature of human ecological demands. One special consequence of mating bonds is the trait of sexual jealousy (which does not appear relevant to species such as the Ugandan kob). Again, this unique feature is presumed to interact with inherent differences in the demands upon male and female mammals in general. Jealousy is presumed somewhat higher among males, as a consequence of the uncertainties of paternity; thus the danger of unknowingly investing resources in another male's offspring. Women are also seen to be jealous, but to be relatively less intolerant of minor infidelities (because they are always certain whether the offspring they care for are their own). Daly and Wilson (1979) review research to support these arguments. For instance, survey data indicate that males are twice as likely to engage in extramarital liaisons (and are 10 times more eager to do so), yet infidelity by the female appears to be more likely to lead to divorce (see also Ford & Beach, 1951).

PROXIMATE MECHANISMS

How are genes presumed to influence behavior? Contrary to the stereotype among social scientists, current comparative approaches (e.g., Alcock, 1979; Lumsden & Wilson, 1981) do not favor unrestrained "genetic determinism" but are attentive to interactions between the organism and the environment. Several mechanisms by which genes and the environment can interact are considered below.

Stimulus Sensitivity

Attention and perception are selectively biased to fit the demands of any given species. Some organisms do not even develop sensory receptors for aspects of the environment that are highly salient for others. For example, carnivorous cats are insensitive to the sugar in their foods (a taste for sugar presumably allows for a discrimination of ripe fruit that is unnecessary to carnivores; Lumsden & Wilson, 1981). Lumsden and Wilson (1981) note that genetic variations in sensitivity to taste, color, and smell stimuli occur between humans as well.

There is evidence that human males and females differ in response to certain classes of stimuli from birth (Friedman & Jacobs, 1981; Lipsitt & Levy, 1959), and adult males and females also differ in sensitivity to certain stimuli, including certain sexual pheromones (Doty, 1981).

Morphology and the Environment

Genes affect the physical structure of the body, and the importance of any physical feature often depends on the environmental response it evokes. It is a basic postulate of evolutionary theory that form and function are inextricably interwoven. The adaptiveness of having wings or a long neck depends on the possession of a corresponding set of behaviors, as well as a responsive physical and social environment. A giraffe's neck on a monkey would not only be a hindrance in performing the required activities of primate daily living, but would also invoke a strange set of social responses from his or her fellow primates. On the other hand, a slightly overdeveloped set of shoulders and arms could be functional both in swinging about in the trees, and in rising through a social dominance hierarchy.

Although Sheldon's classic work (Sheldon & Stevens, 1942) may have overestimated the association between body type and behavior, many of his empirical findings are replicable (Lindzey, 1965; Wells,

1980). One reliable finding is that mesomorphic (muscular) males are greatly overrepresented among criminal populations (Glueck & Glueck, 1956). Such a relationship could arise very simply from the differential response of the environment to different body types. For instance, a mesomorph, who is strong and muscular, will get a very different pattern of reinforcement for "tough" or exploitive behavior than will a skinny ectomorph or a chubby endomorph. Note that this is not due to some arbitrary social labeling convention; muscularity has real effects on the social environment. These may be recognized by social convention, but they are not just "constructed" in an arbitrary manner.

Here the implications for gender are clear. Testosterone at puberty stimulates large muscle growth; estrogen leads to an increased accumulation of fat on the breasts and hips. When fully grown, an average man is 40% muscle and 15% fat; a woman, 23% muscle, 25% fat. Men have wider shoulders, longer arms and legs, and hairier faces with more pronounced features. Women can achieve pound for pound parity in leg strength, but equivalently trained upper body strength in females is one-third to two-thirds that of males (Doyle, 1985). These features have direct effects on the environment, and indirect social stimulus value. Even assuming that children of both sexes engaged in equal amounts of aggressive competition from the start, average sized females would, like ectomorphic males, simply not get as much reinforcement from the outcomes of such interactions as would average sized males.

It seems likely that differences in secondary sex-typed characteristics could account for some of the differences in sex-typing within the sexes as well. This could occur through direct effects on the environment, through the labeling response of others in the social environment, or through a process of self-labeling. Cognition, learning, and biology do not act independently of one another. The male who is constructed like Woody Allen will get a different response from the social environment than the one constructed like O. J. Simpson, will learn from experience, and will label himself accordingly. Likewise for two females constructed like Bella Abzug and Marilyn Monroe.

Response Patterns

It has been suggested that certain human behaviors fit the criteria for what ethologists call "fixed action patterns" (innate movement sequences). For instance, Eibl-Eibesfeldt (1975) notes that smiling appears in deaf and blind children at the same age that it appears in normal children, and, along with several other facial expressions, smiling appears to have a universal meaning across cultures (Ekman & Friesen, 1971). Even more thought-provoking is Eibl-Eibesfeldt's (1975) microanalysis of filmed flirtation gestures in females from several widely disparate cultures. The analysis suggested a universal motor sequence, beginning with a short duration smile and "eyebrow flash" (wide opening of the eyes accompanied by raising the eyebrows) followed by dropping and turning the head, and then a sidelong glance.

Men and women differ in obvious ways in motor behavior. The sexes can generally be distinguished from walking gait alone, a distinction related to differences in the anatomy of the hips. Paralleling Eibl-Eibesfeldt's findings on female microgestures for flirtation, Jensen (1973) noted male flirtation gestures are similar in humans and chimpanzees. Interestingly, these are gestures that are also used in dominance interactions, such as direct staring and "dominance swaggering." On the other hand, the female microgestures found by Eibl-Eibesfeldt suggest "coyness."

Reaction Chains

Reaction chains are sequences of behavior in which the termination of one sequence leads to the onset of another. Such reaction chains are common in mating (Lehrman, 1966; Morris, 1958) where one sex will not move from step *a* to step *b* responses until the mate has completed a response sequence *a'*. Lehrman's (1966) classical work with ring dove mating sequences indicated physiological changes that accompany the stages in the mating sequence, and that appear to differentially inhibit or disinhibit particular mating behaviors. For example, a female will engage in "nest-soliciting" behaviors only when she is in a state of appropriate physiological readiness, and when she has been exposed to appropriate courtship display behaviors on the part of the male. At times of readiness, flirtation gestures by the male lead to estrogen secretion in the female, and concomitant nest-solicitation behaviors. Once the male has been exposed to nest-soliciting on the part of the female, he then shows alterations in his physiological state, as well as a new set of behaviors associated with nest building, and so on.

Kenrick and Trost (1986) discuss the possible applicability of response chaining to human courtship, with particular attention to differences between male and female strategies. A number of sex differences in the human literature are consistent with the parental investment and sexual selection ideas. Females are more likely to find dominance in a male to be sexually attractive (Sadalla, Kenrick, & Vershure, 1987), and are generally more reticent to move tne relationship to sexual intimacy, for instance. These gender differences in sexual sequencing may be related to differences in testosterone production, to be discussed below.

Research on nonverbal "responsivity" (e.g., Rosenthal & DePaulo, 1979) generally finds females to excel in this regard. Along similar lines, there is research showing infant-mother response intercalation, although I am not aware whether this sort of nonverbal microdancing is the sole province of females, or whether males are equally good at it.

Differential Learning and Memory

Genes influence responses to the environment through their effects on learning biases. Certain connections between stimuli or between certain stimuli and certain responses appear to be innately prepotent over others. Feelings of nausea, for instance, condition readily to novel taste stimuli even with a single trial and several hours' delay between the conditioned and unconditioned stimulus (Rozin & Kalat, 1971). Nausea is very difficult to condition to a visual stimulus such as a light, however.

There appear to be human individual differences that are heritable and have effects on learning and cognition (see Rushton, 1984). Eysenck (1970) reviewed evidence that anxiety proneness has (a) some genetic basis, and (b) important implications for learning. Hoffman (1981) reviewed evidence to argue that a tendency to experience empathic arousal facilitates the learning of altruistic responses, and Rushton, Fulker, Neale, Nias, and Eysenck (in press) present evidence that approximately 50% of the variance in their measures of altruism is heritable.

Are there gender differences in learning biases? Several interesting possibilities suggest themselves. In line with the parental investment argument that males will be less selective about a casual mating opportunity, males seem to condition sexual arousal to a novel partner more readily than females do. Males greatly outnumber females in all categories of sexual deviation, for instance (Davison & Neale, 1982), and are several times more likely to become homosexual (despite the greater societal revulsion regarding affection between males than between females). In a related vein, males report much more attraction after a first date, and have been found to fall in love more quickly

(Rubin, Peplau, & Hill, 1981). Masters and Johnson (1966) report that females are less easily sexually aroused. Perhaps gender differences in chronic testosterone levels are relevant here. This hormone appears to be the crucial one in initiating sexual desire in both males and females (Bancroft, 1978). Both sexes produce the hormone in the adrenal glands, although males produce larger quantities in their testes.

Several theorists view empathy as a crucial mediator in the learning of certain positive social behaviors. Eisenberg and Lennon (1983) report significant differences in infant empathic responses between males and females. There are also dramatic differences in adult self-reports of empathy, but not for physiological recordings or observers' behavioral ratings. One possible reason for the discrepancy is that empathy is something for which "objective outside" opinions or weakly reliable physiological recording devices may be less relevant than internal phenomenology. Kenrick and Stringfield (1980) argued that certain traits are more accessible to private than to public observation (emotionality as opposed to friendliness, for example), and several findings have corroborated the usefulness of this distinction (e.g., Cheek, 1982; McCrae, 1982).

Existing research on sex differences in altruistic behavior is not clear. Radke-Yarrow, Zahn-Waxler, and Chapman (1983) suggest that girls are frequently rated by their teachers and peers as more altruistic than boys, but that observational studies reveal few differences. Although it is customary to interpret these sorts of findings as due to "biased perceptions" in the ratings, it could be that the observations are simply not reliable enough to detect differences that are noticed by well-acquainted observers. In support of this possibility, Moskowitz and Schwarz (1982) found that behavioral ratings of children's behavior did not correlate well with teacher ratings, unless very long periods of observation were aggregated. With sufficient aggregation, ratings were substantiated by the behavioral observations.

Anastasi (1985) suggests that the crucial reasons for adult sex differences in cognitive abilities are motivational, and that motivational differences lead to different learning experiences. Consistent with this view, Eccles (1985) reports reliably more persistent and single-minded pursuit of high levels of occupational achievement among males, but only small gender differences in abilities. A related learning bias is that males seem to be less susceptible to learned helplessness (Block, 1983). This may be related to higher incidences of clinical depression among females.

Life Experiences and the Biological Organism

As discussed above, genes predispose the development of certain structures such as body types. The effects of those physical structures, however, will be importantly dependent upon inputs from the social environment. A mesomorph born into a group of even larger meso-morphs, for instance, may not be particularly reinforced for dominance displays. From the interactionist perspective, life experiences are seen to have important influences on the expression of innate dispositions, and a given environment will not affect all genotypes in the same way.

One pathway by which experience influences the organism is through alterations in hormone levels. These can affect behavior directly, or can alter morphology and thereby have indirect effects on behavior and the environment. A fascinating example of the interplay between environ-mental events and the biological organism comes from studies of hermaphroditic fishes (Warner, 1984). In the cleaner wrasse (L. abridae dimidiatus), for instance, large males with territories have access to harems, whereas small males have little or no opportunity to mate. Unless a male is both large and territoried, therefore, his chances of passing on his genes are less than those of a female (who can enter a harem with a polygynous male). Under these circumstances, a very unusual adaptation has evolved. If a large male with a harem is killed or injured, the largest female in his harem goes through a rapid series of hormonal changes, resulting in gender transformation, with concomi-tant alterations in size and coloration. In another species, males change from small drab fish into large and colorful ones when they acquire a territory, and these changes are accompanied by enlargement of the gonads (Fernald, 1984). However, these same changes that make the male attractive to females also make him susceptible to attack by other males. The presence of a large, colorful, territoried male inhibits growth in the small drab males, and this smaller size has the indirect result of protecting the small males from attack while they await a territorial opening. These sorts of findings suggest an adaptive interplay between experience, hormones, and behavior.

Moving closer to our own species, Rose and his colleagues have found that testosterone levels are reciprocally related to dominance in rhesus monkeys (Rose et al., 1971, 1972). Administration of testosterone leads to an increase in antagonistic behaviors and a consequent rise in the dominance hierarchy. On the other hand, placing a monkey in with larger, more dominant males leads to a consequent decrease in testosterone level.

To the extent that these concepts are relevant to human gender, one would expect to find individual differences between members of each sex in hormone production as a function of life experiences. Consistent with Rose's work with monkeys, Mazur and Lamb (1980) have shown that success in a competition leads to an increase in testosterone levels for college males. In a related vein, Bandura (1969) noted that male impotence could be successfully treated by training in general assertiveness. Regarding female hormones, there is evidence of a relationship between body weight and menstruation (Daly & Wilson, 1979). Human females do not begin menarche until body fat reaches 20%, and will terminate menstruation when body fat goes below 17%. Throughout most of the history of our species, levels of body fat lower than this were insufficient to support a nursing infant.

Summary

There are several processes by which genetic differences between males and females could lead to behavioral differences, but these processes are intimately tied to the environment. On the most proximate level, stimulus sensitivities and response patterns are keyed to events in the environment. When we consider learning biases, the general map is provided by the genes, but the specific stimulus topography is provided by experience. Similarly, genes code for the development of certain structural features, but the effects of those features will depend on life experiences. Life experiences also have a reciprocal effect on the biological organism—resulting in chronic alterations in biochemistry.

ONTOGENY: MONEY AND EHRHARDT'S INTERACTIONAL MODEL

Developmental studies of hermaphrodites have provided the basis of perhaps the best known ontogenetic model of sex role development. Money and his colleagues (e.g., Ehrhardt, 1985; Money & Ehrhardt, 1972) have examined the development of individuals whose genitals are ambiguous at birth, and who are occasionally labeled as female when they are genetically male or vice versa. Originally, this research was interpreted as indicating that the label was all important, but this conclusion has subsequently been revised in favor of a strongly interactionist position (Ehrhardt, 1985). Money and Ehrhardt note that sexual hormones can have two sorts of effects on sexual development. Very early (e.g., prenatal) exposure to hormones appears to have a "sensitization" effect, whereas later exposure leads to "activation" in previously sensitized organisms. For instance, animals who are exposed to testosterone *in utero* will later respond to testosterone with increases in sexual advances, whereas animals who have not had such early exposure will not respond in this way (regardless of their genetic sex).

Because hormonal abnormalities can affect not only morphology but also hormonal sensitivity during later development, clinical studies of hermaphrodites do not provide ideal "natural experiments" to pit genes against culture, as was once supposed. If a "genetically" male hermaphrodite who is raised as a female acts generally in line with the female label (which there is some debate about in the first place; Diamond, 1980), this may simply be because he is insensitive to androgen as a function of the same *in utero* dysfunction that led to his incorrect labeling in the first place. More problematic is the fact that hermaphrodites in these studies have frequently been surgically treated at birth (to remove internal testicles, for instance), and hormonally treated afterward in ways that destroy the natural genetic pathways. Imperato-McGinley, Peterson, Gautier, and Sturla's (1979) findings have also been troublesome for the model of sex-typing as a main effect of early social labeling. These researchers found a number of male hermaphrodites who were raised as females, with a syndrome in which they began to produce androgen at puberty, and suddenly appeared to change from females into males. These individuals made the adjustment, and all but one ended up married to, or cohabiting with, females.

Research in this area has indicated other interesting developmental effects of sexual hormones on behavior. For instance, Ehrhardt (1985) reviews evidence that high prenatal androgen is associated with more physically active play in boys, whereas prenatal exposure to progesterone leads to decreased activity.

ONTOGENY: GENE EFFECTS ON THE ENVIRONMENT

From our earlier discussion of morphology and life experiences, it should be clear not only that the environment produces temporary and chronic effects on the developing organism, but that the organism has reciprocal effects on the environment. Behavior geneticists (Plomin, DeFries, & Loehlin, 1977; Scarr & McCartney, 1983) have developed a framework to organize the processes by which the genotype may influence its own developmental environment.

Passive G → E Effects

Parents, who provide the child's home environment, also provide his or her genes. Likewise, the child's siblings, who provide an important part of the learning environment, also share genes with the child. As Scarr and McCartney (1983) note, this makes most of the research on children's socialization hopelessly confounded. Without data from adoption studies, it is impossible to tell whether parent-child resemblances in behavior are due to parental modeling of behaviors or coincidence of genetic determinants.

This applied to the literature on sex-role socialization. For instance, Allgeier (1975) notes that those who grew up in homes with working mothers are less rigidly sex-typed. This may be due to their mother's modeling of "androgynous" role behaviors, but could also be due to shared genetic tendencies that facilitate androgyny. Some indirect evidence that may be relevant to this issue is Baucom, Besch, and Callahan's (1985) finding that androgynous and masculine females have significantly higher testosterone levels than feminine females.

Evocative G → E Effects

Another means by which individuals' genotypes can exert an influence on their environment is by eliciting differential reactions from the social environment. Bell and Harper (1977) have noted how young children with different temperaments could elicit different reactions from the adults around them. An irritable child is likely to produce a different parental environment than is a good-natured one, for instance.

From the earliest periods of observation, little boys and girls differ in ways that are likely to result in differential treatment from their parents, nursery school teachers, and siblings. For instance, little boys are more irritable and active (Frieze et al., 1978) from infancy. Once they become mobile, boys maintain higher activity levels, and are more likely to be physically aggressive. Consistently, boys elicit more punishment (Maccoby & Jacklin, 1966). Some social learning theorists have suggested that boys must find punishment reinforcing in some way because they continue to perform the undesired behaviors. Possibly they enjoy the attention. On the other hand, it is at least as plausible to assume that their differential aggressiveness and rowdiness stem not from adult contingencies but occur despite adult demands. Perhaps boys left to their own inclinations would be rather less like little angels than like the lads in Golding's *Lord of the Flies*.

In sexual interactions at the adult level, social psychological findings suggest that males act to change their environments in exactly the ways that would be expected from the sociobiological framework discussed earlier, and that are consistent with their higher levels of testosterone (Kenrick & Trost, 1986). For instance, males push for intimacy in conversation (Davis, 1978), and initiate touching more frequently (Henley, 1977). When females act friendly in a first encounter, males are likely to interpret this as flirtatious and seductive (Abbey, 1982). Roebuck and Spray (1967) found that males invariably made the advance in the cocktail lounge they observed, and Ford and Beach (1951) reported that males are cross-culturally the initiators of sexual relationships. At later stages of the relationship, males encourage sexual intimacy; females are more likely to discourage it (Peplau et al., 1977).

Active G → E Effects

A third mechanism by which genotype can influence environment is through choice. Individuals can choose environments to fit their innate proclivities. The individual with a chronically high sex drive and a need for sensation can work as a recreational director at a nudist singles resort, the one without much libido who is low in sensation seeking can enter a monastery or a nunnery. Scarr and McCartney (1983) review evidence that the role of genotypes in active choice becomes stronger with age, and the consequent freedom to choose environments compatible with one's inclinations. Adoptees' trait ratings correlate slightly with those of adopted family members when they are young, but after teenage years correlate only with the traits of biological relatives.

Anastasi (1985) suggests a compatible account of adult gender differences in math ability. Young girls do not seem to experience more failure in math, and those who take advanced math classes do as well as males on the average, but Anastasi (1985) notes that females are simply more likely to choose themselves out of math classes. Another role of differential choice may occur in female self-selection out of high dominance situations, as suggested by Gilligan (1982). She reviews research suggesting that boys go out of their way to become involved in activities that involve a high level of quarrel potential, whereas girls opt to leave activities when a quarrel erupts.

Kenrick, Stringfield, Wagenhals, Dahl, and Ransdell (1980) conducted an experiment in which male and female subjects were given the choice between two studies in which to participate. One possible choice involved the perception of geometric figures; the other involved viewing erotica. Consistent with the theory and findings on sexuality discussed above, 90% of sex-typed males (but only 30% of sex-typed females) chose the erotic experiment. In keeping with an interactionist perspective, however, these gender differences were not inevitable. No differences were found for androgynous subjects.

Some sex differences consistent with an evolutionary viewpoint are also found in the literature on *mate choice* (Buss, 1986; Kenrick & Trost, 1986). For instance, females are more likely to choose mates along dimensions that are relevant to their ability to provide resources.

Negative G → E Effects

Plomin et al. (1977) noted that gene → environment effects could be negative as well as positive. Negative passive effects occur when anger-prone parents punish their children's anger, to give one example. In the sex-role realm, this would occur if fathers were more likely to hit their sons for being aggressive, for instance. Negative evocative effects occur in what Cattell referred to as "coercion to the biological mean." Cattell suggested the example of overly dominant individuals, who are often given a dose of humility to bring them back into line. Again, in the sex role realm, this would occur if teachers and other authorities were found to be more likely to punish male aggressiveness and dominance, or female passivity. Negative active effects occur when individuals seek an environment that will act in opposition to their own genotype. Plomin et al. (1977) suggest the example of an anxious person who seeks a calming environment. Females taking classes in assertiveness or karate could provide a parallel example in the gender realm.

In the realm of social and personality psychology, anyone familiar with the literature on "reciprocal person/environment interactions" (e.g., Ickes, 1982; Snyder & Ickes, 1985) should find the processes discussed in this section familiar. In fact, Scarr and McCartney's (1983) interesting analysis leads to the suggestion that person-environment interactions may simply be a special case of gene-environment interactions. Whether or not person-environment interactions can ultimately be reduced to gene-environment interactions, awareness of possible reciprocal gene-environment effects could expand our learning and cognitive models of person-environment interactions.

CULTURE AND GENES

Social scientists have been accustomed to regarding cultural influences as more or less orthogonal to genetic influences. This is consistent with the view of sex roles as "historical accidents" (e.g., Bem, 1985, p. 193). I previously discussed cross-cultural and cross-species correspondences in gender roles regarding male dominance, hypersexuality, and aggressiveness, and female child care (Daly & Wilson, 1979) that are not parsimoniously explained with the view of sex-role norms as historical accidents. To suggest that cultures do not act with total independence of genetic constraints does not imply the converse: an enactment of genetic programs unrestrained by the cultural environment. A consideration of gene-environment interactions suggests that the cultures created by human beings are not orthogonal to genetic influences at all. Instead, human genes and cultures are likely to have coevolved with one another (Lumsden & Wilson, 1981, 1983).

There are at least two ways in which genetic predispositions and culture might have coevolved in the area of gender roles. First, to the extent that males and females differ in certain preferences (as discussed in earlier sections), the choices among various cultural possibilities will be influenced by those preferences. Cultural innovations that stress competitiveness and aggressiveness for females will, with all other pressures being equal, simply be less preferred over time to those that stress child-care. The converse will be true for cultural innovations regarding the male role. In this regard, we may note the "drift" toward conventional sex-roles in the Israeli kibbutz over the last two generations (Tiger & Shepher, 1975). This could be due to the influence of the larger historical context that perhaps provided a stronger pressure than the innovative cultural spirit that spawned the kibbutz. However, the evidence is at least as consistent with a coevolutionary explanation as with one based on arbitrary cultural pressures.

Another form of gene-culture coevolution occurs when gene frequency is altered by cultural practices. In primitive societies, a high level of male violence may have been tolerable and may have even increased a male's chances of mating (Wilson, 1978); in modern urban societies, those same highly aggressive males may be more likely to end up in prison or on the gallows (Kenrick, Dantchik, & MacFarlane, 1983) before their genes have had a chance to capitalize on the outlaw's appeal to the ladies. Daly and Wilson (1979) point out that throughout history, female extramarital meanderings have been more likely to result in death sentences, and Ford and Beach (1951) note that in some societies death could result for females unable to produce evidence of virginity on their wedding nights. Certainly these cultural conventions would act as selection pressures against any individual differences in libido that predisposed promiscuous behaviors in females. In a more general way, those who are good at fulfilling cultural expectancies (including those related to gender) would likely have advantages in mating and resource allocation.

Plomin et al.'s (1977) analysis of gene-environment confounding in individual development has some relevance to this arena, in which the same processes occur *writ large*. Passive gene-culture effects occur to the extent that the larger society possesses the same genetically based proclivities as the individual child who is socialized therein. The institutions that the growing girl or boy confronts (such as selective training in athletic competition and military violence for males) will thus have some a priori compatibility with their innate proclivities. Evocative effects occur when the growing child matches sex-role expectations, and thereby reinforces the norms about sex differences in his or her own microculture (e.g., family, school, and workplace). We have all heard the expression "Boys will be boys" used as a marker of some sex-stereotyped behavior. Active effects occur when males and females differentially choose themselves into (and out of) cultural institutions that match genotypic preferences. Highly qualified female students continue to differentially select occupations related to child care (including elementary education) or nursing instead of higher status careers in medicine, science, or engineering. These passive, evocative, and active effects are not independent of one another. The differential reactions evoked by initial sex-typed behaviors will influence future choices, and individuals who act contrary to sex-role norms may experience "coercion to the biological mean." Through these sorts of processes, what may begin as weak initial predispositions in individuals become magnified in social institutions.

SOCIAL LEARNING, SOCIAL COGNITION, OR SOCIAL BIOLOGY?

Most recent analyses of sex roles by social/personality psychologists can be characterized either as social learning or social cognition approaches, with many models combining the two. In traditional form, social learning analyses have focused upon direct and vicarious reward and punishment as determinants of sex-role behaviors (e.g., Mischel, 1966). Boys will be boys, and girls will be girls, because if they do, they get rewarded; if they don't, they get punished. Social cognition models (e.g., Bem, 1985) emphasize cognitive "schemas" or "scripts" as determinants of sex roles. According to these cognitive models, children learn a fuzzy set of behaviors and physical characteristics that seem to be associated with the sex role in their culture, and they simultaneously learn to label themselves and others with regard to the extent to which they match that prototype. Behaviors will be chosen with reference to that standard, particularly by individuals and in situations in which the sex-role schema is especially available for activation. Social learning and social cognition positions have tended to flow over into one another in recent years, following the lead of Mischel (1973). Although psychologists have tended to view sociobiological approaches as incompatible with emphases on learning and cognition, there is no inherent reason to see genetic influences as incompatible with either learning or thinking (see Kenrick, Montello, & MacFarlane, 1985, for a more detailed discussion of these issues). There are several levels at which a consideration of gene-environment interactions could enrich our own endeavors.

Kenrick et al. (1985) discuss how the three models could be integrated at the most proximate level of analysis, showing, for example, how psychopathological states such as depression could be seen to result from a multiplicative interaction of Organism $\times$ Environmental contingencies $\times$ Cognitive interpretation. A similar analysis could be applied to the analysis of gender-stereotyped behaviors. For instance, whether an act of violent aggressiveness is performed by an individual could be seen to be a function of characteristics of the biological organism (aggression thresholds will differ as a function of sex-related characteristics such as testosterone levels and large muscle development); in interaction with the objective characteristics of the situation (there are contexts in which aggression is appropriate, as in some male-dominated sports); and the subject's interpretation of the situation (males would be more likely to have aggressive behaviors as part of their self-perceived script repertoire; and to have had more recent activation of dominance-threat schemata).

The immediate interpretation of situational contingencies is, of course, dependent upon past inputs from the objective environment, and those past events are likely to have differed as a function of morphological differences between the sexes. Further, current hormonal levels may interact directly with cognitive interpretation. For instance, Stephan, Berscheid, and Walster (1971) found that interpretation of the features of a potential date was influenced by whether or not males were sexually aroused. Chronically higher levels of testosterone in males could also be associated with persistent differences in the interpretation of sex-role relevant situations. From this perspective, variation in either the organism, the contingencies, or cognitive interpretation can lead to differential effects upon sex-typed behavior, and behavior can be modified by intervention at any of the three levels. However, males and females may require very different types of interventions.

At the ontogenetic level, a consideration of gene-environment interactions raises interesting questions for the emerging discipline of developmental social psychology. How do variations in sex-related hormones and morphology influence the learning of sex-role schemas, for instance? Are there learning biases or stimulus sensitivities that are relevant to gender differences in social behavior? How do different social experiences during development influence the production of sex hormones? Recall Mazur and Lamb's finding of increased testosterone levels following successful competition in males. Maturational processes involve biological factors, and perhaps gender-related behaviors vary as a function of onset of puberty, to give one possibility. In this regard, Storms (1981) has implicated variations in puberty onset as a potentially relevant factor in homosexual preference.

In a more ultimate sense, an attention to the gene-environment literature has the advantage of connecting our findings and hypotheses to the powerful adaptational framework of Darwinian theory. Social psychological research is frequently characterized by laundry lists of variables, or at best by disconnected minitheories (Kenrick & Dantchik, 1983). By occasionally adopting a sociobiological frame of reference, we may gain a more integrated perspective on the particular social behaviors of particular college students in particular settings with particular tasks salient. As one example, Kenrick and Trost (1986) used a sociobiological perspective to organize their model of heterosexual relationship formation. From an evolutionary standpoint, gender and sexuality are not only inherently connected, but centrally related to the process of natural selection.

In preparing this chapter, I surveyed my own research for evidence of sex differences, and what I found in several disparate research programs seemed to fit nicely within the gene-environmental perspective. For instance, in a recent heat-aggression study, we found a tendency for men to be more likely to make obnoxious use of their horn when a vehicle was stalled at the light in front of them, particularly if the other passengers were also males (Kenrick & MacFarlane, in press). In a study of the effects of centerfold erotica on interpersonal attraction, we found that men rated their mates as significantly less attractive after exposure to the attractive women in *Playboy*. Our female subjects were not so fickle. Exposing women to the fit specimens in *Playgirl* did little to undermine their commitment to the males with whom they lived (Kenrick, Gutierres, & Goldberg, 1985).

I have already discussed a study in which we gave subjects the option to enter an experiment involving erotica (Kenrick et al., 1980). Males in that study were more likely to approach such a situation, whereas females (sex-typed females in particular) were avoidant. As a final example, Sadalla et al. (1987) found a clear sex difference in the relationship between sexual attractiveness and the nonverbal expression of dominance. Dominant males were seen as more sexually attractive in three studies; no such relationship was found for females. Earlier, some of these findings had seemed puzzling to me. Given the perspective of the literature on differential parental investment and sexual selection discussed earlier, however, they make perfect sense.

EPISTEMOLOGICAL QUESTIONS ABOUT
A BIOSOCIAL MODEL

This chapter is not intended to include a review of the massive literature on the "sociobiology debate" (see Caplan, 1978; Fetzer, 1985; Kitcher, 1985; Lumsden & Wilson, 1983, for various perspectives on that debate). Psychologists' traditional biases have placed us against the sociobiologists, however, and some readers may have objected to my earlier dismissal of the objections to a biosocial perspective. With the substantive features of a biosocial model in place, let me address two features of the sociobiology controversy that could be raised as objections to the model.

One criticism of sociobiological models is that they are untestable (Kitcher, 1985). This criticism does not apply to most of what has been presented above. Hypotheses regarding proximate mechanisms such as biochemical, morphological, or other physiological differences between males and females are testable. It is hard to argue with the direct evidence that such physiological differences exist, and we can have some confidence that those differences have been shown to have at least some implications for behavior. Additional research in needed to explore the full implications of these differences for personality and social psychology, but hypotheses at this level are eminently testable. At the ontogenetic level, hypotheses regarding physiological sex differences and development are also testable, and there is already some reasonably clear evidence of such effects (Ehrhardt, 1985). Likewise, behavior genetic methods can be used to test still less proximate hypotheses about genetic effects on sex differences, and Plomin (1983, 1986) makes convincing arguments for the increased use of behavior genetic methods to test hypotheses in personality and social psychology.

It is, in fact, only at the phylogenetic level that the "untestability" criticism is usually applied. Is the sociobiological scenario regarding sex differences in parental investment and sexual selection able to be validated by evidence? More recent critics might substitute "very difficult to test" for "untestable" (Kitcher, 1985). Kitcher notes that sociobiological hypotheses are, in principle, testable by the same sorts of analyses used to test any other evolutionary hypothesis. Unlike hypotheses about morphological evolution of animals, however, Kitcher argues that hypotheses about the evolution of human cultural behaviors present great difficulties for researchers. Kitcher echoes the tone of earlier critics of sociobiology, giving the impression that the difficulties are practically insurmountable and that the environmentalists therefore win by default.

Others (such as Lumsden & Wilson, 1983) hold that the evidence from paleontological, cross-cultural, and cross-species studies form a compelling nomological network to support the idea of evolutionary constraints on human culture. I side with the latter argument, although it would be naive to ignore the special problems of testing hypotheses at the evolutionary level. Regarding the parental investment and sexual selection hypotheses, however, I find the case to be at least as credible as those for the supposedly better substantiated psychological hypotheses I present in my social and personality lectures.

Although the investigation of biosocial hypotheses at the ontogenetic and proximate levels does not depend on any particular commitment to a set of assumptions about evolutionary adaptiveness, I nevertheless hold that the evolutionary perspective is a useful adjunct. For one thing, it provides a comprehensive organizing framework for a number of disparate findings, connecting research in psychology with a well-established tradition in biology. It provides bridges with the other social sciences, and between the subdisciplines of psychology. In particular, it provides a bridge between the areas of personality and social psychology (Buss, 1984; Hogan, 1982; Kenrick, Montello, & MacFarlane, 1985; Rushton, 1984). Despite the fact that the two areas share a journal and a division of the American Psychological Association, they often seem more like intellectual enemies than allies (Hogan & Emler, 1978; Kenrick, 1986; Kenrick & Dantchik, 1983). In addition to its value in organizing disparate findings, an evolutionary perspective has heuristic value. As psychologists, we usually have neither the interests nor the methodological qualifications to examine evolutionary hypotheses directly. However, the framework makes predictions that we are especially qualified to test, such as the predictions about differences in attraction patterns for men and women that follow from the parental investment and sexual selection hypotheses (Buss, 1986; Sadalla et al., 1981).

Beside the point of testability, however, is the claim that biologically based theories about sex differences are scientific "constructions" that stem from, or at least lend support to, reactionary forces that wish to protect male domination in the political and financial arenas. For theorists like Hubbard (1982), this claim stems from a hypertrophied Kuhnian perspective that presumes that one scientific "construction" is about as good as any other. This position leaves me with a problem explaining how I manage to start my car in the morning, much less how we've ever managed to send humans to the moon.

However, in the social realm, our beliefs have at least some potential to create reality (Snyder, 1981), although I think that social psychologists are prone to exaggerate the extent to which this is true (Kenrick & Dantchik, 1983). I nevertheless find it plausible that a belief in sociobiology could be socially harmful, whatever its truth status. This is analogous to acknowledging that a belief in determinism may lead to more helplessness than a belief in free will, whatever the epistemological problems with the free-will view as a scientific theory.

There are also dangers in letting our political desires a priori dictate our scientific theories, however. In particular, there is potential social harm in ignoring biological realities, even from a social activist position. One need only consider the case of PKU (phenylketonuria—a genetic form of retardation caused by an inappropriate metabolization of the lactose in milk). Behavioral or cognitive intervention will scarcely help children suffering from that syndrome, if their biological differences are ignored. However, simply removing lactose from such a child's diet following diagnosis of the genetic difference will prevent retardation.

Social scientists who refuse to consider genetic influences on social behavior are often guilty of the same naturalistic fallacy of which they accuse sociobiologists. The fallacy here is to presume that because something "is," it therefore "ought to be." Try as we might to reconstruct our social realities, we cannot change the evolutionary history of our species, and some of the differences between us are undoubtedly a function of that history. To say that something is the result of a natural state of affairs, however, does not necessarily mean that it is good in the present social context, or that it is unchangeable. One need only consider heart disease. No doubt this is a biological reality; perhaps it will be found to result from processes that are or were generally functional, but researchers into this biological reality do not presume that it is "good."

Policy decisions about gender that ignore biosocial interactions may be doomed to failure. For instance, Bem (1985, p. 181) suggests that if socialization agents did not make such a big deal about sex-roles, "males and females could finally become as similar as their biology allows," and later argues that, in the interests of the greater social good, "human behaviors and personality attributes should no longer be linked with gender" (p. 222). Given our earlier discussion of the relationships between genotypes and the immediate and general cultural environment, however, that expectation seems naive. Sex differences are inherently salient to the least intelligent sexually reproducing organism, and it is hard to believe that humans would fail to take great notice of those differences if no one brought them up.

Further, the creation of culture is not just a one-way street in which infants are "shaped" by culture. Modern societies were not created solely by random historical accidents, independent of the genotypic preferences of those who subsequently inhabited them. They were created by individuals with similar genotypic preferences, and are continuously reshaped by the preferences of the socialization "objects." In fact, Campbell (1975) makes the argument that many cultural features are designed to act in opposition to biological tendencies. To leave the noble savages to their own devices would be impossible, but even if it were not, there is no reason to believe that they would create anything more egalitarian. In fact, things could get worse.

My own view is that sex differences in behavior may have been relevant to our ancestors gathering roots and hunting squirrels on the plains of Northern Africa, but that their manifestations in modern society are less clearly "adaptive." However, rather than deny the evolutionary underpinnings of our behavior, I side with Wilson (1978) in the belief that before we can build an ideal society, it is necessary to understand the natural mechanisms that might obstruct us.

REFERENCES

Abbey, A. (1982). Sex differences in attributions for friendly behavior: Do males misperceive females' friendliness? *Journal of Personality and Social Psychology, 42*, 830-838.

Alcock, J. (1979). *Animal behavior: An evolutionary approach.* Sunderland, MA: Sinauer.

Allgeier, E. R. (1975). Beyond sowing and growing: The relationship of sex typing to socialization, family plans, and future orientation. *Journal of Applied Social Psychology, 5*, 217-226.

Anastasi, A. (1985). Reciprocal relations between cognitive and affective development with implications for sex differences. In T. B. Sonderegger (Ed.) *Nebraska symposium on motivation, 1984: Psychology and gender* (pp. 1-36). Lincoln: University of Nebraska Press.

Bancroft, J. (1978). The relationship between hormones and sexual behaviour in humans. In J. B. Hutchison (Ed.), *Biological determinants of sexual behaviour.* Chichester, England: John Wiley.

Bandura, A. (1969). *Principles of behavior modification.* New York: Holt, Rinehart, and Winston.

Barash, D. P. (1977). *Sociobiology and behavior.* New York: Elsevier.

Baucom, D. M., Besch, D. K., & Callahan, S. (1985). Relation between testosterone concentration, sex role identity, and personality among females. *Journal of Personality and Social Psychology, 48*, 1218-1226.

Bell, R. Q., & Harper, L. V. (1977). *Child effects on adults.* Hillsdale, NJ: Lawrence Erlbaum.

Bem, S. L. (1985). Androgyny and gender-schema theory: A conceptual and empirical integration. In T. B. Sonderegger (Ed.), *1984 Nebraska symposium on motivation: 1984: Psychology and gender* (pp. 179-226). Lincoln: University of Nebraska Press.

Block, J. H. (1983). Differential premises arising from differential socialization of the sexes: Some conjectures. *Child Development, 54*, 1335-1354.

Buss, D. M. (1984). Evolutionary biological and personality psychology: Toward a conception of human nature and individual differences. *American Psychologist, 39*, 1135-1147.

Buss, D. M. (1986). Sex differences in human mate selection: An evolutionary perspective. In C. Crawford et al. (Eds.), *Sociobiology and psychology: Issues, ideas, and findings.* Hillsdale, NJ: Lawrence Erlbaum.

Campbell, D. T. (1975). On the conflicts between biological and social evolution and between psychology and moral tradition. *American Psychologist, 30*, 1103-1126.

Caplan, A. L. (1978). *The sociobiology debate.* New York: Harper & Row.

Cheek, J. M. (1982). Aggregation, moderator variables, and the validity of personality tests: A peer rating study. *Journal of Personality and Social Psychology, 43*, 1254-1269.

Cook, E. P. (1985). *Psychological androgyny.* New York: Pergamon Press.

Daly, M., & Wilson, M. (1979). *Sex, evolution, and behavior*. N. Scituate, MA: Duxbury.

Davis, J. D. (1978). When boy meets girl: Sex roles and the negotiation of intimacy in an acquaintance exercise. *Journal of Personality and Social Psychology, 36*, 684-692.

Davison, G. C., & Neale, J. M. (1982). *Abnormal psychology* (3rd ed.). New York: John Wiley.

Diamond, H. (1980). Sexual identity and sex roles. In C. Gordon & G. Johnson (Eds.), *Readings in human sexuality: Contemporary perspectives* (pp. 231-234). New York: Harper & Row.

Doty, R. L. (1981). Olfactory communication in humans. *Chemical Senses, 6*, 351-376.

Doyle, J. A. (1985). *Sex and gender*. Dubuque, IA: William C. Brown.

Eccles, J. (1985). Sex differences in achievement patterns. In T. B. Sonderegger (Ed.), *Nebraska symposium on motivation, 1984: Psychology and gender* (pp. 97-132). Lincoln: University of Nebraska Press.

Ehrhardt, A.A. (1985). Gender differences: A biosocial perspective. In T. B. Sonderegger (Ed.) *Nebraska a symposium on motivation, 1984: Psychology and gender* (pp. 37-58). Lincoln: University of Nebraska Press.

Eibl-Eibesfeldt, I. (1975). *Ethology: The biology of behavior*. New York: Holt, Rinehart, and Winston.

Eisenberg, N., & Lennon, R. (1983). Sex differences in empathy and related capacities. *Psychological Bulletin, 94*, 100-131.

Ekman, P., & Friesen, W. V. (1971). Constants across cultures in the face and emotion. *Journal of Personality and Social Psychology, 17*, 124-129.

Eysenck, H. J. (1967). *The biological basis of personality*. Springfield, IL: Charles C Thomas.

Fernald, R. D. (1984). Vision and behavior in an African cichlid fish. *American Scientist, 72*, 58-65.

Fetzer, J. H. (1985). *Sociobiology and epistemology*. Dordrecht, Holland: D. Reidel.

Ford, C. S., & Beach, F. A. (1951). *Patterns of sexual behavior*. New York: Harper & Row.

Friedman, S. L., & Jacobs, B. S. (1981). Sex differences in neonates' behavioral responsiveness to repeated auditory stimuli. *Infant Behavior and Development, 4*, 175-183.

Frieze, I. M., Parsons, J. E., Johnson, P. B., Ruble, D. N., & Zellman, G. L. (1978). *Women and sex roles: A social psychological perspective* (chap. 6). New York: W. W. Norton.

Glueck, S., & Glueck, E. (1956). *Physique and delinquency*. New York: Harper & Row.

Gilligan, C. (1982). *In a different voice: Psychological theory and women's development*. Cambridge, MA: Harvard University Press.

Henley, N. M. (1977). *Body politics: Power, sex, and nonverbal communication*. Englewood Cliffs, NJ: Prentice-Hall.

Hoffman, M. L. (1981). Is altruism part of human nature? *Journal of Personality and Social Psychology, 40*, 121-137.

Hogan, R. T. (1982). A socioanalytic theory of personality. In M. Page & R. Dienstbier (Eds.), *Nebraska symposium on motivation: 1981*. Lincoln: University of Nebraska Press.

Hogan, R. T., & Emler, M. P. (1978). The biases in contemporary social psychology. *Social Research, 45*, 478-534.

Hubbard, R. (1982). Have only men evolved? In R. Hubbard, M. S. Henifin, & B. Fried (Eds.), *Biological woman: The convenient myth*. Cambridge, MA: Schenkman.

Ickes, W. (1982). A basic paradigm for the study of personality, roles, and social behavior. In W. Ickes & E. S. Knowles (Eds.), *Personality, roles, and social behavior*. New York: Springer-Verlag.

Imperato-McGinley, J., Peterson, R. E., Gautier, T., & Sturla, E. (1979). Androgens and the evolution of male-gender identity among male pseudohermaphrodites with a 5-reductase deficiency. *New England Journal of Medicine, 300*, 1233-1237.

Jensen, G. D. (1973). Human sexual behavior in primate perspective. In J. Zubin & J. Money (Eds.), *Contemporary sexual behavior: Critical issues in the 1970s*. Baltimore, MD: Johns Hopkins University Press.

Kenrick, D. T. (1986). How strong is the case against contemporary social and personality psychology: A response to Carlson. *Journal of Personality and Social Psychology, 50*, 839-844.

Kenrick, D. T., & Dantchik, A. (1983). Idiographics, interactions, and the social psychological invasion of personality. *Journal of Personality, 51*, 286-307.

Kenrick, D. T., Dantchik, A., & MacFarlane, S. (1983). Personality, environment, and criminal behavior: An evolutionary perspective. In W. S. Laufer & J. M. Day (Eds.), *Personality theory, moral development, and criminal behavior*. Lexington, MA: D.C. Heath.

Kenrick, D. T., Gutierres, S. E., & Goldberg, L. (1985). *Influence of popular erotica on judged sexual attractiveness of strangers and mates: The uglier side of pretty pictures*. Unpublished manuscript, Arizona State University.

Kenrick, D. T., & MacFarlane, S. (1986). Heat and horn-honking: A field study of interpersonal hostility. *Environment and Behavior, 18*, 179-191.

Kenrick, D. T., Montello, D., & MacFarlane, S. (1985). Personality: Social learning, social cognition, or sociobiology? In R. Hogan & W. Jones (Eds.), *Perspectives in personality* (Vol. 1). Greenwich, CT: JAI Press.

Kenrick, D. T., & Stringfield, D. O. (1980). Personality traits and the eye of the beholder: Crossing some traditional philosophical boundaries in the search for consistency in all of the people. *Psychological Review, 87*, 88-104.

Kenrick, D. T., Stringfield, D. O., Wagenhals, W. L., Dahl, R. H., & Ransdell, H. J. (1980). Sex differences, androgyny, and approach responses to erotica: A new variation on the old volunteer problem. *Journal of Personality and Social Psychology, 38*, 517-524.

Kenrick, D. T., & Trost, M. R. (1986). A biosocial theory of heterosexual relationships. In K. Kelley (Ed.), *Males, females, and sexuality: Theory and research*. Albany: State University of New York Press.

Kitcher, P. (1985). *Vaulting ambition: Sociobiology and the quest for human nature*. Cambridge, MA: MIT Press.

Lehrman, D. S. (1966). The reproductive behavior of ring doves. In S. Coopersmith (Ed.), *Frontiers of psychological research*. San Francisco, CA: W. H. Freeman.

Lindzey, G. (1965). Morphology and behavior. In G. Lindzey & C. S. Hall (Eds.), *Theories of personality: Primary sources and research*. New York: John Wiley.

Lipsitt, L. P., & Levy, N. (1959). Electrotactual threshold in the neonate. *Child Development, 30*, 547-554.

Lumsden, C. J., & Wilson, E. O. (1981). *Genes, mind and culture: The coevolutionary process*. Cambridge, MA: Harvard University Press.

Lumsden, C. J., & Wilson, E. O. (1983). *Promethean fire.* Cambridge, MA: Harvard University Press.

Maccoby, E. E., & Jacklin, C. N. (1974). *The psychology of sex differences.* Stanford, CA: Stanford University Press.

Marshall, D. S. (1971). Sexual behavior on Mangaia. In D. S. Marshall & R. G. Suggs (Eds.), *Human sexual behavior: Variations in the ethnographic spectrum.* New York: Basic Books.

Masters, W. H., & Johnson, V. E. (1966). *Human sexual response.* Boston, MA: Little, Brown.

Mazur, A., & Lamb, T. (1980). Testosterone, status, and mood in human males. *Human Behavior, 14*, 236-246.

McCrae, R. M. (1982). Consensual validation of personality traits: Evidence from self-reports and ratings. *Journal of Personality and Social Psychology, 43*, 293-303.

Messenger, J. C. (1972). Sex and repression in an Irish folk community. In D. S. Marshall & R. C. Suggs (Eds.), *Human sexual behavior: Variations in the ethnographic spectrum.* Englewood Cliffs, NJ: Prentice-Hall.

Mischel, W. (1966). A social learning view of sex differences in behavior. In E. E. Maccoby (Ed.), *Development of sex differences* (pp. 56-81). Stanford, CA: Stanford University Press.

Mischel, W. (1973). Toward a cognitive social learning reconceptualization of personality. *Psychological Review, 80*, 252-283.

Money, J., & Ehrhardt, A. A. (1972). *Man and woman, boy and girl.* Baltimore, MD: Johns Hopkins University Press.

Morris, D. (1958). The reproductive behaviour of the ten spined stickleback (Pygosteus pungitius L.). *Behaviour, 6.*

Moskowitz, D. S., & Schwarz, J. C. (1982). Validity comparison of behavior counts and ratings by knowledgeable informants. *Journal of Personality and Social Psychology, 42*, 518-528.

Peplau, L. A., Rubin, Z., & Hill, C. T. (1977). Sexual intimacy in dating relationships. *Journal of Social Issues, 35*, 86-109.

Plomin, R. (1983). Developmental behavioral genetics. *Child Development, 54*, 253-259.

Plomin, R. (1986). Behavior genetic methods. *Journal of Personality, 54*, 226-261.

Plomin, R., DeFries, J., & Loehlin, L. (1977). Genotype-environment interaction and correlation in the analysis of human behavior. *Psychological Bulletin, 84*, 309-322.

Radke-Yarrow, M., Zahn-Waxler, C., & Chapman, M. (1983). Children's prosocial dispositions and behavior. In P. Mussen (Ed.), *Manual of child psychology* (pp. 469-545). New York: John Wiley.

Roebuck, J. B., & Spray, S. L. (1967). The cocktail lounge: A study of heterosexual relations in a public organization. *American Journal of Sociology, 72*, 386-396.

Rose, R. M., Gordon, T. P., & Bernstein, I. S. (1972). Plasma testosterone levels in the male rhesus: Influence of sexual and social stimuli. *Science, 178*, 643-645.

Rose, R. M., Holaday, J. W., & Bernstein, I. (1971). Plasma testosterone, dominance rank, and aggressive behavior in male rhesus monkeys. *Nature, 231*, 366-368.

Rosenthal, R., & De Paulo, B. M. (1979). Sex differences in eavesdropping on nonverbal cues. *Journal of Personality and Social Psychology, 37*, 273-285

Rozin, P., & Fallon, A. E. (1981). The acquisition of likes and dislikes for foods. In J. Solms & R. Hall (Eds.), *Criteria of food acceptance: How man chooses what he eats. A symposium* (pp. 35-48). Zurich: Forster.

Rozin, P., & Kalat, J. W. (1971). Specific hungers and poison avoidance as adaptive specializations of learning. *Psychological Review, 78*, 459-486.

Rubin, Z., Peplau, L. A., & Hill, C. T. (1981). Loving and leaving: Sex differences in romantic attachments. *Sex Roles, 7*, 821-835.

Rushton, J. P. (1984). Sociobiology: Toward a new theory of individual and group differences in personality and social behavior. In J. R. Royce & L. P. Mos (Eds)., *Annals of theoretical psychology* (Vol. 2). New York: Plenum.

Rushton, J. P., Fulker, D. W., Neale, M. C., Nias, D.K.B., & Eysenck, H. J. (in press). Altruism and aggression: Individual differences are substantially heritable. *Journal of Personality and Social Psychology.*

Sadalla, E. K., Kenrick, D. T., & Vershure, B. (1987). Dominance and heterosexual attraction. *Journal of Personality and Social Psychology.*

Scarr, S., & McCartney, K. (1983). How people make their own environments: A theory of genotype → environment effects. *Child Development, 54*, 424-435.

Sheldon, W. H., & Stevens, S. S. (1942). *The varieties of temperament: A psychology of constitutional differences.* New York: Harper & Row.

Snyder, M. (1981). On the self-perpetuating nature of social stereotypes. In D. L. Hamilton (Ed.), *Cognitive processes in stereotyping and intergroup behavior.* Hillsdale, NJ: Lawrence Erlbaum.

Synder, M., & Ickes, W. (1985). Personality and social behavior. In G. Lindzey & E. Aronson (Eds.), *Handbook of social psychology.* Reading, MA: Addison-Wesley.

Stephan, W., Berscheid, E., & Walster, E. (1971). Sexual arousal and heterosexual perception. *Journal of Personality and Social Psychology, 20*, 93-101.

Storms, M. D. (1981). A theory of erotic orientation development. *Psychological Review, 88*, 340-353.

Tiger, L., & Shepher, J. (1975). *Women in the kibbutz.* New York: Harcourt Brace Jovanovich.

Trivers, R. L. (1972). Parental investment and sexual selection. In B. Campbell (Ed.), *Sexual selection and the descent of man.* Chicago: Aldine.

Warner, R. R. (1984). Mating behavior and hermaphroditism in coral reef fishes. *American Scientist, 72*, 128-134.

Wells, B.W.P. (1980). *Personality and heredity: An introduction to psychogenetics.* London: Longman.

Wilson, E. O. (1978). *On human nature.* Cambridge, MA: Harvard University Press.

2

The Troubled Quest for Masculinity, Femininity, and Androgyny

J. G. MORAWSKI

J. G. Morawski is an Assistant Professor at Wesleyan University. Her research interests include new theory in social psychology, particularly the incorporation of constructivist, interpretive, and structural analysis of gender. Other research interests concern the history of psychology, and in addition to examining early twentieth-century gender research, she has investigated the history of psychology's relation to evolutionary theory, ethics, experimental methods, and political change.

Psychology is a central forum for unraveling the mysteries of male and female difference. On the face of it, psychology's nearly century-long mission represents a progressive move: Exploration of psychic life promised new explanations that would extend beyond biological determinism and the political ideology that justified the unequal status of the sexes. Over time the psychological search into the nature of the sexes has shifted from focus on physiology, behavior, and personality to social identity and cognitive functioning. These shifts have been interpreted as incremental advances in our understanding of males and females. However, a review of the current psychological literature indicates that gender has become a problematic issue in much the same way that it became confusing nearly a century ago. Once again researchers are uncertain or divided over the terms for speaking about sex-related phenomena, be they behavioral, motivational, attitudinal, dispositional, or mentalistic (see Spence, Deaux, & Helmreich, 1985). As in research at the turn of the century, politics and rapid social change surround and infuse the examination of gender.[1]

Conceptual ambiguity is just one of the features shared by the early and recent studies. They have neither a general theory nor any coherent system for organizing knowledge about psychological gender. Noting these similarities is not to imply some invidious circularity in intellectual thought. Much of the earlier discourse would be incredible today (for instance, studies of reading speed and tastes), just as some centerpieces of contemporary work (concepts such as androgyny and gender schemas) might be sheer fantasy to our forebears.

These convergences and divergences offer conceptual anchor points from which we can assess just where the unending search for psychological gender has taken us, and just where it hasn't. This assessment focuses on constructs of psychological gender. It begins with the conjecture, made early in this century, that differences in physiology and overt conduct are inadequate markers of attributes of males and females (Rosenberg, 1982). This awareness spurred the development of the psychological constructs of masculinity and femininity along with fifty years of research evaluating the constructs and their behavioral concomitants. Because the history of these developments has already received attention (Morawski, 1985b), it is appropriate to turn to the eventual criticism or renunciation of the constructs, and detail subsequent attempts to reformulate gender studies according to notions of androgyny. The historical excursion sets a context for reconsidering some central theoretical problems and alternative proposals.

Such a broad review inevitably blurs theoretical subtleties and perturbations but, nevertheless, offers a fair sense of how our understanding of certain constructs has fared. It reveals just how the empirical study of gender has been repeatedly challenged by fundamental thematic problems: the coincidence of feminism and politics within scientific discussions, the complex effects of social change, and the unrelenting search for "real" gender or "core" masculine and feminine characteristics. That is, the study of the psychological attributes of males and females has been marked by several metatheoretical issues, namely, the normative dimensions of scientific inquiry, the transhistorical mutability of social phenomena, and the desire for realism and determinism in human studies.

DISSOLVING AND REAPPEARING DIFFERENCES

Writing in 1902 on the question of coeducation, James Rowland Angell noted that "the prevalent doctrines concerning the mental differences of men and women are matters of dogma readily susceptible of neither proof nor disproof" (p. 90). Oddly enough for a flourishing psychologist, Angell conjectured that even the new scientific psychology harbored such dogmas. He argued that only time—and social experiments such as coeducation—would deliver a true understanding of sex differences and their origins. Such observations of the ideological contamination of much research on sex and gender have been confirmed in historical investigations (Bleier, 1984; Gould, 1981; Shields, 1975, 1982). Despite his skepticism regarding the scientific study of sex differences, Angell nevertheless trained young psychologists, including women, who took up the scientific quest for an understanding of the nature of males and females.

For the most part, interested American psychologists placed their bets on scientific psychology as the means to debunk the myths of masculine and feminine spheres, and the effort to establish knowledge of gender was a significant one in the new psychology (Rosenberg, 1982). In psychology the questions would be examined empirically, the focus would be psychological and hence would differ from dubitable work in biology, and the inquiry would be open-minded as to the true causes— nature or nurture—of sex-related differences. The equivocal if not confusing outcome of these empirical pursuits is described in detail elsewhere (Lewin, 1984a; Morawski, 1985b; Rosenberg, 1982). In summary, these early studies of psychological attributes and conduct indicated that sex differences were either nonexistent, relatively insubstantial, or erratic in their patterns. The reported differences were often so slight that Hollingworth (1918) argued that anyone who attempted to review sex difference research would "automatically tend to do himself out of his review. He would have very little to report" (p. 428).

By the 1920s the effort to attain scientific knowledge of the psychology of gender faltered, caught in a web of inconsistent and inconclusive findings (Allen, 1927; Hollingworth, 1916, 1918). The myriad experiments yielded no discernible sex-related patterns in performance or cognition; they yielded no theory about sex-linked styles or their origins. Some psychologists concluded that differences were largely environmental in origin and would shift or disappear with ongoing cultural changes (see Rosenberg, 1982). Others, undeterred by the inconclusive state of research, proceeded to speculate about the nature of males and females. The conjectures were of two sorts: that the experimentation was faulty (Hall, 1922; Moore, 1922), or that meaningful differences were located beyond the psychological domains mined in the typical experiment (Jastrow, 1918; Leuba, 1926). Both explanations suggested the existence of some deeper structure of gender, and the excavation of this structure was a task that lay ahead. These arguments were bolstered by claims that studies had to be detached from researchers' passionate political interests and designed to minimize the subjects' tendencies to act complicitly when the issue under study related to any aspect of sexuality (Morawski, 1985b).

Of those who persisted in an empirical search for meaningful differences, none were as successful as Lewis Terman and Catherine Cox Miles. In 1936 they published the results of over a decade of work: they had developed a means to identify *and* measure psychological attributes of males and females (Terman & Miles, 1936). The means was a 910-item test that could detect masculinity and femininity. The M-F scale was called the Attitude Interest Analysis Test (AIST) in order to conceal its purpose from subjects. The test embodied highly desirable research standards: It was quantitative and, therefore, objective and above political contamination; it protected against subjects' response biases; and it located psychological gender, femininity and masculinity, at a deeper substrate than could be ascertained by the casual observer or lone introspector—even if they were trained psychologists. With such a powerful instrument, Terman and Miles could conclude that masculinity and femininity "do have behavioral correlates but that ordinary observers lack adeptness in detecting them" (p. 465). Consequently, the test also had diagnostic capabilities. The measures of hidden masculinity or femininity could reveal incongruencies between one's biological sex and one's psychological sex and, therefore, could be used to determine "sexual inversion" (homosexuality) or predict problems in marital adjustment. Although Terman and Miles conceded that the M-F scale did not pronounce on the origins of such differences, they were satisfied with its unambiguous identification of feminine and masculine minds.

REPRODUCING MASCULINITY AND FEMININITY

The psychological gender attributes unearthed by Terman and Miles became the prototype for research on masculinity and femininity for over three decades. But theirs was not to remain the sole measurement tool, and soon other M-F tests were constructed. These subsequent instruments were often designed to assess a more restricted range of psychological phenomena or to complement particular personality theories. Some testmakers introduced psychometric innovations, such as projective techniques, because they were purported to be even more sensitive to hidden or unconscious psychological characteristics (Lewin, 1984b; Morawski, 1985b).

Despite the proliferation of psychometric devices, the various M-F tests shared four root assumptions with the original scale devised by Terman and Miles: (1) Psychological gender was a deep-seated and enduring quality of individuals. (2) That quality evaded ready detection and, perhaps more important, was not signified directly by overt behaviors. Researchers embraced this stipulation despite the ascendancy of behavioral psychology and the correspondent disavowal of mentalism. (3) The deep-seated quality was closely linked to individuals' true inner natures and, hence, to their mental health. Incongruency with biological sex or disorder in one's masculinity or femininity indicated problems in psychological adjustment and well-being. On the basis of this assumption, two technical developments were implemented: the creation of assessment controls, techniques to offset subjects' desires to disguise their true gender orientation, and the use of M-F scales as diagnostic tools for identifying psychological disorders. Together the putative importance of masculinity and femininity in mental health and individuals' inability to articulate their own psychological gender strongly implied that psychologists take precautions to retain control over assessment and diagnosis. (4) The psychological attributes, feminine and masculine, are opposite ends of a bipolar and unidimensional continuum. Masculinity and femininity consist of opposing psychological characteristics, and these characteristics correspond closely to cultural stereotypes of gender. Masculine and feminine minds resemble the gender-role schema of separate spheres that was articulated, exaggerated, and elaborated upon during the Victorian era (Lewin, 1984b, 1984c; Rosenberg, 1982). Masculinity is associated with the extroverted, active, independent, self-confident, and instrumental; femininity with the introverted, timid, dependent, sentimental, and expressive. Together these four assumptions delineated the realms of psychological gender and, in turn, enabled the production of empirical evidence of these realms.

REARRANGEMENT OF THE M-F TYPOLOGY

The M-F tests became a conventional procedure for assessing gender, and despite occasional problems of validity and response bias, the tests were in continued use until the 1970s. By the early 1970s there was considerable disenchantment with psychological gender concepts and the technical procedures used to evaluate them. It is no coincidence that this upheaval occurred when the new wave of feminism of the 1960s had reached scientific psychology. The ensuing criticism of masculine and feminine constructs in particular, and of sex-role research in general, was twofold. First, the research program was found to exaggerate difference: Gender differences had been socially constructed in the course of formulating theories and conducting empirical inquiries into gender. Second, this manufacturing of difference included devaluation of feminine characteristics and perpetuated stereotypic ideas of femininity as deficient and undesirable (Angrist, 1972; Broverman, Vogel, Broverman, Clarkson, & Rosenkrantz, 1972; Carlson, 1972; Helson, 1972; Weisstein, 1971). The critique of the purported sex differences and of the degradation of female attributes challenged some methodological and conceptual foundations. Weisstein's (1971) suggestion that the psychological attributes associated with the biological designations of male and female were constructed and not intrinsic implicated psychologists in an enterprise of creating gender. In addition, Constantinople's (1973) review questioned the bases for assuming the unidimensionality and bipolarity of the constructs and called into question the veridicality of constructs that were validated simply by sex differences in item response.

Beyond questioning the validity of M-F scales, these criticisms imperiled the simple equation of "masculine" with males and "feminine" with females. The most noted test of this reality was Bem's (1974) conceptualization of sex-role "androgyny." The idea that masculinity and femininity are not unidimensional or bipolar suggested the possibility that individuals could display both masculine and feminine attributes. A high level of both attributes, if present in approximately equal amounts, could be taken to indicate that an individual is neither masculine nor feminine but androgynous. It was hypothesized that the androgynous individual, with a balance of gender components, would be psychologically healthier as well as more flexible and independent than either feminine or masculine individuals. Bem (1974, 1977) developed a scale, the Bem Sex Role Inventory (BSRI), to measure masculinity, femininity, and androgyny. Several similar scales were created within a few years (Berzins, Welling, & Wetter, 1978; Heilbrun, 1976; Spence, Helmreich, & Stapp, 1975).

The new androgyny scales are not homogeneous. They share, however, at least nine core assumptions.

(1) Categories of masculinity and femininity are assumed to be independent dimensions, hence not necessarily mutually exclusive.

(2) Masculinity and femininity, as psychological categories, are unrelated to biological sex and to sexuality.

(3) The categories are derived by aggregating responses to stereotypic descriptions that distinguish gender roles and expectations.

(4) These sex-typed characteristics are assumed to be a function of individual traits as well as popular conceptions about masculinity and femininity.

(5) The categories retain the same content as the previous M-F scales; masculine is direct, instrumental, and independent whereas feminine is indirect, expressive, and dependent.

(6) Androgyny is identified as a high level of both femininity and masculinity within an individual.

(7) The categories of feminine, masculine, and androgynous are held to be predictive of certain social behaviors, although the models differ in specifying which behaviors are related to the measures.

(8) Androgyny, or high levels of both masculinity and femininity, is believed to be desirable. Although there are differences between the models, they generally posit that the androgynous person has a greater range of options for behaving and, therefore, is more flexible and adjusted.

(9) The androgyny construct is situated in conventional frameworks of psychology. Whether explained through self- and cognitive-schemas or through trait theory, androgyny adheres to current canons in psychology.

If judged by their use in research, androgyny inventories have been highly successful. In addition to studies of the instruments' validity and behavioral correlates, the measures, like their predecessors, have been used to diagnose psychological disturbances and to counsel for androgyny (Cook, 1985; Gilbert, 1981). Androgyny inventories, primarily those of the BSRI and Personal Attributes Questionnaire (PAQ; Spence et al., 1975), have become standard tools in empirical research and clinical practice. Psychologists have moved toward androgyny just when its cultural presence, as reported in the press, is "gradually but steadily becoming part of the American way of life" (Engel, 1985, p. 24). However, it is far from clear how the androgynous images in popular culture, stunning in dress and performance, relate to the psychological conceptualization.

Like the early twentieth-century studies of sex differences, current research on androgyny illuminates neither psychological gender nor even gender differences. Androgyny research is, indeed, problematical. Admittedly there are those who move onward in limiting or refining androgyny (Bem, 1985; Feather, 1984; Spence, 1983) and there are many other investigators who confidently utilize the models and related inventories. Nevertheless, substantial problems with the new conceptions have been noted, concerning not just those psychometrics or empirical findings but the basic assumptions that sustain them. These foundational problems suggest that either criticism of particular methodological points or simple ridicule of the entire enterprise (an attitude exemplified by some critics of androgyny) is inadequate. Assessment must necessarily cover the full landscape of metatheoretical concerns and not just particular features of the various models. This can be initiated by reviewing the problems that have received most attention: difficulties concerning the structure, content, and contextual relevance of androgyny. These problems can then be related to several aspects of the underlying metatheory.

Structure

Androgyny research has been charged with some of the same misdemeanors associated with M-F scales. The research contains unexamined assumptions about the two-dimensionality and orthogonality of femininity and masculinity just as the earlier scales assumed unidimensionality and bipolarity without warrant. The androgyny models further assume that responses to sex-stereotyped descriptions adequately distinguished what is feminine and what is masculine just as the M-F scales tenuously assumed that sex-differences on item response indicate masculinity and femininity (Locksley & Colten, 1979; Myers & Gonda, 1982). Related to this assumption is a more global presupposition that responses tap not simply cultural stereotypes but personality and cognitive structures—the true "inner" nature of masculine and feminine. With androgyny as with the M-F scales, the positing of a real inner substrate, one not readily accessible except by technical expertise, has wide-ranging implications for how we evaluate human performance (Morawski, 1985b). These issues are compounded by methodological problems in the scoring procedures and by difficulties in relating the different androgyny models to each other (Blackman, 1982; Pedhazur & Tetenbaum, 1979; Strahan, 1984; Taylor, 1983; Wilson & Cook, 1984). Important questions thus remain about the extent to which the scales are structured to measure a unique and singular psychological phenomenon.

Content

After a decade of vigorous research, the meaning of androgyny remains opaque. When introducing the initial scale, Bem (1974) defined androgyny as an individual's ability to act in both masculine and feminine ways, "depending on the situational appropriateness of these various behaviors" (p. 155). Although apparently simple enough, this definition ran against others that were imbedded in the various scales. Was androgyny, in reflecting both the feminine and the masculine, produced by a combination that was additive, interactive, emergent, or balanced? (See Cook, 1985; Hall & Taylor, 1985; Spence, 1985; Taylor & Hall, 1982.)

One might argue that this question ultimately could be settled by empirical research, but such arguments evade even more trenchant problems. First, by using various forms of analysis, several critics have found that what is taken as androgynous behavior is really masculine in essence: Androgynous action is constituted by the presence of masculine components, rather than by some special uniting of both gender dimensions (Jones, Chernovetz, & Hansson, 1978; Lee & Scheurer, 1983; Lubinski, Tellegen, & Butcher, 1983; Olds & Shaver, 1980; Taylor & Hall, 1982). Still other critics claim that the androgyny scales really measure self-esteem (Brown, 1986). It must be noted that the close relation of androgyny to masculinity and self-esteem may be due, in part, to masculine-task bias in many experimental situations and to the fact that there have been few attempts to assess the behavioral impact of femininity. Wheeler, Reis, and Nezlek (1983) have found femininity to be negatively related to loneliness in both males and females, although they did not examine the relation between loneliness and androgyny. Thus, to date there is little evidence for the feminine components of androgynous well-being.

The disparities between the different scales suggest that there is still lack of agreement on what constitutes masculinity and femininity (Wilson & Cook, 1984). There have been two types of commentaries levied about the equivocality of the masculinity and femininity concepts. From one side, defenders argue that the scales represent only specific facets of masculinity and femininity. For example, Spence and Helmreich (1978; Spence, 1983) claim that their scale, the PAQ, merely measures "instrumental" and "expressive" traits (although they and others who use the PAQ persist in using the terms synonymously with masculine and feminine). Bem (1983, 1985) has revised her approach, and, rather than emphasizing surface attributes of gender, is now examining the deeper cognitive processes that determine how individuals employ "schemas" of gender to understand themselves and others.

From another side, the two components of androgyny inventories, and even androgyny itself, can be seen as global stereotypes. Despite their own criticism of the normative (sexist) basis of M-F scales, researchers developed androgyny models according to certain values and interests with several serious implications (Hefner & Rebecca, 1979; Lott, 1981; Morawski, 1985b). Given its utilization of fixed gender concepts that designate what is masculine and what is feminine, androgyny perpetuates, perhaps even reifies, the very prejudices it was intended to remedy. Bem (1979) recognized these value contradictions and argued that because the ascendancy of androgyny would spell the demise of masculinity and femininity, and because androgyny is defined by the joint presence of femininity and masculinity, the concept contains the seeds of its own destruction. Literary critics have made similar claims, arguing that androgyny "embodies its own deconstruction" in that it is built upon internal contradictions (Weil, 1985, p. 3).

Concerning the values imbedded in androgyny itself, the major problems are unlikely to dissolve. Androgyny has been criticized as an undesirable and probably unattainable ideal. Not only does the model stipulate demanding goals of conduct that few fulfill in their life situations, not only does it seem to privilege and promote masculine characteristics, but it also poses an ideal of human action that fails to consider social relations and social processes (Locksley & Colten, 1979; Morawski, 1985b; Myers & Gonda, 1982; Stark-Adamec, Graham, & Pyke, 1980; Taylor & Hall, 1982). The model prescribes what Sampson (1978) identified as "self-contained individualism," and I have suggested that it does more. The androgynous image is a mirror of the ideals of contemporary professional life, reflecting a historical moment when women professionals, in particular, required a model that promoted conventionally masculine (instrumental) actions without compromising the feminine self (Morawski, 1985b). Ehrenreich (1983) has argued that males also have benefited from something akin to an androgynous model insofar as exhibiting attributes and social skills of both genders further frees them from their commitment to women and families. Androgyny, then, can be interpreted as an emerging social style, an adaptation to contemporary life. This interpretation corresponds with the way in which feminists in the 1920s and 1930s used the androgynous ideal to repudiate confining gender conventions. Ironically, these women shed their identity as women and fashioned the androgynous image with male words and symbols only to become alienated not only from women but from men and male sources of power (Smith-Rosenberg, 1985).

Given the insensitivity to social relations, processes, and situations, the so-called androgyny phenomenon is open to other interpretations. Perhaps what we have with androgyny is a "hollow identity" (Sarbin & Scheibe, 1983), a case of the individual's ascribed roles being overshadowed or damaged by attained roles. Thus the social identity traditionally associated with the ascribed roles of "woman" or "man" is only operational at specific times and places, whereas in other situations these ascribed roles are negated by the individual's attained identity. Thus, for instance, the impression of attained roles constrains the male hairdresser's ability to maintain a singular stable identity across situations or the female chief executive officer's enactment of any feminine identity.

Recent social commentaries have employed similar models of fragmented identities to explain the decline of human virtues and communities (Lasch, 1978; MacIntyre, 1981). Or perhaps what we are observing are "multiplicative identities" that, like the uses of androgyny in fictional literature (Weil, 1985), allow the author tremendous textual liberties in designing and executing action. Androgynous characters are mercurial persons, even tricksters, who can draw upon either masculine or feminine attributes, depending on which identity best serves them in a given interaction. This interpretation might be congruent with theories of situated or multiple identities (Kihlstrom & Cantor, 1983; Rosenberg & Gara, 1985). Then again, perhaps what we have is nothing more than idealism, a long-standing quality of American culture whereby psychological androgyny signifies the ideal of full equality of all persons regardless of race or gender. This ideal frequently surfaces in fantasy and utopian literature where the realities of a hierarchical and discriminatory social structure can be suspended (Glenn, 1980; Morgan, 1977).

Contextual Relevance

The case for alternative interpretations of androgyny becomes even more plausible in light of various problems of contextual relevance. Leaving aside the question of whether androgyny or masculinity better predicts successful behavior and the related question of what constitutes successful behavior, empirical studies indicate that androgyny measures do not predict an impressively wide range of behaviors. They seem to be limited predictors of gender-related behaviors and do not predict adaptability and competence equally well for males and females (Heilbrun, 1984; Heilbrun & Pitman, 1979; Helmreich, Spence, &

Holahan, 1979; Spence & Helmreich, 1980; Williams, Leak, & Millard, 1984). They reveal little about the full range of effects of masculinity and femininity in culture, although it should be noted that not all researchers claim that their scales have such extensive predictive power (Helmreich et al., 1979; Spence, 1983, 1985).

The few studies that have attended to cultural meanings of masculinity and femininity find them to be far more diverse than the concepts represented by the scales; subjects relate the terms to physical appearance, movement, and status—not just to personality traits or cognitive orientations (Myers & Gonda, 1982). Some research has challenged the underlying assumptions of independent dimensions of masculinity and femininity, the irrelevance of sexuality, and the personal well-being associated with androgyny. Harris (1981) found that female subjects believed masculinity and femininity to be bipolar and not independent dimensions. Some research even indicates the negative consequences of androgyny, for instance, in parenting (Baumrind, 1982). And Brown (1986) argues that it is more appropriate to use the word "androgyny" in reference to sexuality rather than to some constellation of traits or attributes.

These various predictive problems may well result from eschewal of both contextual-situational and social-structural factors. Judging from the research literature, androgynous individuals seem to operate (effortlessly) in a social vacuum where expectations for gender-related behavior or gender-based constraints on choice of action are noticeably absent. The contextual framework supporting androgyny does not accommodate real gender-based constraints that enable or prohibit human activities (Locksley & Colten, 1979; Sherif, 1982; Skrypnek & Snyder, 1982). The models do not recognize the material constraints deriving from the state of the physical world and the physicalities of the body (some tools can be operated only by individuals with particular physical features); the formal sanctions, laws, or rules that prohibit males or females from certain activities (joining the Kiwanis club, being an attendant in a women's restroom, leaving the top section of the body uncovered in public); or the social constraints that contextually structure cognitive processing, speech, and action (imagining that the physician might be a certain sex, the use of personal space, crying in public). Even the simplest expression of these structural constraints is virtually absent from androgyny models, although some attention is given to them in discussions of gender schemas (Bem, 1983, 1985; Skrypnek & Snyder, 1982).

In overlooking social structure, androgyny models also do not attend to cultural change or to intra- and cross-cultural differences (Hefner & Rebecca, 1979; Kenworthy, 1979). Just as they are static in regard to historical change (Morawski, 1982; Stark-Adamec et al., 1980), so they have no explanatory perspective on individual change across the life span. The neglect of broader contextual features, of the plurality of stereotypes and expectations, and of the dynamics of cultures and personalities renders androgyny a reifying ideal, one that inadvertently perpetuates a very particular constellation of values and virtues.

THE VALUES OF ANDROGYNY

Documenting the particularities of androgyny's shortcomings might seem like an unnecessary diversion in an essay reviewing one hundred years of research on sex-related concepts. But particularities illustrate the crucial if rather basic point that attention to the fine strokes often interferes with seeing the pattern unfolding on the canvas. A preoccupation with technical details obscures the normative features of psychological theory.

The fundamental issues surrounding androgyny are not psychometric, nor do they inhere in the research contests between behavioral, trait, and cognitive models. Rather, they concern the epistemology that structures the theories and the values implicit in that structuring. The epistemology is modeled after that of the physical sciences, which, by its nature, hinders articulation of values. With this worldview, psychology has been able to ignore the implications of human reflexivity—the multiple consequences of humans being both the objects and the subjects of scientific studies (Flanagan, 1981; MacIntyre, 1985; Morawski, 1985a, 1986; Unger, 1983). Across time and situations psychologists have been reluctant to see the degrees to which research mirrors or is a metaphor of our self-conceptions, desires, and intuitions.

Much of North American psychology is guided by an ideal of individual functioning and associated beliefs in an equilibrium of needs and satisfiers, drives and adjustments, information and judgment (Henriques, Hollway, Urwin, Venn, & Walkerdine, 1984; Hogan & Emler, 1978; Israel, 1972; Sampson, 1978, 1985). Yet individual characteristics in themselves do not constitute successful action. No model of individual functioning is coherent without considering social context and structure. Nevertheless, contemporary gender research adheres to the individual-centered stipulations, along with certain political ideals that have been salient in the late twentieth century—most notably the desire to eliminate barriers that prevent individuals from achieving' their potential. In keeping with psychological tradition, androgyny models locate these barriers largely within the individual and offer a recipe for their elimination. And in keeping with the tendency for human rights movements to be most populated by those who are disadvantaged, this corrective research has been sustained largely by female psychologists whose own images are intimately related to the subject under study. However, the fact that many women participate in gender research can be misleading, for it is still the case that scientific and professional standards, established primarily by men (and perhaps with masculine criteria), underlie the gender constructions. In other words, although increases in the number of female psychologists have expanded gender research, these increases have not substantially altered research styles (Lykes & Stewart, 1986; Parlee, 1979). As discussed later, feminist psychologists may be in the same quandary as earlier feminists who appropriated the language and symbols of men, only to remain socially marginal and without power.

Gender research reflects a history of political interests, sometimes in favor of revealing differences (as in the 1920s) and at other times in favor of minimizing differences (Bleier, 1984; Hall, 1974; Newman, 1985; Shields, 1975). Like their predecessors (the M-F scales), masculinity, femininity, and androgyny inventories reflect concern with differences between females and males but obscure the sociopolitical implications of difference. Androgyny research was motivated by a liberal feminism that, in seeking equality for women, assumed that many reputed differences were actually superficial and that reducing the imposed differences would engender equal treatment. In psychology this feminism has fostered ideals of gender-neutral human characteristics. Few researchers considered the extent to which these gender-neutral ideals may have actually represented masculine characteristics or the appropriate ingredients for successful action in a male-centered world (skills at instrumental tasks, high self-esteem). The move toward androgyny now seems ironic and certainly puzzling. In the face of critiques of the science's devaluation of the feminine and endorsement of the masculine as exemplifying mental health (Broverman et al., 1972; Weisstein, 1971), androgyny was introduced despite its incorporation of those very asymmetrical standards. To be fair, it must be recognized that in scientific research the asymmetry of gender is not always readily detected—for example, masculine task bias—nor is it easy to locate the impact of femininity on behavior.

Although individualism and liberal feminism were influencing research, the field of psychology was hardly touched by new ventures in feminist thought that emerged during the 1970s and 1980s (Eisenstein, 1983). It was not involved in the critical analysis of masculine and feminine values and experiences, or of the social structure that sustains such values and experiences. In fixing on the need to examine gender and sex-related attributes in quantitative terms, to insist above all that they be measurable, psychological research could not readily accommodate these more global factors; conventional research required context-stripping. By focusing on gender within the individual and by eliminating issues of sexuality from discussion of gender (albeit for corrective reasons), androgyny research overlooked a crucial component of gender—that of social power. Yet, gender is not simply related to social power, it is constitutive of power relations and is a stable component in social hierarchies of power.

Also lost to psychology were some trenchant and compelling conceptual critiques of androgyny that might have saved substantial expenditures in empirical research (Beardsley, 1982; Eisenstein, 1983; Gelpi, 1974; Harris, 1974; Secor, 1974). These and other commentaries identified the underlying masculine bias, the promotion of "male androgynies" (Gelpi, 1974, p. 157). They further discussed how such models idealistically glossed over the asymmetries of social power, rights, and privileges that constitute our contemporary social structure and that are ascribed to individuals according to their biological sex, not their personal styles or skills. Given the inherent contradictions and political implications of androgyny, some writers declared it a word that should not be spoken (Rich, 1977) or a concept that distorts descriptions of gender and gender relations (Daly, 1978; Eisenstein, 1983; Gelpi, 1974).

The political orientations that motivated androgyny in particular, and research on gender in general, did not encourage examination of the social institutions that are sustained by and, in turn, sustain gender distinctions. Yet some perspectives being developed (mostly) outside psychology do address these issues as well as questions about the gender bases of science and our scientific models (Gould, 1984; Harding & Hintikka, 1983; Jaggar, 1983; Keller, 1985; Merchant, 1980). These reflexive practices reveal the ways in which gender structures even social scientific epistemology and methodology, from the masculine conceptions of "objectivity" to the failure to legitimize female experience (Mies,

1983; Sampson, 1978; Unger, 1983; Weskott, 1979). With few exceptions, the varied implications of political values, power, and scientific epistemology are not part of psychologists' conversations about gender. Yet these conversations are necessary if research is to move beyond the impasse so clearly embodied in the concept of androgyny.

RELOCATING GENDER

Situating androgyny research in its social-political context—within a science influenced by the interest of late twentieth-century American society—affords a new understanding of the tradition of psychological research on gender. Considerations of normative interests, rigid conceptual frameworks, and historical change do more than challenge the status or intelligibility of gender research; they provide outlines for profoundly altering our theoretical understandings. Based on such considerations, innovative metatheories of social action are appearing both within and outside of psychology (Gergen, 1985; Giddens, 1984; Harré, 1983; Henriques et al., 1984; Morawski & Gergen, 1980; Rabinow & Sullivan, 1979; Rosnow & Georgoudi, 1986; Sampson, 1985; Shotter, 1984). These metatheories vary considerably but they all recognize the normative bases of theory, the historical nature of sociality, the limits (through not necessarily the irrelevance) of experimental techniques, and the importance of incorporating constructs of social structure and human agency in any theory of social action. The exploration of such routes first requires an even more detailed understanding of current research on gender.

All scientific epistemology or practical metatheories are constituted by certain interests, political and moral (Habermas, 1971). There is more to the normative bases of gender research than assumptions of individualism and liberal feminism. Gender research, like most contemporary psychology, was designed according to a conventional and now dated philosophy of science (Leahey, 1980; Morawski, 1985a; Toulmin & Leary, 1985). Given its underlying edicts of determinism and realism, the research attempts to locate "real" gender; the search has moved through periods in which this real essence was objectified and reified as well as through periods in which the real was disassembled and relocated. Regardless of such shifts, and regardless of psychologists' prescient decision to rescue sex and gender from the reductionist shoals of biology, gender research continues to adhere to essentialism. In the study of men and women, one consequence of this orientation is the obscuring of prescriptions by claims of essentialist truths. That is, descriptions of the attributes of personhood provide mandates for what qualities are required for someone to be recognized as a person. Perhaps the best documented example of masking prescriptive intents is the scientific study of sexuality (Bleier, 1984). In examining these prescriptions, Foucault (1980a, 1980b) has argued that science produced discourses on sex that established or secured certain social relations of power and pleasure.

Another consequence of essentialist commitments is the retention and perpetuation of conceptual dualisms that have no clear empirical grounding (Jaggar, 1983). Instrumental-expressive, agentic-communal, abstract-relational, and masculine-feminine are theoretical conveniences that have been passed down through generations of social science (and social mythmaking). With dubious heritages and a paucity of empirical warrant, these dichotomies inspire preferences and hierarchies, usually in the form of privileging instrumental over expressive and what is male over what is female. The conventional philosophy of science is in part a product of such dichotomous hierarchies: Stereotypical masculine attributes of objectivity, rationality, disinterestedness, and instrumentality are privileged over feminine ones of emotion, relatedness, subjectivity, and expressivity (Keller, 1985; Merchant, 1980; Sampson, 1978). New methodologies are required that bracket these dualist heuristics, reflect critically on hierarchical dimensions, and submit them to critical tests of social experience (Lott, 1985; Mies, 1983; Morawski, 1984, 1986; Unger, 1983; Weskott, 1979).

Essentialism also appears in analytic distinctions. Restricting the central unit of analysis to the individual, sometimes even to his or her cognitions, reflects a "poetics of the individual" (Sarbin & Scheibe, 1983) that neglects the ways in which identity and action are social and in which psychological reality is negotiated between actors and within socially structured constraints (Gergen, 1985; Giddens, 1984). Analysis in terms of individual units has theoretical as well as political implications. Unger (1985) cogently described the failure of conventional theorizing to disclose the double-binds in women's lives and the social negotiations constituting these contradictions. Deaux (1984) has argued similarly that conventional theory focuses on static categories and individual-centered explanations rather than exploring the social processes of gender. Such recommendations are not endorsing the opposite sides of dualisms—say, of individual versus social analysis—but suggest the dynamic relations of such polar constructs.

To suggest the necessity of recognizing social negotiations and processes is to endorse a more contextual research enterprise. Current understandings of gender are framed within a narrowly bounded cultural and historical context and, as noted, fail to encompass even ordinary interpretations of masculine and feminine. As a consequence, there is almost no work (outside that done by historians) on the temporal dynamics of gender in individuals or on variations within or across cultures. For instance, contextual study of the reading of romance novels by American housewives (Radway, 1984) reveals more of a gender subculture than is explained by the psychometric label of "traditional feminine," "feminine schematic," or "expressive." The recent rise in the degree to which American women show an external locus of control (Doherty & Baldwin, 1985) may indicate cultural changes whereby the emergence of androgyny is being mitigated by women's realization that their choices are limited by social structures. Also unexamined is the possible plurality of gender forms. Any idea of proliferating genders is preempted by the persistent construal of gender as dichotomous. This assumption is not necessary, and there is some evidence that, when given the opportunity, individuals use more gender categories than simply those of male and female (England & Hyland, 1985; McCarthy et al., 1985).

These dynamics of gender cannot be understood without considering the full context—the ways in which social structures constrain certain enactments of gender and enable others. The question of social structure and the social relations of power that it creates are central to gender theories (Lott, 1985; Parlee, 1979; Sherif, 1982; Unger, 1985). Weisstein (1971) has delineated the ways in which psychology furnishes the image and psychological reality of the female; it is also the case that the constructing of gender, regardless of the social ends, occurs within a social world of which the dynamics analyzed by conventional psychology are just one part. Considerable research on the creation of psychological gender in terms of its rootedness in a democratic, corporate, and patriarchal social matrix has been done by scholars working within a feminist psychoanalytic tradition (Chodorow, 1978; Dinnerstein, 1976; see Steele, 1985) or documenting the social experiences of women (for example, Hartmann, 1979; Radway, 1984; Rosaldo, 1980; Smith-Rosenberg, 1985). The material and cultural bases of gender and its reproduction reveal the necessity of looking beyond disciplinary borders (Parlee, 1979) and cultural boundaries (Gewertz, 1984; Marks & de Courtivron, 1981; Rosaldo, 1980).

CONCLUSION

The quest for psychological gender seems to be far from finished, although the aims of the quest now require sober reconsideration. Psychologists took up the search with a resolute belief that the essentialist accounts of the biological imperative were inadequate. Yet somehow, along the way of elucidating the environmental, social, and cognitive constituents of gender, a modified version of essentialist categories was adopted. These categories emerged in the form of universal dichotomies along with naive realist notions about an integrated, internal reality of gender. Although probably few psychologists would deny the impact of social structure and interpersonal relations of power, gender came to be located primarily in the interior of individuals. The commonplace ideas about the separate spheres of feminine and masculine were confirmed and reified just as they were accorded reality within science.

Feminist psychologists have questioned the categorical realities of gender and have introduced a more liberal model of human functioning. But they have done so within a conventional philosophy of science that maintains the irrelevance of politics, values, and history. The study of gender, therefore, remains embedded in conventional interpretive frameworks that view human action as corresponding to some stable, identifiable, and internal state that is to some extent unalterable by history, culture, politics, or economics. Thus feminist psychologists face some of the same dilemmas that, according to Smith-Rosenberg (1985), feminists faced earlier in this century: In turning to androgyny to expand the options for women's lives, they are caught in the male language and symbols they appropriated, and yet they are still largely without material power. During the same period, an interest in gender has spread across the disciplines, generating challenges to conventional canons of research in fields as diverse as English, anthropology, philosophy, and history. The new scholarship is intimating the poverty of fundamentally psychological interpretations of gender, and could signal the decline of psychology's place in explaining gender. The challenges suggest that as psychologists we need to ask new questions, including questions about the interests and politics inherent in our scientific philosophy. Unless we stop inquiring, in essentialist and universalist terms, merely about what gender is and begin to examine more seriously the processes that confirm and sustain gender, the search for psychological gender might well remain at its current impasse.

NOTE

1. There are no ready conventions for the use of the terms "sex" and "gender" in psychology. My preference is to use "sex" to refer to the biological assignment of males and females and "gender" to refer to all other characteristics assigned to male and females. However, it is sometimes anachronistic to apply such distinctions to historical materials, and wherever possible I have tried to preserve the terminology of these materials.

REFERENCES

Allen, C. (1927). Studies in sex differences. *Psychological Bulletin, 24,* 294-304.

Angell, J. R. (1902). Some reflections upon the reaction from coeducation. *Popular Science Monthly, 62,* 5-26.

Angrist, S. (1972). The study of sex roles. In J. M. Bardwick (Ed.), *Readings on the psychology of women* (pp. 101-106). New York: Harper & Row.

Baumrind, D. (1982). Are androgynous individuals more effective persons and parents? *Child Development, 53,* 44-75.

Beardsley, E. L. (1982). On curing conceptual confusion: Response to Mary Ann Warren. In M. Vetterling-Braggin (Ed.), *"Femininity," "masculinity," and "androgyny": A modern philosophical discussion* (pp. 197-203). Totowa, NJ: Littlefield, Adams.

Bem, S. L. (1974). The measurement of psychological androgyny. *Journal of Consulting and Clinical Psychology, 42,* 155-162.

Bem, S. L. (1977). On the utility of alternative procedures for assessing psychological androgyny. *Journal of Consulting and Clinical Psychology, 45,* 196-205.

Bem, S. L. (1979). Theory and measurement of androgyny: A reply to Pedhazur-Tetenbaum and Locksley-Colton critiques. *Journal of Personality and Social Psychology, 37,* 1047-1054.

Bem, S. L. (1983). Gender schema theory and its implications for child development: Raising gender-aschematic children in a gender-schematic society. *Signs, 8,* 598-616.

Bem, S. L. (1985). Androgyny and gender schema theory: A conceptual and empirical integration. *Nebraska Symposium on Motivation, 32,* 179-226.

Berzins, J. I., Welling, M. A., & Wetter, R. E. (1978). A new measure of psychological androgyny based on the personality research form. *Journal of Consulting and Clinical Psychology, 46,* 126-138.

Blackman, S. (1982). Comments on three methods of scoring androgyny as a continuous variable. *Psychological Reports, 51,* 1100-1102.

Bleier, R. (1984). *Science and gender: A critique of biology and its theories on women.* New York: Pergamon Press.

Broverman, I. K., Vogel, S. R., Broverman, D. M., Clarkson, F. E., & Rosenkrantz, P. S. (1972). Sex role stereotypes: A current reappraisal. *Journal of Social Issues, 28*, 59-78.

Brown, R. (1986). *Social psychology, the second edition*. New York: Free Press.

Carlson, R. (1972). Understanding women: Implications for personality theory and research. *Journal of Social Issues, 28*, 17-32.

Chodorow, N. (1978). *The reproduction of mothering: Psychoanalysis and the sociology of gender*. Berkeley: University of California.

Constantinople, A. (1973). Masculinity-femininity: An exception to a famous dictum. *Psychological Bulletin, 80*, 389-407.

Cook, E. P. (1985). *Psychological androgyny*. New York: Pergamon Press.

Daly, M. (1978). *Gyn/ecology*. Boston: Beacon Press.

Deaux, K. (1984). From individual differences to social categories: Analysis of a decade's research on gender. *American Psychologist, 39*, 105-116.

Dinnerstein, D. (1976). *The mermaid and the minotaur: Sexual arrangements and human malaise*. New York: Harper & Row.

Doherty, W. J., & Baldwin, C. (1985). Shifts and stability in locus of control during the 1970s: Divergence of the sexes. *Journal of Personality and Social Psychology, 48*, 1048-1053.

Ehrenreich, B. (1983). *The hearts of men: American dreams and the flight from commitment*. Garden City, NY: Anchor.

Eisenstein, H. (1983). *Contemporary feminist thought*. Boston: G. K. Hall.

Engel, P. (1985, February). Androgynous zones. *Harvard Magazine*, pp. 24-33.

England, E. M., & Hyland, D. T. (1985). *Male categories: Are all men "masculine"?* Paper presented at the annual meetings of the Eastern Psychological Association, Boston.

Feather, N. T. (1984). Masculinity, femininity, psychological androgyny, and the structure of values. *Journal of Personality and Social Psychology, 47*, 604-620.

Flanagan, O. J., Jr. (1981). Psychology, progress, and the problem of reflexivity: A study in the epistemological foundations of psychology. *Journal of the History of the Behavioral Sciences, 17*, 375-386.

Foucault, M. (1980a). *Herculine Barbin: Being the recently discovered memoirs of a nineteenth-century French hermaphrodite* (R. McDougall, Trans.). New York: Pantheon.

Foucault, M. (1980b). *The history of sexuality: Volume I: An introduction* (R. Hurley, Trans.). New York: Vintage.

Gelpi, B. C. (1974). The politics of androgyny. *Women's Studies, 2*, 151-160.

Gergen, K. J. (1985). The social constructionist movement in modern psychology. *American Psychologist, 40*, 266-275.

Gergen, K. J., & Morawski, J. G. (1980). An alternative metatheory for social psychology. *Review of Personality and Social Psychology, 1*, 326-352.

Gewertz, D. (1984). The Tchambuli view of persons: A critique of individualism in the works of Mead and Chodorow. *American Anthropologist, 86*, 615-629.

Giddens, A. (1984). *The constitution of society*. Berkeley: University of California Press.

Gilbert, L. A. (1981). Toward mental health: The benefit of psychological androgyny. *Professional Psychology, 12*, 29-38.

Glenn, E. W. (1980). *The androgynous woman character in the American novel*. Unpublished dissertation, University of Colorado, Denver.

Gould, C. C. (1984). *Beyond domination: New perspectives on women and philosophy*. Totowa, NJ: Rowman & Allanheld.

Gould, S. J. (1981). *The mismeasure of man.* New York: W. W. Norton.

Habermas, J. (1971). *Knowledge and human interests* (J. J. Shapiro, Trans.). Boston: Beacon Press.

Hall, D. L. (1974). Biology, sex hormones, and sexism in the 1920s. *Philosophical Forum, 5,* 81-96.

Hall, G. S. (1922). Flapper Americana novissima. *Atlantic Monthly, 129,* 771-780.

Hall, J. A., & Taylor, M. C. (1985). Psychological androgyny and the masculinity and femininity interaction. *Journal of Personality and Social Psychology, 49,* 429-435.

Harding, S., & Hintikka, M. B. (Eds.). (1983). *Discovering reality: Feminist perspectives on epistemology, metaphysics, methodology, and philosophy of science.* Boston: D. Reidel.

Harré, R. (1983). *Personal being.* Oxford: Basil Blackwell.

Harris, D. A. (1974). Androgyny: The sexist myth in disguise. *Women's Studies, 2*(2), 171-184.

Harris, M. B. (1981). Women runners' views of running. *Perceptual and Motor Skills, 53,* 395-402.

Hartmann, H. (1979). Capitalism, patriarchy, and job segregation by sex. In Z. R. Eisenstein (Ed.), *Capitalist patriarchy and the case for socialist feminism* (pp. 206-247). New York: Monthly Review Press.

Hefner, R., & Rebecca, M. (1979). The future of sex roles. In M. Richmond-Abbott (Ed.), *The American woman: Her past, her present, her future* (pp. 243-264). New York: Holt, Rinehart & Winston.

Heilbrun, A. B., Jr. (1976). Measurement of masculine and feminine sex role identities as independent dimensions. *Journal of Consulting and Clinical Psychology, 44,* 183-190.

Heilbrun, A. B., Jr. (1984). Sex-based models of androgyny: A further elaboration of competence difference. *Journal of Personality and Social Psychology, 46,* 216-229.

Heilbrun, A. B., Jr., & Pitman, D. (1979). Testing some basic assumptions about psychological androgyny. *Journal of Genetic Psychology, 135,* 175-188.

Helmreich, R. L., Spence, J. T., & Holahan, C. K. (1979). Psychological androgyny and sex role flexibility: A test of two hypotheses. *Journal of Personality and Social Psychology, 37,* 1631-1644.

Helson, R. (1972). The changing image of the career woman. *Journal of Social Issues, 28,* 33-46.

Henriques, J., Hollway, W., Urwin, C., Venn, C., & Walkerdine, V. (Eds.). (1984). *Changing the subject: Psychology, social regulation, and subjectivity.* London: Methuen.

Hogan, R. T., & Emler, N. P. (1978). The biases in contemporary social psychology. *Social Research, 45,* 478-534.

Hollingworth, L. S. (1916). Sex differences in mental traits. *Psychological Bulletin, 13,* 377-384.

Hollingworth, L. S. (1918). Comparison of the sexes in mental traits. *Psychological Bulletin, 15,* 427-432.

Israel, J. (1972). Stipulations and construction in the social sciences. In J. Israel & H. Tajfel (Eds.), *The context of social psychology: A critical assessment* (pp. 123-211). New York: Academic Press.

Jaggar, A. M. (1983). *Feminist politics and human nature*. Sussex: Harvester Press.

Jastrow, J. (1918). The feminine mind. In J. Jastrow (Ed.), *The psychology of conviction* (pp. 280-325). New York: Houghton Mifflin.

Jones, W., Chernovetz, M. E., & Hansson, R. O. (1978). The enigma of androgyny: Differential implications for males and females? *Journal of Consulting and Clinical Psychology, 46*, 298-313.

Keller, E. F. (1985). *Reflections on gender and science*. New Haven: Yale University Press.

Kenworthy, J. A. (1979). Androgyny in psychotherapy: But will it sell in Peoria? *Psychology of Women Quarterly, 3*, 231-240.

Kihlstrom, J. F., & Cantor, N. (1983). Mental representations of the self. In L. Berkowitz, (Ed.), *Advances in experimental social psychology* (Vol. 15). New York: Academic Press.

Lasch, C. (1978). *The culture of narcissism: American life in an age of diminishing expectations*. New York: W. W. Norton.

Leahey, T. (1980). The myth of operationism. *The Journal of Mind and Behavior, 1*, 127-143.

Lee, A., & Scheurer, V. L. (1983). Psychological androgyny and aspects of self-image in women and men. *Sex Roles, 9*, 289-306.

Leuba, J. H. (1926). The weaker sex. *Atlantic Monthly, 137*, 454-460.

Lewin, M. (Ed.). (1984a). *In the shadow of the past: Psychology portrays the sexes*. New York: Columbia University Press.

Lewin, M. (1984b). Psychology measures femininity and masculinity. II: From "13 Gay Men" to the instrumental-expressive distinction. In M. Lewin (Ed.), *In the shadow of the past: Psychology portrays the sexes* (pp. 197-204). New York: Columbia University Press.

Lewin, M. (1984c). Rather worse than folly? Psychology measures femininity and masculinity. I: From Terman and Miles to the Guilfords. In M. Lewin (Ed.), *In the shadow of the past: Psychology portrays the sexes* (pp. 155-178). New York: Columbia University Press.

Locksley, A., & Colten, M. E. (1979). Psychological androgyny: A case of mistaken identity? *Journal of Personality and Social Psychology, 37*, 1017-1031.

Lott, B. (1981). A feminist critique of androgyny: Toward the elimination of gender attributions for learned behavior. In C. Mayo & N. M. Henley (Eds.), *Gender and nonverbal behavior* (pp. 171-180). New York: Springer-Verlag.

Lott, B. (1985). The potential enrichment of social/personality psychology through feminist research and vice versa. *American Psychologist, 40*, 155-164.

Lubinski, D., Tellegen, A., & Butcher, J. N. (1983). Masculinity, femininity, and androgyny viewed and assessed as distinct concepts. *Journal of Personality and Social Psychology, 44*, 428-439.

Lykes, M. B., & Stewart, A. J. (1986). Evaluating the feminist challenge in psychology: 1963-1983. *Psychology of Women Quarterly, 10*.

MacIntyre, A. (1981). *After virtue: A study in moral theory*. Notre Dame: University of Notre Dame Press.

MacIntyre, A. (1985). How psychology makes itself true—or false. In S. Koch & D. Leary (Eds.), *A century of psychology as science* (pp. 897-903). New York: McGraw-Hill.

Marks, E., & de Courtivron, I. (Eds.). (1981). *New French feminisms: An anthology*. New York: Schocken.

McCarthy, W. J., Hamilton, M., Leaper, C., Pader, E., Rushbrook, S., & Henley, N. (1985). Social influences on what to call her: "Woman," "girl," or "lady." Paper presented at the annual meeting of the American Psychological Association. Los Angeles.

Merchant, C. (1980). *The death of nature: Women, ecology, and the scientific revolution.* New York: Harper & Row.

Mies, M. (1983). Toward a methodology for feminist research. In G. Bowles & R. D. Klein (Eds.), *Theories of women's studies.* London: Routledge & Kegan Paul.

Moore, H. T. (1922). Further data concerning sex differences. *Journal of Abnormal and Social Psychology, 17,* 210-214.

Morawski, J. G. (1982). On thinking about history as social psychology. *Personality and Social Psychology Bulletin, 8,* 393-401.

Morawski, J. G. (1984). Historiography as metatheoretical text for social psychology. In K. J. Gergen & M. Gergen (Eds.), *Historical social psychology* (pp. 37-60). New York: Lawrence Erlbaum.

Morawski, J. G. (1985a). *Historical transformation of the cultures of psychology.* Lecture at the Boston Colloquium for the Philosophy of Science, Boston.

Morawski, J. G. (1985b). The measurement of masculinity and femininity: Engendering categorical realities. *Journal of Personality, 53,* 196-223.

Morawski, J. G. (1986). Contextual discipline: The unmaking and remaking of sociality. In R. L. Rosnow & M. Georgoudi (Eds.), *Contextualism and understanding in behavioral science.* New York: Praeger.

Morawski, J. G., & Gergen, K. J. (1980). An alternative metatheory for social psychology. In L. Wheeler (Ed.), *Review of personality and social psychology* (Vol. 1, pp. 326-352). Beverly Hills, CA: Sage.

Morgan, E. (1977). The feminist novel of androgynous fantasy. *Frontiers, 11,* 40-49.

Myers, A. M., & Gorda, G. (1982). Utility of the masculinity-femininity construct: Comparison of traditional and androgyny approaches. *Journal of Personality and Social Psychology, 43,* 514-522.

Newman, L. M. (Ed.). (1985). *Men's ideas/women's realities: Popular science, 1870-1915.* New York: Pergamon Press.

Olds, D. E., & Shaver, P. (1980). Masculinity, femininity, academic performance, and health: Further evidence concerning the androgyny controversy. *Journal of Personality, 48,* 323-341.

Parlee, M. B. (1979). Psychology and women. *Signs, 5,* 121-133.

Pedhazur, E., & Tetenbaum, T. J. (1979). Bem sex-role inventory: A theoretical and methodological critique. *Journal of Personality and Social Psychology, 37,* 996-1016.

Rabinow, P., & Sullivan, W. M. (Eds.). (1979). *Interpretive social science: A reader.* Berkeley: University of California Press.

Radway, J. A. (1984). *Reading the romance: Women, patriarchy, and popular literature.* Chapel Hill: University of North Carolina Press.

Rich, A. (1977, December). Natural resources. *MS.*

Rosaldo, M. Z. (1980). The use and abuse of anthropology: Reflections on feminism and cross-cultural understanding. *Signs, 5,* 389-417.

Rosenberg, R. L. (1982). *Beyond separate spheres: Intellectual origins of modern feminism.* New Haven, CT: Yale University Press.

Rosenberg, S., & Gara, M. A. (1985). The multiplicity of personal identity. In P. Shaver (Ed.), *Review of personality and social psychology* (Vol. 6, pp. 87-113). Beverly Hills, CA: Sage.

Rosnow, R. L., & Georgoudi, M. (Eds.). (in press). *Contextualism and understanding in behavioral science*. New York: Praeger.

Sampson, E. E. (1977). Psychology and the American ideal. *Journal of Personality and Social Psychology, 35*, 767-782.

Sampson, E. E. (1978). Scientific paradigms and social values: Wanted—a scientific revolution. *Journal of Personality and Social Psychology, 36*, 1332-1343.

Sampson, E. E. (1985). The decentralization of identity: Toward a revised concept of personal and social order. *American Psychologist, 40*, 1203-1211.

Sarbin, T. R., & Scheibe, K. E. (1983). A model of social identity. In T. R. Sarbin & K. E. Scheibe (Eds.), *Studies in social identity*. New York: Praeger.

Secor, C. (1974). Androgyny: An early appraisal. *Women's Studies, 2*, 161-169.

Sherif, C. W. (1982). Needed concepts in the study of gender identity. *Psychology of Women Quarterly, 6*, 375-398.

Shields, S. A. (1975). Functionalism, Darwinism, and the psychology of women. *American Psychologist, 31*, 739-751.

Shields, S. A. (1982). The variability hypothesis: The history of a biological model of sex differences in intelligence. *Signs, 7*, 769-797.

Shotter, J. (1984). *Social accountability and selfhood*. Oxford: Basil Blackwell.

Skrypnek, B. J., & Snyder, M. (1982). On the self-perpetuating nature of stereotypes about women and men. *Journal of Experimental Social Psychology, 18*, 277-291.

Smith-Rosenberg, C. (1985). *Disorderly conduct: Visions of gender in Victorian America*. New York: Alfred A. Knopf.

Spence, J. T. (1983). Comment on Lubinski, Tellegen, and Butcher's "masculinity, femininity, and androgyny viewed and assessed as distinct concepts." *Journal of Personality and Social Psychology, 44*, 440-446.

Spence, J. T. (1985). Gender identity and its implications for the concepts of masculinity and femininity. *Nebraska Symposium on Motivation, 32*, 59-96.

Spence, J. T., Deaux, K., & Helmreich, R. L. (1985). Sex roles in contemporary American society. In G. Lindsey & E. Aronson (Eds.), *Handbook of social psychology* (3rd ed.), (pp. 149-178). New York: Random House.

Spence, J. T., & Helmreich, R. L. (1978). *Masculinity and femininity: Their psychological dimensions, correlates, and antecedents*. Austin: University of Texas Press.

Spence, J. T., & Helmreich, R. L. (1979). The many faces of androgyny: A reply to Locksley & Colten. *Journal of Personality and Social Psychology, 37*, 1032-1046.

Spence, J. T., & Helmreich, R. L. (1980). Masculine instrumentality and feminine expressiveness: Their relationships with sex role attitudes and behaviors. *Psychology of Women Quarterly, 5*, 147-163.

Spence, J. T., Helmreich, R., & Stapp, J. (1975). Ratings of self and peers on sex role attributes and their relation to self-esteem and conceptions of masculinity and femininity. *Journal of Personality and Social Psychology, 32*, 29-39.

Stark-Adamec, C., Graham, M. J., & Pyke, S. W. (1980). Androgyny and mental health: The need for a critical evaluation of the theoretical equation. *International Journal of Women's Studies, 3*, 490-507.

Steele, R. (1985). Paradigm lost: Psychoanalysis after Freud. In C. Buxton (Ed.), *Points of view in the modern history of psychology*. New York: Academic Press.

Strahan, R. F. (1984). More on scoring androgyny as a single continuous variable. *Psychological Reports, 55*, 241-242.

Taylor, M. C. (1983). Masculinity, femininity, and androgyny: Another look at three androgyny scoring systems. *Psychological Reports, 53,* 1149-1150.

Taylor, M. C., & Hall, J. A. (1982). Psychological androgyny: Theories, methods, and conclusions. *Psychological Bulletin, 92,* 347-366.

Terman, L. M., & Miles, C. C. (1936). *Sex and personality.* New York: McGraw-Hill.

Toulmin, S., & Leary, D. E. (1985). The cult of empiricism in psychology, and beyond. In S. Koch & D. E. Leary (Eds.), *A century of psychology as science* (pp. 594-617). New York: McGraw-Hill.

Unger, R. K. (1983). Through the looking glass: No wonderland yet! (The reciprocal relationship between methodology and models of reality.) *Psychology of Women Quarterly, 8,* 9-32.

Unger, R. K. (1985). *Between the "no longer" and the "not yet": Reflections on personal and social change.* Invited address at the annual meetings of the American Psychological Association, Los Angeles.

Weil, K. (1985). The aesthetics of androgyny in Balzac and Woolf or the difference of difference. *Critical Matrix, 1*(6), 1-21.

Weisstein, N. (1971). Psychology constructs the female. In V. Gornick & B. K. Moran (Eds.), *Women in sexist society* (pp. 207-224). New York: Signet.

Weskott, M. (1979). Feminist criticism of the social sciences. *Harvard Educational Review, 49,* 422-456.

Wheeler, L., Reis, H., & Nezlek, J. (1983). Loneliness, social interaction, and sex roles. *Journal of Personality and Social Psychology, 45,* 943-953.

Williams, D., Leak, G., & Millard, R. (1984). Relationships between androgyny and self monitoring. *Psychological Reports, 55,* 197-198.

Wilson, F. R., & Cook, E. P. (1984). Concurrent validity of four androgyny instruments. *Sex Roles, 11,* 813-837.

3

Social Constructionism and the Study of Human Sexuality

LEONORE TIEFER

Leonore Tiefer received her Ph.D. in experimental psychology from the University of California at Berkeley in 1969. She has been engaged in clinical and research work on human sexuality for the past ten years, and has worked as a feminist on issues of sexual assault, anticensorship, and economic justice. She is Clinical Associate Professor of Psychiatry at the New York University School of Medicine and Staff Psychologist at the Beth Israel Medical Center.

In the last 10 years, a radical transformation has been taking place in scholarship on human sexuality, but only within certain disciplines. New theories "potentially explosive in their implications for our future understanding and behavior in regard to sex" (Vicunus, 1982, p. 137) have been proposed, but psychology seems not to have noticed. The need for new ideas and research in the psychology of sexuality comes with some real-world urgency; the study of sexual discourses is no mere intellectual enterprise. As feminist anthropologist Gayle Rubin (1984) puts it,

> There are historical periods in which sexuality is more sharply contested and more overtly politicized. In such periods, the domain of erotic life is, in effect, renegotiated. . . . Periods such as the 1880s in England and the 1950s in the United States recodify the relations of human sexuality. The struggles that were fought leave a residue in the form of laws, social practices, and ideologies which then affect the way sexuality is experienced long after the immediate conflicts have faded. All signs indicate that the present era is another of those watersheds. (pp. 267, 274)

Since *Brown v. Board of Education,* the 1954 U.S. Supreme Court decision outlawing school segregation, social scientists have contributed their theories and data to the public debate over momentous social issues. As I write, public places of sexual activity are being closed "for health reasons" because of AIDS and quarantine is being discussed;

censorship statutes are being passed to limit the production and dissemination of explicit sexual images to "protect" women and children; penal codes specify in ever greater detail illegal sexual activities between adults and children; and the U.S. Attorney General's Commission on Pornography (the Meese Commission) is conducting hearings on the causes of sexual violence in our society.

History may show that the academic community did not, and perhaps could not, take a leadership role in these great sociosexual issues. Perhaps academia speaks with too fragmented a voice or on too slow a time scale. Most recent histories of sexuality (e.g., Weeks, 1981), however, agree that social scientists, physicians, mental health professionals, and other sexuality "experts" are increasingly relied on for advice and authority regarding social sexual policy. Whether this represents part of the problem or part of the solution need not concern us at the moment. It provides sufficient reason to be aware of the range of scholarship concerning sexuality.

In this chapter I will present some key elements in the social constructionist approach and indicate how and why current psychological writing and research about human sexuality is dominated by a limiting, medicalized perspective. I hope to show how a transformed perspective offers social and personality psychologists exciting opportunities for scholarship on issues already familiar to them as these pertain to human sexuality.

THE SOCIAL CONSTRUCTIONIST APPROACH

In a recent essay, Gergen (1985) defined the social constructionist approach as a form of inquiry indebted to intellectual trends such as symbolic interactionism, symbolic anthropology, ethnomethodology, literary deconstructionism, existentialism, phenomenology, and, to some degree, conventional social psychological theories. What these disciplines have in common is an emphasis on the person's active role, guided by his or her culture, in structuring reality. This "endogenic" perspective is to be contrasted with empiricism and positivism, which emphasize the objective existence and reality of topics of scientific inquiry, an "exogenic" perspective.

Gergen identified four assumptions made by social constructionists:

(1) The way we go about studying the world is determined by available concepts, categories, and methods. Our concepts often incline us toward or even dictate certain lines of inquiry while precluding

others, making our results the products more of our language than of empirical discovery. For example, the assumption that there are two and only two genders is taken for granted. We don't ask where gender conceptions come from, and gender, then, becomes only an independent variable (Kessler & McKenna, 1978/1985; Morawski, this volume; Tiefer, 1983).

(2) The concepts and categories we use vary considerably in their meanings and connotations over time and across cultures. Scholars without sufficient historical or cultural awareness may not realize this. Gergen lists concepts such as romantic love, childhood, mother's love, the self, and emotion, which have meant very different things at different points historically and culturally. Insofar as these concepts are often uncritically assumed to relate to permanent human experiences or functions, their relativity is an important limitation on theory and method.

(3) The popularity or persistence of a particular concept, category, or method depends more on its usefulness (particularly its political usefulness for social influence and control) than on its validity. For example, the "hard" science, positivist-empiricist model of psychological research has been criticized for its limitations and omissions, yet it persists because of prestige, tradition, and unexamined congruence with cultural values (Sherif, 1979; Unger, 1983).

(4) Descriptions and explanations of the world are themselves forms of social action and have consequences. Gergen cites Gilligan's (1982) discussion of the consequences of prominent theories of moral development to show how theoretical concepts and categories have systematically ignored and denied certain (in this case, women's) ethical values and processes.

Social Constructionism and Sexuality Scholarship

Many scholars credit French philosopher Michel Foucault's 1976 essay with first showing how the modern idea of sexuality has been constructed in a particular social-historical context (Foucault, 1976/ 1978). Foucault argues that, contrary to popular belief, sexuality has not been repressed and suppressed during a long, Victorian era only to gradually reawaken under the warming influence of twentieth-century permissiveness. In fact, he argues, there is no essential human quality or inner drive, sexuality, that can be repressed in one era and liberated in another. Rather, there is a human potential for consciousness, behavior, and physical experience available to be developed ("incited") by social forces of definition, regulation, organization, and categorization. Sexualities, he argued, are constantly produced, changed, and modified, and the nature of sexual discourse and experience changes accordingly.

In one of the most accessible explications of this approach, Plummer (1982) contrasts, point by point, the conventional drive-based sexologic view of the sources of human sexuality with a social constructionist (here, symbolic interactionist) position. Is sexuality "really" a powerful universal biological drive that can be shaped by sociocultural forces and individual learning, or is it more akin to a learned "script," expressed in physical performance, fundamentally created, not just shaped, by the sociocultural moment?

Plummer shows how the dramaturgic metaphor of sexual script introduced and elaborated by Gagnon and Simon (1973) leads to a vision of sexuality (1) as emergent in relationships and situations rather than as universal essence; (2) as needing to be constructed rather than as needing to be controlled; (3) as a shaper of conduct (as when sex is used to satisfy needs for affection, protection, and gender-validation); (4) as a contingent (depending on particular lives) rather than a necessary (mandated by some inevitable internal energy) form of human behavior; and (5) as an aspect of life that is qualitatively different for children and adults.

Histories and anthropologies of sexuality are being altered by the new constructionist emphasis. If intercourse has always and everywhere felt, meant, and been the same, if a kiss is just a kiss, a sigh just a sigh, then it doesn't matter whether you are Roman or Barbarian, ancient or modern, 5 or 55, in love or just earning a living. This, of course, is counterintuitive, and indicates the fallacy of universal assumptions (Tiefer, 1978a). Whereas earlier scholarship merely reviewed cultural and historical variations in acts and attitudes (e.g., Ford & Beach, 1951; Lewinsohn, 1958), newer history (e.g., Weeks, 1981) and anthropology (e.g., Ortner & Whitehead, 1981) trace the variations of the categories and concepts themselves. "In any approach that takes as predetermined and universal the categories of sexuality, real history disappears" (Padgug, 1979, p. 5).

Most sexologists appear unaware of these developments. Weeks (1982, p. 295) points out that "even in the case of writers like Kinsey, whose work radically demystified sexuality, and whose taxonomic efforts undermined the notions of 'normality,' the [naturalistic] concept is still traceable in the emphasis on sexual 'outlet' as opposed to beliefs or identities." Naturalistic assumptions are often related to belief in an evolution-related universal sex drive. Kinsey, whose biological background and fundamental allegiance have been described by Robinson (1976), ultimately assumed a hydraulic model of sexual drive not unlike Freud's despite their differences concerning the source of sexual energy.

Why this universalization? Although all human conduct, from eating to dancing to thinking, is expressed through the body, scholars of these subjects do not see the role of anatomy and physiology as primary for understanding human experience. Hastrup (1978), in analyzing the concepts of virginity and abortion, for example, contrasts the limited role of physiological realities with the multiple social and symbolic meanings, obvious cultural and historical variations, and so on. Yet this emphasis is reversed in the case of erotic sexuality.

Miller and Fowlkes (1980), among others, have suggested that the sociological perspective on sexuality has been limited because the few sociologists who are interested in sex have focused on deviance and social control, and have studied prostitutes, nudists, transvestites, and homosexuals much more than conventional patterns and populations. Deviations became the subject, rather than the problematic nature of psychological sexuality itself. Although occasional social scientists, such as Simon (1973), have argued that it is an "illusion" that the body is a source of compelling sexual messages, controls sexual conduct, or is universal in its sexual expressions, the symbolic interactionist message has remained a minor voice in sexuality scholarship. It has taken the recent burst of publication from constructionist historians to make a noise loud enough to disturb the prevailing naturalism:

> Biological sexuality is the necessary precondition for human sexuality. But biological sexuality is only a precondition, a set of potentialities, which is never unmediated by human reality, and which becomes transformed in qualitatively new ways in human society. (Padgug, 1979, p. 9)

Aspects of the Social Constructionist Approach

It may be useful to outline some elements of a social constructionist approach to the psychology of human sexuality that builds on the platform introduced above.

Analysis and Challenge of Categories and Concepts

The most basic, and also most difficult, aspect of the study of sexuality is defining the subject matter. Any study must begin with an attempt to say both what is and what is not to be included. How much of the body is relevant? How much of the life span? How much of human behavior is to be considered sexual? How much of thought and feeling? Which interpersonal activities are sexual? Which group activities? Can we use similar language for animals and people? How do we deal with historical change and cultural variation?

The challenge, obviously, is to be inclusive enough to capture a meaningful amount of human variation while being selective enough not to study everything and its relation to everything else! As Kinsey plaintively wrote in describing his method,

> In spite of the long list of items included in the present [interview] study, [anywhere from 300 to 521 items per interview] and in spite of the fact that each history has covered five times as much material as in any previous study, numerous students have suggested, and undoubtedly will continue to suggest after the publication of the present volume, that we should have secured more data in the fields of their special interests. Specifically it has been suggested that the following matters should have had more thorough investigation: racial ancestry . . . somatotypes . . . hormonal assays . . . physical examination of the genitalia . . . marital adjustment . . . early childhood and parental relations . . . motivations and attitudes . . . cultural and community backgrounds . . . sperm counts. (Kinsey, Pomeroy, & Martin, 1948, p. 56)

Sexologists have occasionally addressed issues of "terminology," but the assumptions of essentialism and naturalism prevent their seeing that the discussion of language is not a search for the "real" or "best" or "clearest" terms and definitions, but an exercise in boundary legitimation. What will we choose to see as sexual?

During a 1977 interdisciplinary conference, Katchadourian, a psychiatrist, made an unusual effort to discuss "the many meanings of sex." His list included the fact of being male or female ("biological" sex), sexual behavior (including "internal" behavior such as fantasy), sexual experience (private feelings and thoughts), sex as behavior leading to orgasm (Kinsey's definition), sex as whatever is sexually motivated (Freud's definition), sexuality (the quality of being sexual, possessing of sexual capacity, or being capable of sexual feelings), sexual identity (including partner preference and sex-role identity), and core gender identity (the sense of being a man or a woman). However, the entire discussion was a superficial review of terminological diversity, with no critical analysis (Katchadourian, 1979). Had his discussion taken a constructionist turn, Katchadourian might have observed that almost all the terms relate to individuals and to functions. Is that what the many meanings of sex boil down to? If so, why? And, are we satisfied with that vocabulary?

Contrast this discussion with the one offered in a dialogue between Foucault and Sennett (1982) on the modern vocabulary of sexology. They explicitly wonder where the individualized focus of the language (e.g., libido, desire, fantasy) comes from, and their study takes them to the contributions of early Christian theology and nineteenth-century medicine. Both theology, preoccupied with sexual purity and personal obedience, and medicine, preoccupied at that time with sexual excess and insanity, emphasized sexuality as an individual matter. Sexuality fit into the domains of personal responsibility and personal medical disorder. The modern vocabulary has inherited this focus, in contrast to an emphasis on sexuality as a domain of interpersonal relations. Foucault and Sennett's historical discussion of terminology construes concepts as fluid, responsive, and constructed within a particular context, rather than as objectively valid. In such a discussion, there is no expectation that "the" definition of sexuality will ever emerge.

Another illuminating conceptual analysis is Robinson's (1976) discussion of how Masters and Johnson's (1966) commitment to equal sexual rights for women led them to force their physiological findings to fit a procrustean bed of uniform human function, the "human sexual response cycle." After selecting a homogeneous sample and testing subjects in an environment where the definition of sexual behavior was physical arousal and orgasm, Masters and Johnson "found" similar physical patterns between men and women, which they described in terms of a fixed four-stage "cycle." The persistence of this concept is due to its political and professional usefulness, an example of one of Gergen's fundamental points about social constructions in science.

For the social constructionist, categories and concepts (such as gender, orgasm, homosexuality, genitals, desire, sexual offender, and sexual response cycle) organize our personal and professional approach to sexuality. These concepts cannot simply be taken as objectively valid or given brief "factual" definitions.

Imagery and Metaphor

As significant from a social constructionist point of view as terminology is the question of metaphor: What other kinds of things is sexuality like? What metaphors are useful?

As mentioned above, Gagnon (1973) and Simon (1973) have found the language of dramatic scripts helpful for discussing sexuality. Such a metaphor directs our attention to learned, planned, external sources of sexual behavior. Person (1980), a psychoanalyst, shifts the metaphor to sexuality as a "sex print ... in the sense of fingerprint, unchangeable and unique ... an individualized script that elicits erotic desire" (p. 620). She wants to focus on the learned sources of eroticism, but also to retain a Freudian early-life determinism. By using "script," Simon (1973) had explicitly wanted to reject psychoanalytic ideas of irreversibility with a metaphor that would underscore

> a continuing potential for reordering of meanings, ... a reordering that has permanent consequences in the sense that later changes are at the very least as significant in informing current behavior as were the original or earlier meanings and, in many instances, more significant. (p. 70)

Metaphors such as "script" and "fingerprint" carry significantly different implications that relate in important ways to their originators' assumptions.

In one of the earliest social-constructionist papers, McIntosh (1968) contrasted the models of homosexuality as a "condition" and as a "role," and concluded that "role" imagery was more conducive to examining social, historic, and individual sexual variability, aspects that seemed central to her.

The 1973 struggle over diagnostic nomenclature within the American Psychiatric Association provided a dramatic illustration of the power of imagery in sexuality discourse (Bayer, 1981). Should homosexuality continue to be listed in the official APA manual of psychiatric disorders? Bayer describes how both proponents and opponents of "declassification" argued that the presence of homosexuality in the manual carries a powerful message to young people, parents, legislators, patients, teachers, and homosexuals. Decades of research on the effects of labeling (both halo and stigma effects) validate the impression that, in many cases, the metaphor is the message.

Poets have favored the language and imagery of sexual "pleasure" and "appetite" to emphasize the rich diversity of personal meaning and experience. Social scientists, however, have limited their discussions of sexual appetite and pleasure only to learned expectations that result from the reinforcing effects of "innate" enjoyment of genital stimulation (Hardy, 1964). Perhaps this is to distinguish learned human anticipation of sexuality from the primarily innate appetitive patterns of animals that indicate arousal and predict imminent mating (Beach, 1976). Even psychoanalytic usage seems to restrict discussion to the acquisition of sexual appetites based on the experiences of early childhood. But the metaphor of appetite could also lend itself to exploring personal connections among appetites for sex, food, beauty, power, and so on. Similarly, a social constructionist approach could analyze the relationships among various pleasures for an individual or a cultural group. Do they feel the same? Can they be substituted? What effect does one type of enjoyment have on others? Once learned, can they be lost or forgotten?

The metaphors of work and play offer many images of individual and interpersonal activity and expression. The sex therapy literature seems to favor the work language of skills, practice, scheduling, technique, and mastery, even as it stresses the importance of a playful attitude (Lewis & Brissett, 1967). There may be interesting connections between an individual's values and models of work and play and how she or he perceives sexuality.

Images, as much as technical terms, organize our thinking, and are not to be taken lightly. They provide a fertile field for analysis, and the choice of metaphor in one's own communication about sexuality offers an opportunity to persuade at a level different from the factual.

Historical Dimensions of Sexuality Language

Historical analysis is especially effective in disputing essentialist biases. Social constructionism is attentive to the appearance, disappearance, and changes of many sexological concepts. Plummer's (1981) recent collection, *The Making of the Modern Homosexual*, for example, contains extended discussions of how the modern terms for describing physical and emotional closeness between two men or two women has evolved, and, furthermore, how the actors themselves have been affected by the linguistic changes.

Recently, Elliott (1985) counted the prevalence of the terms "impotence" and "frigidity" in the psychological literature between 1940 and 1983. He found that each term appeared in titles indexed in *Psychological Abstracts* between two and eight times per year until 1970, when titles including "impotence" escalated dramatically. Despite numerous calls in the 1970s sexological literature for the elimination of both terms because of imprecision and pejorative connotations, "impotence" continued to flourish whereas "frigidity" almost disappeared. These observations open the door to a variety of contructionist analyses, and I have elsewhere suggested some social and economic explanations (Tiefer, 1986).

Methods for Studying Sexuality

Feminists have examined the limitations and biases in traditional scholarship that prevent appreciation of the personal and social impact of gender. Many believe that the overwhelming emphasis on positivist-empiricist truth criteria in social science thwarts full understanding, a restriction not found in the interpretive traditions of history, anthropology, and literature (Stacey & Thorne, 1985).

The social scientific study of human sexuality is similarly fettered by professional standards and reward systems that value only "experimentally rigorous" research in the most "objective" tradition (Tiefer, 1978b). The prestige hierarchy in psychology, with applied, correlational, descriptive work at the bottom and experimental, controlled, highly quantitative methods at the top (Sherif, 1979), holds true in sexuality research. The small, prestigious, admission-by-election-only International Academy of Sex Research, for example, will not elect anyone to associate membership, much less full membership, without a suitable number of "empirical" sexuality publications. Annual arguments occur at the business meeting over the suitability of work in history or anthropology (to my knowledge, no literary expert in sexuality has applied for admission), but thus far the gates hold fast. It is not that such work is not worthy, the argument goes, it's just not science!

Contrast this position with Gergen's (1985) assertion that a constructionist analysis must

> eschew the empiricist account of scientific knowledge . . . the traditional Western conception of objective, individualistic, ahistorical knowledge . . . [and embrace criteria such as] the analyst's capacity to invite, compel, stimulate, or delight the audience . . . virtually any methodology can be employed so long as it enables the analyst to develop a more compelling case. (pp. 271, 272, 273)

To understand human sexuality fully, we need to see experimental, correlational, and clinical methods as complementary, not competing (Carlson, 1971). The popularity of sexual surveys (e.g., Hite, 1976) lies in their combination of quantitative and qualitative methods, generalizations derived from data together with personal stories and vignettes. Individual constructions of sexuality involve an interplay of social and psychological factors, and cannot be explored with only one method. When and how does a person construe a situation as sexual? How do people negotiate a sexual script? How does this change over the history of a relationship, a lifetime, a social generation?

Bell (1975) has recommended that researchers interested in homosexuality need to involve themselves more in the lives of their research subjects in order to appreciate fully the meanings of sexuality for their subjects. Carlson (1971) called for new methods bridging former categories: short-term longitudinal studies, anonymous accounts of subjects' experiences during experimental research (wouldn't these have added a great deal to Masters and Johnson's physiological report?), and the publication of "incidental" phenomenological information that now rarely appears in the social science literature.

Suppose we were to start with a speculation such as the following:

> It is the recollection rather than the anticipation of the act that assumes a primary importance in homosexual relations. That is why the great homosexual writers of our culture can write so elegantly about the sexual act itself, because the homosexual imagination is for the most part concerned with reminiscing about the act rather than anticipating it . . . this is all due to concrete and practical considerations and says nothing about the intrinsic nature of homosexuality. (Foucault, 1982/1983, p. 19)

Following Gergen's lead, our reaction would not merely be to formulate empirical research to decide whether and under what circumstances it is "true" that homosexuals feel and behave this way (although that agenda would be a welcome part of the exploratory enterprise), but rather to use a variety of avenues to explore and understand the who, what, when, where, and why of this speculation. What does clinical work on the nature of fantasy have to say? What about theories on the nature of artistic and literary representation? How might this change in an era with mass availability of erotic images? What differences do cultural variations in the encouragement of myth, fantasy, and individual imagination make?

Vance (1983), analyzing a two-week sexology workshop, pointed out that "though sex research is inevitably based on theoretical and conceptual models, researchers and therapists alike maintain that they have no theory, no basic assumptions, no axe to grind. They are just collecting the facts" (p. 376). This Mr. Clean image is in part a reaction against centuries of sexuality authorities' axes, but it serves to isolate and impoverish scholarship. A recent conference on sex research methodology sponsored by the National Institute of Mental Health underscored the field's commitment—at least that of the people who were invited—to "unambiguous concepts," "objective measurement," "operationalism," and "control" of many sorts (Green & Wiener, 1980). Nevertheless, there were occasional suggestions for more constructionist scholarship, including life histories, analyses of the role of sex in diverse relationships, and the choice of real situations to study over laboratory analogs.

THE MEDICALIZATION OF SEXUALITY

The major obstacle to a social constructionist approach to sexuality is the domination of theory and research by the biomedical model.

> The term medicalization refers to two interrelated processes. First, certain behaviors or conditions are given medical meaning—that is, defined in terms of health and illness. Second, medical practice becomes a vehicle for eliminating or controlling problematic experiences that are defined as deviant. (Riessman, 1983, p. 4)

The central ideological support for the medicalization of sexuality is essentialist, naturalist, biological thinking. The major constructionist project is to define and locate sexuality primarily in personal and relational, rather than physical, terms.

Analyzing the Privileged Position of Biology in Sexuality

Take a typical example of writing about sexuality:

> The scientific picture of sexual behavior has become so distorted that we must make a serious attempt to rediscover the obvious. In any attempt of this kind, it is always well to begin again at the beginning, in this case with a brief reexamination of the evolutionary differentiation of the sexes, and the physiologic basis of sexual activity.... In the most primitive protozoa, the individual propagates by its long self. (Rado, 1949, p. 159)

Even in a psychoanalytic article about sexuality we hear the familiar intonation: In the beginning were the birds and the bees . . . and the genes and the genitals and the protozoa. Every sexuality textbook gives the same testimony. The privileged position of biology in sexual discourse is based on the assumption that the body comes before everything else; it is the original source of action, experience, knowledge, and meaning for the species and the individual.

But isn't this just biological determinism and reductionism? Hasn't this fight already been successfully fought? Why is sexuality still so beholden to the body when other aspects of human conduct have long since been disengaged? The answer is complex, and will take far more unraveling than I can do here. I can touch on a bit of the answer, involving an analysis of the special position of sex in our Western Judeo-Christian sociocultural history, wherein sexual desire came to be located in the body, and spirit and reason in the mind (Petras, 1973).

In his dialogue with Foucault, Sennett credits Tissot, the French-Swiss physician who believed masturbation was powerful and addictive, with translating the Christian moral agenda of sexuality (self-purification through sexual self-knowledge) to the biomedical idea that sexual desire exists in the individual, prior to any sexual attraction or relationship. The role of science became to examine sexuality as an individual phenomenon, and, incidentally, to support the hidden moral agenda (Foucault & Sennett, 1982).

Weeks (1985) has traced the deep faith of early sexologists that in the struggle between sexual ignorance and enlightenment, the surest weapon would be biological science. He tells how German sexologist Magnus Hirschfeld, founder of sexology journals, research institutes, and international congresses, saw his Berlin Institute seized and its papers burned by the Nazis in 1933, yet could still write,

> I believe in Science, and I am convinced that Science, and above all the natural Sciences, must bring to mankind, not only truth, but with truth Justice, Liberty, and Peace. (Hirschfeld, 1935, cited in Weeks, 1985, p. 71)

The hope that science would overcome prejudice and bring morality was widely shared.

> The laws which Science was uncovering would turn out to be the expression of the will of God—revelations of the divine Plan. Thus, science could provide moral guidelines for living. (Ehrenreich & English, 1978, p. 66)

Sexual biology, at first the study of instincts, later the study of brain centers, germ plasm, hormones, genes, biochemical reactions, and fetal development, and most recently the study of vaginal blood flow, anal orgasm contractions, and clitoral histochemistry, would provide nature's direction for human sexual conduct. Set free from religious orthodoxy, science would allow what *is* to dictate what *ought to be*. Sexual biology would reveal true human sexual nature.

Biology's privileged position within contemporary sexuality discourse thus descends from the early researchers' hope that "objective science" would free us from the orthodoxies of the past. Yet the choice of biological variables limits our construction of sexuality even as empirical results do correct old prejudices. An example of this is the impact of Masters and Johnson's (1966) research on female sexuality, already mentioned. At the same time that their description and measurement of female orgasm documented some women's physical capacities, their focus on sexual desire and pleasure as measurable bodily states has mechanized, trivialized, and perhaps even further mystified the social and psychological aspects of sexuality (Segal, 1983). Their work "corrected" past inaccuracy, but its sociological impact may ultimately be measured in terms of its effect on the social construction of sexual choices. The belief that a "true" understanding of biology must precede all other work is an assumption that requires detailed critical analysis.

Increasing Importance of Sexual "Adequacy"

The social support for sexual medicalization arises in part from the increasing importance of sexuality itself in modern life. Like fitness, sexuality seems to gain importance as part of society's glorification of youth and health, its "denial of death." German sexologist Gunther Schmidt (1983) identifies three "compensatory" functions that sexuality serves in our time:

> [Sexuality] is supposed to hold marriages and relationships together because they scarcely fulfill material functions any longer; it is supposed to promote self-realization and self-esteem in a society that makes it more and more difficult to feel worth something and needed as an individual; it is supposed to drive out coldness and powerlessness in a world bureaucratized by administration, a world walled-up in concrete landscapes and a world of disrupted relationships at home and in the community.... All discontent—political, social, and personal—is meant to be deflected into the social and relationship sector in order to be compensated. (pp. vii-viii)

In a world where gender remains important while the proofs of gender adequacy become more elusive, sexual knowledge and performance, for both men and women, need to serve that function, too.

Media and the Hegemony of Sexual Medicine

As sexual interest and adequacy gain in social importance, weaknesses in one's preparation become more significant. The major source of information for the young has become mass media, both because of parents' shyness and because of the dearth of sex education in the current conservative climate (Gagnon, 1985).[1] We know little of the impact of such dependence on commercial media.

In the twentieth century, mass media shape popular consciousness by providing language, experts, information, and fictional scripts. Nonfiction media are dominated by a health model of sexuality, with physicians, psychologists, or other health specialists the authorities. Sex enters the print media either because of a newsworthy event ("new" research or technology, sexual crimes, escapades of celebrities) or a feature article in which authorities give their opinions on issues of "normal" people's adjustment ("How to Have Great New Sex with Your Same Old Spouse," Sarrel & Sarrel, 1983) or deviance ("The Anguish of the Transsexuals," Churcher, 1980). Perhaps because of the history of obscenity censorship, media are more comfortable with the aspects of sexuality that seem most proper, that is, closer to medicine and public health than to pornography. The media use this health-model emphasis with little regard for scientific accuracy. A recent example is the promotion of a "new" sexual finding, "the 'G' spot," in 1981/1982.[2]

A trade book (Ladas, Whipple, & Perry, 1982), based on skimpy research that even prior to publication had been contradicted in professional journals and scientific meetings, became a bestseller in 1982. Its authors had appeared on national television a year earlier, drawing thousands of letters of interest from viewers. Newslike reports of a scientific "discovery," an area of unusual erotic sensitivity on the anterior wall of the vagina that appeared related in some way to the ability of women to ejaculate fluid at orgasm, had appeared in numerous women's magazines, newspapers, and sex-oriented magazines. Seven book clubs purchased the book before publication. The insatiability of the media for the commercial potential of sexual topics results in an endless search for news and advice whereas disconfirming evidence receives little or no publicity.

The romantic and passion-filled portrayals of sexuality in the fiction media increase the public's expectations. If sex can provide such power, meaning, and material rewards, if it can make or break relationships, if it is such a large part of people's lives, then the public's dependence on experts and authorities for guidance in this maelstrom increases. A constructionist approach to sexuality can elucidate how individuals, couples, and social groups are affected by the media's various messages.

Political and Economic Aspects of Professional Expansion

Cultural authority in the area of sexuality is not passively conferred on health authorities; it is actively sought and consolidated. Through individual and group efforts, professionals act to ensure their autonomy, promote economic opportunities, and increase their public status (Larson, 1977). Dominance is maintained through licensure (creating a monopoly by making it a crime for others to practice a particular craft), shaping service-providing institutions, multiplying subspecialties with high rates of cross-referral, eliminating "quacks" and other competitors through adverse publicity and legislation, controlling professional education, maintaining solidarity through professional conferences, journals, and jargon, and increasing the need for services in the eyes of the public (Mishler, 1981; Starr, 1982).

In sexology, professional expansion and control have been promoted through specialty organizations with restricted memberships, locating "approved" service providers in medical institutions, using institutional public relations to advertise new services and disseminate research findings, holding frequent congresses and conferences open to the press, giving awards and other forms of recognition, and publishing numerous specialized technical journals and newsletters. The development of impotence treatment as a subspecialty within urology illustrates some of these processes (Tiefer, 1986). The male gender role constructs potency narrowly as regular, resilient, rigid penile erections. In recent years, physicians (and the media) have challenged earlier claims that most erectile difficulties were not caused by medical problems, although this challenge is made without reliable data. At the same time, a surgical "cure" for erectile difficulties (the intrapenile implanting of a prosthesis) has been widely publicized through the media and patient education materials developed by prosthesis manufacturers. Social constructionist methods can analyze the ways such problems develop, solutions are provided, and individual men choose courses of action.

The recent establishment of female "anorgasmia" as a psychiatric disorder (American Psychiatric Association, 1980)[3] provides another example of medicalization. Based on her wide familiarity with sexual patterns around the world, Margaret Mead (1949/1955) had observed some decades ago,

> There seems to be a reasonable basis to assuming that the human female's capacity for orgasm is to be viewed much more as a potentiality that may or may not be developed by a given culture, or in the specific life history of an individual, than as an inherent part of her full humanity. (p. 166)

Just like playing the piano or grinding corn for tortillas, having an orgasm is probably a universal human potential the development of which depends on opportunity, training, and goals. But rather than making orgasms a matter of talent and predilection, our medicalized era has made them a matter of health (and their absence a matter of disorder). The impact of this on women's experience remains to be studied—a gold mine for social constructionism.

The Public's Role in the Medicalization of Sexuality

The last factor to be acknowledged is the desiring public itself. The public is no tabula rasa, passively responding to the proselytizing of health experts and insatiable media. Rather, for various personal and political reasons, medicalized discourse about sexuality is actively sought.

The public's need for information and guidance has been established by centuries of indoctrination on the centrality of sexuality in judgments of sin and salvation. As sexual performance assumes a more conspicuous role in personal life satisfaction, the need for authoritative direction and self-protective attributions increases. A medicalized discourse, with its locus of explanation in the involuntary universe of hormones and blood vessels, allows face-saving for inadequacy the way "the Devil made me do it" permitted exoneration from sin.

In addition, the public's desire for expert advice is fueled by an eager and abiding interest in erotic pleasure. The "true" human nature the public expects to be revealed by research on sexual biology will include the capacity for sensual enjoyment, and the public looks to scientific research for elucidation of that assumed basic capacity.

Politically, groups stigmatized or oppressed because of their sexuality welcome the morally neutral, biologically authoritative discourse of "objective medical science" to promote their own ends. Feminists, for example, embraced Masters and Johnson's (1966) medical model of sexuality because those authors insisted that their research "proved" women were entitled by their biology to sexual activity, pleasure, and orgasm. The American Psychiatric Association's battle over the classification of homosexuality as a disorder found both sides of the question citing medical research as evidence. And the gay community has gone on to cite their APA "victory" as evidence of the biological normalcy of homosexuality.

The assumption that the "bedrock" of biology will define and direct our choices as sexual beings provides the justification for the medicalization of sexuality and the major obstacle for social constructionism.

The variety of political, economic, and personal motives for maintaining a medicalized discourse makes it a formidable obstacle, indeed.

SEXUALITY AND SOCIAL-PERSONALITY PSYCHOLOGY

Throughout this chapter, I have made suggestions as to research topics and directions for a social-constructionist approach to human sexuality. Let me conclude, however, by focusing more directly on several areas where social-personality psychology can have an important impact.

Refocusing on Social and Personality Dimensions of Sexuality

Personality and social psychologists could contribute to the social constructionist, rather than the medical, model. Any research that emphasizes individual and social group variations in sexual meaning and experience will undermine the assumptions of universalism that are so important to the medical model.

Major issues that need to be addressed include: (1) How, from the universe of possible physical and mental activities, do people come to call certain ones sexual and conduct them in particular ways? (2) What are the personal meanings with which people invest these sexual activities? (3) How do these individual constructions change over the lifetime of a person or of a relationship?

We know very little, for example, about the social and psychological meanings of words used very often in sexology: pleasure and intimacy. Young people, at least, rate pleasure as the most important element of sexual satisfaction (Perlman & Abramson, 1982); yet if we cease assuming a universal inborn experience, what do we know of how people acquire the label "pleasure" for what they do and feel in sexual relations? How does sexual "pleasure" relate to other activities also labeled "pleasure?" The sex therapy literature is full of claims about the importance of intimacy to adequate sexual performance and experience (e.g., Levay & Kagle, 1977), although it is safe to assume that the vast majority of genital unions over the centuries have occurred without the presence of anything remotely like our modern idea of intimacy! Again, we know very little about the ways in which people feel intimate in sexual relations, or about how this can change. How does power imbalance between lovers affect their feelings of intimacy? What images do people have of their own bodies and those of their sexual partners, and what connections occur between those images and perceptions of intimacy? How do personality and social influences on self-disclosure and interpersonal trust affect sexual intimacy (Cunningham, 1981; Johnson-George & Swap, 1982)?

Medicalized discourse, with its smooth, unanalyzed prescriptions for what sexual experience ought ideally to be assumes that deviations from the ideal are pathological and the result of conflict or deficiency. But this position has been defined without real exploration of the ways sexuality develops, and the range of variations. In contrast to the individualized, physicalized focus of the medical model, it is particularly important that we develop ways to construe the relational aspects of sexuality. Unfortunately, as psychologists, our tendency is to look at individual variables, which leads inevitably to an emphasis on the body as source and focus. If there is one central image in our efforts to refocus our thinking about sexuality, it should be to see sexuality as a construct that emerges in interaction as a result of expectations and negotiations, not something "inside" each of us.

Sexual Attributions

A rich area for social-personality psychologists at the moment is the study of sexual attributions. When we speak of the social construction of sexuality, we are literally referring to attributional processes, something that social and personality psychologists have studied extensively in recent years. How do people select attributions for sexual behavior (for themselves and others)? How many motives for sexual feelings and activities do people find plausible? How do the patterns of sexual attribution relate to gender, age, social class, sexual history—and to other patterns of attribution?

In my work in a hospital urology department with men who are complaining of erectile difficulties, I am aware of the extraordinary range of attributions they make for their problem, at least in the medical office setting. Other attributions emerge during interviews conducted separately with their primary sexual partners (Tiefer & Melman, 1983). The use of physical attributions for sexual dysfunction seems a prime example of the "self-handicapping" strategy to maintain self-esteem and competency that Snyder and Smith (1982) have discussed in relation to other labels and symptoms. I wonder to what extent self-enhancing and self-protecting attributions for sexual "success" and "failure" follow the same rules as for others forms of performance (Miller & Ross, 1975).

CONCLUDING COMMENTS

John Gagnon, who has been one of the very few social-constructionist voices in sexology, believes that

> people become sexual in the same way they become everything else. Without much reflection, they pick up directions from their social environment. They acquire and assemble meanings, skills and values from the people around them. . . . The study of sex is best realized not through the creation of a special discipline called sexology and special scientists called sexologists, but rather by using the same theories and methods that are used to study other aspects of human conduct. (Gagnon, 1977, p. 2)

Any social-personality psychologist who becomes interested in sex research will rapidly realize that, although Gagnon may theoretically be right in saying that sexual behavior is "just like" any other form of human conduct in its acquisition, it is emphatically not just like any other form of human conduct in the public mind. By seeing how sexuality concepts and metaphors have been the subject of struggle over the centuries, I hope the reader will be in a better position to appreciate why sexuality scholarship has had and continues to have a hard time achieving legitimacy, not to mention funding.

Sexology as a discipline developed as much for the mutual protection of those interested in the subject as in any deliberate effort to create a dominant ideology and expand cultural authority. Because a major function of the medical cloak has been that of respectability for the sexologist (Weeks, 1985), engaging in nonbiomedical sexuality research will almost certainly be controversial. Nevertheless, the social constructionist agenda offers the social and personality psychologist some support and camaraderie in challenging the biomedical monolith, and the encouragement that beyond lies a form of human conduct rich, fascinating, and only barely understood.

A PERSONAL POSTSCRIPT ON SCHOLARSHIP

Some of the scholars I have cited in this chapter developed their thinking within the political frameworks of feminism, gay and lesbian studies, or the antisociobiology critique. Others came from an appreciation of various European trends in social theory and cultural analysis. I was drawn to the critique of essentialism in sexology by my feminist political interests and contacts, contrary to the mythology of empiricism and positivism that research and theory are completely objective—uninfluenced by the lives, values, or demographics of scholars. Numerous recent analyses of this mythology have disputed its validity, and challenged its desirability even in principle (e.g., Unger, 1983; Wallston, 1981). Thus it is important, as part of the development of new methods and theories for examining our lives, that we indicate the sources of our commitments.

Furthermore, my and others' choice of sexuality as a subject area in the first place is not random. An abiding concern throughout Western history has been the relation of sexual thought and action to sin. Nonprocreative acts or acts between inappropriate partners have consistently been devalued and degraded. We know some details of how religious control was exerted from, for example, the early manuals by which Roman Catholic clergy-confessors determined the proper penance for people's sexual sins (Conrad & Schneider, 1980). Beginning in the late Middle Ages, Western secular law incorporated the same disapproval of nonprocreative sexuality in the category "crimes against nature." During the eighteenth century, as secular authority grew, "unnatural" sexual activities, or even approved activities enjoyed in "excess," began to be of medical interest as putative causes of physical disorder and debilitation (Bullough, 1976). Indulgence in nonprocreative acts was said to lead to "worse" sexual problems such as homosexuality or impotence. The resulting nineteenth-century crusade in England and America against the "disease" of masturbation has been well documented (Engelhardt, 1974). The authority to define "correct" sexuality (as well as deviance and its treatment) has become firmly localized in the medical domain in the twentieth century. Most importantly, as Plummer (1984) has pointed out, "It is not just that medicine has constructed the perverse, it has also constructed the normal" (p. 235).

Scholarship that challenges the prevailing empiricist, medical model of sexuality thus confronts more than merely a prevailing theory. It will inevitably have political impact. Although an individual researcher may choose not to be politically active, his or her work will inevitably be cited to support some group's position.

The emergence in the 1960s and 1970s of the "sexual liberation" movements (especially the women's and gays' movements) has radically challenged the "naturalness" and "inevitability" of sex roles, identities, and behaviors. . . . What the early sex radical movements claimed to do was to speak for sexualities which were seen as having been distorted or denied. . . . But in speaking positively of much that had seemed, literally, unspeakable, these movements ultimately demonstrated the historically constructed nature of the categories that shape our ways of thinking, and living, sex. (Weeks, 1982, p. 293)

Scholarship affects politics; politics affects scholarship. If we are in a watershed period for sexual definitions, as Rubin (1984) effectively argues we are, then the research we do, and the way we decide what research to do, both become concerns with broad ramifications.

NOTES

1. I wrote sexual advice columns in the popular magazines *Playgirl* and *Playgirl Advisor* in 1975-1976, as well as a series of essays about sex in *The New York Daily News* in 1980-1981. I still have the hundreds of desperate and ignorance-filled letters I received at those times.

2. This discussion is based on an unpublished manuscript by Carol Tavris and Leonore Tiefer, 1983, "The 'G' Spot, the Media, and Science."

3. There were no sexual dysfunctions per se listed in the previous editions of the APA's *Diagnostic and Statistical Manual of Disorders* (1955, 1968), although "impotence" and "dyspareunia" (pain during intercourse) were mentioned as "psychophysiological genito-urinary disorders" in the 1968 edition. There are eight "psychosexual dysfunctions" listed in the 1980 (3rd) edition of the Manual, including "Inhibited Female Orgasm" (and "Inhibited Male Orgasm").

REFERENCES

American Psychiatric Association. (1980). *Diagnostic and statistical manual of mental disorders* (3rd ed.). Washington, DC: Author.

Bayer, R. (1981). *Homosexuality and American psychiatry*. New York: Basic Books.

Beach, F. A. (1976). Sexual attractivity, proceptivity, and receptivity in female mammals. *Hormones and Behavior, 7,* 105-138.

Bell, A. P. (1975). Research in homosexuality: Back to the drawing board. *Archives of Sexual Behavior, 4,* 421-431.

Bullough, V. L. (1976). *Sexual variance in society and history* . New York: John Wiley.

Carlson, R. (1971). Where is the person in personality research? *Psychological Bulletin, 75,* 203-219.

Churcher, S. (1980, June 16). The anguish of the transsexuals. *New York*, pp. 40-49.

Conrad, P., & Schneider, J. W. (1980). *Deviance and medicalization*. St. Louis, MO: C. V. Mosby.

Cunningham, J. D. (1981). Self-disclosure intimacy: Sex, sex of target, cross-national and "generational" differences. *Personality and Social Psychology Bulletin, 7*, 314-319.

Ehrenreich, B., & English, D. (1978). *For her own good: 150 years of the experts' advice to women*. Garden City, NY: Anchor Press/Doubleday.

Elliott, M. (1985). The use of "impotence" and "frigidity": Why has "impotence" survived? *Journal of Sex and Marital Therapy, 11*, 51-56.

Engelhardt, H. T. (1974). The disease of masturbation: Values and the concept of disease. *Bulletin of the History of Medicine, 48*, 234-248.

Ford, C. S., & Beach, F. A. (1951). *Patterns of sexual behavior*. New York: Harper & Row.

Foucault, M. (1978). *The history of sexuality* (Vol. 1: *An Introduction*). New York: Pantheon. (Original work published 1976)

Foucault, M. (1982/1983). An interview with Michel Foucault. *Salmagundi*, No. 58-59, 10-24.

Foucault, M., & Sennett, R. (1982). Sexuality and solitude. *Humanities in Review, 1*, 3-21.

Gagnon, J. H. (1973). Scripts and the coordination of sexual conduct. *Nebraska Symposium on Motivation, 21*, 27-60.

Gagnon, J. H. (1977). *Human sexualities*. Glenview, IL: Scott, Foresman.

Gagnon, J. H. (1985). Attitudes and responses of parents to pre-adolescent masturbation. *Archives of Sexual Behavior, 14*, 451-466.

Gagnon, J. H., & Simon, W. (1973). *Sexual conduct: The social sources of human sexuality*. Chicago: Aldine.

Gergen, K. J. (1985). The social constructionist movement in modern psychology. *American Psychologist, 40*, 266-275.

Gilligan, C. (1982). *In a different voice*. Cambridge, MA: Harvard University Press.

Green, R., & Wiener, J. (1980). *Methodology in sex research* (Report No. 80-1502). Washington, DC: Department of Health and Human Services.

Hardy, K. R. (1964). An appetitional theory of sexual motivation. *Psychological Review, 71*, 1-18.

Hastrup, K. (1978). The semantics of biology: Virginity. In S. Ardener (Ed.), *Defining females: The nature of women in society* (pp. 49-65). New York: John Wiley.

Hite, S. (1976). *The Hite report: A nationwide study on female sexuality*. New York: Macmillan.

Johnson-George, C., & Swap, W. C. (1982). Measurement of specific interpersonal trust: Construction and validation of a scale to assess trust in a specific other. *Journal of Personality and Social Psychology, 43*, 1306-1317.

Katchadourian, H. A. (1979). The terminology of sex and gender. In H. A. Katchadourian (Ed.), *Human Sexuality: A comparative and development perspective* (pp. 8-34). Berkeley: University of California Press.

Kessler, S. J., & McKenna, W. (1985). *Gender: An ethnomethodological approach*. Chicago: University of Chicago Press. (Original work published in 1978).

Kinsey, A. C., Pomeroy, W. B., & Martin, C. E. (1948). *Sexual behavior in the human male*. Philadelphia: W. B. Saunders.

Ladas, A. K., Whipple, B., & Perry, J. D. (1982). *The G spot and other recent discoveries about human sexuality*. New York: Holt, Rinehart & Winston.

Larson, M. S. (1977). *The rise of professionalism: A sociological analysis.* Berkeley: University of California Press.

Levay, A. N., & Kagle, A. (1977). Ego deficiencies in the areas of pleasure, intimacy, and cooperation: Guidelines in the diagnosis and treatment of sexual dysfunctions. *Journal of Sex and Marital Therapy, 3,* 10-18.

Lewinsohn, R. (1958). *A history of sexual customs.* New York: Harper & Row.

Lewis, L. S., & Brissett, D. (1967). Sex as work: A study of avocational counseling. *Social Problems, 15,* 8-18.

Masters, W. H., & Johnson, V. E. (1966). *Human sexual response.* Boston: Little, Brown.

McIntosh, M. (1968). The homosexual role. *Social Problems, 16,* 182-192.

Mead, M. (1955). *Male and female: A study of the sexes in a changing world.* New York: Mentor. (Original work published 1949)

Miller, D. T., & Ross, M. (1975). Self-serving biases in the attribution of causality: Fact or fiction? *Psychological Bulletin, 82,* 213-225.

Miller, P. Y., & Fowlkes, M. R. (1980). Social and behavioral construction of female sexuality. *Signs, 5,* 783-800.

Mishler, E. G. (1981). The health-care system: Social contexts and consequences. In E. G. Mishler et al. (Eds.), *Social contexts of health, illness, and patient care* (pp. 195-217). Cambridge: Cambridge University Press.

Ortner, S. B., & Whitehead, H. (Eds.). (1981). *Sexual meanings: The cultural construction of gender and sexuality.* Cambridge: Cambridge University Press.

Padgug, R. A. (1979). On conceptualizing sexuality in history. *Radical History Review,* No. 20, 3-23.

Perlman, S. D., & Abramson, P. R. (1982). Sexual satisfaction among married and cohabiting individuals. *Journal of Clinical and Consulting Psychology, 50,* 458-460.

Person, E. S. (1980). Sexuality as the mainstay of identity: Psychoanalytic perspectives. *Signs, 5,* 605-630.

Petras, J. W. (1973). *Sexuality in society.* Boston: Allyn & Bacon.

Plummer, K. (Ed.). (1981). *The making of the modern homosexual.* London: Hutchinson.

Plummer, K. (1982). Symbolic interactionism and sexual conduct: An emergent perspective. In M. Brake (Ed.), *Human sexual relations: Towards a redefinition of sexual politics* (pp. 223-241). New York: Pantheon.

Plummer, K. (1984). Sexual diversity: A sociological perspective. In K. Howells (Ed.), *The psychology of sexual diversity* (pp. 219-253). Oxford: Basil Blackwell.

Rado, S. (1949). An adaptational view of sexual behavior. In P. Hoch & J. Zubin (Eds.), *Psychosexual development in health and disease* (pp. 159-189). New York: Grune & Stratton.

Riessman, C. K. (1983). Women and medicalization: A new perspective. *Social Policy, 14,* 3-18.

Robinson, P. (1976). *The modernization of sex.* New York: Harper & Row.

Rubin, G. (1984). Thinking sex: Notes for a radical theory of the politics of sexuality. In C. S. Vance (Ed.), *Pleasure and danger: Exploring female sexuality* (pp. 267-319). Boston: Routledge & Kegan Paul.

Sarrel, L., & Sarrel, P. (1983, March). How to have great new sex with your same old spouse. *Redbook,* pp. 75-77, 172.

Schmidt, G. S. (1983). Foreword. In J. Bancroft, *Human sexuality and its problems* (pp. v-viii). Edinburgh: Churchill-Livingstone.

Segal, L. (1983). Sensual uncertainty, or why the clitoris is not enough. In S. Cartledge & J. Ryan (Eds.), *Sex & love: New thoughts on old contradictions* (pp. 30-47). London: The Women's Press.

Sherif, C. W. (1979). Bias in psychology. In J. A. Sherman & E. T. Beck (Eds.), *The prism of sex* (pp. 93-133). Madison: University of Wisconsin Press.

Simon, W. (1973). The social, the erotic, and the sensual: The complexities of sexual scripts. *Nebraska Symposium on Motivation, 21*, 61-82.

Snyder, C. R., & Smith, T. W. (1982). Symptoms as self-handicapping strategies: The virtues of old wine in a new bottle. In G. Weary & H. L. Mirels (Eds.), *Integration of clinical and social psychology* (pp. 104-127). New York: Oxford University Press.

Stacey, J., & Thorne, B. (1985). The missing feminist revolution in sociology. *Social Problems, 32*, 301-316.

Starr, P. (1982). *The social transformation of American medicine.* New York: Basic Books.

Tiefer, L. (1978a, July). The kiss. *Human Nature*, pp. 149-158.

Tiefer, L. (1978b). The context and consequences of contemporary sex research: A feminist perspective. In T. E. McGill, D. A. Dewsbury, & B. D. Sachs (Eds.), *Sex and behavior: Status and prospectus* (pp. 363-385). New York: Plenum.

Tiefer, L. (1983, November). *A political perspective on the use of gender as independent variable.* Paper presented at the meeting of the International Academy of Sex Research, Harriman, NY.

Tiefer, L. (1986, May). In pursuit of the perfect penis: The medicalization of male sexuality. *American Behavioral Scientist, 29*, 579-600.

Tiefer, L., & Melman, A. (1983). Interview of wives: A necessary adjunct in the evaluation of impotence. *Sexuality and Disability, 6*, 167-175.

Unger, R. K. (1983). Through the looking-glass: No wonderland yet! (The reciprocal relationship between methodology and models of reality). *Psychology of Women Quarterly, 8*, 9-32.

Vance, C. S. (1983). Gender systems, ideology, and sex research. In A. Snitow, C. Stansell, & S. Thompson (Eds.), *Powers of desire: The politics of sexuality* (pp. 371-384). New York: Monthly Review Press.

Vicunus, M. (1982). Sexuality and power: A review of current work in the history of sexuality. *Feminist Studies, 8*, 133-156.

Wallston, B. S. (1981). What are the questions in psychology of women? A feminist approach to research. *Psychology of Women Quarterly, 5*, 597-617.

Weeks, J. (1981). *Sex, politics, and society: The regulation of sexuality since 1800.* London: Longman.

Weeks, J. (1982). The development of sexual theory and sexual politics. In M. Brake (Ed.), *Human sexual relations: Towards a redefinition of sexual politics* (pp. 293-309). New York: Pantheon.

Weeks, J. (1985). *Sexuality and its discontents.* London: Routledge & Kegan Paul.

4

Sexual Violence in the Mass Media

SOCIAL PSYCHOLOGICAL IMPLICATIONS

DANIEL LINZ
EDWARD DONNERSTEIN
STEVEN PENROD

Daniel Linz is a postdoctoral fellow in the Department of Psychology at the University of Wisconsin—Madison and Coordinator for Health Services Research and Development at the William S. Middleton Memorial Veterans Hospital in Madison, Wisconsin. His primary research interests include psychology and law, the effects of sexual and violent mass media depictions on viewers, and the prediction and control of violent behavior.

Edward Donnerstein is a Professor of Communications at the Center for Communication Research at the University of Wisconsin—Madison. His interests include the effects of sexual violence in the media and techniques for mitigating the impact of these effects on male viewers.

Steven Penrod is an Associate Professor of Psychology at the University of Wisconsin—Madison. His research interests include jury decision making, eyewitness identification, and media.

Recently, controversies concerning the proliferation of "pornographic" and violent depictions in the mass media have assumed national political and legal importance. Feminists, fundamentalist religious groups, and civil libertarians are currently debating whether these materials should be permitted to flourish in American society. In 1984, the Reagan administration reacted to this concern by establishing a Presidential Commission within the Attorney General's office. The surgeon general of the United States, C. Everett Koop, preempting the findings of the commission, has gone so far as to claim that

AUTHORS' NOTE: The research described in this chapter was partially funded by National Science Foundation Grant No. BNS-8216772 to the second and third authors.

we have enough evidence to implicate pornography as a serious contributing factor to certain disorders of human health and as a kind of accessory, if you will, to certain antisocial actions. . . . We suspect that for men who are slightly predisposed to such behavior, this material may provide the impetus that propels them from the unreal world of fantasy to the real world of overt action. (*Washington Post*, 1985)

Feminists (Dworkin, 1985; MacKinnon, 1985) are concerned about the possibility that pornographic materials foster sex discrimination in American society. Several ordinances defining pornography as a form of sex discrimination are being considered or enacted in various cities across the country (e.g., Indianapolis; see Linz, Penrod, & Donnerstein, in press, for a discussion of the use of social science evidence in the context of the Indianapolis ordinance).

Recent debates about pornography have been partially fueled by findings from the social psychological research that has accumulated since the time of the first Presidential Commission on Obscenity and Pornography in 1970. In the sixteen years following the Commission's report, social psychologists have been engaged in research on the effects of exposure to sexually explicit and sexually violent materials. In this chapter we will summarize many of these findings.

DEFINING EROTICA, PORNOGRAPHY, AND SEXUAL VIOLENCE

The term "pornography" has been loosely applied to many forms of explicit and nonexplicit depictions of human sexual activity. The kinds of depictions encompassed by the term vary and depend on the political and religious orientation of those who use it. For some, pornography is defined as depictions that elicit or are intended to elicit sexual arousal in the viewer (e.g., Falwell, 1980; Gould, 1977). Others (e.g., Longino, 1980) have suggested that depictions be labeled pornographic only if they include degrading and dehumanizing portrayals of women, not simply if they are sexually arousing.

Steinem (1980), for example, emphasizes that the dehumanizing aspect of pornography distinguishes it from erotica. According to Steinem, the message in pornography "is violence, dominance, and conquest. It is sex being used to reinforce some inequality, or to create one, or to tell us that pain and humiliation . . . are really the same as pleasure" (p. 37). On the other hand, erotica portrays "mutually pleasurable, sexual expression between people who have enough power to be there by positive choice. It may or may not strike a sense-memory in the viewer, or be creative enough to make the unknown seem real; but it doesn't require us to identify with a conqueror or victim" (p. 37).

Although this distinction between pornography and erotica has occasionally been used by researchers, most often the distinction has been blurred. Terms that may appear incompatible or contradictory (e.g., "aggressive erotica" or "nonviolent pornography") have unfortunately become part of the research language. This has created difficulty in interpreting research results, particularly among readers unfamiliar with the stimulus materials used in experimental studies.

There is another source of ambiguity in the interpretation of the research findings. When people think of pornography, they usually think of explicit portrayals of human sexual activity in magazines and movies. Therefore, when researchers discuss the effects of pornography on attitudes or behavior, it is assumed by the casual reader that the central concern is with this sexual explicitness; and that this explicitness alone accounts for the outcomes of many experiments. The research over the last decade has demonstrated, for the most part (we will discuss the exceptions in detail), that sexually explicit images, per se, do not in the short run facilitate aggressive behavior against women, change attitudes about rape, or influence other forms of antisocial behavior. Instead, the research indicates that it is the violent images embedded in some forms of pornography, or even the violent images alone, that account for many of the antisocial effects observed in experimental studies.

To guide our analysis of the experimental research on pornography and sexual violence, we have created a rough typology of the variety of stimulus materials used by social psychologists in their investigations. The typology includes six categories. The first two categories contain nonviolent sexually explicit stimuli that are either high or low in their tendency to degrade women. The third and fourth categories include films that portray the myth that women benefit from rape or desire it. The difference between the two categories is the level of sexual explicitness. The fifth and sixth categories include R-rated films[1] that are not sexually explicit but that either juxtapose sex and violence or are portrayals of brutal rape.

(1) Nonviolent, low-degradation sexually explicit stimuli. This material is most consistent with Steinem's definition of erotica (e.g., nonviolent, noncoercive, and nondegrading, but sexually explicit). These materials are usually X-rated, although many researchers have employed X-rated materials in the past (early 1970s) that would carry an

R rating by today's standards. These stimuli have been presented to research subjects in the form of audio depictions of mutually consenting sexual activity, pictures, verbal descriptions, or films.

(2) Nonviolent, high-degradation sexually explicit stimuli. More recently researchers have employed materials that, although not expressly violent, are, according to many, demeaning and degrading to women. These materials take two forms: feature length, X-rated pornographic films; and shorter, less well-produced depictions. An example of the former would be the popular X-rated film entitled *Debbie Does Dallas.* Examples of the latter would include the 10- to 12-minute "stag" or "peep show" films once widely available in pornographic bookstores. What both kinds of material have in common is the debasing depiction of women as willing receptacles of any male sexual urge (excluding rape) or as oversexed, highly promiscuous individuals with insatiable sexual urges.

(3) Violent pornography. This material depicts sexual coercion in a sexually explicit context. Usually a man uses force against a women in order to obtain sexual gratification (e.g., scenes of rape and other forms of violent sexual assault). The unique feature of many of these depictions is the tendency to portray "positive victim outcomes." Rape and other forms of sexual assault are depicted as pleasurable, sexually arousing, and beneficial to the female victim. This theme contrasts with other forms of media violence (e.g., most forms of TV violence) in which victims usually are not portrayed as enjoying their victimization. Researchers have presented violent pornographic depictions to subjects via film presentations, audiotapes, and written portrayals.

(4) Nonexplicit sexual aggression against women. This category includes depictions of sexual violence against women that are conceptually similar to violent pornography but are less sexually explicit. There may be a rape scene, but it is often of the kind that would be permissible under television broadcast standards. In this sense, the sex is far less explicit than in the X-rated materials described above. However, the idea that women derive positive benefit from sexual abuse is a recurring theme.

(5) Sexualized explicit violence against women. The materials considered here are R-rated due to the lack of explicit portrayals of sex but are typically much more graphically violent than X-rated aggressive pornography. These materials do not depict "positive victim outcomes," but contain images of torture, murder, and mutilation. The victims of

this violence are usually women. Further, the unique feature of these films is the sexual context in which the violence against women occurs. As film critic Janet Maslin notes,

> The carnage is usually preceded by some sort of erotic prelude: footage of pretty young bodies in the shower, or teens changing into nighties for the slumber party, or anything that otherwise lulls the audience into a mildly sensual mood. When the killing begins, this eroticism is abruptly abandoned, for it has served its purpose, that of lowering the viewer's defenses and heightening the film's physical effectiveness. The speed and ease with which one's feelings can be transformed from sensuality into viciousness may surprise even those quite conversant with the links between sexual and violent urges. (Maslin, 1982, p. 2)

(6) R-rated rape films. These materials depict graphic and brutal rapes, but are unlike violent pornography, with no indication that the victim enjoys being raped. The sexual activity is simulated in order to avoid an X-rating.

It must be emphasized that these six categories do not orthogonally classify the materials examined by researchers interested in the effects of pornography or violence against women. It is often difficult to fit specific stimuli into an appropriate category due to vague descriptions given in research reports. The scheme does, however, allow for ready classification of the vast majority of stimulus materials, and is a useful framework within which to examine the major experimental investigations conducted over the last two decades.

THE EFFECTS OF EXPOSURE TO NONVIOLENT, LOW-DEGRADATION SEXUAL MATERIALS

An examination of early research and reports examining nonviolent, noncoercive material would suggest that the effect of exposure to it is minimal. For instance, the President's Commission on Pornography and Obscenity (1970) concluded that

> pornography is an innocuous stimulus which leads quickly to satiation and that the public concern over it is misplaced. (Howard, Liptzin, & Reifler, 1973, p. 133)

> Results . . . fail to support the position that viewing erotic films produces harmful social consequences. (Mann, Sidman, & Starr, 1971, p. 113)

> If a case is to be made against "pornography" in 1970, it will have to be made on grounds other than demonstrated effects of a damaging personal

or social nature. (President's Commission on Obscenity and Pornography, 1970, p. 139)

A number of criticisms of these findings (e.g., Cline, 1974; Dienstbier, 1977; Wills, 1977) led to reexamination of potential links between exposure to pornography and subsequent aggressive behavior. Some researchers (e.g., Cline, 1974) argued that there were major methodological and interpretive problems with the Pornography Commission report; others (e.g., Liebert & Schwartzberg, 1977) believed that the observation that exposure to pornography is harmless was premature. The relationship between exposure to pornography and subsequent aggressive behavior is more complex than first thought. Indeed, recent research has shown that exposure to nonviolent, noncoercive pornography can increase aggressive behavior under some circumstances and decrease it under others.

For example, a number of experiments in which individuals have been predisposed to aggress and later exposed to nonaggressive pornography have produced increases in aggressive behavior (e.g., Baron & Bell, 1977; Donnerstein, Donnerstein, & Evans, 1975; Malamuth, Feshbach, & Jaffe, 1977; Meyer, 1972; Zillmann, 1971, 1979). Other experiments (e.g., Baron, 1974a, 1974b, 1977; Baron & Bell, 1973; Donnerstein et al., 1975; Frodi, 1977; Zillmann & Sapolsky, 1977) indicate the opposite—that exposure to nonaggressive pornography reduces subsequent aggressive behavior.

Some researchers (e.g., Baron, 1977; Donnerstein, 1983; Donnerstein et al., 1975; Zillmann, 1979) have begun to tease apart the apparent inconsistencies. It is now believed that as these materials become more sexually explicit, and thus more arousing to the viewer, they give rise to increases in aggression. Zillmann (1978, 1979, 1982, 1984) has argued, for example, that exposing subjects to highly arousing stimuli may cause them to behave more aggressively because of the transfer of arousal from one situation to the next. Others (e.g., Bandura, 1973; Donnerstein, 1983) have argued that if subjects are disinhibited about aggression, or aggression is a dominant response in a given situation, any source of emotional arousal will tend to increase aggressive behavior. At a low level of arousal, however, the stimulus may act as a distractor. This may be especially true if the stimulus is rated as pleasant, in which case the subject's attention is directed away from previous anger.

Acting aggressively toward a target is theorized to be incompatible with the pleasant feelings associated with low-level arousal (Baron, 1977; Donnerstein, 1983). Evidence in support of this notion suggests that individuals who find the materials "displeasing" increase their aggression after exposure, whereas those who have more positive reactions to the material will not increase their aggression even to highly arousing materials (e.g., Zillmann, 1984). It is probable that excitation transfer and pleasant versus unpleasant feelings about the material act together to affect aggressive behavior after exposure to nonviolent pornography (see Zillmann, Bryant, Comisky, & Medoff, 1981, for supportive evidence).

The research noted above is concerned primarily with male-to-male aggression. Studies of the influence of nonaggressive sexual stimuli on male aggression against women in the laboratory have produced different results. In studies by Donnerstein and Barrett (1978) and Donnerstein and Hallam (1978), it was found that nonaggressive sexually explicit materials had no effect on subsequent aggression unless constraints against aggression were reduced by the experimenter. Constraints have been lowered both by having a woman anger male subjects and by giving male subjects multiple chances to aggress. In an additional study, Donnerstein (1983) tried to reduce aggressive inhibitions by providing an aggressive model. However, this resulted in no increase in aggression after exposure to an X-rated nonviolent film.

In general, these studies indicate that nonaggressive sexual material does not contribute substantially to aggression against women except under specific conditions. Furthermore, in circumstances where aggression did increase, it appears to have been due to the material's arousing and displeasing nature. In this sense, effects of nonviolent pornography may be indistinguishable from the effects of any other instigator of arousal (such as physical exercise) and/or negative affect.

LONG-TERM EXPOSURE TO IMAGES OF FEMALE DEGRADATION

Research on exposure to nonviolent sexually explicit stimuli has at least two limitations that make it difficult to determine whether exposure to these stimuli actually produces antisocial attitudes and behaviors in consumers. Almost without exception, studies reporting on the effects of nonviolent sexual materials have relied on short-term exposure (only a few minutes). Furthermore, the studies noted above usually employed pictures of nudes or short film clips depicting nudes or mutually consenting sexual behaviors. In other words, many of the materials chosen for these experiments might more appropriately be classified as erotica rather than pornography. If male subjects were exposed to sexually explicit materials for longer periods of time and / or if they were exposed to materials that, while not overtly violent, were demeaning or debasing in some way to women, the effects might be different.

A major concern of political activists attempting to pass ordinances designed to control pornography is the effect of prolonged exposure to pornography that is not overtly violent but allegedly objectifies and dehumanizes women. These ordinances have been introduced in a variety of communities including Minneapolis and Indianapolis. The Indianapolis ordinance passed the city council but was ruled unconstitutional in Federal Court and now awaits further appeal. One of the central tenets of the Indianapolis ordinance (and one of its most controversial features from a legal point of view) is that pornography is considered to be the graphic, sexually explicit subordination of women, by presenting them "as sexual objects for domination, conquest, violation, exploitation, possession or use, or through postures or positions of servility or submission or display" (City County General Ordinance No. 35, City of Indianapolis, 1984). The suggestion among the framers of the ordinance is that, after viewing such material, "a general pattern of discriminatory attitudes and behavior, both violent and nonviolent, that has the capacity to stimulate various negative reactions against women will be found" (Defendants' memorandum, United States District Court for the Southern District of Indiana, Indianapolis Division, 1984, p. 8).

Zillmann and Bryant (1982, 1984) conducted a study on long-term exposure (4 hours and 48 minutes over a six-week period) to sexually explicit materials (8mm "stag films"), which the authors claim do not contain overt aggressiveness but depict women as sexual objects for exploitation. According to these researchers, the films depicted women as "socially nondiscriminating, as hysterically euphoric in response to just about any sexual or pseudosexual stimulation, and eager to accommodate seemingly any and every sexual request" (Zillmann & Bryant, 1984, p. 134). Zillmann and Bryant found that male and female subjects exposed to these depictions (1) became more tolerant of bizarre and violent forms of pornography, (2) became less supportive of statements about sexual equality, and (3) became more lenient in assigning punishment to a rapist whose crime was described in a newspaper account. Furthermore, extensive exposure to this material significantly increased males' sexual callousness toward women, as evidenced by increased acceptance of statements such as, "A man should find them, feel them, fuck them, and forget them," "A woman doesn't mean 'no' until she slaps you," and "If they are old enough to bleed, they are old enough to butcher."

Zillmann and others (e.g., Berkowitz, 1984; Berkowitz & Rogers, in press) have offered a possible explanation for these effects. As noted earlier, although the films do not feature infliction of pain or suffering, women are portrayed as extremely permissive and promiscuous, quite willing to accommodate any male sexual urge. Brief periods of exposure to this view of women may not be sufficient to bring viewers' attitudes into line with these messages. Attitudinal changes might be expected under conditions of long-term exposure, however. Continued exposure to the idea that women will do practically anything sexual may prime or encourage other, similar thoughts (Wyer & Srull, 1980). This increase in the availablility of thoughts about female promiscuity, or the ease with which viewers can imagine instances in which a female has been sexually insatiable, may lead viewers to inflate their estimates of how willingly and frequently women engage in such behavior. The availability of thoughts about female insatiability may also inflate judgments about the frequency or normality of sexual behaviors such as rape, bestiality, and sadomasochism. Further, these ideas, once instated, may be enduring. Zillmann and Bryant (1982), for example, found that male subjects still had a propensity to trivialize rape three weeks after exposure to nonviolent pornography.

It is important to note that long-term exposure to this type of pornography did not increase aggressive behavior in these studies. In fact, subsequent aggression declined with continued exposure. This finding supports the studies noted above that indicate that nonviolent sexual materials do not play a major role in the elicitation of aggressive behavior.

Unfortunately, we can only speculate about the role that images of female promiscuity and insatiability play in fostering callous perceptions of women. No one has systematically manipulated film content in an experiment designed to facilitate or inhibit these kinds of viewer cognitions. It is possible that simple exposure to large numbers of sexually explicit depictions (regardless of their "insatiability" theme) accounts for the attitudinal changes found in the Zillmann and Bryant study. But it is also possible that long-term exposure to images of women that are not sexually explicit or pornographic but are sexually demeaning to women may produce negative attitude changes in male viewers. Sexual explicitness and themes of insatiability are experimentally confounded in the existing work.

A recent experiment by Check (1985) is a step toward disentangling the effects of prolonged exposure to sexually explicit images from the effects of exposure to images that are dehumanizing or degrading. In Check's study, a sample of male college students and other adult males from the greater Toronto metropolitan area was solicited through newspaper ads. Subjects were assigned to one of three conditions; two of these conditions consisted of 90 minutes of sexually explicit film clips that the authors labeled "nonviolent dehumanizing pornography" and "nonviolent erotica." The third condition was a no-exposure control group.

Check describes a scene from the sexually dehumanizing condition in which a male who is waiting to be treated by a female physician sexually harasses her in the following way:

> In spite of the male's abuse (e.g., aspersions regarding her promiscuous nature, obscene language, and the exposing of his genitals), the doctor merely threatens action. The doctor, for the most part, ignores the abuse. When the male exposes his penis, the doctor becomes mesmerized or entranced. She becomes, as described by Zillmann and Bryant (1982), hysterically euphoric and, in fact, cannot delay the sexual gratification offered by the male. Later, the doctor even wonders why she initially put up such a fight. (Check, 1985, p. 116)

The results indicated that exposure to pornographic film clips of this kind affected subjects' subsequent self-reports about certain antisocial behaviors. Compared to control subjects and to subjects exposed to the erotic film clips, subjects exposed to the dehumanizing material were more likely to indicate that they might commit a rape if assured that no one would know and they would not be punished. A similar result was found for a scale constructed to measure the degree to which subjects would use force to coerce a female into other forms of unwanted sexual activity. This study suggests that relatively long-term exposure to sexually explicit depictions of mutually consenting sexual activity ("erotica") probably does not facilitate negative changes in antisocial attitudes among males. However, long-term exposure to dehumanizing or demeaning depictions may have such effects.

Unfortunately, two aspects of the procedures employed in Check's study undermine the confidence that might otherwise be placed in its outcome. The time periods during which subjects viewed the stimulus material and the interval between the last pornographic film presentation and completion of the dependent measures varied across subjects.

Because there is no assurance that the time intervals were randomly distributed across film-viewing groups, and because these varying time periods are not considered as a factor in the analyses of the results, it is difficult to assess their potential impact on subsequent self-reports. Further, Check used a series of sexually explicit excerpts taken from feature-length X-rated films. The end result (as in Zillmann & Bryant, 1982) is a long series of sexually explicit images with no context that could provide viewers with information about the characters' motivations, goals, and so on.

Recent work by the first author (Linz, 1985), in which male subjects were exposed to nearly eight hours of unedited, feature length X-rated films (five complete films; e.g., *Debbie Does Dallas*) over a two-week period, does not yield the same results. These films contain portrayals similar to those used by Check in his dehumanizing, nonviolent condition. The difference is that these portrayals were embedded in the context of larger, feature-length films rather than appearing as a series of sexually explicit scenes strung together by the experimenter. After exposure to these films, subjects exhibited no significant increases in the tendency to (1) hold calloused attitudes about rape, (2) view women as sexual objects, (3) judge the victim of a reenacted rape trial as more responsible for her own assault, or (4) view the defendant as less responsible for the victim's assault.

The films used in this experiment contain numerous scenes that portray women in a degrading or dehumanizing fashion like the clips excerpted from the full-length movies in Check's (1985) study. Failure to find the effects for the nonviolent but degrading depictions of women embedded in these feature-length films suggests that it is not simply frequency of images of female promiscuity that produce the effects, but rather the ratio of these images to other (not necessarily sexually related) images that might account for negative changes in attitudes about women. In other words, the commercially released X-rated films used in the present study, although just as sexually explicit and at times as dehumanizing as the "stag" films used by Zillmann and Bryant and the excerpts used by Check, contain a plethora of other scenes and ideas about women (sexual and nonsexual) that are unrelated to depictions of promiscuity and insatiability.

This is not to say that the "plots" contained in any of the films used in this study are anything but predictable and sophomoric. But the films are shot in scenic locations and women are depicted as traveling in cars, eating in restaurants, going to movies, holding jobs, and so on. Although the films contain scenes that are insulting and demeaning to women, other ideas compete or interfere with notions about female promiscuity and insatiability that may be activated by the films. This suggests that either a more concentrated dosage of scenes depicting women as sexually insatiable, such as the ones to which viewers were subjected in the Zillmann and Bryant and Check studies, is necessary for the trivialization of rape and bestiality to occur, or that a longer term of exposure (more than the five films used by Linz) may be necessary for these effects to emerge. Further research on long-term exposure to nonviolent sexual materials is needed before definitive conclusions can be drawn.

RESEARCH ON THE EFFECTS OF VIOLENT PORNOGRAPHY

In the years following the Report of the Commission on Obscenity and Pornography in 1970, pornography gradually changed: It became more violent. For example, Smith (1976a, 1976b), in an examination of "hard core" paperback novels, found that the incidence of rape depicted in these novels doubled between 1968 and 1974. Malamuth and Spinner (1980) found similar increases in sexual violence in "soft core" magazines such as *Playboy* and *Penthouse*. Social psychologists have investigated the impact of these forms of pornography, and we will briefly examine their major findings.

Aggressive Pornography and Sexual Arousal

Although it was once believed that only rapists would become sexually aroused by depictions of rape and other forms of aggression against women (e.g., Abel, Barlow, Blanchard, & Guild, 1977), research by Malamuth and his colleagues (e.g., Malamuth, 1981b, 1984; Malamuth & Check, 1983; Malamuth & Donnerstein, 1982; Malamuth, Haber, & Feshbach, 1980; Malamuth, Heim, & Feshbach, 1980) indicates that even nonrapists will show sexual arousal to certain kinds of media-presented images of rape. This increased arousal occurs primarily to depictions of rape in which the female victim shows signs of pleasure and arousal. However, certain male college students—those who indicate that there is some likelihood that they themselves would rape if assured of not being caught—display increased sexual arousal in response to rape depictions even when the victim is portrayed as suffering (e.g., Malamuth, 1981b; Malamuth & Donnerstein, 1982). This reaction is similar to those of known rapists. Researchers have suggested that sexual arousal to rape depictions may be an objective and reliable index of a proclivity to engage in rape (e.g., Abel et al., 1977; Malamuth, 1981a; Malamuth & Donnerstein, 1982). An individual whose sexual arousal to rape themes was found to be similar to or greater than his arousal to nonaggressive depictions would be considered to have a proclivity to rape.

Aggressive Pornography and Attitudes Toward Rape

Aggressive pornography may also foster the belief that women desire and derive pleasure from sexual assault. Images of women eventually succumbing to and finally enjoying sexual violence may suggest to male viewers that even if a woman seems to be initially repelled by a pursuer, she will eventually respond favorably to overpowering, aggressive advances (e.g., Brownmiller, 1975). Male consumers of aggressive pornography might come to think, at least for a while, that actually engaging in sexual aggression might be personally profitable, thus reducing their inhibitions about this form of aggression (Bandura, 1973). Beliefs such as these may be important in producing or sustaining violent behavior. Men who possess these beliefs might be more likely to attack a woman after they see the supposedly "pleasurable" rapes depicted in violent pornography.

There is now considerable evidence that exposure to aggressive pornography alters observers' perceptions of the act of rape and of rape victims themselves. For example, exposure to a sexually explicit rape scene in which the victim shows a "positive" reaction tends to produce decreased sensitivity toward and identification with the rape victim (e.g., Malamuth & Check, 1983), increased acceptance of rape myths and interpersonal violence against women (e.g., Malamuth & Check, 1981), and increases in the self-reported likelihood of raping (e.g., Malamuth, 1981a). This self-reported likelihood of committing rape is highly correlated with (a) sexual arousal to rape stimuli, (b) aggressive behavior and a desire to hurt women, and (c) a belief that rape would be a sexually arousing experience for the rapist (see Malamuth, 1981a; Malamuth & Donnerstein, 1982). There is also data to suggest that exposure to aggressive pornography can lead to self-generated rape fantasies (i.e., Malamuth, 1981b).

Aggressive Pornography and Aggression against Women in the Laboratory

Several studies (e.g., Donnerstein, 1980a, 1980b, 1983, 1984; Donnerstein & Berkowitz, 1981) have found that exposure to aggressive pornography increases aggression by men against women in a laboratory context. This same exposure does not seem to influence aggression against other men, however. This effect occurs for angered as well as nonangered subjects, and increases in aggressive behavior are most pronounced when the violent pornography portrays a positive outcome for the victim.

RESEARCH ON NONSEXUALLY VIOLENT PORTRAYALS OF VIOLENCE AGAINST WOMEN

Obviously, violent pornography both contains a message about violence against women and is emotionally arousing because of its sexual explicitness. The important question is, What is the relative contribution of the sexual and aggressive components of violent pornography to changes in attitudes and aggressive behavior? Is it the sexual nature of the material or the messages about violence that are crucial in facilitating laboratory aggression by males against females? As noted earlier, many policy-oriented discussions of this research omit the fact that the material studied is aggressive as well as sexual in nature (Scott, 1985). It is sometimes assumed that the experimental effects occur only because the material is sexually explicit and sexually arousing. In this section we examine two studies that suggest this is not true.

Images of violence against women have increased not only in pornographic materials but also in much more readily accessible mass media materials. Scenes of rape and violence have appeared with some frequency in daytime television soap operas, movies shown on network television, and in numerous magazine advertisements. These images are often accompanied by the theme, common in aggressive pornography, that women enjoy or benefit from sexual violence. For example, in the daytime drama *General Hospital*, produced by the American Broadcasting Company, several episodes were devoted to the rape of one of the popular female characters by an equally popular male character. At first the victim was humiliated; later the two characters married. A similar theme was expressed in the popular film *The Getaway* starring Steve McQueen and Ali McGraw. In this film, the protagonist

> kidnaps a woman . . . and her husband. He rapes the woman but the assault is portrayed in a manner such that the woman is depicted as a willing participant. She becomes the protagonist's girlfriend and they

both taunt her husband until he commits suicide. The woman then willingly continues with the assailant and at one point frantically searches for him. (Malamuth & Check, 1981, p. 439)

Malamuth and Check (1981) attempted to determine whether the nonexplicit depiction of sexual violence contained in *The Getaway* and in a mass-released film with similar content (*Swept Away*) influenced the viewers' perceptions of women as well as their attitudes toward women. In the investigation, 271 male and female students participated in what they thought was a study of movie ratings. One group of subjects watched, on two different evenings, *The Getaway* and *Swept Away*. A group of control subjects watched neutral feature-length movies. The movies were viewed in campus theaters as part of the "Campus Film Program." The dependent measures assessed acceptance of inter-personal violence against women (AIV) and rape myth acceptance (RMA). (See Burt, 1980.) The measures were embedded in a larger questionnaire containing many items as part of a "Sexual Attitudes Survey." The survey was conducted several days after the movie sessions. Subjects reported seeing no connection between the survey and the movies. The results indicated that viewing the sexually aggressive films significantly increased male but not female acceptance of inter-personal violence and tended to increase acceptance of rape myths. The important point here is that these effects occurred not with X-rated materials but with images more suitable for "prime time" television.

In a more recent pair of studies, Donnerstein, Berkowitz, and Linz (1986) systematically examined the relative contributions of the aggressive and sexual components of violent pornography. In the first study, male subjects were angered by either a male or female confederate of the experimenter and then shown one of four different films. The first was similar to aggressive pornography used in studies discussed earlier. The second was X-rated but contained no aggression or coercion. Subjects rated it just as sexually and physiologically arousing as the first film. The third contained scenes of aggression against women but without any sexual content. Subjects rated it as less sexually and physiologically arousing than the previous two films. The final film was of neutral content.

After viewing the films, subjects were given the opportunity to aggress against either a male or a female confederate of the experimenter. The results indicated that while the aggressive pornographic film resulted in the highest level of aggression against the woman, the aggression-only film produced more aggression against the woman than the sex-only film. In fact, there were no differences in aggression against the female target for subjects in the sex-only film condition and the neutral film condition.

In the second study, the aggressive cue value of the female target was strengthened by establishing a name connection between the female victim in the film and the female confederate in the study (see Berkowitz, 1974, for details of the name association procedure). In this study, subjects were first angered or treated in a neutral manner by a female confederate and then exposed to three versions of the same film. The first version contained a scene of sexual aggression in which a woman is tied up, threatened with a gun, and raped. The second version contained only the violent portions of the scene, with the sexually explicit content removed. The third version contained the sexually explicit portions of the scene with most of the violence deleted. After viewing the films, it was made apparent to half of the subjects that the female in the film had the same name as the confederate whom they now had the opportunity to punish. The other half of the subjects were not encouraged to make this association. The results indicated that whereas subjects who viewed the combination of sex and violence showed higher levels of aggressive behavior than subjects in the sex-only group, subjects exposed to the violence-only depiction under certain conditions also exhibited higher levels of aggression than the sex-only group. Subjects in the violence-only condition who either were given the name association cue or were angered by the experimenter showed higher levels of aggression against the female target than the sex-only subjects. Attitudes about rape and subjects' willingness to say they might commit a rape were also measured. The most callous attitudes and the largest percentage of subjects indicating some likelihood of raping if assured of not being caught were found in the aggression-only film condition. Subjects in the X-rated sex-only film condition scored lowest on these measures.

When considered together these studies strongly suggest that violence against women need not occur in a pornographic or sexually explicit context to have a negative impact on viewer attitudes and behavior. The study by Malamuth and Check (1983), cited earlier, suggested that sexual violence against women need not be portrayed in a pornographic fashion for greater acceptance of interpersonal violence and rape myths to result. In this study, the victim's reaction to sexual violence was always positive in the end. Presumably, the viewer came to accept the view that aggression against women is permissible because women enjoy sexual violence. In the experiments by Donnerstein, Berkowitz, and Linz, other processes may have been at work. In these experiments, exposure to nonpornographic depictions of aggression against women resulted in the highest levels of aggressive behavior when subjects were first angered by a female confederate of the experimenter or when the victim of aggression in the film and the female confederate were linked by the same name. Subjects need not come to perceive violence as acceptable because victims in this material enjoyed violence. Instead, the association of the female victim in the laboratory with the female characters in the films (Berkowitz, 1974) and the possibility that pain cues stimulated aggression in angry individuals better account for the findings. When a male is placed in a situation in which cues associated with aggressive responding are salient (e.g., a situation involving a female victim) or one in which he is predisposed to aggress because he is angered, he will be more likely to respond aggressively because of the stimulus-response connections previously accumulated through exposure to the films and/or because the pain and suffering of the victim reinforces already established aggressive tendencies.

Regardless of the best theoretical explanation of these data, the studies by Malamuth and Check (1983) and Donnerstein et al. (1986) suggest that an important element, if not the most important element, accounting for effects of exposure to aggressive pornography is the violent nature of the depiction, not exposure to explicit, arousing sexual behavior. And, as noted above, the mass media contain an abundance of such non-sexually explicit images. In fact, the wide availability of non-sexually explicit images of violence against women and the apparent popularity of films containing these images have prompted researchers to examine them in more detail.

Of particular interest are R-rated "slasher" films that portray graphic and brutal violence against women in a mildly sexual context, and that are particularly popular among teenage viewers. Slasher films do not fit the general definition of pornography, but their impact on the viewer is probably more detrimental. In the next section we examine the impact of these movies on young males who view them.

THE EFFECTS OF EXPOSURE TO R-RATED SEXUALIZED VIOLENCE

The depictions of increasingly graphic violence, especially in feature-length movies shown in theaters and available for home viewing on videocassettes, has caused concern among officials at the National Institute of Mental Health (1982):

> Films [have] to be made more and more powerful in their arousal effects. Initially, strong excitatory reactions (may grow) weak or vanish entirely with repeated exposure to stimuli of a certain kind. This is known as "habituation." The possibility of habituation to sex and violence has significant social consequences. For one, it makes pointless the search for stronger and stronger arousers. But more important is its potential impact on real life behavior. If people become inured to violence from seeing much of it, they may be less likely to respond to real violence by, for example, helping the victim. (p. 29)

This loss of "sensitivity" to real violence after repeated exposure to films containing sexualized violence, or the dilemma of the detached bystander in the presence of violence, is the concern of our current research program. We are investigating the effects of long-term exposure to R-rated sexually violent, commercially released mass media portrayals. In particular we are investigating how extensive exposure to commercially released violent and sexually violent films influence (1) general physiological and emotional desensitization to violence, (2) viewer perceptions of violence, (3) judgments about sexual violence and victims of sexual violence, and (4) aggressive behavior. Unlike many previous studies in which subjects have seen only 10-30 minutes of material, the current studies examine 10 hours of exposure. Because of this long exposure period, we are able to monitor the process of desensitization in subjects over an extended period. Also, because of the longer period of exposure we have multiple opportunities to examine perceptual and judgmental changes regarding violence, and particularly violence against women.

Linz, Donnerstein, and Penrod (1984) conducted an experiment to monitor males' desensitization to filmed violence against women and to determine whether this desensitization "spilled over" into other decision making about victims in more realistic situations. Male subjects watched nearly 10 hours of R-rated sexually violent films (five commercially released feature-length films, one per day for five days) such as *Tool Box Murders*, *Vice Squad*, *I Spit On Your Grave*, and *Texas Chainsaw Massacre*. These films contain far more graphic violence than explicit sex. After each movie, the men completed a mood questionnaire and evaluated the films on several dimensions. The films were counterbalanced so that comparisons could be made of the same films being shown on the first and last day of viewing. After the week of movie viewing the subjects watched another film, this time a realistic videotaped reenactment of a rape trial. After the trial, subjects were asked to render judgments as to how much injury the victim had suffered.

Before participation in the study all subjects were screened for hostility and psychoticism (the latter being an individual-difference variable particularly useful in determining which subjects may be most reactive to sexual violence). Only subjects with comparatively low scores on these variables were included in the study. This was done to help guard against the possibility of an overly hostile individual imitating the filmed violence during the week of the films. The screening is also noteworthy because it suggests that any effects that might be found in our experiments might occur within populations relatively low in predispositions toward aggression. It has generally been assumed by critics of media violence research that only people who are already predisposed toward aggressive behavior are influenced by exposure to media violence. In this study, and in others we have conducted, such individuals have probably been eliminated.

After the first day of viewing, the men rated themselves as significantly above college norms for depression and anxiety on a mood adjective checklist. A comparison of anxiety and depression scores for the first and last days of participation indicated, however, that by the last day of viewing subjects' levels of anxiety and depression had dropped significantly. What happened to the viewers as they watched more and more violence?

We argue that they were becoming desensitized to violence, particularly against women. But this entailed more than a simple lowering of arousal to the movie violence. The men also began to perceive the films differently as time went on. For example, on Day 1 the men estimated (on the average) that they had seen four "offensive scenes." By the fifth day, however, subjects reported only half as many offensive scenes (the films were presented in counterbalanced order to half the subjects so the same movies are evaluated on the first and fifth days). Likewise, subjects' ratings of level of violence decreased from Day 1 to Day 5. By the last day, the men rated the movies as less graphically violent and less gory, and estimated a smaller number of violent scenes than on the first day of viewing. Most startling, by the last day of viewing, the men were rating the material as significantly less debasing and degrading to women, more humorous and more enjoyable, and they were more willing to see this type of film again.

The subjects' evaluations of a rape victim (following their viewing of a reenacted rape trial) were also affected by the repeated exposure to brutality against women. The victim of rape was rated as significantly more worthless, and her injury as significantly less severe, by those exposed to the R-rated filmed violence as compared to a control group of men who saw only the rape trial and did not view any films. Desensitization to the violence in the films on the last day was also significantly correlated with assignment of greater responsibility to the assault victim.

Another study (Linz, 1985) was designed to answer additional questions about desensitization to sexualized violence. First, how much exposure is required for the effect to occur? Subjects viewed either five films over a two-week period or two films over a one-week period. Second, how long does the desensitization effect last? In this study subjects viewed the simulated rape trial almost immediately after viewing the last experimental film. The rape trial was shown two days following the last viewing session.

Results of this second study supported our earlier findings. When subjects are continually exposed to graphically depicted film violence against women, initial feelings of anxiety and depression begin to dissipate. Material that was once anxiety-provoking and depressing became less so with prolonged exposure. Perceptual changes found in the first study also prove to be reliable. Subjects reported seeing less violence with continued exposure. They also evaluated the material differently after continued exposure. Material once found somewhat degrading to women was judged to be less so after prolonged exposure.

How much exposure is necessary for these effects to appear? The second investigation suggests that two movies (the equivalent of about three hours of viewing time and approximately 20-25 violent acts) are sufficient to obtain a desensitization effect similar to that obtained after five movies. We found no statistically significant interactions between film dosage and the repeated measure factor (first day/last day film evaluations) on any of the dependent measures, suggesting that desensitization to filmed violence occurs rather rapidly. Once viewer discomfort in the face of violence has been reduced to a certain level, continued exposure may not further inure the viewer to the material to any significant degree.

The Linz (1985) study also revealed several consistent relationships between measures of general empathy for rape victims and sympathy for the specific victim portrayed in a videotaped reenactment of a rape trial. Subjects exposed to R-rated filmed violence against women were less sympathetic to the victim of rape portrayed in the trial and less able to empathize with rape victims in general as compared to no-exposure control subjects and subjects exposed to other kinds of films. Level of film exposure, however, affected specific sympathy and general empathy differently—longer exposure was necessary to affect the general empathic response.

This study also showed that reactions to victims portrayed in more realistic circumstances need not be measured immediately after exposure to violence for effects to be observed. Subject evaluations of the victim portrayed in the rape trial and of rape victims in general, made two days after the last film exposure, were nonetheless affected by the violent films. The time between the last film exposure and subjects' subsequent judgments about the victim of rape was not experimentally manipulated, however. To be certain that the effects are robust across a greater time period, the interval between exposure and victim evaluation should be manipulated.

NEGATIVE OUTCOME RAPE FILMS

For most subjects, exposure to rape depictions in which the victim abhors the experience results in relatively little sexual arousal, fewer negative evaluations of rape victims, and little increase in aggressive behavior. There is evidence, however, that a substantial proportion of college-age male subjects are sexually aroused by rape depictions in which the victim expresses negative reactions. In one study, for example, Malamuth and Check (1983) classified subjects on the basis of a single questionnaire item assessing the likelihood of committing a rape if assured of not being caught or punished. On the basis of this item 62 subjects were classified as having a low likelihood of raping (a rating of 1 on a 5-point scale corresponding to the response "not at all likely"). A total of 42 subjects were classified as having a high likelihood of raping (a 2 or above on the scale). Equivalent distributions of subjects have been found in several other studies (Malamuth, 1981a, 1981b; Malamuth, Haber, & Feshbach, 1980; Tieger, 1981).

Several days after completing the likelihood-of-raping item, subjects listened to one of three audiotapes (similar in sexual content and length): (1) a rape depiction wherein the victim abhors the experience; (2) a rape portrayal in which the rapist perceives the victim as becoming sexually aroused; and (3) a mutually consenting depiction. Measures of subjects' penile tumescence were taken while they listened to the audiotapes. Subjects who indicated that they had a low likelihood of raping were more sexually aroused by the mutually consenting depictions than by the negative outcome depictions, whereas subjects indicating a high likelihood of raping displayed an opposite pattern of results. Of course, as suggested by the research reviewed earlier, the most arousing depiction for all subjects was the positive outcome sexually violent condition. Most important for our discussion in this section, however, is the identification of a group of subjects more sexually aroused by the rape depiction in which the victim abhorred the experience than by the depiction of mutually consenting sex. As noted earlier, the reactions of the high-likelihood-of-raping subjects are quite similar to responses of convicted rapists studied by other investigators (e.g., Abel et al., 1977).

More recently, researchers have turned their attention to the response to depictions of rape of persons who score relatively high on various measures of psychoticism. These persons might be especially susceptible to depictions of rape in which the victim abhors the experience. Subjects high in psychoticism as measured by Eysenck's (1975) Personality Questionnaire (which contains a subscale to measure psychoticism, the P scale) have been examined in several studies by Malamuth and his colleagues (e.g., Barnes, Malamuth, & Check, 1984a, 1984b; Malamuth & Check, 1983). Malamuth and Check (1983) noted Eysenck and Nias's (1978) hypothesis that higher scores on the P scale would be associated with aggressive and impersonal sex. They examined subjects' levels of psychoticism as part of an experiment in which they manipulated the disgust, level of consent, and pain in an audiotaped depiction of sexual intercourse between a man and a woman. Malamuth and Check found that self-reported sexual arousal to the nonconsenting (rape) depictions was associated with higher scores on the P scale (although actual sexual arousal as measured by penile tumescence was not).

In a more recent study designed to test the relationship between the P scale and sexual arousal to rape depictions, Barnes et al. (1984b) exposed subjects to sexually explicit audio messages varying in degree of violence (rape versus nonrape) and pain experienced by the victim. A significant interaction between psychoticism and the level of violence variable was obtained. Subjects high in psychoticism showed greater self-reported sexual arousal and greater penile tumescence in response to the rape depictions. The opposite pattern of results was found for low P scorers. In a separate correlational study, Barnes et al. (1984a) found that, in addition to positive reactions to depictions of rape, high P scores were associated with (1) less interest in love and affection as a motivation for sex, (2) a greater tendency to fantasize about the use of force in sexual relations, (3) less positive evaluations of conventional sexual activities, and (4) greater self-reported likelihood of participating in unconventional sexual activities such as rape and pedophilia. These findings are largely consistent with those reported by Eysenck (1976) showing that high P scorers had greater levels of self-reported sexual promiscuity along with hostility and lack of satisfaction, and findings from an unpublished study by Eysenck (1976) that indicated that sex offenders were high P scorers.

A study by Linz, Donnerstein, Penrod, and Collins (1985) extends the research on psychoticism and sexual arousal to rape depictions. Instead of examining sexual arousal to these depictions, they examined how sexually violent media depictions interact with predispositions toward hostility and psychoticism to influence attitudes toward victims of violence. Subjects who scored high on measures of hostility and psychoticism as measured by the SCL-90 (Derogatis, 1977) were exposed to feature-length commercially released R- and X-rated films depicting sexual violence against women. Subjects were exposed to one of three types of film: (1) R-rated, mildly sexually violent films, (2) X-rated films that contain one ambiguous outcome rape (i.e., it was not clear if the victim experienced sexual arousal or derived benefit from the rape), and (3) R-rated brutally violent rape films (e.g., *I Spit on Your Grave*). After viewing, subjects watched a videotaped reenactment of a rape trial and made evaluations of the rape victim. Several interactions between psychoticism and film exposure were found. Subjects high in psychoticism and exposed to the brutal rape films showed a marginal decline in general empathy for rape victims and significant increases in endorsement of force in sexual relations. They also rated the rape victim in the trial as significantly less credible, less attractive, and somewhat more responsible for her own assault than did subjects in any of the other experimental conditions.

These studies on negative outcome rape depictions indicate that there may be individuals who are especially susceptible to the effects of the most brutal portrayals of violence against women. This research suggests that persons high in psychoticism may be more likely to become sexually aroused to negative outcome portrayals of rape, and more likely to rate victims of sexual assault less favorably after exposure to rape films in which there is no hint that the victims enjoy such treatment.

MITIGATING THE EFFECTS OF EXPOSURE TO SEXUAL VIOLENCE

There is some evidence that the negative attitudes and perceptions regarding rape and violence against women resulting from exposure to violent pornography can be changed in a positive direction if subjects are debriefed properly (see Linz, Donnerstein, Bross, & Chapin, in press, for a review). Malamuth and Check (1983), for example, found that male subjects who participated in an experiment in which they were exposed to pornographic rape depictions and later administered a carefully constructed debriefing were actually less accepting of myths about rape (i.e., the belief that women are in general responsible for their own rapes) than control subjects exposed to consenting intercourse depictions (without a rape debriefing). A similar finding has been obtained by Check and Malamuth (1984). Research by Donnerstein and Berkowitz (1981) suggests that not only are the negative effects of previous exposure eliminated, but even up to four months later, well-debriefed subjects have more "sensitive" attitudes toward rape than control subjects.

Generally, the content of the debriefings has consisted of (1) cautioning men that the portrayal of rape they have just seen is completely fictitious in nature, (2) educating them about the violent nature of rape, (3) pointing out that rape is illegal and punishable by imprisonment, and (4) dispelling "rape myths" that are perpetrated in the portrayal (e.g., in the majority of rapes the victim is promiscuous or has a bad reputation, or that many women have a subconscious desire to be raped).

Tests of the effectiveness of debriefings for male subjects in our work with R-rated sexual violence have yielded similar results (Linz, 1985). Immediate and long-term assessments of the impact of debriefings on male attitudes about sexual violence have shown that subjects who participated in the week-long film exposure study followed by a debriefing changed their attitudes in a positive direction (Linz, 1985; Linz, Donnerstein, Bross, & Chapin, 1982). These debriefings emphasize the fallacious nature of movie portrayals suggesting that women deserve to be physically violated and emphasize that processes of desensitization may have occurred due to long-term exposure to violence. The results indicated an immediate effect for debriefing, with subjects scoring lower on rape myth acceptance after participation than before participation in the film viewing sessions. These effects generally persisted six weeks later. The effectiveness of the debriefing for subjects who participated in two later experiments (one involving two weeks of exposure to R-rated violent films) was also examined. The results indicated that even after seven months, subjects' attitudes about sexual violence showed significant positive change (less rape myth acceptance) compared to preparticipation levels.

This research suggests that callous attitudes about rape and violence presented in aggressive pornography and other media representations of violence against women can be modified. Furthermore, if the debriefings used in the studies cited above contribute to the elimination of these negative effects, it would seem possible to develop effective "pre-briefings" to be administered to subjects before viewing sexual violence. In the future, social psychologists should begin the task of constructing and evaluating educational materials designed to reduce the impact of sexual violence on young viewers.

NOTE

1. The Motion Picture Association Film Rating Board assigns one of five possible ratings to films released in the United States: G, PG, PG-13, R, and X. An R-rated film is one to which children under the age of 17 may not be admitted unaccompanied by their parent or guardian. An X-rated film is one to which no one under the age of 18 may be admitted.

REFERENCES

Abel, G., Barlow, D., Blanchard, E., & Guild, D. (1977). The components of rapists' sexual arousal. *Archives of General Psychiatry, 34,* 395-403, 895-903.

Bandura, A. (1973). *Aggression: A social learning process.* Englewood Cliffs, NJ: Prentice-Hall.

Bandura, A. (1977). *Social learning theory.* Englewood Cliffs, NJ: Prentice-Hall.

Barnes, G. E., Malamuth, N. M., & Check, J.V.P. (1984a). Personality and sexuality. *Personality and Individual Differences, 5*(2), 159-172.

Barnes, G. E., Malamuth, N. M., & Check, J.V.P. (1984b). Psychoticism and sexual arousal to rape depictions. *Personality and Individual Differences, 5*(3), 273-279.

Baron, R. A. (1974a). Sexual arousal and physical aggression: The inhibiting influence of "cheesecake" and nudes. *Bulletin of the Psychonomic Society, 3,* 337-339.

Baron, R. A. (1974b). The aggression-inhibiting influence of heightened sexual arousal. *Journal of Personality and Social Psychology, 30*(3), 318-322.

Baron, R. A. (1977). *Human aggression.* New York: Plenum.

Baron, R. A. (1984). The control of human aggression: A strategy based on incompatible responses. In R. Geen & E. Donnerstein (Eds), *Aggression: Theoretical and empirical reviews* (Vol. II). New York: Academic Press.

Baron, R. A., & Bell, P. A. (1973). Effects of heightened sexual arousal on physical aggression. *Proceedings of the 81st Annual Convention of the American Psychological Association, 8,* 171-172.

Baron, R. A., & Bell, P. A. (1977). Sexual arousal and aggression by males: Effects of type of erotic stimuli and prior provocation. *Journal of Personality and Social Psychology, 35,* 79-87.

Berkowitz, L. (1974). Some determinants of impulsive aggression: Role of mediated associations with reinforcements for aggression. *Psychological Review, 81,* 165-179.

Berkowitz, L. (1984). Some effects of thoughts on anti- and prosocial influences of media events: A cognitive-neoassociation analysis. *Psychological Bulletin, 95,* 410-427.

Berkowitz, L., & Rogers, K. H. (in press). A priming effect analysis of media influences. In D. Zillmann (Ed.), *Advances in media effects research.* Hillsdale, NJ: Lawrence Erlbaum.

Brownmiller, S. (1975). *Against our will: Men, women and rape.* New York: Simon & Schuster.

Burt, M. R. (1980). Cultural myths and supports for rape. *Journal of Personality and Social Psychology, 38,* 217-230.

Check, J.V.P. (1985). *The effects of violent and nonviolent pornography* (Department of Supply and Services Contract No. 05SV 19200-3-0899). Ottawa, Ontario: Canadian Department of Justice.

Check, J.V.P., & Malamuth, N. (1983). Violent pornography, feminism, and social learning theory. *Aggressive Behavior, 9*(2), 106-107.

Check, J.V.P., & Malamuth, N. (1984). Can there be positive effects of participation in pornography experiments? *Journal of Sex Research, 20,* 14-31.

City County General Ordinance No. 35. (1984). City of Indianapolis, Indiana.

Cline, V. B. (Ed.). (1974). *Where do you draw the line?* Salt Lake City, UT: Brigham Young Press.

Defendants' memorandum. (1984). United States district court for the Southern District of Indiana, Indianapolis division, p. 8.

Derogatis, L. R. (1977). *The SCL-90 manual I: Scoring administration and procedures for the SCL-90.* Baltimore, MD: Johns Hopkins University School of Medicine, Clinical Psychometrics Unit.

Dienstbier, R. A. (1977). Sex and violence: Can research have it both ways? *Journal of Communication, 27,* 176-188.

Donnerstein, E. (1980a). Pornography and violence against women. *Annals of the New York Academy of Sciences, 347,* 277-288.

Donnerstein, E. (1980b). Aggressive-erotica and violence against women. *Journal of Personality and Social Psychology, 39,* 269-277.

Donnerstein, E. (1983). Erotica and human aggression. In R. Geen & E. Donnerstein (Eds.), *Aggression: Theoretical and empirical reviews.* New York: Academic Press.

Donnerstein, E. (1984). Pornography: Its effect on violence against women. In N. Malamuth & E. Donnerstein (Eds.), *Pornography and sexual aggression.* New York: Academic Press.

Donnerstein, E., & Barrett, G. (1978). The effects of erotic stimuli on male aggression toward females. *Journal of Personality and Social Psychology, 36,* 180-188.

Donnerstein, E., & Berkowitz, L. (1981). Victim reactions in aggressive-erotic films as a factor in violence against women. *Journal of Personality and Social Psychology, 41,* 710-724.

Donnerstein, E., Berkowitz, L., & Linz, D. (1986). *Role of aggressive and sexual images in violent pornography.* Manuscript submitted for publication.

Donnerstein, E., Donnerstein, M., & Evans, R. (1975). Erotic stimuli and aggression: Facilitation or inhibition. *Journal of Personality and Social Psychology, 32,* 237-244.

Donnerstein, E., & Hallam, J. (1978). Facilitating effects of erotica on aggression against women. *Journal of Personality and Social Psychology, 36,* 1270-1277.

Donnerstein, E., & Linz, D. (1984, January). Sexual violence in the media, a warning. *Psychology Today,* pp. 14-15.

Dworkin, A. (1983). *Pornography: Men possessing women.* New York: Perigee.

Dworkin, A. (1985). Against the male flood: Censorship, pornography, and equality. *Harvard Women's Law Journal, 8.*

Eysenck, H. J. (1976). *Sex and personality.* London: Open Books.

Eysenck, H. J., & Eysenck, S.B.G. (1975). *Manual of the Eysenck personality questionnaire.* London: Hodder & Stoughton.

Eysenck, H. J., & Nias, H. (1978). *Sex, violence, and the media.* London: Spector.

Falwell, J. (1980). *Listen America.* Garden City, NY: Doubleday.

Frodi, A. (1977). Sexual arousal, situational restrictiveness, and aggressive behavior. *Journal of Research in Personality, 11,* 48-58.

Gould, L. (1977). Pornography for women. In T. H. Gagmen (Ed.), *Human sexuality in today's world.* Boston: Little, Brown.

Howard, J. L., Liptzin, M. B., & Reifler, C. B. (1973). Is pornography a problem? *Journal of Social Issues, 29,* 133-145.

Liebert, R. M., & Schwartzberg, N. S. (1977). Effects of mass media. *Annual Review of Psychology, 28,* 141-173.

Linz, D. (1985). *Sexual violence in the media: Effects on male viewers and implications for society.* Unpublished doctoral dissertation, University of Wisconsin—Madison.

Linz, D., Donnerstein, E., Bross, M., & Chapin, M. (1986). Mitigating the effects of sexual violence in the media. In R. Blanchard (Ed.), *Advances in the study of aggression* (vol. 2). New York: Academic Press.

Linz, D., Donnerstein, E., & Penrod, S. (1984). The effects of long-term exposure to filmed violence against women. *Journal of Communication, 34,* 130-147.

Linz, D., Donnerstein, E., Penrod, S., & Collins, R. (1985). *Individual differences in hostility and psychoticism, exposure to sexual violence and reactions to a victim of sexual violence.* Unpublished manuscript, University of Wisconsin—Madison.

Linz, D., Penrod, S., & Donnerstein, E. (in press). Media violence and antisocial behavior: Some alternative legal policies. *Journal of Social Issues.*

Longino, H. E. (1980). Pornography, oppression, and freedom: A closer look. In L. Lederer (Ed.), *Take back the night: Women on pornography.* New York: William Morrow.

MacKinnon, C. A. (1985). Pornography, civil rights, and speech. *Harvard Civil Rights-Civil Liberties Law Review, 20*(1).

Malamuth, N. (1981a). Rape proclivity among males. *Journal of Social Issues, 37,* 138-157.

Malamuth, N. (1981b). Rape fantasies as a function of exposure to violent-sexual stimuli. *Archives of Sexual Behavior, 10,* 33-47.

Malamuth, N. (1984). Aggression against women: Cultural and individual causes. In N. Malamuth & E. Donnerstein (Eds.), *Pornography and sexual aggression.* New York: Academic Press.

Malamuth, N., & Check, J.V.P. (1981). The effects of mass media exposure on acceptance of violence against women: A field experiment. *Journal of Research in Personality, 15*, 436-446.

Malamuth, N., & Check, J.V.P. (1983). Sexual arousal to rape depictions: Individual differences. *Journal of Abnormal Psychology, 92*, 55-67.

Malamuth, N., & Donnerstein, E. (Eds.). (1984). *Pornography and sexual aggression.* New York: Academic Press.

Malamuth, N., & Donnerstein, E. (1982). The effects of aggressive pornographic mass media stimuli. In L. Berkowitz (Ed.), *Advances in experimental social psychology* (Vol. 15). New York: Academic Press.

Malamuth, N., Feshbach, S., & Jaffe, Y. (1977). Sexual arousal and aggression: Recent experiments and theoretical issues. *Journal of Social Issues, 33*(2), 110-133.

Malamuth, N., Haber, S., & Feshbach, S. (1980). Testing hypotheses regarding rape: Exposure to sexual violence, sex differences, and the normality of rape. *Journal of Research in Personality, 14*, 121-137.

Malamuth, N., Heim, M., & Feshbach, S. (1980). The sexual responsiveness of college students to rape depictions: Inhibitory and disinhibitory effects. *Journal of Personality and Social Psychology, 38*, 399-408.

Malamuth, N., & Spinner, B. (1980). A longitudinal content analysis of sexual violence in the best-selling erotica magazines. *Journal of Sex Research, 16*(3), 226-237.

Mann, J., Sidman, J., & Starr, S. (1971). Effects of erotic films on sexual behavior of married couples. In *Technical report of The Commission on Obscenity and Pornography* (Vol. 8). Washington, DC: Government Printing Office.

Maslin, J. (1982, November 11). Bloodbaths debase movies and audiences. *New York Times*, p. 2.

Meyer, T. (1972). The effects of viewing justified and unjustified real film violence on aggressive behavior. *Journal of Personality and Social Psychology, 23*, 21-29.

National Institute of Mental Health. (1982). *Television and behavior: Ten years of scientific progress and implications for the eighties, Vol. 1: Summary report.* Rockville, MD: National Institute of Mental Health.

President's Commission on Pornography and Obscenity. (1970). *Technical report of The Commission on Obscenity and Pornography* (Vol. 8). Washington, DC: Government Printing Office.

Scott, D. A. (1985, March). Pornography and its effects on family, community, and culture. *Family Policy Insights, 4*(2).

Smith, D. D. (1976a). *Sexual aggression in American pornography: The stereotype of rape.* Paper presented at the annual meeting of the American Sociological Association, New York City.

Smith, D. D. (1976b). The social content of pornography. *Journal of Communication, 26*, 16-33.

Steinem, G. (1980). Erotica and pornography: A clear and present difference. In L. Lederer (Ed.), *Take back the night: Women on pornography* (pp. 35-39). New York: William Morrow.

Tieger, T. (1981). Self-rated likelihood of raping and the social perception of rape. *Journal of Research in Personality, 15*, 147-158.

Washington Post. (1985, October 15).

Wills, G. (1977, November). Measuring the impact of erotica. *Psychology Today*, pp. 30-34.

Wyer, R. S., & Srull, T. K. (1980). The processing of social stimulus information: A conceptual integration. In R. Hastie et al. (Eds.), *Person memory: The cognitive basis of social perception.* Hillsdale, NJ: Lawrence Erlbaum.

Zillmann, D. (1971). Excitation transfer in communication-mediated aggressive behavior. *Journal of Experimental Social Psychology, 7,* 419-433.

Zillmann, D. (1978). Attribution and misattribution of excitatory reactions. In J. H. Harvey, W. J. Ickes, & R. F. Kidd (Eds.), *New directions in attribution research* (Vol. 2, pp. 335-368). Hillsdale, NJ: Lawrence Erlbaum.

Zillmann, D. (1979). *Hostility and aggression.* Hillsdale, NJ: Lawrence Erlbaum.

Zillmann, D. (1982). Transfer of excitation in emotional behavior. In J. T. Cacioppo & R. E. Petty (Eds.), *Social psychophysiology.* New York: Guilford.

Zillmann, D. (1984). *Victimization of women through pornography.* Proposal to the National Science Foundation.

Zillmann, D., & Bryant, J. (1982). Pornography, sexual callousness, and the trivialization of rape. *Journal of Communication, 32,* 10-21.

Zillmann, D., & Bryant, J. (1984). Effects of massive exposure to pornography. In N. Malamuth & E. Donnerstein (Eds.), *Pornography and sexual aggression.* New York: Academic Press.

Zillmann, D., Bryant, J., Comisky, P. W., & Medoff, N. J. (1981). Excitation and hedonic valence in the effect of erotica on motivated intermale aggression. *European Journal of Social Psychology, 11,* 233-252.

Zillmann, D., & Sapolsky, B. S. (1977). What mediates the effect of mild erotica on annoyance and hostile behavior in males? *Journal of Personality and Social Psychology, 35,* 587-596.

5

Gender, Justice, and the Psychology of Entitlement

BRENDA MAJOR

Brenda Major is Associate Professor of Psychology at the State University of New York at Buffalo. She received her Ph.D. in 1978 from Purdue University, where she worked with Kay Deaux. Her research interests include determinants of gender-linked social behaviors, the role of the self in social interaction, and the impact of outcome expectancies on coping behaviors.

Do women and men differ in their sense of their own entitlement, in what they feel they deserve from their jobs or relationships? If so, under what circumstances and for what reasons? These questions, which are the focus of this chapter, concern distributive justice—the conditions under which outcome distributions (e.g., of rewards, goods, services) are perceived as fair. Social scientists generally have addressed questions of justice from one of two theoretical perspectives, that of equity theory (Adams, 1965; Walster, Walster, & Berscheid, 1978) or relative deprivation theory (Crosby, 1976). Both theories share several core assumptions about the nature of justice (Martin & Murray, 1983). First, it is the *subjective* evaluation of outcomes rather than their objective status that determines whether one feels fairly or unfairly treated, satisfied, or deprived. Second, individuals must want or *value* an outcome in order to feel deprived or inequitably treated if they do not have it. Third, perceptions of justice are the result of a *comparison process*, in which the outcomes of one individual (the comparer) are compared to those of a comparative referent.

The precise nature of this comparative referent, however, varies according to the particular theory in question. According to relative deprivation theories (Crosby, 1976), this comparative referent may be another person or group, what one received in the past, expects to receive in the future, or even what one wants. According to equity theory (Adams, 1965), justice is achieved when the ratio of the comparer's inputs (contributions) to outcomes (rewards) is equal to the input/outcome ratio of a comparison other. More recently, Folger (1984; Mark &

Folger, 1984) has proposed that these comparative referents be conceptualized as *referent cognitions*. These include *referent outcomes*—outcomes that one could feasibly imagine oneself receiving under different circumstances, and *justifications*—the perceived appropriateness or moral acceptability of the procedures that could have produced existing or referent outcomes. Referent outcomes may derive from several sources, including social comparisons, prior expectations, and even imagined or theoretically ideal outcomes. According to this view, individuals feel deprived to the extent that they lack some outcome (or enough of that outcome) and they (a) desire that outcome, (b) have high referent outcomes, and (c) perceive the justification for existing outcomes (relative to referent outcomes) as low.

Both equity and relative deprivation theories predict that when outcomes are perceived as unjust (e.g., less than those of referent outcomes), a variety of cognitive, affective, and behavioral reactions ensue, ranging from psychological justifications of the injustice to behavioral attempts to redress it.

Although psychological theories of justice have generally ignored the question of individual differences, a number of researchers have compared the sexes in their approach to issues of distributive justice. As with so many areas of psychological research, this initial interest in sex comparisions appears to have been spurred, in part, by the ease of measuring the sex of research participants rather than by any coherent theoretical framework regarding gender. This research, derived from divergent theoretical frameworks, disciplinary roots, and research methodologies, has revealed two striking patterns: Despite objectively similar performance inputs, women generally allocate fewer rewards to themselves than men do, and despite objectively lower job-related rewards, women are generally just as satisfied with their jobs and pay as men are.

In the current chapter, I will present a brief overview of this research (see Crosby, 1982; Kahn, O'Leary, Krulewitz, & Lamm, 1980; Major & Deaux, 1982, for reviews) and consider several explanations for these patterns. The most prevalent explanation proposes that men and women differ in what they value or want from their social or work relationships, hence their tendencies to allocate rewards differently and evaluate their jobs similarly. In contrast to this view, I will propose that women and men use different comparative referents when they evaluate their existing outcomes or when they estimate what they deserve or are entitled to receive. In addition, I will consider the role of psychological justifications of victimization in producing and maintaining gender differences in perceived entitlement.

GENDER AND REWARD ALLOCATION PREFERENCES

Social psychologists testing predictions from equity theory frequently compare the manner in which men and women allocate rewards between themselves and others. This research typically employs an experimental paradigm in which a subject is asked to work with another person on some mutual task, with payment contingent on their joint performance. False performance feedback from the experimenter indicates that one of the coworkers was the superior performer and one was the inferior performer. Subjects are then assigned the task of allocating the reward (usually money) between themselves and their coworker.

Although a substantial amount of research using this paradigm has supported predictions from equity theory, it has also revealed frequent differences in the ways that men and women allocate rewards between themselves and others (Kahn et al., 1980; Major & Deaux, 1982). Specifically, when asked to split rewards between themselves and a partner with performance inferior to theirs, men tend to allocate the rewards equitably (i.e., in proportion to inputs or performance) whereas women tend to allocate the rewards equally. When the partner's performance is superior to theirs, both men and women tend to divide the rewards equitably, but women generally take less for themselves than men do. Even when the allocator's and partner's performances are equal (Lane & Messé, 1971, Experiment 1), women tend to take less reward for themselves and give more to their partners than men do. A number of authors have suggested that women's allocations appear to adhere more to the norm of equality, whereas men's allocations appear to adhere more to the norm of equity (Kahn et al., 1980; Sampson, 1975).

Although a number of possible explanations for these gender differences have been proposed, certainly the most popular and most enduring explanation is that gender differences in interpersonal values, styles, or goals are responsible. Women are assumed to be more communal, more status-neutralizing, and more oriented toward maximizing the interpersonal aspects of their relationships with their partners. Men, in contrast, are assumed to be more agentic, more status-assertive, and more concerned with performing the task and maximizing material rewards (Bakan, 1966; Deaux, 1976; Kahn et al., 1980). Proponents of value-based explanations for sex differences in allocation behavior have noted the correspondence between the presumed interaction goals of females and the goals fostered by equal allocations as compared to the presumed interaction goals of males and the goals fostered by equitable allocations (Deutsch, 1975; Sampson, 1975). A substantial literature indicates that equal allocations tend to be preferred when the goal is to promote harmonious relationships, whereas equitable allocations tend to be preferred when the goal is to promote productivity (Leventhal, 1976).

Noting this correspondence post hoc, however, is not the same as demonstrating that sex differences in values or goals underlie sex differences in allocation behavior. Although the sexes are widely assumed to differ in their interaction goals or values, comparisons of the social behaviors of women and men rarely show the consistent cross-situational sex differences that such an assumption implies (Deaux, 1984). Women's and men's allocation preferences are frequently moderated by situational factors such as the sex of the coworker (Reis & Jackson, 1981), the sex-linkage of the task (Reis & Jackson, 1981), the salience of impression management concerns (Kidder, Bellettirie, & Cohn, 1977), and the type of reward being allocated (Major & Adams, 1984).

Furthermore, the research paradigm typically used to examine reward allocation preferences confounds issues of personal entitlement with interpersonal concerns. That is, the use of a fixed-sum reward requires that allocators who take more for themselves must of necessity give less to others. In an attempt to separate these processes, Callahan-Levy and Messé (1979, Experiment 1) asked men and women to work on a task for a specified period of time and then to pay privately either themselves or another person (male or female) what they thought was fair pay for their performance. The researchers found that women paid themselves significantly less money and reported that less money was fair pay for their work than men did. Women and men did not differ, however, in the amount of money they paid to others. Thus gender differences in allocations occurred primarily in allocations to the self. Other research has also found few differences in women's and men's patterns of allocations to others when they themselves are not corecipients (Major & Deaux, 1982).

The most serious challenge to the value-based explanation comes from three studies designed to test this explanation directly (Major & Adams, 1983; Swap & Rubin, 1983; Watts, Vallacher, & Messé, 1982). These studies examined allocations to self and others using designs in which men and women were preselected so as to be matched on some measure of interpersonal values (e.g., measures of interpersonal orientation or agency/communion). Hence, according to the value-based explanation, allocations in these studies should vary as a function of allocator's values rather than allocator's sex. As predicted, the measures of interpersonal values generally were related to allocation behavior in the expected direction (e.g., those who were high in interpersonal orientation were more generous to their partners than were those low in interpersonal orientation). Nevertheless, in all three studies gender differences in allocations were still observed. That is, despite the fact that gender differences in interpersonal values were presumably controlled for by subject selection, the typical pattern of women allocating rewards more equally and men more equitably between themselves and others still was obtained. Although these results obviously may be due to imperfect measurement of interpersonal values, they nevertheless pose a serious problem for the value-based explanation. In short, despite its intuitive appeal and post hoc capabilities, attempts to put the value-based explanation to empirical test suggest that by itself it is insufficient to explain women's and men's patterns of reward allocation.

GENDER AND JOB SATISFACTION

A different approach to distributive justice is to examine how individuals react to existing reward distributions. Comparisons of how women and men evaluate their jobs and pay are relevant to this issue. Both equity and relative deprivation theories suggest that individuals should feel anger, resentment, and/or dissatisfaction when they perceive that their outcomes are less than those received by a comparative referent, such as similar others doing similar work. Consequently, one should expect that field research investigating the job and pay satisfaction of men and women would reveal striking sex differences. Full-time working women in the United States are concentrated in lower paying, lower prestige jobs than men, and women are paid less than similarly qualified men doing comparable work (Treiman & Hartmann, 1981). This difference holds even when men and women are matched on numerous job characteristics that typically covary with sex, such as age, education, organizational tenure, tenure in present position, and occupational prestige (Nieva & Gutek, 1981; Treiman & Hartmann, 1981).

Despite this objectively unjust situation, however, most field studies of job and pay satisfaction find little evidence that women are subjectively more dissatisfied than men with their pay or with their jobs (e.g., Crosby, 1982; Sauser & York, 1978). In one of the more recent and comprehensive investigations of this issue, Crosby (1982) surveyed 345 male and female full-time workers, matched for occupational prestige, on a number of dimensions relevant to satisfaction at work. Consistent with earlier research, she found that the women in her sample were objectively underpaid relative to the men. Further, she found that although the women were aware of and aggrieved about the underpayment of women in general, they reported no evidence of personal deprivation or dissatisfaction with their own pay, jobs, or treatment. In other words, although these women realized that other women were being discriminated against, they did not believe that this inequitable situation applied to themselves.

It has frequently been proposed that differences in what men and women value or want from their jobs can explain their paradoxically similar levels of job and pay satisfaction (e.g., Crosby, 1982; Sauser & York, 1978). The logic of this argument is that women are "contented" with their jobs and pay despite their objectively inequitable treatment because there is little discrepancy between what they want and what they receive. Three major assumptions are inherent in this explanation: first, that women and men value or want different things from their jobs; second, that women and men obtain from their jobs the things they want; and third, that sex differences in job values or wants explain the similarity in women's and men's job satisfaction. In support of the first assumption, a number of studies have found that men are more interested in pay and promotion than women are, whereas women value social relations on the job and "comfortable" working conditions (e.g., good hours, easy transportation, pleasant physical surroundings) more than men do (see Nieva & Gutek, 1981, for a review). With regard to the second assumption, there is ample evidence that men receive higher pay and more promotional opportunities than women (Treiman & Hartmann, 1981), and some evidence that women's jobs tend to be higher on comfort factors than men's (Quinn & Shepard, 1974). There is no evidence, however, that women experience higher levels of positive social relationships on the job than men (Nieva & Gutek, 1981). The third assumption, that sex differences in job values or wants explain women's paradoxically high levels of job and pay satisfaction, remains a post hoc explanation without direct empirical support.

A major confound in much of the data indicating that men and women differ in job values is the frequent failure of researchers to control adequately for sex differences in structural factors, such as organizational level, opportunities, and/or occupational sex-segregation. The American work force is highly sex-segregated, and most individuals work in jobs dominated by their own sex (Treiman & Hartmann, 1981). Furthermore, pay and promotional opportunities are far greater in "men's jobs" than "women's jobs" (Treiman & Hartmann, 1981). Thus differences in what women and men may realistically expect to obtain from their jobs may shape their values and aspirations (Kanter, 1977; Nieva & Gutek, 1981).

Several studies provide support for the hypothesis that expectations affect aspirations and values (see Kanter, 1977, for a thorough discussion of this issue). For example, Crowley, Levitin, and Quinn (1973) found that when sex differences in the expectation that one would be promoted were controlled, sex differences in the desire for promotion disappeared. Crosby's (1982) survey also provides support. To measure job values, she asked male and female workers, matched for level of occupational prestige (but not for specific occupation), to describe the things about their work that they found especially gratifying or rewarding. Results revealed that women and men in high prestige jobs were remarkably similar in their responses. These two groups, for example, were almost identical in the degree to which they cited pay, interpersonal relations, and the desire for independence and control as sources of job gratifications. Furthermore, high prestige men as well as women in general cited a sense of accomplishment and interpersonal relations as greater sources of job gratification than pay. Differences between women and men in low prestige jobs (which are more apt to be sex-segregated) were more pronounced and conformed more to stereotypical sex preferences. More recently, Golding, Resnick, and Crosby (1983) found that women and men in the same occupation (lawyers) showed no differences in job values. When value differences were observed, they varied by job level (secretary versus lawyer) rather than sex.

The argument that women and men differ in their job values or preferences has been used not only to explain women's and men's job satisfaction but also, as Nieva and Gutek (1981) point out, to justify the low rewards that women receive from their jobs relative to men. For example, it has been suggested that women's lesser interest in money and greater interest in comfort factors make women less willing than men to do the kind or amount of work necessary to acquire high pay (O'Neill, 1985). This tendency to "blame the victim" may perpetuate occupational sex-segregation and discrimination. As Kahn and Gaeddert (1985) note, it is but a small step to argue that if women and men want or value different things, they might be best suited for different work organizations, different social organizations, and/or different family and societal roles.

In summary, women and men paradoxically fail to differ in their satisfaction with their own job-related rewards, despite the objectively documented underpayment of women. The prevailing explanation for this paradox is that women and men differ in what they want from their jobs. As with the literature on gender differences in reward allocations, however, this value-based explanation has seldom been tested directly, and when so tested, has often been found wanting. One of the major limitations of this explanation is its failure to consider the impact of structural factors, such as restricted opportunities and unequal status, on women's and men's values, aspirations, and attitudes.

GENDER AND PERSONAL ENTITLEMENT

In contrast to the prevailing focus on gender differences in outcome values, my research has examined the comparative referents used by women and men when making justice-related judgments. Although not ruling out the possibility that women and men may differ to some extent in what they value, I have argued that cognitive processes can also explain why men and women allocate and evaluate rewards as they do. This argument explicitly recognizes the impact of the differential social status of women and men on their attitudes and behaviors. In particular, I have proposed that women's sense of personal entitlement or deservingness is lower than men's, especially with regard to monetary outcomes, and I have sought to identify possible determinants of such entitlement differences.

The construct of personal entitlement is synonymous with that of deservingness; the person who feels entitled to a particular outcome or level of outcomes feels that he or she should receive that outcome. Entitlement is a key mediating construct in theories of equity (Adams, 1965), relative deprivation (Crosby, 1976, 1982), and outcome satisfaction (Lawler, 1971). But what produces a sense of entitlement or deservingness? Why might some individuals feel more "entitled" than others? All of the antecedents to feelings of relative deprivation or inequity are potentially relevant here. For example, we may feel entitled to receive what we have always received in the past or what we perceive similar others receive. Folger's analysis (1984) suggests that procedural justice considerations also are important. Specifically, people feel entitled to receive desirable outcomes that they can feasibly imagine themselves receiving under alternative justifiable circumstances (i.e., through just procedures).

But why might women and men differ in their sense of entitlement? A consideration of the differing positions of and rewards received by men and women in society suggests several reasons why this might occur, especially with regard to pay. First, entitlement differences may occur as a consequence of a history of occupational and wage discrimination against women. Specifically, women may develop lower adaptation levels for their pay or lower pay expectations than men (Sauser & York, 1978). These lower pay expectations may then serve as a lower comparative referent against which women evaluate how much pay they deserve. A second possible mechanism is restricted social comparisons. For example, in judging what they deserve, women and men may compare primarily with same-sex and/or same-job others. Because women typically are paid less than men, and people working in female-dominated jobs are paid less than those working in male-dominated jobs (Treiman & Hartmann, 1981), the comparative referents acquired by such similarity-based social comparisons may be lower for women than men. Hence, on the basis of such comparisons, women may feel entitled to less than men do.

A third possible mechanism is related to the ways in which male and female performances, attributes, and tasks are valued in our society. Research indicates that female performances often tend to be seen as less competent than identical male performances (Deaux, 1976; Nieva & Gutek, 1981), successful performances by women frequently are attributed to external or unstable causes (Hansen & O'Leary, 1985), and a task or job labeled as feminine is seen as easier than an identical task labeled as masculine (Deaux, 1984). Furthermore, research suggests that women and men often make parallel judgments about their own work. That is, relative to men, women tend to evaluate their own performances more harshly in the absence of performance feedback (Lenney, 1977) and are less likely to take credit for their successes and more likely to accept responsibility for their failures (Deaux, 1984; Hansen & O'Leary, 1985). Consequently, women may feel that their (objectively identical) work is less deserving of reward than men's.

Note that none of these hypotheses proposes that women and men have different goals or values. Rather, each suggests a cognitive process as a possible explanation for women's and men's patterns of reward allocations and satisfaction. The studies described in the following section were designed to test these hypotheses. They suggest that women and men not only differ in their sense of personal entitlement with respect to monetary outcomes, but that differences in comparative referents may underlie these differences.

Gender Differences in Self-Payment for Work

As noted above, Callahan-Levy and Messé (1979, Experiment 1) found that women and men differed in the amount of money they paid themselves, but did not differ in the amount of money they paid to others. Our first experiment (Major, McFarlin, & Gagnon, 1984, Experiment 1) attempted to replicate these findings and assess the impact of social comparison information on this process. Some research (e.g., Austin, McGinn, & Susmilch, 1980) suggests that people rely on the comparison that is most salient when judging what they deserve. That is, judgments of entitlement are based on social comparisons when those are available, but on internally generated referents, such as prior expectations, when social comparisons are unavailable.

We hypothesized that if women and men differ in their sense of personal entitlement with respect to pay, gender differences in self-pay should occur when social comparison referents are unavailable. In contrast, gender differences in self-pay should be absent when similar social comparison standards are available, providing that impression management and interpersonal concerns are minimized. Furthermore, in order to examine whether people's judgments of personal deservingness are based on restricted social comparisons (e.g., with same-sex others) we manipulated the content of the available social comparison standards so that in some conditions the pay of comparison women and men was discrepant.

Undergraduate students were recruited for the experiment for an unspecified amount of pay, and were asked to work individually on a sex-neutral prediction task for a fixed amount of time. In order to manipulate the content and availability of comparison information, a bogus "student expenditure list," which presumably had been filled out by four male and four female subjects (in the social comparison present conditions) or was blank (in the social comparison absent condition), had been placed on top of the desk at which they were working. The purpose of this list, subjects were told, was to keep an anonymous record of expenditures in the experiment. For one-third of the subjects in the social comparison present conditions, information on the list indicated that other women in the experiment had paid themselves more (M = $2.50) than had men (M = $1.50), for one-third the information indicated that men (M = $2.50) had paid themselves more than had women (M = $1.50), and for one-third the information indicated that men and women had paid themselves the same average amounts (M = $2.00). In a procedure similar to that used by Callahan-Levy and Messe, after subjects had completed the task and a posttask questionnaire, they were asked to pay themselves privately, from a $4.00 "pot," what they thought was fair pay for their work.

As predicted by the hypothesis that women and men differ in their personal entitlement with respect to pay, when no social comparison standards were available, women paid themselves less ($1.95) than men did ($3.18; $p < .01$), and said that less money was fair pay for their work ($1.89) than men did ($3.61; $p < .06$). In contrast, no gender differences in self-pay were observed when social comparisons were present. Furthermore, although subjects in the unequal social comparison conditions perceived the discrepancy between the self-pay of comparison women and men, this discrepancy had no impact on their own self-payment. Women and men in all three social comparison conditions paid themselves approximately the average amount taken by comparison others, regardless of sex (means ranged from $1.88 to $2.19).

Exploration of possible determinants of these gender differences in personal entitlement revealed that men and women did not differ in the importance they placed on the money earned or in their ratings of the enjoyability of the task. Nor did they differ in their evaluations of or attributions for their performance. Women had earned somewhat lower pay than men in their past jobs, but self-pay was not significantly correlated with past pay history for either sex. Surprisingly, however, both women and men in the social comparison standard absent condition believed that other males in the experiment had paid themselves significantly more ($3.16) than had females ($2.55; $p < .01$). Furthermore, for the subjects in this condition, their own self-pay was highly and significantly correlated with what they thought same-sex, but not cross-sex, others had paid themselves. Although this finding may reflect a "false consensus effect" (Ross, Greene, & House, 1977), it is nevertheless suggestive that when social comparisons are unavailable, men and women may determine their deservingness on the basis of internalized reference group comparisons, specifically, their beliefs about the behavior or deservingness of others of their own sex.

Gender Differences in Work for Pay

In our second experiment (Major, McFarlin, & Gagnon, 1984, Experiment 2) we hypothesized that if women and men differ in their sense of personal entitlement with regard to pay, gender differences should also be observed in the amount of inputs (e.g., time, work) that women and men feel they should expend in return for fixed outcomes. That is, in the absence of salient and similar social comparison standards, women should work longer and do more work for a fixed, prepaid amount of money than should men. We also examined the competing hypothesis that gender differences in self-allocations of money or work primarily reflect the greater influence of impression management or interpersonal concerns on women than men. According to this perspective, women might be expected to take fewer rewards for themselves than men or work longer and harder for the same amount of reward only when there are interpersonal benefits to be gained from this strategy, such as when behavior is public rather than private (Kahn et al., 1980; Callahan-Levy & Messe, 1979).

Male and female university students were recruited for pay via advertisements, but were not informed in advance of the length of time the experiment would require. Each person participated individually and was asked to work on a lengthy task that involved counting 50 sets of dots in various spatial configurations. Prior to beginning work on the task, all were paid $4.00 and informed that although there were quite a few pages of dots, our only requirement was that they do as much work as they thought was fair for the amount of money they were paid. Furthermore, they were told that the $4.00 was theirs to keep regardless of how long they worked or how many sets of dots they counted. Half of the subjects were asked to put their names on all forms and were told that the experimenter would wait outside for them to finish. The other half worked anonymously and were told that the experimenter had a scheduling conflict and thus would not be able to monitor their work. They were told to let themselves out when they had finished.

As predicted by the hypothesis that women's sense of personal entitlement with respect to pay is lower than men's, women worked significantly longer, did more work, completed more correct work, and worked more efficiently than men. Furthermore, these sex differences occurred in both monitored and unmonitored conditions. Some support, however, also was obtained for the hypothesis that women's judgments of entitlement are more susceptible to interpersonal or impression management concerns, in that women worked longer when their behavior was monitored than when it was unmonitored (67.46 min. versus 50.05 min.) whereas men did not (44.18 min. versus 40.88 min.).

Exploration of other possible determinants of these gender differences revealed that, as in the first experiment, women and men did not differ in their ratings of how important the pay was to them or in their ratings of task enjoyment. Furthermore, despite the fact that women's performance was objectively superior to men's, women and men did not differ in their performance evaluations, attributions, or satisfaction. In addition, although women's past pay history again was somewhat lower than men's, it was unrelated to any of the work input variables. Once again, however, the role of referential comparisons in judgments of deservingness was implicated. Women thought most people (sex unspecified) would work longer on the task (M = 53.58 min.) than men thought (M = 39.53; $p < .01$), regardless of the public or private nature of the situation. These estimates of how long others would work were, in turn, highly correlated with how long the women and men themselves worked. Furthermore, both men and women thought females would work far longer (M = 51.00 min.) than males (M = 39.33 min., $p < .01$).

Gender Differences in Pay Expectations

Our third study tested the hypothesis that women have lower pay expectations than men. Although several authors had speculated that gender differences in pay expectations might explain women's tendency to be as satisfied as men despite lower pay (Major & Deaux, 1982; Sauser & York, 1978) or to place a lower value on pay (Kanter, 1977; Nieva & Gutek, 1981), no research had demonstrated this difference among similarly qualified men and women. To test this hypothesis, Ellen Konar and I surveyed the career-entry and career-peak pay expectations of 50 male and female management students enrolled in a work internship program (Major & Konar, 1984). We also explored whether these women and men differed on a number of other factors that might relate to gender differences in pay expectations.

As predicted, men and women differed in their career-entry and career-peak salary expectations. Male management students expected to earn approximately $2,600 more than female management students expected to earn at career-entry ($p < .05$), and almost $20,000 more at career-peak ($p < .01$). Men and women did not differ in their qualifications or job performance, either as self-perceived or as rated by their internship supervisors. They did, however, differ in three other areas: career-path, job values, and social comparisons. Specifically, relative to men, women were more likely to be enrolled in the BA rather than the MBA program, were more likely to be specializing in personnel (a somewhat lower paying specialty), placed a lower value on a high salary and a higher value on interesting work, and thought that others in their field (sex unspecified) earned less at both career-entry and career-peak.

Analyses examining the extent to which these factors could explain the gender difference in pay expectations revealed that although each of these factors explained a significant portion of the discrepancy, the factor that explained the most was comparison standards. That is, differences in women's and men's estimates of what others earned accounted for more of the gender difference in career-entry and career-peak pay expectations than any other single factor. Furthermore, comparison standards were a significant predictor of gender differences in pay expectations even after all other factors (e.g., career-paths) were controlled for. In a follow-up survey of 168 management students, we replicated not only the significant gender differences in pay expectations but also the finding that social comparisons were by far the strongest predictor of pay expectations (McFarlin, Major, Frone, & Konar, 1984). In addition, we found that women's and men's perceptions of what same-sex others earn were more strongly related to their own pay expectations than were their perceptions of what cross-sex others earn (p < .01).

Gender, Entitlement, and Social Comparison Processes

The above studies not only suggest that women and men differ in their sense of personal entitlement with respect to pay and in their pay expectations, but also repeatedly implicate the role of social comparison processes in producing these differences. Thus our next set of studies examined the hypothesis that similarity biases in social comparison processes may produce observed gender patterns in outcome evaluations and distributions. We proposed that (1) similarity biases (e.g., preferences for same-sex and same-job comparisons) occur in the acquisition of information about the outcomes of others; that (2) this leads to gender differences in wage standards (comparative referents) acquired when women are paid less than men and/or people in female-dominated occupations are paid less than people in male-dominated occupations; and (3) these different standards affect women's and men's judgments of what to expect, what they deserve, and their assessments of whether their wage is fair or satisfactory.

Our first experiment (Major & Forcey, 1985) examined the first of these hypotheses. Several field studies have found that working men and women are more likely to name same-sex than cross-sex others and same-job than different-job others when asked with whom they compare their wages or jobs (Crosby, 1982; Goodman, 1974; Oldham et al., 1982; Patchen, 1961). Because most people work in jobs dominated by their own sex, however, same-job and same-sex comparisons are confounded in field settings. Thus our first experiment examined whether same-sex and/or same-job comparisons are preferred in a controlled setting where the outcomes of other males and females in one's own job as well as comparable jobs are equally available for comparison.

Male and female undergraduates were randomly assigned to work on a job described as masculine, feminine, or sex-neutral. The identical sex-neutral prediction task was used in each condition. Subjects were informed in advance that they would be paid according to their performance and job assignment. After working on the job, all were given privately an ambiguous performance score and paid an identical wage. They were then given the opportunity to rank order their preferences for seeing the average wage paid to nine different groups of individuals—the average male, average female, and average combined-sex wage for each of the three jobs. (They did not actually see this information.) They also indicated how fair they thought the wage they received was and how satisfied they were with it.

Despite the availability of the combined-sex wage, most men and women preferred to maximize similarity in their wage comparisons, with the majority (63%) choosing to see the pay of a same-sex and same-job group first. Same-job others were chosen first regardless of the sex-linkage of one's assigned job. Sex-linkage of job did, however, affect same-sex preferences. Subjects in the "sex-appropriate" job (men assigned to the masculine job and women assigned to the feminine job) showed a significant preference for acquiring the pay of same-sex others first (80%), as did those in the sex-neutral job (67%). Those assigned to the sex-inappropriate jobs, in contrast, displayed a more even preference for same-sex (47%), average-sex (32%), and cross-sex (21%) first comparisons. The finding that same-sex others were preferred for comparisons in the sex-neutral job (where sex was presumably irrelevant to pay) suggests that social comparisons are made not only with others who are similar on criterion-relevant (e.g., job) attributes, but also with others who are similar on self-relevant (e.g., sex) attributes. These findings parallel those of recent research on the social comparison of abilities (e.g., Miller, 1984).

Consistent with our prior research (Major, McFarlin, & Gagnon, 1984), women felt they deserved less pay for their work (M = $1.93) than did men (M = $2.31), regardless of job assignment (p < .05). In addition, however, women thought that they had performed worse than did men (p < .05), and these performance evaluations were positively correlated with deservingness for both sexes. Furthermore, despite the fact that the three jobs had been described and were perceived by the subjects as comparable in difficulty (and were in fact identical), individuals assigned to the "feminine" job expected to earn less pay prior to doing the job and thought that the pay they subsequently received was more fair than did individuals assigned to the "masculine" job. Pay expectations and fairness ratings of those assigned to the sex-neutral job fell in between.

A second study (Major & Testa, 1985, Experiment 1) was designed to test the second and third hypotheses presented above, namely, that (a) similarity biases in social comparisons can lead to the acquisition of different wage standards when some groups (e.g., women) are paid less than other groups (e.g., men), and (b) these standards then produce differences in judgments of entitlement and satisfaction. Women and men were asked to work on one of two sex-neutral tasks (which were in fact identical) and were then privately paid an identical wage ($2.50). They were then given the opportunity to acquire information about the pay received by one other student who had presumably participated in the experiment earlier. They could select this student from a list of eight—two males and two females for each of the two jobs. Unbeknownst to the subjects, in one job the pay to males was higher ($3.75) than that to females ($1.25); whereas in the other job this was reversed. We then gave the subject the wage information corresponding to whatever comparison other he or she had selected.

Results generally confirmed our hypotheses. As expected, we found strong similarity biases in outcome comparisons: 92% of subjects selected a same-sex/same-job comparison other. Second, as a result of this biased search, those assigned to a job in which their own sex was more highly paid perceived a higher referent outcome than did those assigned to a job in which their own sex was lower paid. That is, the former believed that a higher wage standard existed for everyone (e.g., in general, in their own job, in the other job, for men, and for women). Third, those in the former group, regardless of sex, also felt personally entitled to a higher wage and were less satisfied with the wage they were paid than were those in the latter group. Thus in the presence of similar salient external comparisons, women and men did not differ overall in their outcome entitlement or satisfaction. Women's judgments, however, were more strongly affected by the external comparisons than were men's. Women and men did not differ in their evaluations of their own performance.

In summary, this series of studies suggests that in the absence of explicit comparison standards, men and women differ in what they feel personally entitled to receive in terms of pay for work. These studies also suggest that differences in referent outcomes, that is, the outcomes women and men feasibly imagine receiving, may underlie observed gender patterns in evaluations and distributions of pay. The sources of these different referent outcomes include (a) expectations based on the perceived sex-linkage of the task or job one is performing, (b) expectations based on past pay history, and (c) expectations derived from similarity biases in the acquisition of social comparison information. In addition, evidence indicated that under some circumstances women evaluate their own performance less positively than men, and consequently feel deserving of less reward (Major & Forcey, 1985). This factor seems not to be the primary determinant of gender differences in entitlement, however, because the majority of studies have found no link between women's and men's self-evaluations of performance and their patterns of allocations to self and others (e.g., Major & Adams, 1983; Reis & Jackson, 1981), allocations to self only (e.g., Major, McFarlin, & Gagnon, 1984, Experiment 1), or pay expectations (Major & Konar, 1984).

CONCLUSIONS

This chapter began by asking whether men and women differ in their sense of their own entitlement or in what they feel they deserve from their jobs or relationships, and if so, why. Research reviewed indicates that although women and men generally allocate rewards similarly to others, women take less for themselves than do men (Callahan-Levy & Messé, 1979). Although women are aware that other women obtain less than they deserve from their jobs, they fail to acknowledge that this applies to themselves as well (Crosby, 1982). In attempting to explain these paradoxes, it is helpful to reconsider the antecedents and consequences of a sense of injustice outlined at the beginning of this chapter. It was proposed that individuals feel deprived to the extent that they lack some outcome (or enough of that outcome) and they (a) desire or value that outcome, (b) have high referent outcomes, that is, can easily imagine receiving better outcomes under alternative circumstances, and (c) perceive the justification for existing outcomes (relative to the justification for referent outcomes) as low. These three antecedents correspond to three different possible explanations for gender differences in reward allocations and evaluations: outcome values, referent outcomes, and justifications.

Outcome Values

As I have noted above, the typical explanation for gender differences in justice-related judgments is that men and women differ in the outcomes they value. According to this view, women's greater concern for interpersonal relationships and lesser interest in outcomes such as money leads them (a) to prefer more equal reward distributions among themselves and others, and (b) to be similarly satisfied with their jobs and pay despite their underpayment relative to comparable men.

This approach reflects the dominant view of psychologists with respect to gender, which is that due either to socialization or biological predisposition, adult women and men develop differing personality characteristics and values. Although research suggests that gender differences in values do indeed exist (Eagly, in press), their role as a mediator of gender differences in reward allocations and evaluations has yet to be established. Furthermore, this view tends to ignore or minimize the impact of structural factors, such as the unequal status and rewards received by men and women in society, and the unequal distribution of men and women into communal (e.g., domestic) and agentic (e.g., work) roles, on women's and men's aspirations, values, and social behaviors. Finally, this approach suggests a greater cross-situational consistency in gender-linked social behaviors than typically is observed (Deaux, 1984).

This argument also suggests that different patterns should be observed when the focus is on outcomes that are presumably of more value to women than men. Surprisingly, research addressing this issue is almost nonexistent. We might, for example, ask whether women have a lower sense of entitlement than men for nonmonetary outcomes or in nonexchange relationships, such as intimate relationships. There is some suggestion that they might (Steil, 1983). Studies of family power and task allocations have consistently revealed that wives have less say in important decisions and spend more time on household chores and child care than their husbands even in marriages where both spouses work full-time (Spence, Deaux, & Helmreich, 1985). Nevertheless, studies of marital satisfaction rarely show evidence of greater dissatisfaction among wives than husbands (Crosby, 1982; Kidder, Fagan, & Cohn, 1981). Such patterns suggest that women may be "paradoxically contented" in their marriages as well as in their jobs.

Referent Outcomes

In contrast to the outcome-value approach, I have suggested that gender patterns in reward allocations and evaluations may better be explained by focusing on the second antecedent to a sense of deprivation—women's and men's referent outcomes. Specifically, research reviewed here suggests that as a consequence of differences in the degree to which women and men are valued and monetarily rewarded in society, the referent outcomes generated by women when evaluating their existing outcomes or estimating what they deserve are lower than men's. According to this perspective, the female worker appears "contented" not because she values money less than men (or values good relationships more), but because she feels she is paid what she deserves (a) relative to what she expects based on her past pay; (b) relative to what she expects based on what people doing "women's jobs" are typically paid; and (c) relative to the people with whom she compares (primarily other underpaid women). Other factors may also suppress women's referent outcomes. For example, due to restricted employment opportunities or greater home responsibilities, women may imagine fewer and more limited alternatives as realistically attainable.

Of all of these referent outcomes, those based on social comparisons are perhaps most important. Evidence indicates that when social comparisons are salient, people base their satisfaction and judgments of deservingness more on these referents than on internally generated referent outcomes (e.g., expectancies based on prior wages). (See Austin et al., 1980.) We found that gender differences in judgments of entitlement disappeared when women and men were exposed to the same social comparisons, regardless of the sex of these comparison others. In addition, although we found no evidence that individuals preferentially used same-sex comparison information when cross-sex comparison information was also presented (Major, McFarlin, & Gagnon, 1984, Experiment 1), we did find that individuals preferred to acquire information about the outcomes of same-sex others.

A major problem for theories of social justice (and comparison theories more generally) is specifying in advance *who* will be chosen for comparison purposes. Many comparisons are possible, and social comparisons are often motivated by self-protective as well as outcome-evaluative purposes. Social comparisons also serve a normative function to the extent that they are used to set and enforce standards of how the comparer "ought" to behave. A tendency to rely on same-sex comparisons may provide a critical link between the self-system and the larger social context in which behavior occurs.

Justifications

A third antecedent to feelings of deprivation is the perceived justifiability of the procedures that produced existing outcomes (relative to the justification for referent outcomes). Individuals should feel more distressed about their (relatively) low outcomes to the extent that they believe these outcomes occurred through unfair procedures. This suggests a third explanation for women's lower sense of personal entitlement and failure to recognize personal deprivation: They may perceive that the procedures that produced their (lower) outcomes are justifiable. Such perceptions may be motivated by efforts to maintain a belief that the world is just (Lerner, 1975), to maintain a sense of personal control over outcomes (Wortman, 1976), or to protect self-esteem. Indeed, there is evidence that people who are treated unjustly but who cannot change their situation may come to believe that they are entitled to less, or that they deserved their fate, rather than believe that they are victims of injustice (Crosby, 1982; Kanter, 1977; Wortman, 1976). In short, this explanation suggests that women may not want to acknowledge the extent to which they are unjustly treated by society.

This analysis may account for the paradoxical findings that although women underpay themselves, they do not believe that other women deserve less (Callahan-Levy & Messé, 1979), and that although women fail to recognize the unjust nature of their own work situations, they recognize injustice in the work situations of other women (Crosby, 1982). Motivational factors, such as a desire for control, the need to believe in a just world, or the motive to protect self-esteem, may be most aroused and hence most likely to affect perceptions when one's own outcomes are at stake. Indeed, Wortman (1976) suggests that it is easier for individuals to see the influence of situational factors (such as unjust procedures) in producing others' misfortunes than in producing one's own.

Alternative Responses to Unjust Situations

The above argument highlights the fact that there are a variety of responses individuals might make to injustices. Theories of social justice stress that being unfairly treated is a negative emotional state that individuals are motivated to resolve. Further, they note that a variety of responses may be used to eliminate this distress. Nevertheless, research has considered only a restricted set of responses. Mark and Folger (1984) have proposed that responses to injustice may be categorized as being directed toward the system, the self, or the outcome of which one is deprived. Most research has considered system-directed responses. For example, the deprived person may try to change the system (e.g., lobby or strike for better treatment) or change his or her attitude toward the system (e.g., feel resentful and angry). If it is impossible for people to change an unfair system or improve their situations, however, they may try to resolve the injustice through psychological means. For example, they may devalue the outcome of which they are deprived (e.g., money isn't all that important to me) or enhance the value of outcomes that are attainable (e.g., my work is very meaningful). Alternatively, they may devalue themselves or their contributions (e.g., my work isn't as good; my job is easier) or enhance the value of those who obtain higher outcomes (e.g., his work is better; his job is more demanding). They may also revise their comparative referents (e.g., I'm really more similar to Sally than George; I guess my expectations were out of line). (See, e.g., Wood, Taylor, & Lichtman, 1985.) Repeated exposure to outcomes that are unjust or beyond one's personal control, however, may exacerbate tendencies toward self-blame and lead to feelings of helplessness and depression (Abramson, Seligman, & Teasdale, 1978). Further research is clearly needed on the extent to which women and men differ in their tendencies to make system-, object-, or self-directed responses to injustices and victimization.

In summary, several alternatives to the traditional value-difference explanation for gender differences in reward allocations and evaluations have been proposed in this chapter. None of these by itself is sufficient to explain these patterns. Despite the wish for parsimony, complex social behaviors such as these are most likely multiply determined. Furthermore, none of these explanations has as yet been clearly demonstrated to mediate observed gender patterns in reward allocations or job evaluations.

What might we conclude from the analyses presented in this chapter? Some might argue that there is no reason to change the status quo because raising women's sense of their own entitlement without also making major social changes in the ways in which female attributes, performances, and jobs are valued and rewarded will only foster women's frustration and discontent. In response, I suggest that only by recognizing the injustice of their own situations will women succeed in getting what they deserve. The preceding discussion suggests that at least two changes are needed to raise women's sense of their own entitlement: (1) elevate referent outcomes, and (2) increase recognition of the influence of unjustifiable procedures on current reward structures.

Because social comparisons tend to have priority over prior expectancies in determining referent outcomes, changing the nature of women's social comparisons seems a prime candidate for remedial action. Such change might be accomplished by publishing pay norms for both sexes in same and comparable jobs, doing away with pay secrecy rules, or in other ways increasing the salience of men's pay or the pay of comparable male-dominated jobs. Clearly such changes will produce discontent. A recent study indicates that the few women who compare their job outcomes exclusively or predominantly with men's are least satisfied with their jobs (Zanna, Crosby, & Loewenstein, 1984). Discontent may motivate constructive attempts to change the system, such as the push for equal pay for equal work and the more recent push for pay equity. Elevating expectations may also circumvent a self-limiting cycle in which those who expect fewer outcomes ask for less and in turn are paid less than those who expect and ask for more (Major, Vanderslice, & McFarlin, 1984).

Changing perceptions of the fairness of the procedures by which rewards are allocated is a more difficult challenge. For women to recognize the degree to which they are victimized and undervalued by society and its agents entails psychic costs. So too, however, does blaming oneself rather than the system for failing to obtain desired rewards. Relative to men, women are more likely to suffer from lack of self-confidence, blame themselves for their failures, and are far more likely to suffer from depression (Radloff, 1975). In short, "contentment" may be an illusion purchased at too high a price.

REFERENCES

Abramson, L. H., Seligman, M.E.P., & Teasdale, J. D. (1978). Learned helplessness in humans: Critique and reformulation. *Journal of Abnormal Psychology, 87*, 49-74.

Adams, J. S. (1965). Inequity in social exchange. In L. Berkowitz (Ed.), *Advances in experimental social psychology* (Vol. 2, pp. 267-299). New York: Academic Press.

Austin, W., McGinn, N. C., & Susmilch, C. (1980). Internal standards revisited: Effects of social comparisons and expectancies on judgments of fairness and satisfaction. *Journal of Experimental Social Psychology, 16*, 426-441.

Bakan, D. (1966). *The quality of human existence*. Chicago: Rand McNally.

Callahan-Levy, C. M., & Messe, L. A. (1979). Sex differences in the allocation of pay. *Journal of Personality and Social Psychology, 37*, 443-446.

Crosby, F. (1976). A model of egotistical relative deprivation. *Psychological Review, 83*, 85-113.

Crosby, F. (1982). *Relative deprivation and working women*. New York: Oxford University Press.

Crowley, J., Levitin, T. E., & Quinn, R. P. (1973). Seven deadly half-truths about women. In C. Tavris (Ed.), *The female experience*. Del Mar, CA: CRM.

Deaux, K. (1976). *The behavior of women and men*. Monterey, CA: Brooks/Cole.

Deaux, K. (1984). From individual differences to social categories: Analysis of a decade's research on gender. *American Psychologist, 39*, 105-116.

Deutsch, M. (1975). Equity, equality, and need: What determines which value will be used as the basis of distributive justice? *Journal of Social Issues, 31*, 137-149.

Eagly, A. H. (in press). *Sex differences in social behavior: A social-role interpretation*. Hillsdale, NJ: Lawrence Erlbaum.

Folger, R. (1984, July). *Rethinking equity theory: A referent cognitions model*. Paper presented at the NSF Cross-National Conference on Justice in Intergroup Relations, Morburg, West Germany.

Golding, J., Resnick, A., & Crosby, F. (1983). Work satisfaction as a function of gender and job status. *Psychology of Women Quarterly, 1*, 286-290.

Goodman, P. S. (1974). An examination of referents used in the evaluation of pay. *Organizational Behavior and Human Performance, 12*, 170-195.

Hansen, R. D., & O'Leary, V. E. (1985). Sex-determined attributions. In V. E. O'Leary, R. K. Unger, & B. S. Wallston (Eds.), *Women, gender, and social psychology* (pp. 67-100). Hillsdale, NJ: Lawrence Erlbaum.

Kahn, A. S., & Gaeddert, W. P. (1985). From theories of equity to theories of justice: The liberating consequences of studying women. In V. E. O'Leary, R. K. Unger, & B. S. Wallston (Eds.), *Women, gender, and social psychology* (pp. 129-148). Hillsdale, NJ: Lawrence Erlbaum.

Kahn, A., O'Leary, V., Krulewitz, J. E., & Lamm, H. (1980). Equity and equality: Male and female means to a just end. *Basic and Applied Social Psychology, 1*, 173-197.

Kanter, R. M. (1977). *Men and women of the corporation*. New York: Basic Books.

Kidder, L. H., Bellettirie, G., & Cohn, E. S. (1977). Secret ambitions and public performances. *Journal of Experimental Social Psychology, 13*, 70-80.

Kidder, L. H., Fagan, M. A., & Cohn, E. S. (1981). Giving and receiving. In M. J. Lerner & C. S. Lerner (Eds.), *The justice motive in social behavior: Adapting to times of scarcity and change* (pp. 255-259). New York: Plenum.

Lane, I. M., & Messe, L. A. (1971). Equity and the distribution of rewards. *Journal of Experimental Social Psychology, 20*, 1-17.

Lawler, E. E. (1971). *Pay and organizational effectiveness: A psychological view*. New York: McGraw-Hill.

Lenny, E. (1977). Women's self-confidence in achievement settings. *Psychological Bulletin, 84*, 1-13.

Lerner, M. J. (1975). The justice motive in social behavior: An introduction. *Journal of Social Issues, 31*, 1-19.

Leventhal, G. S. (1976). The distribution of rewards and resources in groups and organizations. In L. Berkowitz & E. Walster (Eds.), *Advances in experimental social psychology* (Vol. 9, pp. 92-133). New York: Academic Press.

Major, B., & Adams, J. B. (1983). The role of gender, interpersonal orientation, and self-presentation in distributive justice behavior. *Journal of Personality and Social Psychology, 45*, 598-608.

Major, B., & Adams, J. B. (1984). Situational moderators of gender differences in reward allocations. *Sex roles, 11*, 869-880.

Major, B., & Deaux, K. (1982). Individual differences in justice behavior. In J. Greenberg & R. L. Cohen (Eds.), *Equity and justice in social behavior* (pp. 43-76). New York: Academic Press.

Major, B., & Forcey, B. (1985). Social comparisons and pay evaluations: Preferences for same-sex and same-job wage comparisons. *Journal of Experimental Social Psychology, 21*, 393-405.

Major, B., & Konar, E. (1984). An investigation of sex differences in pay expectations and their possible causes. *Academy of Management Journal, 27*, 777-792.

Major, B., McFarlin, D., & Gagnon, D. (1984). Overworked and underpaid: On the nature of gender differences in personal entitlement. *Journal of Personality and Social Psychology, 47*, 1399-1412.

Major, B., & Testa, M. (1985). *The role of social comparison processes in judgments of entitlement and satisfaction.* Manuscript under review, State University of New York at Buffalo, Psychology Department, Buffalo, N.Y.

Major, B., Vanderslice, V., & McFarlin, D. B. (1984). Effects of pay expected on pay received: The confirmatory nature of initial expectations. *Journal of Applied Psychology, 14*, 399-412.

Mark, M. A., & Folger, F. (1984). Responses to relative deprivation: A conceptual framework. In P. Shaver (Ed.), *Review of personality and social psychology* (Vol. 5, pp. 192-218). Beverly Hills, CA: Sage.

Martin, J., & Murray, A. (1983). Distributive injustice and unfair exchange. In D. M. Messick & K. S. Cook (Eds.), *Equity theory: Psychological and sociological perspectives* (pp. 169-205). New York: Praeger.

McFarlin, D. B., Major, B., Frone, M., & Konar, E. (1984, August). *Predicting management students' pay expectations: The importance of social comparisons.* Paper presented at the meeting of the American Psychological Association, Toronto, Canada.

Miller, C. T. (1984). Self-schemas, gender, and social comparison: A clarification of the related attributes hypothesis. *Journal of Personality and Social Psychology, 46*, 1222-1229.

Nieva, V. F., & Gutek, B. A. (1981). *Women and work: A psychological perspective.* New York: Praeger.

Oldham, G. R., Nottenburg, G., Kassner, M. W., Ferris, G., Fedor, D., & Masters, M. (1982). The selection and consequences of job comparisons. *Organizational Behavior and Human Performance, 29*, 84-111.

O'Neill, J. (1985). Role differentiation and the gender gap in wage rates. In L. Larwood, A. H. Stromberg, & B. A. Gutek (Eds.), *Women and work: An annual review* (Vol. 1, pp. 50-75). Beverly Hills, CA: Sage.

Patchen, M. (1961). *The choice of wage comparisons.* Englewood Cliffs, NJ: Prentice-Hall.

Quinn, R. L., & Shepard, L. (1974). *The 1972-73 quality of employment survey.* Ann Arbor, MI: Survey Research Center.

Radloff, L. (1975). Sex differences in depression: The effects of occupation and marital status. *Sex Roles, 1*, 249-265.

Reis, H. T., & Jackson, L. A. (1981). Sex differences in reward allocation: Subjects, partners, and tasks. *Journal of Personality and Social Psychology, 3*, 465-478.

Ross, L., Greene, D., & House, P. (1977). The false consensus phenomenon: An attributional bias in self-perception and social perception processes. *Journal of Personality and Social Psychology, 13*, 279-301.

Sampson, E. E. (1975). Justice as equality. *Journal of Social Issues, 31*, 45-61.

Sauser, W. I., & York, M. (1978). Sex differences in job satisfaction: A reexamination. Personnel Psychology, 31, 537-547.

Spence, J. T., Deaux, K., & Helmreich, R. L. (1985). Sex roles in contemporary American society. In G. Lindzey & E. Aronson (Eds.), *Handbook of social psychology* (3rd ed., Vol. 2), (pp. 149-178). New York: Random House.

Steil, J. M. (1983). Marriage: An unequal partnership. In B. B. Wolman & G. Stricker (Eds.), *Handbook of family and marital therapy* (pp. 49-60). New York: Plenum.

Swap, W., & Rubin, J. Z. (1983). Measurement of interpersonal orientation. *Journal of Personality and Social Psychology, 44*, 208-219.

Treiman, D. J., & Hartmann, H. I. (1981). *Women, work and wages: Equal pay for jobs of equal value.* Washington, DC: National Academy Press.

Walster, E., Walster, G. W., & Berscheid, E. (1978). *Equity: Theory and research.* Boston: Allyn & Bacon.

Watts, B. L., Vallacher, R. R., & Messé, L. A. (1982). Toward understanding sex differences in pay allocations: Agency, communion, and reward distribution behavior. *Sex Roles, 12*, 1175-1188.

Wood, J. V., Taylor, S. E., & Lichtman, R. R. (1985). Social comparison and adjustment to breast cancer. *Journal of Personality and Social Psychology, 49*, 1169-1183.

Wortman, C. B. (1976). Causal attributions and personal control. In J. H. Harvey, W. J. Ickes, & R. F. Kidd (Eds.), *New directions in attribution research* (Vol. 1, pp. 23-52). Hillsdale, NJ: Lawrence Erlbaum.

Zanna, M. P., Crosby, F., & Loewenstein, G. (1984). *Male reference groups and job satisfaction among female professionals.* Paper presented at the meeting of the American Psychological Association, Toronto, Canada.

6

Gender and Communication

ELIZABETH ARIES

Elizabeth Aries is Associate Professor of Psychology at Amherst College. She received her Ph.D. from Harvard University in social psychology. She has published articles on interaction patterns and thematic content in single-sex and mixed-sex conversations.

There are many widely held beliefs about gender differences in communication.[1] Male speech is perceived to be loud, dominating, forceful, aggressive, authoritarian, blunt, and straight to the point. Female speech is perceived to be gentle, friendly, emotional, polite, enthusiastic, open, self-revealing, and showing concern for the listener, but also to be "gibberish," "gossip," and "talk about trivial topics" (Kramer, 1977). Male speech is held to be argumentative, insistent on reason and logic, whereas female speech attempts to "raise the status of the other, relieve tension, agree, concur, comply, understand, accept" (Bernard, 1972, p. 137). Jespersen (1922), who provided one of the first treatments of the topic, claimed that women use more refined, euphemistic, and hyperbolic expressions, men more slang and innovative language; Jespersen even declared that "women much more often than men break off without finishing their sentences, because they start talking without having thought out what they are going to say" (p. 250).

Despite such widely held stereotypes about gender differences in communication, until the early 1970s evidence for actual gender differences tended to be based on anecdotal observation, speculation, and untested hypotheses (Thorne & Henley, 1975). Since that time there has been a burgeoning of serious scholarship on gender and communication by scholars from diverse disciplines—linguistics, speech communication, anthropology, sociology, and psychology. Some reviewers of the literature on actual gender differences in interaction, however, have still concluded that this literature primarily contains myths about language, and only limited corroborating evidence (e.g., Frank, 1978; Haas, 1979; Philips, 1980).

149

In order to determine whether research evidence supports any clearly identifiable gender differences in communication, this chapter will provide a review of the literature on verbal communication processes and topics of discourse, and will include a brief discussion of nonverbal behavior as well. Given the current magnitude of the field, the chapter will provide a broad overview rather than a comprehensive review, highlighting seminal studies and issues in the field. Gender differences will be considered in the context of situational factors that influence communication; for example, the impact of interacting in intimate or nonintimate contexts, and in single-sex or mixed-sex groups. The differential perception and evaluation of males and females as speakers, and of communication behaviors associated with each sex, will then be discussed. Finally, the major hypotheses that have been put forth to explain gender differences in communication will be assessed.

Although sex roles are undergoing profound change, in the area of communication gender differences have remained fairly constant over time. Interaction patterns and nonverbal behaviors that are out of conscious awareness are slower to change than behaviors that are more directly affected by conscious intentions and attitudes (Aries, 1982). What have changed over time, however, are the researchers' perspectives and the perceived implications of their research findings, and these changes will be considered here.

This chapter is restricted in the following ways. First, it will be concerned primarily with the interactions of adults rather than children. Second, it will focus on actual speech, rather than on sexism in the language itself. Third, it will omit a discussion of paralanguage—such things as pitch, loudness, intonation, pronunciation, laughing, crying, and hesitations in speech. (See Thorne, Kramarae, & Henley, 1983, for an excellent annotated bibliography of gender differences in these areas.)

PATTERNING OF VERBAL INTERACTION

Early interest in gender differences in communication was shown by a few researchers of small group behavior. Parsons and Bales (1955) suggested that role differentiation occurs within the nuclear family, with the father being concerned with adaptive-instrumental activity and the mother with integrative-expressive activity. Strodtbeck and Mann (1956) demonstrated that the same role differentiation occurs in mixed-sex task groups. Using Bales's (1950) twelve-category scoring system,

"Interaction Process Analysis," to classify interaction during jury deliberations, men were found to exceed women in the task area, giving suggestions, opinions, and information, whereas women exceeded men in the social-emotional area, showing solidarity, tension release, and agreement. Strodtbeck and Mann concluded that "men *proact*, that is, they initiate relatively long bursts of acts directed at the solution of the task problem, and women tend more to *react* to the contributions of others" (p. 635). Both task and socioemotional behaviors exist in the repertoires of men and women, but they are used with different frequencies by the two sexes. Numerous studies using Bales's original scoring system, or some modification of it, have also found that men devote a greater proportion of their interaction to task behavior, and women to social-emotional behavior (Aries, 1982; Heiss, 1962; Kenkel, 1963; Leik, 1963; Lockheed & Hall, 1976; Nemeth, Endicott, & Wachtler, 1976; Piliavin & Martin, 1978).

Strodtbeck and Mann (1956) suggested that the differential socialization of boys and girls creates a latent personality basis for role selection in interactions. Both Meeker and Weitzel-O'Neill (1977) and Lockheed and Hall (1976) provide evidence that these findings are best explained in terms of status rather than role differentiation. The theory of status characteristics and expectation states (Berger, Cohen, & Zelditch, 1972) holds that in task-oriented groups requiring instrumental competence, if members differ on one diffuse status characteristic, they will assume that individuals with the highly valued state of the characteristic will have greater performance ability. These high status persons will be given more opportunities to participate, and will be more likely to initiate performance. If sex functions as a diffuse status characteristic, with the male state more highly valued than the female, then men will be more likely to hold positions of power and prestige in mixed-sex groups.

Status differences, however, do not fully account for gender differences in interaction. Gender differences emerge even when women are made more competent at a task than men. Leet-Pellegrini (1980) analyzed the discussions of male, female, and mixed-sex pairs. In equally informed pairs, partners discussed the topic as nonexperts, whereas in unequally informed pairs, one person was given topically relevant information before the conversation began. Men with expertise talked proportionately longer than women with expertise, and were perceived by judges as more dominant and more controlling of the conversation. Individuals without expertise used more assent terms ("yeh," "right," "uh-huh") than individuals with expertise in all situations except when a female expert was with a male nonexpert. Women with expertise assisted partners more than men with expertise, repeating words or completing thoughts. Competent women, therefore, appear to compensate for their power with social-emotional behaviors and avoidance of dominant responses.

There has been considerable interest in the relative expression of dominance by men and women in mixed-sex settings. One of the most widely used indicators of dominance is the amount of interaction initiated by individuals. To take up time speaking is an exercise of power (Bales, 1970). Those who talk the most in decision-making groups also tend to be the most influential persons (Kenkel, 1963; Strodtbeck, 1951). When analyses are done of the amount of interaction initiated by men and women in mixed-sex conversation, men have fairly consistently been found to initiate more interaction than women (e.g., Aries, 1976; Lockheed & Hall, 1976; Strodtbeck & Mann, 1956; Willis & Williams, 1976).

Another behavior often used as an indicator of dominance is interruption. Interruptions can be seen as a mechanism of topic control—a signal of nonsupport for continued development of a topic (Zimmerman & West, 1975). Men have frequently been found to interrupt women more than women interrupt men. Zimmerman and West (1975), for example, recorded 31 conversational segments in public places and private residences. In same-sex conversations interruptions were equally divided between the two speakers, whereas in cross-sex conversations 96% of all of the interruptions were by men. Zimmerman and West collapsed the results for same-sex conversations, making it impossible to determine whether male-male dyads did more interrupting than female-female dyads, but Bohn and Stutman (1983) reported that male dyads engaged in more interruptions than female dyads. Both West and Zimmerman (1977) and Greif (1980) have reported a similar pattern of interruptions between parents and children. Women, like children, have restricted rights to speak and may be ignored or interrupted. Greater use of interruptions by men in mixed-sex groups has also been reported by Bohn and Stutman (1983), Esposito (1979), LaFrance and Carmen (1980), McMillan, Clifton, McGrath, and Gale (1977), Natale, Entin, and Jaffe (1979), and West and Zimmerman (1983).

The proper interpretation of interruptions is open to question, however. Interruptions may be related to involvement and spontaneity rather than to dominance (Vrugt & Kerkstra, 1984). Shaw and Sadler (1965) found that women use more interruptions than men in hetero-sexual dyads, but suggested that these interruptions might have been comments showing agreement and support. LaFrance and Carmen (1980) classified interruptive questions and interruptive statements separately, and found the two to be uncorrelated. Women used significantly more interruptive questions than men, indicative of greater responsiveness rather than greater assertiveness.

The studies of interruptions raise two general problems in the study of gender differences that will become increasingly evident as the discussion proceeds. First, there has too often been a tendency to interpret a behavior in a particular way without direct evidence to validate that inference. (Interruptions, for example, are equated with dominance.) Second, operational definitions of specific behaviors vary across studies, resulting in inconsistent research findings and calling into question the assumption that the different measures can be interpreted similarly.

Two additional measures have been used by some researchers as indicative of dominance: length of speaking turns and overlaps in speaking between participants. Results are inconsistent. Duncan and Fiske (1977), Frances (1979), and Rosenfeld (1966) found that men used longer utterances than women, whereas Markel, Long, and Saine (1976) found that women use longer utterances than men. Zimmerman and West (1975) found that men initiated more overlaps than women; Esposito (1979) found no gender difference in overlaps.

It is difficult to account for the inconsistent findings from these studies and others to be cited because the studies vary in sample size, interaction context, relationship between participants, task of the participants, length of the interaction, sex and number of the partici-pants, and the operational definition of the dependent variables. Often, studies have failed to control for the quantity of speech produced by each sex. These variables can serve either to maximize or minimize the extent to which gender differences are found.

Other gender differences have been documented in single-sex and mixed-sex groups or dyads consistent with the proactive, dominant position of men and social-emotional, responsive orientation of women. Goodwin (1980) recorded black working-class children ages 8-13, a group of boys making slingshots, and a group of girls making rings from bottle rims. She found that boys created a more hierarchical organi-zation. The male leader issued direct commands, contradicted proposals and requests of others, and usurped others' turn space by responding to requests directed to those others. By contrast, girls participated jointly in decision making. Girls' directives were suggestions rather than commands. Girls, unlike boys, used "let's," the model forms "can" or "could," or more tentative language such as "maybe." Where girls used imperative forms, they said "we gotta." Girls' disagreements, unlike boys', did not attempt to affirm the relative superiority of one party over another.

Similar themes were reflected in groups of college-age students and adults. Aries (1976) found that all-male groups established a stable dominance hierarchy, whereas all-female groups maintained a more flexible rank order of speaking over time. Active female speakers expressed discomfort with their leadership positions and in some sessions drew out more silent members and assumed lower ranks. Aries also found that men addressed a greater proportion of their interaction than women to the group as a whole, which has been viewed as an exercise of power or influence in a group (Bales, 1970). Women addressed almost all of their interaction to individuals.

Systematic studies of consciousness-raising groups are few, but they also show women's lack of emphasis on dominance and hierarchy, and preference for an orientation that is collaborative and supportive (Jenkins & Kramer, 1978). Ellis (1982), for example, studied two women's consciousness-raising groups and analyzed contiguous pairs of acts. Three-quarters of the interaction pairs included acts that were neither dominant nor submissive followed by the same. There was little evidence for dominance followed by dominance, or dominance followed by submissiveness. The groups discouraged the establishment of leaders or any hierarchy.

Studies of intimate couples as well as small laboratory groups show men to be more directive and women to be more expressive. In an in-depth study of the ongoing conversation of a vacationing couple, Soskin and John (1963) found that the man used significantly more directive responses that control behavior by restriction and prescription, or that channel behavior through demands, prohibitions, invitations, or permissions. He also used more informational statements, reporting facts, identifying, and classifying. The woman used more affect-discharging or expressive messages, utterances that induce others to provide a verbal response.

Communication studies in large organizations yield similar results. Employees reporting about managerial communication behavior claim that women place a greater emphasis on happy interpersonal relations, are more receptive to subordinates' ideas, and are more encouraging of subordinates, whereas men are more dominant, directive, and quick to challenge others (Baird & Bradley, 1979). There is also an expectation that women will do these things; it was more important for employee morale for women than men to appear friendly, express approval, promote happy relations, and show encouragement, concern, and attentiveness.

The studies reviewed here employ very different methodologies and subject samples. Some of the sample sizes are small, although in-depth and detailed analyses of behavior have been carried out. The evidence would be stronger if there were replications of the individual findings based on larger and more varied samples. Yet a fairly consistent pattern emerges from the diverse data sets: Men put a greater emphasis on hierarchical organization, on interactions that assert direction and dominance, whereas women engage in more egalitarian, cooperative participation, and more expressive, receptive, encouraging, and supportive interactions.

A considerable amount of research has been sparked by Lakoff's (1973, 1975, 1977) claims about the differential speech styles of women and men. Lakoff used introspection, observation, and intuition in extending linguistic principles to the analysis of communication styles. She argued that women more frequently than men use a number of speech forms that are indicative of hesitancy, uncertainty, deference, and imprecision. Among such characteristics of women's speech are the use of questions, tag questions (statements with a short question "tagged" on; e.g., "John is here, isn't he?"), question forms with declarative functions, modals, and hedges.

Studies designed to gather empirical data to test some of Lakoff's claims yield complex and inconsistent results. Some studies are supportive. When a range of language features described by Lakoff have been added together to form single indices, women have been found to use this "female register" (Crosby & Nyquist, 1977) or "women's language" (O'Barr & Atkins, 1980) more frequently than men. Women have been found to use questions with declarative functions more than men (Fishman, 1980; McMillan et al., 1977). However, contradictory results have also been reported. Dubois and Crouch (1975), for example, found that men use tag questions more frequently than women do.

Some of the inconsistencies between studies can be attributed to differences in setting, topic, sex, and number of participants, as well as operational definitions of Lakoff's variables. A more serious problem is that inadequate attention has been paid to the fact that the language features described by Lakoff may be used to serve different functions. For example, Lakoff's interpretation of tag questions as indicative of hesitancy and deference is open to debate. Although tags may express the speaker's degree of uncertainty, they may also express a degree of solidarity toward the addressee by facilitating the addressee's contribution to discourse, or may express politeness by attenuating the force of a speech act (Holmes, 1984). When tags were classified by their function, Holmes (1984) found that women used more tags than men (also reported by Fishman, 1980; McMillan et al., 1977), but also that tags function most frequently in women's speech to express solidarity by facilitating the addressee's contribution to discourse. Tags that served this function were used three times more often by women than by men.

Research that looks at particular communicative strategies is more informative than research that looks simply at gender differences in the use of a particular speech form. Given that multiple functions may be served by a single speech form (e.g., tags), it may not be meaningful to add together multiple occurrences of the same speech form, and may be even more problematic to sum occurrences of a particular range of disparate language features that vary in function into a "female register" or "women's language." Such indices obscure what the participants are trying to convey in a particular instance.

Fishman (1978, 1980, 1983) adopted a functional approach in her research, looking at the ways in which particular speech forms are used to realize particular communicative strategies. Fishman studied the interaction of three couples by placing tape recorders in their apartments for a period of 4-14 days and looked at devices used by women to keep conversations going. Fishman found that women ask questions almost three times as often as men. Questions demand answers and therefore strengthen the possibility of getting a response. Women had a harder time starting a conversation and keeping it going, as evidenced by the fact that women initiated 62% of the topics, men only 38%, but none of the men's topic initiations failed to evolve into a conversation, whereas only 38% of the topics women raised developed into a conversation.

Fishman found that women used a variety of other verbal strategies to keep conversations going. Women used more attention-getting devices than men as a conversational opening; for example, "Do you know what?" Children also say "Do you know what?" as a conversational opening to provide for a next utterance and ensure their right to speak. Women used the phrase, "This is really interesting more frequently than men, to establish their remarks as worthy of joint interest. Women said "you know" five times as often as men. Fishman argued that this was not just a hedge reflecting insecurity. Women used "you know" in places where they were unsuccessfully trying to pursue a topic. The term displays conversational trouble and is an attention-getting device designed to solve the trouble. "You know" was concentrated in long turns at talk, after pauses in women's speech where men might have responded but didn't.

Hirschman (1973) also found that women used more fillers than men (e.g., "you know") and that women tended to elaborate more on each other's utterances, whereas men were more likely to offer no response or acknowledgement at all to the comment of the other speaker. Fishman (1983) found women used terms like "yeah" and "um-hum," which analysts call back-channeling, differently from men. Women used them as "support work," inserted throughout streams of talk to indicate attention and interest. Men used such terms at the end of statements. Fishman (1980) concluded that if women feel insecure, it is not because of early socialization. Rather, it is because women's attempts at conversation are faltering or failing, and they are forced to do what she terms the "shitwork" of routine interaction (Fishman, 1983) to keep conversations going.

Research findings do not consistently support Lakoff's assertions, but of more importance, they call into question her interpretation of women's speech characteristics as indicators of hesitancy, insecurity, and deference. Research sparked by Lakoff suggests instead that women use speech forms such as questions, tag questions, and back-channeling to indicate involvement and connection in conversations and to facilitate conversations by soliciting responses from listeners. These findings are consistent with the communication processes described above to be more characteristic of women, their social-emotional orientation, and supportive, encouraging style of interaction.

Although there are clearly differences in the communication processes used by men and women, the portrayal of men and women as possessing different global styles of communication should not be overdrawn. Speaking always occurs within a social context, and in each situation the encounter makes demands on the participants and is governed by particular rules for initiation and termination, and for turn taking (Goffman, 1964; Hymes, 1967).[2] Authors have too often seen gender differences as absolute and too seldom seen the social context of speech as problematic. Let us consider some of the evidence for the influence of the situational context on gender differences.

Men tend to initiate more interaction than women in mixed-sex groups, but gender relations are dictated by the culture. Over thirty years age Strodtbeck (1951), in a cross-cultural study of decision making in couples from three cultures, demonstrated that the person who talked most and won the most decisions was determined in part by elements in the larger social and cultural organization. In the patriarchal culture he studied, husbands won most decisions, whereas in the matriarchal culture, wives won most decisions. In a study of bright, career-oriented men and women who did not differ on measures of dominance, masculinity, and femininity, Aries (1982) found females to contribute more interaction than men in six out of eight mixed-sex group discussions. Similarly, in the interaction of couples where wives were active in the women's liberation movement, wives spoke longer than husbands, whereas husbands spoke longer than wives in couples where wives were not active in the movement (Hersley & Werner, 1975). Thus men take more active roles in interaction only when the larger social and cultural values support such behavior.

Further evidence for the variability of gender differences with status differences comes from research by O'Barr and Atkins (1980), who, in the analysis of testimony of witnesses in a North Carolina superior court, found that individuals who used "women's language" with the lowest frequency were high in social status, well-educated, and professional. Men who frequently used women's language had lower social status or were unemployed. "Women's language," then, was attributable to women's relatively powerless social positions.

Gender differences in language have also been found to vary with social role. Women's language—that is, "the female register"—has been found to occur more frequently in clients' speech than in the speech of police personnel (Crosby & Nyquist, 1977). However, tag questions, one component of the "female register," are used more frequently by people in leadership/facilitator roles than by nonleaders (Holmes, 1984). Because Crosby and Nyquist (1977) did not report results for tag questions separately, it is impossible to resolve this inconsistency.

Gender differences in language are related to the social opportunities available to men and women. Nichols (1980, 1983) studied the use of creole and nonstandard variants of speech in an all-black speech community in coastal South Carolina. Where women had opportunities for jobs in sales, nursing, and elementary school teaching, there was an increase in the use of standard speech forms. Where women worked in motels as maids in jobs requiring little language interaction, they used more creolized speech. Women used less standard forms than men in their group where education and occupational opportunities were limited. Nichols concluded that it is linguistically naive to speak of "women's language" outside the context of life experiences available to each sex that affect linguistic choices.

Men generally show more of a task-orientation and women more of a social-emotional orientation, but role differentiation has been found to decrease with increased intimacy. The more intimate the relationship, the more substantial the task contributions made by women (Heiss, 1962; Leik, 1963). These findings may be accounted for by the general tendency for people in established relationships to show a wider repertoire of communication behaviors than do individuals in initial or developing relationships (Altman & Taylor, 1973).

The demands of the immediate setting influence the extent of gender differences in communication. Gender differences are greatly reduced in interactions that are formal and public. For example, no gender differences have been reported in interactions at an information booth (Crosby & Nyquist, 1977) or in the speech of subjects buying a train ticket (Brouwer, Gerritsen, & Haan, 1979). Soskin and John (1963) offered a married couple an expense-free vacation at a resort community in exchange for having each partner carry a radio transmitter throughout the day so that macrosamples of spontaneous talk could be studied. Although the equipment was antiquated by today's standards, the results remain timely. Soskin and John found that the type of communication used varied with the setting. The greatest gender differences occurred when the couple was out of public view in intimate social contexts, where the woman used more expressive messages. The talk of the two spouses was most similar in social settings that call for a relatively heavy reliance on informational language, objective statements about oneself and the world. It is interesting to note that even though task/social-emotional differentiation decreases as couples become more intimate, gender differences in communication still exist in intimate couples.

Gender differences have been found to vary within a single interaction setting. Edelsky (1981) studied informal committee meetings of a mixed-sex faculty committee. Edelsky discovered that there were actually two types of "floor." The first was orderly, with one-at-a-time interaction and monologues. The second involved almost a time-out from the agenda, with two or more people talking at once, jointly building an idea, operating on the same wavelength, with deep overlaps. Men held forth in the first type of floor, and took longer turns, though not more of them. Women became more proactive in the second type of floor, their turns were equal in length to men's, and occasionally they talked more than men. Men joked, argued, directed, and solicited responses more in the first type of floor; women in the second. Edelsky concluded that when the floor is an informal, collaborative venture women display a fuller range of language ability. When the floor involves hierarchical interaction where turn takers stand out and floors are lost and won, women have not learned to assert themselves. Hirschman (1973) found in female dyads that women interrupted and overlapped each other more than in mixed-sex or male dyads, creating an interaction similar to Edelsky's (1981) second type of floor.

An important aspect of the situation that has an impact on gender differences is the sex composition of the group. Numerous studies report less stereotypic behavior by men in mixed-sex groups than in single-sex groups. For example, men in mixed groups have been found to disagree less (Piliavin & Martin, 1978), to use more supportive statements (Bohn & Stutman, 1983), to talk longer about personal problems (Marlatt, 1970), to use more of the "female register" (Crosby & Nyquist, 1977), and to address more interaction to individuals rather than to the group as a whole (Aries, 1976) than men in all-male groups. Although men may initiate more interaction than women in mixed-sex groups, women clearly have a strong influence on the situation, as male communication behavior comes closer to the female pattern. The presence of women increases the frequency of supportive, personal interaction, and decreases combativeness. The results are not as clear concerning whether female behavior in mixed-sex groups becomes more sex-role stereotypic (e.g., McMillan et al., 1977) or less sex-role stereotypic (e.g., Piliavin & Martin, 1978) than in all-female groups. Gender differences in nonverbal behavior are also reduced in mixed-sex groups, as will be discussed below (e.g., Hall, 1984).

There is ample evidence that gender differences are affected by social context. In particular, criteria for status in the larger society, social role, occupational and educational experiences, the degree of intimacy of the participants, the interaction setting, and the sex of the participants have all been found to have an influence on communication processes, and hence interact with gender in producing behavior. Too often, studies have failed to consider these kinds of situational variables, so there is still lack of clarity in the field about the complex interaction effects of gender and other contextual variables on communication.

NONVERBAL COMMUNICATION

Parallels can be drawn between gender differences in verbal and in nonverbal interaction. Certain nonverbal cues are commonly interpreted as communicating dominance or high status, others as communicating emotional warmth, and gender differences tend to be maximized on these dimensions of dominance and warmth (Frieze & Ramsey, 1976). Henley's (1975, 1977) work was particularly instrumental in stimulating interest and research in this area. Henley drew together numerous studies of nonverbal communication as evidence for her argument that nonverbal behaviors do not simply facilitate social intercourse, but are micropolitical gestures intimately linked to power. Whether these nonverbal behaviors "are seen as simply *associated* with power, *affecting* it, or *resulting* from it; as *symbols* or *expressions*; as *describing*, *establishing* or *maintaining* power, power and nonverbal behavior are intimately and fruitfully linked" (Henley, 1977, p. 25). Careful attention to the literature suggests, however, that the meaning of gender differences in nonverbal behavior is less certain than Henley presumed.

Many gender differences in nonverbal behavior have been well established and are greater in magnitude than most other psychological gender differences (Hall, 1984). For example, in her comprehensive review of the literature, Hall (1984) reported that women smile more, gaze more, are approached more closely than men, and assume less relaxed, expansive body positions. Whether these behaviors are expressions of the dimensions of dominance and status, or of warmth and affiliation, remains open to interpretation. Major reviews of this literature by both Hall (1984) and Vrugt and Kerkstra (1984) argue that it exhibits "an extraordinary lack of direct evidence bearing on explanations for the sex differences" (Hall, 1984, p. 141), and that firm conclusions about the motives and intentions behind the sex differences are not warranted based on available research. Gender differences are most pronounced in single-sex interactions and are reduced in cross-sex encounters. If these gender differences were simply expressions of power and status, one would expect them to be maximized in male-female encounters (Hall, 1984).

Before turning to gender differences in the content of discourse, it is important to note that some researchers hold that behavior cannot be predicted as well by the sex of the individual as by his or her gender-role orientation: masculinity, femininity, or androgyny. Attempts have been made to relate both verbal and nonverbal communication to the gender-role categories using either the BSRI (Bem Sex Role Inventory; Bem, 1974) or the PAQ (Personal Attributes Questionnaire; Spence, Helm-reich, & Stapp, 1968). (For example, see Crosby, Jose, & Wong-McCarthy, 1981; Ickes & Barnes, 1978; Ickes, Schermer, & Steeno, 1979; LaFrance, 1981; Lamke & Bell, 1981 as cited in Ickes, 1981; Lavine & Lombardo, 1974; Lombardo & Lavine, 1981.) Some of the results are promising, showing meaningful connections between gender-role categories and communication behaviors (e.g., Ickes, 1981), some results are complex or confusing (e.g., LaFrance, 1981), and still others find gender-role categories to have little utility in explaining com-munication (e.g., Crosby et al., 1981). Given the lack of consistency in classification of subjects between the BSRI and the PAQ (Isenhart, 1982), the validity of the findings using these measures remains questionable.

TOPICS OF DISCOURSE

Let us turn now to the evidence for gender differences in topics of discourse. As early as 1924 Landiss and Burtt (1924) reported differences in the conversations of men and women observed unobtrusively in public places, but only in the past 15 years has new interest developed in gender differences in the content of discourse. Women's talk, considered stereotypically as "gossip," "gibberish," and "talk about trivial topics" (Kramer, 1977), has been given more serious scholarly attention, and has come to be viewed in a more positive light, as evidenced by essays such as that of Jones (1980) on women's gossip. For example, Jones (1980) described gossip as the language of intimacy between women. Gossip functions as an exchange of information and resources connected with the female role, as a catharsis for the expression of anger at women's restricted role, as entertainment, and as emotional sustenance through intimate mutual self-disclosure.

The literature on conversation content in close friendships is consistent. Self-reports from questionnaire and interview studies of adolescent and adult samples find that women have more conversations than men about personal issues that involve expression of feelings about themselves and their close relationships (Aries & Johnson, 1983; Davidson & Duberman, 1982; Douvan & Adelson, 1966; Johnson & Aries, 1983b; Jourard, 1971; Williams, 1985; Wright, 1982). Men focus their conversations more on sports, work, or issues external to the individual. Conversation is also viewed by women friends to be more central to their relationships, as a source of support, encouragement, and self-validation (Johnson & Aries, 1983a).

Cozby's (1973) review of the literature on self-disclosure established that although some studies find no gender differences, none have found men to be more self-disclosing than women, whereas many have shown women to be more self-disclosing than men. Morgan (1976) has found that men are just as self-disclosing as women on many topics, but are less self-disclosing than women on high intimacy topics. However, when a different definition was used for high intimacy topics, men and women were equally self-disclosing (Lavine & Lombardo, 1984; Lombardo & Lavine, 1981).

Gender differences in conversation appear in studies of the actual conversations of strangers as well as acquaintances. A computer-aided content analysis of the discussion content of laboratory groups of strangers getting to know one another showed that all-female groups shared a great deal of information about themselves, their feelings, homes, and relationships with family, friends, and lovers, whereas all-male groups talked very little about these topics (Aries, 1976). Members of all-male groups were very concerned about where they stood in relation to each other, and engaged in brain picking—sizing up the competition by finding out who was the best informed on a variety of topics. There were frequent references to practical joking, tricking someone out of something or into something, or simply being one up. Males engaged in dramatizing and storytelling, achieving camaraderie and closeness through stories and laughter, whereas females achieved closeness through more intimate self-revelation. Similarly, Ayres (1980) found that in 15 minutes of free conversation male dyads said little about their feelings and their home lives as compared to female dyads, but talked more about entertainment-oriented topics such as sports and rock concerts.

When one looks at the conversation content in developing and ongoing relationships, women are again found to discuss personal feelings and relationships more than men are. Wheeler and Nezlek (1977) had entering freshmen record all interactions lasting at least 10 minutes during two 2-week periods. Women classified more interactions as involving an exchange of immediate feelings or perceptions about one's self or others. Levin and Arluke (1985) unobtrusively recorded 194 instances of gossip, defined as conversation about third parties, and found that women devoted a larger proportion of their conversations to gossip than men did, although women are not more derogatory in these discussions than men. Women were more likely to gossip about close friends and family members, whereas men were more likely to talk about celebrities including sports figures and acquaintances on campus.

As is true in both verbal and nonverbal interaction, the conversation of men becomes less sex-role stereotypic in mixed-sex groups than in single-sex groups. In her study of laboratory groups, Aries (1976) found that the themes of aggression, competition, victimization, and practical joking prevalent in the all-male groups were no longer frequent in mixed groups. Men showed a dramatic change to more frequent references to themselves and their feelings, and decreased talk of sports and amusements in mixed groups. In conversation content, as in interaction style, men adopt a more personal orientation in interaction with women. Despite men's more personal style with women, they may not reach a level acceptable to women. Johnson and Aries (1983a) found that half the married women in their sample said they could talk to female friends in ways they could not to husbands, who had a difficult time listening or understanding what was being said. Komarovsky (1962) found that female friends provide an emotional balance to the difficult and meager communication with husbands in working-class families.

There are mixed results from self-disclosure studies as to whether men disclose more to women than to same-sex friends (e.g., Komarovsky, 1974) or vice versa (Jourard & Lasakow, 1958; Mulcahy, 1973). Women tend to be more self-disclosing than men in cross-sex friendships (Hacker, 1973) and the content of those disclosures needs to be considered. Hacker (1981) found that one-third of the women in her sample reported that they reveal only weaknesses in friendships with men, whereas almost a third of the men revealed only strengths in relationships with women. Men may be interpreted as maintaining positions of dominance through withholding information about their own vulnerabilities or may be seen as constrained in their capacities for self-exploration and open communication.

PERCEPTIONS AND EVALUATIONS OF SPEECH

Whereas many researchers have been interested in actual gender differences in interaction and speech, others have focused on the differential perception and evaluation of men and women as speakers, and of the speech features associated with each sex.

Researchers have presented subjects with identical communications that varied speech characteristics used more typically by one sex or the other. When asked to guess the sex of the speaker, subjects attribute tag questions to women and strong assertions to men (Siegler & Siegler, 1976). Even when the frequency of tag questions was equal for both sexes, subjects perceived women as using more tag questions than men (Newcombe & Arnkoff, 1979). When subjects are given information about a speaker's status subsequent to hearing him or her speak, they alter their perceptions of the communicator's rate of speech and accent in line with stereotypes of the speech associated with that status (Thakerar & Giles, 1981). Knowledge about speakers' lives and status can thus elicit vocal stereotypes before or after the fact.

These stereotypes bias judgments about speakers in part because different valuations are put on specific styles of speech. A number of studies have manipulated the speech of speakers to include particular features of "male" or "female" language in order to see whether speakers were evaluated differently based on these speech features. When "female speech features" are used singly or in combination, speech is viewed as less intelligent (O'Barr & Atkins, 1980; Siegler & Siegler, 1976), less assertive (Newcombe & Arnkoff, 1979), less commanding (Berryman & Wilcox, 1980), less convincing, truthful, competent, and trustworthy (O'Barr & Atkins, 1980), with contradictory results as to whether it is more credible (Berryman, 1980) or less credible (Erickson, Lind, Johnson, & O'Barr, 1978). Female speech has also been judged as warmer and more polite (Newcombe & Arnkoff, 1979).

Bradley (1981) found that the same linguistic device is viewed differently, however, depending on whether it is used by a male or female. Females who used tag questions and disclaimers were viewed as less intelligent and knowledgeable than men who used them. Furthermore, these language forms weakened women's image, but not men's. Females were viewed as less intelligent and knowledgeable when they used them, whereas perceptions of men were not affected. Similarly, females who advanced arguments without support were viewed as less intelligent, knowledgeable, and influential than men who advanced arguments without proof. Whereas use of supportive arguments caused women to be seen as more intelligent, knowledgeable, and influential, it did not affect ratings of men. Bradley (1981) argued that when men use linguistic devices commonly used by women, they may be taken not as indicators of uncertainty or nonassertiveness but as tools of politeness and other-directedness. However, when used by women the same linguistic devices may be devalued because of the lower status of women.

The same speech may be evaluated differently depending on the sex of the speaker. Whittaker and Meade (1967) found that subjects perceived men as more honest, as doing a better job in giving the facts, and as better justifying the conclusions by the facts than women reading the same speech. Thus female speakers as well as female speech features are perceived as less credible. However, female speakers reading a prose passage were perceived as more competent and socially attractive on the basis of speech than men (Smith, 1980).

Although there are not many data in this area, existing evidence suggests that people do attribute certain speech features to each sex (e.g., tag questions to women, assertive speech to men) and that these attributes can influence judgments of speakers. When a great many "female" speech features are present, especially those connoting uncertainty and hesitancy, the speaker is viewed as less assertive, commanding, competent, intelligent, and knowledgeable. However, women seem to be more detrimentally affected by use of these speech features, as the effect combines with a general tendency to see women speakers as less intelligent, credible, and knowledgeable. Although women speakers are also perceived as warmer and more polite, more competent and socially attractive, these features cannot make up for the barriers against women being perceived on an equal status basis with men.

EXPLANATION OF GENDER DIFFERENCES

I would like now to consider the changing but interrelated explanations put forward to account for gender differences in communication. Most earlier researchers (e.g., Lakoff, 1975; Strodtbeck & Mann, 1956) postulated that gender differences result from differential socialization of men and women. The greater social-emotional or expressive emphasis of women and the greater instrumental and dominance orientation of men are acquired aspects of masculinity and femininity. As Douvan and Adelson (1966, pp. 192-193) suggest,

> The girl is socialized to place great importance on personal relations; her task, as wife and mother, requires her to cultivate such traits as sensitivity, warmth, tact, and empathy. The boy, to put matters oversimply, is trained towards activity and achievement; he needs to cultivate assertiveness and independence.

Many researchers in the past decade insisted that a broader sociocultural perspective be taken (e.g., Henley, 1977; Kramarae, 1981; Spender, 1985). Male dominance is built into the familial, economic, political, religious, and legal structures of society. Power structures the relations between individuals and is reflected in their communication patterns. Women's language is the language of the powerless (O'Barr & Atkins, 1980). The greater power of men is reflected in their tendency to take more turns at speaking, to interrupt others more, to use more directive responses, and to control the topics of conversation. These patterns of communication perpetuate male dominance at the individual and interpersonal level (Borker, 1980).

A closely connected argument is that these gender differences derive from the traditional division of labor by sex, which still has a powerful influence on women's lives despite considerable sex-role change. Certain work, activities, privileges, and responsibilities are still assigned to individuals on the basis of sex. Men's place in the public sphere is associated with and generates power and authority. Women are assigned to the domestic sphere, to child-care and home-related activities. This division of labor creates differences in women's vocabularies and the content of their discourse specific to their own interests. Women's talk centers around relationships and the interpersonal sphere, men's around work and the public sphere.

Kramarae (1981, p. 119) argues that "as a consequence of the division of labor, the separation of spheres, and the differential allocation of resources and legitimate power, men and women use different strategies to influence others and shape events." From this perspective, communicative behaviors are strategies that evolve from situational constraints to meet social expectations. The inexpressivity of men can be seen as a strategy to hide vulnerability and guard positions of power (Sattel, 1983); the use of politeness by women can be seen as strategically advantageous given their position of vulnerability and inferiority (Brown, 1980). Thus the speech of women is not "ineffective," but creative, rational behavior (Kramarae, 1981).

A rather different and more convincing argument has been articulated by Maltz and Borker (1982). They postulate that men and women in this culture "come from different sociolinguistic subcultures, having learned to do different things with words in a conversation, so that when they attempt to carry on conversations with one another, even if both parties are attempting to treat one another as equals, cultural miscommunication results" (p. 200). Rules for carrying on friendly conversation are learned from peers from age 5 to 15, when children interact primarily in single-sex groups. During those years, "Members of each sex are learning self-consciously to differentiate their behavior from that of the other sex and to exaggerate these differences" (p. 203). Men and women thus acquire different rules for conversation.

As a consequence, in interactions with each other each sex wrongly interprets cues according to its own rules. For example, back-channel responses such as "yeah" and "um hum" have different meanings for men and women. For women, these mean "I'm listening, please continue"; for men these mean agreement. If a man is not agreeing, a woman feels he is not listening. Women may see questions as conversational maintenance; men see questions as requests for information. Women's rules may call for an explicit acknowledgement of what has been said by the previous speaker and a connection made to it, whereas men have no such rule and some male strategies call for ignoring it. Women share experiences and problems and respond by offering reassurance, whereas men see the presentation of problems as requests for solutions and respond by giving advice, lecturing, acting as experts. Reik (1954) suggested thirty years ago that "men and women speak different languages even when they use the same words. The misunderstanding between men and women is thus much less a result of linguistic and semantic differences, but of the emotional divergencies when the two sexes use identical expressions" (p. 15). When men and women speak of marriage, love, home, and babies, they use the same words, but the thoughts and feelings connected with these words and the ideas expressed by them are different.

From this perspective it is not surprising that communication between heterosexual couple members is often difficult. Another example of the type of problem that arises is provided by a couple seen in therapy (Surrey, 1985). Surrey reported that the man was ready to argue and debate, treating his partner as an equal who could argue her position. This stance created confusion, disorganization, and disconnection for the woman, rather than fostering what she considered to be communication. She wanted him to listen actively and to help in the developing movement of her ideas toward greater focus and clarity. They held different assumptions about what it meant to communicate. Aries (1976) found that in single-sex groups members shared implicit assumptions about how to proceed, whereas in mixed-sex groups there were more awkward silences and hesitations about how to proceed, and speech was more qualified and defensive.

Although the explanations based on sex-role socialization, male dominance, and the division of labor in society can each account for some of the gender differences in communication, the description of the course of development of gender differences put forth by Maltz and Borker (1982) draws upon these explanations and takes these themes a step further. It is the only argument that can account not only for gender differences in communication, but for the numerous findings that gender differences are most pronounced in single-sex groups.

Along with the changing explanations for the findings over time have come changes in researchers' values and in the implications researchers draw from their findings. Johnson (1983) suggested that three attitudinal positions on women's language can be identified. The first to prevail was the *deficit* position. Many early researchers took male speech as the norm and described female speech as deficient by comparison (e.g., Jespersen, 1922; Lakoff, 1975). Such researchers believed that women's language might benefit from becoming more like men's. The *difference* position then emerged, a position that assumes that there are no inherent liabilities in women's language, but that negative value often becomes attached to behavior patterns typical of low status groups. From this perspective some researchers suggested that each sex should draw equally on the communication strengths of the opposite sex with the goal of reducing gender differences (e.g., Eakins & Eakins, 1978). The *code-switching* position retains the notion of maintaining gender differences, and emphasizes the need for men and women to use "male" or "female" speech styles depending on the demands of the situation. There has been a clear shift over time reflected in the latter two positions from a greater valuation of male behavior to a more equal valuation of male and female behaviors. In some cases, greater valuation has even been put on female behavior. This shift in perspective and attitude may well be due to the growing preponderance of women researchers now in this field.

CONCLUSION

There has been a burgeoning of research on gender and communication in the past 15 years, and our understanding of the topic no longer rests on anecdotal observation and speculation. Although there are still many gaps in the evidence, there is a broad base of research evidence that reveals consistent findings despite considerable variability in methodologies employed, samples tested, and social contexts examined. There are clearly gender differences in the patterning of both verbal and nonverbal communication and in the topics of discourse. The interactions of men can be characterized as more task-oriented, dominant, directive, hierarchical; and women's as more social-emotional, expressive, supportive, facilitative, cooperative, personal, and egalitarian. These characteristics are not possessed exclusively by either sex, but are used by the two sexes with different frequencies (Bodine, 1975).

These gender differences must not be overdrawn. They are not absolute across situations, and are greatly reduced or even reversed in some contexts. The data so far only begin to provide an understanding of the ways in which specific situational variables affect gender differences in communication. As Hass (1979, p. 624) noted, "Sex is not the only variable to influence speech style. There is a complex interaction of personal characteristics such as sex, age, education, occupation, geographical region, ethnic background and socioeconomic status and contextual factors such as communication, situation, environment and participants."

Although many gender differences have been established, the major problem remains the proper interpretation of these differences. Both verbal and nonverbal communication behaviors (e.g., tag questions, interruptions, smiling) may serve multiple functions, and may take on different meanings depending on the social context or even the sex of the speaker. To complicate the picture further, verbal and nonverbal behaviors, though treated separately in most research, may in fact be used separately or in combination in interaction. When researchers focus on a single behavior, or even a selected number of behaviors, the total impression conveyed at a particular moment by a speaker through all available channels becomes distorted. In most studies, the motives, intentions, and expectations of the communicators are not systematically studied. Research efforts must focus now on providing direct evidence for the specific function served by communication behaviors used singly and in combination as they occur in context in conversation. Such research will provide a deeper understanding of the meaning of the gender differences that clearly exist in communication.

NOTES

1. I have chosen to speak of gender differences rather than sex differences in this chapter. The latter term refers to biological differences, the former to cultural expressions

of masculinity and femininity, and as there is no known biological basis for the communication behaviors to be discussed, the term "gender" seems to be more appropriate.

2. One interaction setting that has been frequently examined for gender differences is the classroom. The literature on gender and classroom interaction has been reviewed by Brophy and Good (1974) and Safilios-Rothschild (1979), and is discussed more recently by Treichler and Kramarae (1983). Obviously the rules that govern classroom behavior will differ from those that govern other settings. This chapter will not go into studies of conversation in more structured settings.

REFERENCES

Altman, I., & Taylor, D. (1973). *Social penetration: The development of interpersonal relationships*. New York: Holt, Rinehart & Winston.

Aries, E. (1976). Interaction patterns and themes of male, female, and mixed groups. *Small Group Behavior, 7*, 7-18.

Aries, E. (1982). Verbal and nonverbal behavior in single-sex and mixed-sex groups: Are traditional sex roles changing? *Psychological Reports, 51*, 127-134.

Aries, E., & Johnson, F. (1983). Close friendship in adulthood: Conversational content between same-sex friends. *Sex Roles, 9*, 1183-1196.

Ayres, J. (1980). Relationship stages and sex and factors in topic dwell time. *Western Journal of Speech Communication, 44*, 253-260.

Baird, J. E., & Bradley, P. H. (1979). Styles of management and communication: A comparative study of men and women. *Communication Monographs, 46*, 101-111.

Bales, R. F. (1950). *Interaction process analysis*. Chicago: University of Chicago Press.

Bales, R. F. (1970). *Personality and interpersonal behavior*. New York: Holt, Rinehart & Winston.

Bem, S. L. (1974). The measurement of psychological androgyny. *Journal of Consulting and Clinical Psychology, 42*, 155-162.

Berger, J., Cohen, B. P., & Zelditch, M. (1972). Status characteristics and social interaction. *American Sociological Review, 37*, 241-255.

Bernard, J. (1972). *The sex game*. New York: Atheneum.

Berryman, C. (1980). Attitudes toward male and female sex-appropriate and sex-inappropriate language. In C. Berryman & V. Eman (Eds.), *Communication, language and sex* (pp. 195-216). Rowley, MA: Newbury House.

Berryman, C. L., & Wilcox, J. R. (1980). Attitudes toward male and female speech: Experiments on the effects of sex-typed language. *Western Journal of Speech Communication, 444*, 50-59.

Bodine, A. (1975). Sex differentiation in language. In B. Thorne & N. Henley (Eds.), *Language and sex: Difference and dominance* (pp. 130-151). Rowley, MA: Newbury House.

Bohn, E., & Stutman, R. (1983). Sex-role differences in the relational control dimension of dyadic interaction. *Women's Studies in Communication, 6*, 96-104.

Borker, R. (1980). Anthropology: Social and cultural perspectives. In S. McConnell-Ginet, R. Borker, & N. Furman (Eds.), *Women and language in literature and society* (pp. 26-44). New York: Praeger.

Bradley, P. H. (1981). The folk-linguistics of women's speech: An empirical investigation. *Communication Monographs, 48*, 73-90.

Brophy, J. E., & Good, T. L. (1974). *Teacher-student relationships: Causes and consequences.* New York: Holt, Rinehart & Winston.

Brouwer, D., Gerritsen, M. M., & De Haan, D. (1979). Speech differences between women and men: On the wrong track? *Language in Society, 8*, 33-50.

Brown, P. (1980). How and why are women more polite: Some evidence from a Mayan community. In S. McConnell-Ginet, R. Borker, & N. Furman (Eds.), *Women and language in literature and society* (pp. 111-136). New York: Praeger.

Cozby, P. C. (1973). Self-disclosure: A literature review. *Psychological Bulletin, 79*, 73-91.

Crosby, F., Jose, P., & Wong-McCarthy, W. (1981). Gender, androgyny and conversational assertiveness. In C. Mayo & N. Henley (Eds.), *Gender and nonverbal behavior* (pp. 151-169). New York: Springer-Verlag.

Crosby, F., & Nyquist, L. (1977). The female register: An empirical study of Lakoff's hypotheses. *Language in Society, 6*, 313-322.

Davidson, L. R., & Duberman, L. (1982). Friendship: Communication and interactional patterns in same-sex dyads. *Sex Roles, 8*, 809-822.

Douvan, E., & Adelson, J. (1966). *The adolescent experience.* New York: John Wiley.

Dubois, B., & Crouch, I. (1975). The question of tag questions in women's speech: They don't really use more of them, do they? *Language in Society, 4*, 289-294.

Duncan, S., & Fiske, D. (1977). *Face-to-face interaction.* Hillsdale, NJ: Lawrence Erlbaum.

Eakins, B. W., & Eakins, R. G. (1978). *Sex differences in human communication.* Boston: Houghton Mifflin.

Edelsky, C. (1981). Who's got the floor? *Language in Society, 10*, 383-421.

Ellis, D. G. (1982). Relational stability and change in women's consciousness-raising groups. *Women's Studies in Communication, 5*, 77-87.

Erickson, B., Lind, E. A., Johnson, B. C., & O'Barr, W. (1978). Speech style and impression formation in a court setting: The effects of "power" and "powerless" speech. *Journal of Experimental Social Psychology, 14*, 266-279.

Esposito, A. (1979). Sex differences in children's conversation. *Language and Speech, 22*, 213-220.

Fishman, P. (1978). What do couples talk about when they're alone? In D. Butturff & E. Epstein (Eds.), *Women's language and style* (pp. 11-22). Akron, OH: L & S Books.

Fishman, P. M. (1980). Conversational insecurity. In H. Giles, W. P. Robinson, & P. M. Smith (Eds.), *Language: Social psychological perspectives.* New York: Pergamon.

Fishman, P. M. (1983). Interaction: The work women do. In B. Thorne, C. Kramarae, & N. Henley (Eds.), *Language, gender and society* (pp. 89-101). Rowley, MA: Newbury House.

Frances, S. (1979). Sex differences in nonverbal behavior. *Sex Roles, 5*, 519-535.

Frank, F. W. (1978). Women's language in America: Myth and reality. In D. Butturff & E. Epstein (Eds.), *Women's language and style* (pp. 47-61). Akron, OH: L & S Books.

Frieze, I., & Ramsey, S. J. (1976). Nonverbal maintenance of traditional sex roles. *Journal of Social Issues, 32*, 133-141.

Goffman, E. (1964). The neglected situation. *American Anthropologist, 66*, Part 2, 133-136.

Goodwin, M. H. (1980). Directive-response speech sequences in girls' and boys' task activities. In S. McConnell-Ginet, R. Borker, & N. Furman (Eds.), *Woman and language in literature and society* (pp. 157-173). New York: Praeger.

Greif, E. B. (1980). Sex differences in parent-child conversations. *Women's Studies International Quarterly, 3*, 253-258.

Haas, A. (1979). Male and female spoken language differences: Stereotypes and evidence. *Psychological Bulletin, 86*, 616-626.

Hacker, H. M. (1981). Blabbermouths and clams: Sex differences in self-disclosure in same-sex and cross-sex friendship dyads. *Psychology of Women Quarterly, 5*, 385-401.

Hall, J. (1984). *Nonverbal sex differences: Communication accuracy and expressive style.* Baltimore, MD: Johns Hopkins University Press.

Heiss, J. (1962). Degree of intimacy and male-female interaction. *Sociometry, 25*, 197-208.

Henley, N. (1975). Power, sex and nonverbal communication. In B. Thorne & N. Henley (Eds.), *Language and sex: Difference and dominance* (pp. 184-203). Rowley, MA: Newbury House.

Henley, N. (1977). *Body politics: Power, sex and nonverbal communication.* Englewood Cliffs, NJ: Prentice-Hall.

Hersley, S., & Werner, E. (1975). Dominance in marital decision-making in women's liberation and non-women's liberation families. *Family Process, 14*, 223-233.

Hirschman, L. (1973). *Female-male difference in conversational interaction.* Paper given at the meeting of the Linguistic Society of America, San Diego, CA.

Holmes, J. (1984). Women's language: A functional approach. *General Linguistics, 24*, 149-178.

Hymes, D. (1967). Models of interaction of language and social setting. *Journal of Social Issues, 23*, 8-28.

Ickes, W. (1981). Sex-role influences in dyadic interaction: A theoretical model. In C. Mayo & N. Henley (Eds.), *Gender and nonverbal behavior* (pp. 95-128). New York: Springer-Verlag.

Ickes, W., & Barnes, R. D. (1978). Boys and girls together and alienated: On enacting stereotyped sex roles in mixed-sex dyads. *Journal of Personality and Social Psychology, 36*, 669-683.

Ickes, W., Schermer, B., & Steeno, J. (1979). Sex and sex-role influences in same-sex dyads. *Social Psychology Quarterly, 42*, 373-385.

Isenhart, M. (1982). A review of critical issues in the measurement of psychological gender role. *Women's Studies in Communication, 5*, 56-64.

Jenkins, L., & Kramer, C. (1978). Small group process: Learning from women. *Women's Studies International Quarterly, 1*, 67-84.

Jespersen, O. (1922). *Language: Its nature, development and origin.* London: Allan & Urwin.

Johnson, F. L. (1983). Political and pedagogical implications of attitudes towards women's language. *Communication Quarterly, 31*, 133-138.

Johnson, F., & Aries, E. (1983a). The talk of women friends. *Women's Studies International Forum, 6*, 353-361.

Johnson, F., & Aries, E. (1983b). Conversational patterns among same-sex pairs of late adolescent close friends. *Journal of Genetic Psychology, 142*, 225-238.

Jones, D. (1980). Gossip: Notes on women's oral culture. *Women's Studies International Quarterly, 3*, 193-198.

Jourard, S. (1971). *Disclosure: An experimental analysis of the transparent self.* New York: John Wiley.

Jourard, S., & Lasakow, P. (1958). Some factors in self-disclosure. *Journal of Abnormal and Social Psychology, 56,* 91-98.

Kenkel, W. F. (1963). Observational studies of husband-wife interaction in family decision-making. In M. Sussman (Ed.), *Sourcebook in marriage and the family* (pp. 144-156). Boston: Houghton Mifflin.

Komarovsky, M. (1962). *Blue collar marriage.* New York: Random House.

Komarovsky, M. (1974). Patterns of self-disclosure of male undergraduates. *Journal of Marriage and the Family, 36,* 677-686.

Kramarae, C. (1981). *Women and men speaking.* Rowley, MA: Newbury House.

Kramer, C. (1977). Perceptions of female and male speech. *Language and Speech, 20,* 151-161.

LaFrance, M. (1981). Gender gestures: Sex, sex-role and nonverbal communication. In C. Mayo & N. Henley (Eds.), *Gender and nonverbal behavior* (pp. 129-150). New York: Springer-Verlag.

LaFrance, M., & Carmen, B. (1980). The nonverbal display of psychological androgyny. *Journal of Personality and Social Psychology, 38,* 36-49.

Lakoff, R. (1973). Language and woman's place. *Language in Society, 2,* 45-79.

Lakoff, R. (1975). *Language and woman's place.* New York: Harper & Row.

Lakoff, R. T. (1977). Women's language. *Language and Style, 10,* 222-247.

Lamke, L., & Bell, N. (1981). *Sex-role orientation and relationship development in same-sex dyads.* (Available from L. Lamke, Dept. of Home Economics, Arizona State University, Tempe, AZ 85281.)

Landis, M. H., & Burtt, H. E. (1924). A study of conversations. *Journal of Comparative Psychology, 4,* 81-89.

Lavine, L. O., & Lombardo, J. P. (1984). Self-disclosure: Intimate and nonintimate disclosures to parents and best friends as a function of Bem Sex-Role Category. *Sex Roles, 11,* 735-744.

Leet-Pellegrini, H. M. (1980). Conversational dominance as a function of gender and expertise. In H. Giles, W. P. Robinson, & P. M. Smith (Eds.), *Language: Social psychological perspectives* (pp. 97-104). New York: Pergamon.

Leik, R. K. (1963). Instrumentality and emotionality in family interaction. *Sociometry, 26,* 131-145.

Levin, J., & Arluke, A. (1985). An exploratory analysis of sex differences in gossip. *Sex Roles, 12,* 281-286.

Lockheed, M. E., & Hall, K. P. (1976). Conceptualizing sex as a status characteristic: Applications to leadership training strategies. *Journal of Social Issues, 32,* 111-124.

Lombardo, J. P., & Lavine, L. O. (1981). Sex-role stereotyping and patterns of self-disclosure. *Sex Roles, 7,* 403-411.

Maltz, D., & Borker, R. (1982). A cultural approach to male-female miscommunication. In J. J. Gumperz (Ed.), *Language and social identity* (pp. 196-216). New York: Cambridge University Press.

Markel, N. H., Long, J. J., & Saine, T. J. (1976). Sex effects in conversation interaction: Another look at male dominance. *Human Communication Research, 2,* 356-364.

Marlatt, G. A. (1970). A comparison of vicarious and direct reinforcement control of verbal behavior in an interview setting. *Journal of Personality and Social Psychology, 16,* 695-703.

McMillan, J. R., Clifton, A. K., McGrath, D., & Gale, W. (1977). Women's language: Uncertainty or interpersonal sensitivity and emotionality. *Sex Roles, 3*, 545-559.

Meeker, B. F., & Weitzel-O'Neill, P. A. (1977). Sex roles and interpersonal behavior in task-oriented groups. *American Sociological Review, 42*, 91-105.

Morgan, B. S. (1976). Intimacy of disclosure topics and sex differences in self-disclosure. *Sex Roles, 2*, 161-166.

Mulcahy, G. A. (1973). Sex differences in patterns of self-disclosure among adolescents: A developmental perspective. *Journal of Youth and Adolescence, 2*, 343-356.

Natale, M., Entin, E., & Jaffe, (1979). Vocal interruptions in dyadic communication as a function of speech and social anxiety. *Journal of Personality and Social Psychology, 37*, 865-878.

Nemeth, C., Endicott, J., & Wachtler, J. (1976). From the '50s to the '70s: Women in jury deliberations. *Sociometry, 39*, 293-304.

Newcombe, N., & Arnkoff, D. (1979). Effects of speech style and sex of speaker on person perception. *Journal of Personality and Social Psychology, 37*, 1293-1303.

Nichols, P. (1980). Women in their speech communities. In S. McConnell-Ginet, R. Borker, & N. Furman (Eds.), *Women and language in literature and society* (pp. 140-149). New York: Praeger.

Nichols, P. (1983). Linguistic options and choices for black women in the rural South. In B. Thorne, C. Kramarae, & N. Henley (Eds.), *Language, gender and society* (pp. 54-68). Rowley, MA: Newbury House.

O'Barr, W., & Atkins, B. (1980). "Women's language" or "Powerless language"? In S. McConnell-Ginet, R. Borker, & N. Furman (Eds.), *Women and language in literature and society* (pp. 93-110). New York: Praeger.

Parsons T., & Bales, R. F. (1955). *Family socialization and interaction processes.* New York: Free Press.

Pedersen, T. B. (1980). Sex and communication: A brief presentation of an experimental approach. In H. Giles, W. P. Robinson, & P. M. Smith (Eds.), *Language: Social psychological perspectives* (pp. 105-114). New York: Pergamon.

Philips, S. (1980). Sex differences and language. *Annual Review of Anthropology, 9*, 523-544.

Piliavin, J. A, & Martin, R. R. (1978). The effects of the sex composition of groups on style of social interaction. *Sex Roles, 4*, 281-296.

Reik, T. (1954). Men and women speak different languages. *Psychoanalysis, 2*, 3-15.

Rosenfeld, H. M. (1966). Approval-seeking and approval-inducing functions of verbal and nonverbal responses in the dyad. *Journal of Personality and Social Psychology, 4*, 597-605.

Safilios-Rothschild, C. (1979). *Sex role socialization and sex discrimination: A synthesis and critique of the literature.* Washington, DC: National Institute of Education.

Sattel, J. W. (1983). Men, inexpressiveness, and power. In B. Thorne, C. Kramarae, & N. Henley (Eds.), *Language, gender and society* (pp. 118-124). Rowley, MA: Newbury House.

Shaw, M. E., & Sadler, O. (1965). Interaction patterns in heterosexual dyads varying in degree of intimacy. *Journal of Social Psychology, 66*, 345-351.

Siegler, D. M., & Siegler, R. S. (1976). Stereotypes of males' and females' speech. *Psychological Reports, 39*, 167-170.

Smith, P. M. (1980). Judging masculine and feminine social identities from content-controlled speech. In H. Giles, W. P. Robinson, & P. M. Smith (Eds.), *Language: Social psychological perspectives* (pp. 121-126). New York: Pergamon.

Soskin, W. F., & John, V. P. (1963). The study of spontaneous talk. In R. Barker (Ed.), *The stream of behavior* (pp. 228-281). New York: Appleton-Century-Crofts.

Spence, J. T., Helmreich, R., & Stapp, J. (1968). The Personal Attributes Questionnaire: A measure of sex-role stereotypes and masculinity-femininity. *Journal Supplement Abstract Service Catalog of Selected Documents in Psychology, 32,* 287-295.

Spender, D. (1985). *Man made language* (2nd ed.). London: Routledge and Kegan Paul.

Strodtbeck, F. L. (1951). Husband-wife interaction over revealed differences. *American Sociological Review, 16,* 468-473.

Strodtbeck, F. L., & Mann, R. D. (1956). Sex role differentiation in jury deliberations. *Sociometry, 19,* 3-11.

Surrey, J. (1985). *Self-in-relation: A theory of women's development.* Work in progress. Wellesley, MA: Stone Center for Developmental Services and Studies.

Thakerar, J., & Giles, H. (1981). They are—so they spoke: Noncontent speech stereotypes. *Language and Communication, 1,* 255-261.

Thorne, B., & Henley, N. (1975). Difference and dominance: An overview of language, gender and society. In B. Thorne & N. Henley (Eds.), *Language and sex: Difference and dominance* (pp. 5-42). Rowley, MA: Newbury House.

Thorne, B., Kramarae, C., & Henley, N. (1983). *Language, gender and society.* Rowley, MA: Newbury House.

Treichler, P., & Kramarae, C. (1983). Women's talk in the ivory tower. *Communication Quarterly, 31,* 118-132.

Vrugt, A., & Kerkstra, A. (1984). Sex differences in nonverbal communication. *Semiotica, 50,* 1-41.

West, C., & Zimmerman, D. H. (1977). Women's place in everyday talk: Reflections on parent-child interaction. *Social Problems, 24,* 521-529.

West, C., & Zimmerman, D. H. (1983). Small insults: A study of interruptions in cross-sex conversations between unacquainted persons. In B. Thorne, C. Kramarae, & N. Henley (Eds.), *Language, gender and society* (pp. 102-117). Rowley, MA: Newbury House.

Wheeler, L., & Nezlek, J. (1977). Sex differences in social participation. *Journal of Personality and Social Psychology, 35,* 742-754.

Whittaker, J., & Meade, R. (1967). Sex of communicator as a variable in source credibility. *Journal of Social Psychology, 72,* 27-34.

Williams, D. G. (1985). Gender, masculinity-femininity, and emotional intimacy in same-sex friendship. *Sex Roles, 12,* 587-600.

Willis, F. N., & Williams, S. T. (1976). Simultaneous talking in conversation and sex of speakers. *Perceptual and Motor Skills, 43,* 1067-1070.

Wright, P. H. (1982). Men's friendships, women's friendships and the alleged inferiority of the latter. *Sex Roles, 8,* 1-20.

Zimmerman, D. H., & West, C. (1975). Sex roles, interruptions and silences in conversation. In B. Thorne & N. Henley (Eds.), *Language and sex: Difference and dominance* (pp. 105-129). Rowley, MA: Newbury House.

7

On Explaining Gender Differences

THE CASE OF NONVERBAL COMMUNICATION

JUDITH A. HALL

Judith A. Hall received her doctorate in social psychology from Harvard University in 1976. She served on the faculty of Johns Hopkins University from 1976 to 1980 and has had affiliations with the Harvard School of Public Health and the Harvard Medical School. She is now in the Psychology Department of Northeastern University. Her research has focused on gender differences and on social psychological factors in physician performance.

It is impossible to think about gender differences without wondering about their origins. The nature-nurture war is still being waged, as recent exchanges over aggression and mathematical ability illustrate (Benbow & Stanley, 1983, versus Beckwith & Woodruff, 1984; Tieger, 1980, versus Maccoby & Jacklin, 1980); and an interactionist position has also emerged (Bleier, 1984). Even among those who dismiss "nature" arguments altogether, there is little agreement over the roots of the differences.

In spite of debates, or perhaps because of them, investigators continue to amass basic descriptive evidence for the gender differences that theory seeks to explain. On what attributes do males and females differ, to what extent, and under what circumstances? Meta-analysis, the quantitative summary of research, is an important tool in understanding the extensive literature available (e.g., Hyde & Linn, 1986).

The present chapter is about gender differences in nonverbal communication skills and expressive behaviors, an area of study that has received increasing attention of both a descriptive and theoretical nature. The chapter is mainly concerned with the problem of explaining such differences. To set the stage, the chapter begins with an overview of a meta-analysis of nonverbal gender differences (Hall, 1984). Then comes a discussion of the challenge of developing a theory, and a

AUTHOR'S NOTE: Sincere thanks are extended to the reviewers of this chapter as well as to Elizabeth Aries, Amy Halberstadt, Sarah Snodgrass, Marylee Taylor, and Anneke Vrugt for their detailed criticisms and suggestions.

summary of various explanations that have been proposed. The final sections address the problem of relating theory to data via different research designs, and the thorny issue of what kind of overall evaluation should be placed on nonverbal gender differences.

SUMMARY OF NONVERBAL GENDER DIFFERENCES

Obviously, a literature involving over a dozen nonverbal variables and hundreds of studies cannot be done justice in a short summary. But for the present purpose, which is to discuss explanations for the major differences, it is not too distorting to present a broad overview. Such an overview is contained in Table 7.1. Data are presented for different age groups if the trends were noticeably different and if there were enough studies.

Gender-difference results for each variable are presented in several ways. First is the mean effect size across studies. The effect size index is d, the most commonly used one for comparing two group means (Cohen, 1977). It is defined as the difference between two means divided by their pooled within-group standard deviation. This index of effect size is not usually presented in research reports, but it can often be calculated from available statistics such as r or t (see Rosenthal, 1984, for formulas). In Table 7.1 positive effect sizes indicate that females had the larger mean.

After the effect size is the proportion of results favoring males versus females, out of those studies that showed any difference at all. Next is the proportion of studies that favored males versus females significantly, based on all studies, with those of unknown significance included in the nonsignificant category. In evaluating these last proportions, one should keep in mind that by chance alone (alpha = .05, two-tail), one would expect to find only 2.5% of studies favoring males or females significantly. With few exceptions all studies summarized within each variable are independent. For variables where studies were entered more than once, introducing some nonindependence among the entries, no tests of significance for the "direction of effect" proportions are given.

Nonverbal communication skills include the ability to judge accurately the affective meanings of nonverbal cues, the accuracy with which one's nonverbal expressions (whether conveyed via face, body, or voice) can be judged, and the ability to know a face that one has seen before. For all three skills, females were more accurate than males. For decoding skill and for face-recognition skill, the magnitude of the

TABLE 7.1

Summary of Nonverbal Gender Differences

Variable	Age Group	N	Mean Effect Size(d) (N = 133)	Direction of Effects	Direction of Significant Results
Decoding skill (PONS test only)	C, Adol, Adult	133	.41[a] (N = 133)	80% (106/133) favor F*	Not available
Decoding skill (all studies)[b]	C, Adol, Adult	125	.43 (N = 64)	83% (77/93) favor F*	26% (33/125) favor F, 2% (2/125) favor M
Face-recognition skill	C, Adol, Adult	40	.32 (N = 17)	73% (19/26) favor F*	12% (5/40) favor F, 2% (1/40) favor M
Expression accuracy	C, Adult	49	.52 (N = 35)	66% (25/38) favor F	31% (15/49) favor F, 6% (3/49) favor M
Facial expressiveness	Adult	6	1.00 (N = 5)	100% (5/5) favor F	83% (5/6) favor F, none favors M
Social smiling	C	20	−.04 (N = 5)	47% (8/17) favor F	10% (2/20) favor F, none favors M
Social smiling	Adult	23	.63 (N = 15)	94% (17/18) favor F*	52% (12/23) favor F, none favors M
Gazing	C	25	.39 (N = 10)	82% (14/17) favor F*	16% (4/25) favor F, none favors M
Gazing	Adult	61	.68 (N = 30)	83% (35/42) favor F*	34% (21/61) favor F, 3% (2/61) favor M
Gazing (target sex effect)	Adult	16	.65 (N = 6)	90% (9/10) favor F*	12% (2/16) favor F, none favors M
Distance[d]	C	28	−.22 (N = 4)	67% (14/21) favor M	18% (5/28) favor M, 4% (1/28) favor F
Distance[d]	Adult	59	−.56 (N = 17)	80% (32/40) favor M*	27% (16/59) favor M, 3% (2/59) favor F
Distance (target sex effect)[d]	C, Adult	25	−1.06 (N = 11)	93% (14/15) favor M*	36% (9/25) favor M, none favors F
Directness of orientation	C, Adult	23	.28 (N = 6)	88% (14/16) favor F*	22% (5/23) favor F, 4% (1/23) favor M
Touch	C	20	—[c]	70% (12/17) favor F**	5% (1/20) favor F, 10% (2/20) favor M
Touch	Adult	18	—[c]	67% (10/15) favor F	22% (4/18) favor F, none favors M

(continued)

179

TABLE 7.1 Continued

Variable	Age Group	N	Mean Effect Size(d)		Direction of Effects	Direction of Significant Results
Body restlessness[e]	Adult	14	−.72	(N = 6)	100% (9/9) favor M	50% (7/14) favor M, none favors F
Body relaxation[f]	Adult	6	−.70	(N = 4)	100% (5/5) favor M	67% (4/6) favor M, none favors F
Body expansiveness[g]	Adult	6	−1.04	(N = 6)	100% (6/60 favor M	100% (6/6) favor M, none favors F
Body involvement[h]	Adult	18	.32	(N = 7)	57% (4/7) favor F	22% (4/18) favor F, 6% (1/18) favor M
Body expressiveness[i]	Adult	15	.58	(N = 7)	73% (8/11) favor F	33% (5/15) favor F, 7% (1/15) favor M
Body self-consciousness[j]	Adult	11	.45	(N = 5)	67% (4/6) favor F	36% (4/11) favor F, 9% (1/11) favor M
Speech errors	C, Adol, Adult	14	−.68	(N = 7)	100% (8/8) favor M*	28% (4/14) favor M, none favors F
Filled pauses	C, Adol, Adult	7	−1.18	(N = 6)	100% (6/6) favor M	86% (6/7) favor M, none favors F

NOTE: All effects refer to subject-sex main effects except where "target sex" is indicated, in which cases the result is the target sex main effect. C = children. Adol = adolescents under college age. PONS test refers to Profile of Nonverbal Sensitivity (Rosenthal et al., 1979), a 220-item audiovisual test of nonverbal decoding skill.

a. Median.

b. This group of 125 studies includes only a few studies of the PONS test.

c. Effect sizes not often available and usually in different effect-size metric. Those that are available tend to be very small (see Stier & Hall, 1984, for complete report).

d. Naturalistic observation.

e. Includes fidgeting, manipulating objects, foot and leg movements, shifts of body position, and posture shifts.

f. Includes trunk tilt to side or back, relaxation in arms, and feet on table.

g. Includes leg or body openness, wide arms or knees.

h. Includes nods, forward lean, head tilt.

i. Includes gesticulating, expressive gestures, head movements.

j. Includes manipulation of any part of own body, preening clothes or hair, hands near face, nervous gestures.

*p < .05; **p < .10.

difference (d) was approximately the same for all ages tested. For expression accuracy there was a nonsignificant tendency for the difference to become larger as samples were older; most of this effect was due to Buck's (1977) study of preschool children's spontaneous facial accuracy, in which boys were much more accurate than girls.

After nonverbal skills in Table 7.1 come a variety of specific behaviors. Among adults, females smiled and gazed substantially more than males; had much more expressive faces; stood closer to others when unobtrusively observed; faced others more directly; touched others more; showed less restless, relaxed, and expansive body movements; showed more involved, expressive, and self-conscious body movements; made fewer speech errors (tongue slips, false starts, and so on); and used fewer pause-fillers during their own speech ("er," "ah," "um").

Regarding interpersonal distance, studies using reactive measures are also available; these include staged measures, in which subjects announce when a confederate gets too close (25 studies), and projective measures, which involve manipulating representations of people or responding to paper-and-pencil questions (42 studies). For reactive measures, differences between the behavior of males and females were practically nonexistent. The gender of the interactant made a great difference, however, for these measures as well as for unobtrusive measures of distance (see Table 7.1), with females being accorded smaller distances than males. For gazing, also, the other's gender made a large difference (Table 7.1), with females being gazed at more than males.

For children's smiling, gazing, distance, and possibly also for touch, the differences were smaller than they were for adults. Indeed, for children's social smiling there was no consistent evidence of a difference. Differences for children's and adults' laughter, not shown in Table 7.1, showed similar age trends as smiling (Hall, 1984).

Analysis of gender differences according to the gender composition of the dyad revealed a predominant pattern. For gazing, distance, smiling, and touch there was evidence (particularly strong for gazing and distance) that the biggest differences were between male-male and female-female dyads, with mixed dyads showing behavioral levels midway between these extremes. This is the pattern associated with the gender-of-subject and gender-of-target main effects presented in Table 7.1. This pattern has important theoretical implications that will be discussed later. For only one nonverbal behavior, visual dominance ratio (Dovidio & Ellyson, 1985; Ellyson, Dovidio, & Fehr, 1981), is there any evidence that gender differences are more extreme in mixed dyads than in male-male or female-female dyads, but even this evidence is equivocal as of this writing (Dovidio & Ellyson, 1985; Kimble & Musgrove, 1985).

The effects shown in Table 7.1 are by no means large in terms of variation accounted for. Even the largest gender difference, for filled pauses, accounts for only 26% of variation on this trait. Most explain much less; for example, the decoding-skill difference accounts for only 4%. However, a number of these differences are medium or large with reference to the magnitude of group differences typical in behavioral science (Cohen, 1977). In evaluating the magnitude of these differences, therefore, we must adopt an appropriate frame of reference. We should ask how these effects compare to other correlates of these same nonverbal variables, and how these gender differences compare to other gender differences. The answers to these questions are not fully known, but it does seem that a number of these differences are larger than the gender differences that have been documented for a range of other psychological variables (Hall, 1984).

In interpreting all of these results, one must consider possible biases in measurement, reporting, and sampling. The three accuracy measures are not highly subject to measurement bias because their scoring is done using standard criteria for right and wrong answers. The results for these measures may, however, be subject to publication (or some other) bias, for Eagly and Carli (1981) found that male authors reported smaller gender differences in decoding nonverbal cues than female authors did.

In comparison with the accuracy measures, the behavioral measures are more likely to contain measurement bias. Coding of behavior is done by human observers who, though typically trained to achieve good reliability, are not necessarily immune to the effects of stereotypes. Most of the variables in Table 7.1 would probably elicit expectations for gender differences in the minds of observers, based on the coder's personal experience or material taught in college psychology courses.

One bias in these studies is the unrepresentativeness of the situations in which observations were made. Several writers have criticized the accuracy measures for their artificiality because most do not involve actual interpersonal interaction but rather responses to canned stimuli or the investigator's instructions (Cunningham, 1977; Halberstadt, 1986; Snodgrass, 1985). Moreover, Hall and Halberstadt (1986) have commented on the extreme unrepresentativeness of most of the observational studies of nonverbal behaviors. Despite a wealth of studies, we actually know surprisingly little about nonverbal gender differences in everyday situations and among well-acquainted individuals, or about the nonverbal behavior of adolescents younger than college age. Most nonverbal behaviors have been studied in college students in laboratory situations during waiting periods, experiments ostensibly on other topics, and "get acquainted" sessions. These situations are probably marked by strong implicit demands to be nice, by self-consciousness, and by social anxiety in the presence of strange experimenters and fellow subjects. Hall and Halberstadt (1986) found evidence that the magnitude of some nonverbal gender differences varies with these kinds of situational factors. Thus overall estimates such as those in Table 7.1 are possibly unrepresentative of the nonverbal differences that exist in everyday life.

THEORETICAL ISSUES

The meanings of nonverbal behavior are highly variable. The same behavior can mean different things depending on situational context, other associated verbal and nonverbal behaviors, and the expressor's intentions. In interpreting nonverbal gender differences we are faced with multiple ambiguities—what a behavior was intended to mean, as opposed to what a perceiver might judge it to mean; whether the same nonverbal behaviors may mean different things to males versus females, or whether different behaviors mean the same thing; why males and females differ in their use of nonverbal behaviors; and whether we, as psychologists and as members of society, think these differences have a net impact that is good or bad for men and women.

Although research has made inroads on some of these questions, in my view psychology has not provided an adequate, empirically grounded explanation of nonverbal gender differences. The development of a comprehensive theory of nonverbal gender differences would be an awesome task, not only because of the difficulty of knowing what nonverbal behavior means but also because a theory would have to encompass a large and complex data base. Such a theory would have to take the following into account:

(1) The varying magnitudes of gender differences across various nonverbal skills and behaviors. Why do differences occur more for some nonverbal variables than others? Should one assume that one explanation must apply to all differences, and does this not depend in part on the degree of relationship among different nonverbal variables? What significance should be placed on developmental trends?

(2) The varying magnitudes of differences as functions of the subject's gender and the gender of others with whom the subject is interacting. Why do male-male and female-female interactions often differ so much?

(3) The varying magnitudes of differences across situations that vary on degree of acquaintanceship of the people in them, identity of others, roles, location, or social tension. Why do situations suppress or exaggerate behavioral styles differently for males versus females?

(4) The need to specify the causal relationships among various contending explanatory variables.

This last point deserves elaboration. As I have pointed out elsewhere (Hall, 1984), in a causal sequence several variables may be implicated, with some having more immediate impact on a given behavior than others. What appear to be competing explanations may simply involve variables at different positions in a causal stream; what one identifies as "the" cause depends on where in the stream one looks and on how many mediating variables one is willing to take into consideration.

To illustrate this point, imagine a causal stream that begins historically with cultural, political, and physical oppression of women by men, and proceeds to gender-role standards that exist at the start of any person's life; from there the stream moves to the specific learning experiences of that person, and ends with the fact that females smile more than males. Authors who have discussed the oppression of women as a source of nonverbal gender differences (e.g., Henley, 1973, 1977; Henley & LaFrance, 1984) have been vague about the exact causal role of oppression. If a woman smiles to appease her violent husband, then oppression plays a very significant and direct role in her nonverbal behavior; but if she smiles because it is an ingrained habit shared by most others of her gender, a habit that is engendered by gender-role expectations that stem only historically from oppression, then oppression plays a remote role in her behavior, one that may be of little importance either in her own motivation or in the reactions of others.

Other factors could be added to this hypothetical model. For example, because smiling is generally rewarded by smiling (Mackey, 1976), and women have been shown to receive more smiles than men (Rosenthal, 1976), then females may experience more rewarding interactions, which could lead them to smile even more. One could also add a physiological explanation for some nonverbal variables, such that learning experiences alter hemispheric lateralization in a way that favors females as nonverbal decoders (Safer, 1981). Constructing a model that can encompass all such factors would be a large job indeed.

The simple examples given here demonstrate that it is not very profitable to talk about "the" cause of nonverbal gender differences. Rather, we should recognize that many factors can work in concert and have varying direct and indirect paths, as well as proximal and distal relations, and that a model that seems to work for one behavior may not work for another.

I shall make one more comment before turning in more detail to specific explanations that have been offered. Nearly always, investigators of nonverbal gender differences (myself included) talk of women as doing more of this and that—rarely of men doing less. Partly this is because of our convention of describing a result in terms of the group that shows the larger mean. But such rhetoric inevitably influences how we interpret these differences. We seek explanations for why women smile more, gaze more, and so on, not for why men do so less. Our emphasis is on women's motives, and on factors that influence women, as though making the implicit assumption that men's behavior is normal and needs no explanation. Such implicit assumptions reflect and color our evaluations of these differences, as well as our opinions of their social ramifications.

CURRENT EXPLANATIONS

Credit for propelling the topic of nonverbal gender differences into the consciousness of social psychologists goes to Nancy Henley. She suggested (1973, 1977) that status differences between men and women play an important role in their nonverbal behavior and that nonverbal gender differences help perpetuate that social inequality.

Nearly all nonverbal gender differences have been hypothesized by some author to reflect dominance-status differences. Thus women's greater smiling is said to convey submissiveness and appeasement; their gazing and decoding skills are said to reflect the needs of a socially weak person who must constantly monitor others, either to please them or to plan their own strategy as best they can; their closer interpersonal distances are said to reflect lack of respect paid to socially weak individuals; their more restrained body movements are said to reflect society's demands that they be unassertive and take up as little space as possible; their speech patterns have been said to reflect social weakness and forced politeness (see Aries, this volume); and it has been suggested that women are touched more than men and initiate less touch than men, by virtue of their low social power, though both of these purported differences are actually debatable (see Table 7.1 and Stier & Hall, 1984).

The ability of this "oppression" point of view to encompass many findings conceptually and its compatibility with feminist ideology have contributed to its wide acceptance. One can find few criticisms of this interpretation. Recently, however, Vrugt and Kerkstra (1984), Hall (1984), Stier and Hall (1984), and Halberstadt and Baird (1985) have all argued that nonverbal gender differences may not be so easily explained. Vrugt and Kerkstra (1984) summarized the current state of theory this way:

> Furthermore, there is a profound lack of sound theoretical background. The observed differences between men and women are often loosely interpreted and thus unjustly viewed as expressions of the supposedly different characteristics of men and women, as for example male dominance. Such interpretations, which start to live a life of their own and gain common acceptance, are not beneficial to the building of a sound theoretical framework for this area of research. (p. 29)

It is important to state explicitly that theoretical perspectives other than oppression have been proposed; for these, the reader can consult Aries (this volume), Hall (1984), and Henley and LaFrance (1984). I shall review various explanations briefly here. Of course, as noted earlier, these perspectives may not be mutually exclusive but may represent different points in a causal process.

Many nonverbal gender differences fit a friendliness/affiliation explanation. Smiling, facial expressiveness, gazing, close distances, direct orientation, touch, responsive body movements, and communication skills can all be messages and reflections of friendly attention and warmth, both given and received. If females are more friendly or affiliative (or relatedly, trusting, capable of intimacy, and so on), then these traits could account for the nonverbal differences.

Relevant to some behaviors, such as smiling and laughing, nervous body movements, and speech errors, is anxiety. These behaviors all seem to increase under anxiety, and also show some interestingly different patterns in males versus females as a function of anxiety (Hall, 1984; Hall & Halberstadt, 1986). If women experience more anxiety in social situations than men, some differences might be explained.

For interpersonal distance, it is possible that height differences help determine men's versus women's preferences, and the differing approach distances of men and women. Shorter people, within gender, seem to command less space (Hall, 1984).

Personality traits of masculinity and femininity have been proposed to account for expression-skill differences (Zuckerman, DeFrank, Spiegel, & Larrance, 1982) and decoding-skill differences (Hall & Halberstadt, 1981). Decoding-skill differences have also been discussed in terms of gender differences in attention to, and practice in, nonverbal communication; women's gaze habits fit with this hypothesis, especially because the greatest decoding gender differences are for facial cues (Hall, 1984).

Rosenthal and DePaulo (1979) have suggested that some nonverbal differences result from women's greater motives to be "accommodating," which they propose is manifest (among other things) in women's decreasing advantage for channels that are more "leaky"—that is, likely to convey cues accidentally emitted by the expressor. An accommodating person would avoid reading these leaky cues, out of deference or out of greater wisdom about what behaviors meet with others' positive reactions. Although such accommodatingness could reflect low status, Rosenthal and DePaulo do not emphasize that possibility.

All nonverbal gender differences could stem from social learning and "self-socialization" experiences (Maccoby & Jacklin, 1974), with boys and girls gradually internalizing the characteristics of same-gender models as they perceive them, and being rewarded, both intrinsically and extrinsically, for doing so. One can argue that this is not a useful hypothesis because it presupposes the very differences we wish to explain—that is, children adopt nonverbal behaviors that already exist in models around them. But this kind of explanation is important for two reasons. First, the self-perpetuation of gender-role norms may actually be the predominant causal process as far as an individual is concerned because it is possible that the original forces that shaped these norms (oppression, for instance) are no longer directly operative. Second, if one acknowledges that these norms are learned largely in one's same-gender group, then a very different avenue of hypothesizing is opened up.

The idea that same-gender norms control behavior has been elaborated by Maltz and Borker (1982) in the context of gender differences in conversational behavior (see also Aries, this volume). Maltz and Borker's thesis is that gender differences in conversational style emerge from male and female subcultures whose norms are learned from, and reinforced by, gender mates from early childhood on.

Drawing on developmental studies, these authors see the "girl's world" as occurring in small groups, most often pairs; private; cooperative; noncompetitive; differentiated in terms of relative closeness, not power; based on talk, especially talk that is supportive, shared equally, and respectful of each other. Direct criticism is avoided, with the following consequences:

> Girls must become increasingly sophisticated in reading the motives of others, in determining when closeness is real, when conventional, and when false, and to respond appropriately. . . . Given the indirect expression of conflict, girls must learn to read relationships and situations sensitively. Learning to get things right is a fundamental skill for social success, if not just social survival. (p. 207)

The world of boys, by contrast, is more hierarchical, marked by the constant manipulation of relative status, and filled with posturing and counterposturing to assert dominance, attract an audience, and assert oneself when other speakers have the floor. Verbal challenge is a hallmark of boys' interactions.

What might this hypothesis mean for our understanding of nonverbal gender differences? It might mean that, in contrast to the assumptions that underlie the oppression hypothesis, nonverbal gender differences may stem from adherence to the norms operating within one's same-gender group, and not from status differences that supposedly become so salient when males and females interact with each other. The finding that several nonverbal differences are more pronounced between males and females in same-gender dyads than between males and females in mixed dyads supports the idea that same-gender norms are the prevailing, and controlling, ones. Further, the specific "female" and "male" nonverbal styles are consistent with Maltz and Borker's characterization of their respective worlds: Much of women's style can be seen as fitting with the heightened affiliation and egalitarianism that mark female-female interaction, and their communication skills could follow from their needs to express and perceive subtle degrees of within-group social inclusion and exclusion. At the same time, men's greater use of filled pauses (which serve to keep the floor), more frequent speech disturbances, faster speech, and more frequent interruptions (Aries, this volume; Hall, 1984) could all follow from their increased within-group competition over conversational floor time.

The socialization hypothesis does not, of course, tell us why same-gender groups have divergent norms. This question reaches beyond the scope of this chapter. For present purposes, however, that limitation should not overshadow the potential contribution of this hypothesis to our understanding of gender differences in communication behaviors. A mainstay of oppression-hypothesis reasoning is the sexual-politics nature of male-female interaction, that is, the assumption that the different statuses of men and women have specific significance for their communications with each other. According to the socialization hypothesis, in contrast, men and women come together as citizens of different cultures; in their own cultures, they have different patterns and norms for communication, but when they come together, those norms have less force and more behavioral latitude is possible. Indeed, the idea that the rules of mixed-gender interaction are not well specified in advance may help explain why such interaction is exciting and stressful.

Although, like Maltz and Borker, Henley and LaFrance (1984) have depicted male-female nonverbal differences as reflecting male and female cultures, they also seem to view the domination of females by males as directly important for nonverbal behavior. Maltz and Borker would probably see social inequality as historically relevant, at best.

METHODS FOR ASSESSING EXPLANATIONS

Elsewhere, I have reviewed the evidence that is relevant to various explanations of nonverbal gender differences (Hall, 1984). It is impossible to summarize this material here, and to try to do so would do injustice on many fronts. It is also premature to lay out the evidence and determine which explanations fare best, because the empirical evidence is too limited in most areas. It is safe to say that no one explanation has received unequivocal support. Rather than argue about particular theories, I would rather focus on the difficult question of how we can decide if a given explanation is supported. What follows is an effort to analyze some forms of theory-relevant evidence, to appraise their worth in general terms, and to point to some applications.

Comparing Bivariate Relations

The evidence most commonly cited to support explanations of nonverbal gender differences consists of bivariate relations that point logically to a possible causal role for some variable that is correlated with gender. For example, one might hypothesize that gender differences in smiling are caused by women's lower status, as lower-status people smile more and women are of lower status than men. One would seek to confirm all three of these hypothetical relations, using either results pieced together from different studies or results originating from one study.

This is a weak basis for assessing the cause of a gender difference, though it is a first step. If the predicted bivariate relations can be documented, further steps can be taken to demonstrate (a) that a hypothesized third variable can account for the gender difference statistically, and (b) that it does so better than rival explanatory variables can.

Unfortunately, this form of argument is not only applied often, but it is often applied with little rigor. Sometimes one or more of the requisite bivariate relations have not actually been observed. For example, though the smiling-status-gender argument has been made often, empirical documentation of the smiling-status link in humans is virtually never offered.

Moreover, the missing links, when they are observed, can be inconsistent with the hypothesis at hand. For example, in discussing personal space, it has been repeatedly suggested that people's closer approaches to females than to males are grounded in the way low-status individuals are treated; but evidence relating status to distance does not give much support to the assumption that low-status individuals are accorded smaller interpersonal distances (Hall, 1984). Similarly, it has been argued that women cant (tilt) their heads to one side in conversation more than men and that this is a submissive gesture; logically, female submissiveness is supported as the explanation of the gender difference (Henley, 1977). Halberstadt and Baird (in press) have cast doubt on this argument by demonstrating that the gender difference is minimal in empirical studies and also that head canting is not perceived by college raters as reflecting submissiveness.

Modeling the Gender Differences

One problem with the previous method is the possibility that the explanatory variable does not, despite observed bivariate relations, account for the gender difference. This problem can be dealt with by actually testing to see if a gender difference can be reduced in magnitude by measuring all theoretically relevant variables in the same study and controlling statistically for explanatory variables when assessing the gender difference. For example, does the difference in approach distances disappear if participants' heights are partialed out? Explanations involving several variables, ordered according to theory, could be tested using causal modeling techniques. A particularly good discussion and application of this method for a gender difference (though not a nonverbal one) is provided by Verbrugge and Steiner (1981).

Few studies of nonverbal gender differences have performed such analyses, even using the simplest models. Investigators who have applied this method include Rosenthal, Hall, DiMatteo, Rogers, and Archer (1979), who partialed interpersonal gaze out of the decoding difference, and Hall and Halberstadt (1981) and Zuckerman et al. (1982), who partialed masculinity and femininity out of encoding and decoding differences.

Application of the causal modeling approach would greatly benefit this field because investigators would be forced to (1) develop multivariate models, and in the process think carefully about various causal possibilities, (2) include variables for sound theoretical reasons, and (3) develop alternate testable models. Showing that one model is consistent with the data does not, of course, preclude the possibility that another, with a competing explanatory variable, would fit as well or better. Nevertheless, this approach is a big improvement over the preceding method because its conclusions are based on the actual fit of models to data and because it forces investigators to think more carefully about their causal models (Reis, 1982).

Experimental Designs

Some investigators have used experimental designs as a basis for arguing the cause of a gender difference. Typically, a variable that could be the explanatory factor is experimentally manipulated, crossed with gender, and used to predict some nonverbal dependent variable. Although such experiments do demonstrate whether a causal relation exists between an independent variable and a nonverbal behavior, it is much less clear what they demonstrate about the cause of a gender difference.

First, there is the problem of the gap between experimental operationalizations and the many variables that are confounded with gender in the real world. The experimental manipulation of, say, dominance-subordination via a teacher-learner paradigm does not necessarily capture the most salient role or status differences naturally occurring between men and women. It is therefore a leap to conclude that the explanation of a gender difference in "real life" has been found. The second problem is that the connections between theories of gender differences and actual empirical results have not been adequately developed. The following two studies make this point.

Using a measure of communication accuracy as a dependent variable, Snodgrass (1985) experimentally varied teacher/learner roles as an operationalization of dominant/subordinate status in dyads of varying gender composition. She reasoned that, owing to the confounding of gender with dominant/subordinate roles in everyday life, the gender difference traditionally found for interpersonal sensitivity may be based on these role differences. Thus she hypothesized that when role and gender are unconfounded in an experiment, there will be no gender main effect. Instead there will be a main effect of role, with subordinate individuals being more accurate in discerning others' opinions of them than vice versa. Both of these hypotheses were supported, leading Snodgrass to conclude that she had found "strong support for the subordinate role explanation for female superiority in interpersonal sensitivity" (p. 152).

Wittig and Skolnick (1978) experimentally varied male and female confederates' relative status and measured interpersonal distance in male and female subjects. In contrast to Snodgrass, these authors predicted gender main effects, presumably on the grounds that a one-shot experimental manipulation would not erase habits learned over a lifetime. Like Snodgrass, they also predicted a status main effect. They obtained a confederate gender effect but no status main effect; they also obtained an interaction between confederate gender and status. Because of this interaction, the authors concluded that status was probably the important variable accounting for differences in approach to males versus females.

These two studies, so similar in their initial theoretical positions, their designs, and their conclusions, yet so different in their results, reveal that there is no obvious relationship between a theory and what pattern of data can be said to support it. In these examples, one investigator predicted gender effects, the other did not; one found "the" explanation in a status main effect, one found it in an interaction. When this kind of inconsistency occurs, it indicates investigators should engage in more discourse about theory-data relations so that implicit predictions become explicit and unshared assumptions come to light.

Interaction effects seem always to present a challenge to interpretation, no matter what the field of inquiry. Other investigators besides Wittig and Skolnick have found interactions of gender with experimental variables. For example, it has been demonstrated that gender differences in gazing change as a function of the experimentally manipulated physical distance between two interactants (e.g., Aiello, 1972). These kinds of results are not irrelevant to theory, for they demonstrate, causally, that situations can trigger different behaviors in men and women. But situational moderating variables, even experimentally manipulated ones, do not explain an overall gender difference (for example, why females are almost always approached closer than men, regardless of situational variables), and also do not explain why the behavior varies over situations. Why do close distances make men gaze relatively less than women? Why do subjects react differently to a status manipulation for a male versus female confederate? These interaction effects may help to narrow the range of plausible answers, but they do not themselves supply an answer.

Meta-Analysis

An increasing number of investigators apply meta-analysis to gender differences, and would like to use that tool to further theoretical understanding. An example of such a meta-analysis is Eagly and Carli's (1981) review of gender differences in persuasion and conformity. They showed that women conform to a group more than men only when they believe the group has knowledge of their behavior. This result lends itself easily to the interpretation that women are particularly sensitive to group opinion, an interpretation that connotes female weakness and dependency. But a meta-analysis that codes gender *differences* cannot tell about gender by condition group *means*, which are crucial to an interpretation of this kind. Indeed, when Eagly, Wood, and Fishbaugh (1981) performed an experiment that manipulated the presence or absence of group surveillance, the means showed that the only change under surveillance was in males' behavior, which promotes a very different interpretation. It seems that women are not particularly dependent on the group, but rather men feel an exaggerated need to assert independence when under group surveillance. Thus meta-analysis can set us to thinking about likely explanations for why gender differences change over situations, but we should be very cautious in our conclusions without further primary research testing particular hypotheses.

In a meta-analysis of smiling and gazing gender differences, Hall and Halberstadt (1986) coded situational variables such as role, acquaintanceship, age, and presumed comfort. There were many significant relationships between these situational predictors and the gender differences. As alluded to earlier, situational effects on a gender difference can tell us something about the external validity of gender differences reported in the literature (Eagly, 1986). For example, the smiling difference was greatly increased when the circumstances were laboratory based; observations in the field showed much smaller differences (a result confirmed in Halberstadt & Baird, in press). Because most of the smiling literature is laboratory based, it is possible that the overall documented difference is an exaggeration of the "real life" difference.

Our meta-analysis did not, however, provide very much evidence about causal explanations. As in Eagly and Carli (1981), we could document an overall gender difference (analogous to a gender main effect in a primary study) and the extent to which that difference varied over situations (analogous to a gender by situational variable interaction in a primary study). The meta-analysis did not document effects of situations on nonverbal behavior, nor did it document naturally occurring differences in the distributions of men and women over situations. Both of these relations would be essential for any claim that situational factors explain gender differences.

Interpretation of the changes in the smiling and gazing gender differences over different situations is also problematic given that situations were not experimentally manipulated between studies. Thus although the smiling difference was larger for situations that were rated as more uncomfortable, one does not know that it was the situations that accounted for this effect rather than some correlated variable; even if one were sure it was the situations that caused the gender difference to change, one would not know which aspect of the situations was responsible.

To make matters more confusing, even if we could be reasonably sure that more uncomfortable situations do cause an increase in the gender difference, we would still not know the psychological mechanisms involved. Though this general point was made in the previous section, I want to illustrate the interpretational complexity for the benefit of any reader who thinks explanations for nonverbal differences are obvious. First, smiling, as a strongly prescribed and overlearned aspect of the female role, may be a readier response for women under anxious circumstances than for men. Second, perhaps in socially anxious situations females try harder to ease the interaction for the other party; thus their enhanced smiling would not indicate their own anxiety but would indicate the adoption of a supportive, facilitative role. Finally, perhaps males are less socially competent (Sarason, Sarason, Hacker, & Basham, 1985), and as a consequence cope more poorly with anxiety-provoking situations than females do; this could lead to reduced male smiling under anxiety that reflects their greater discomfort. The existence of such different possibilities demonstrates how complex it will be to unravel the causes of nonverbal gender differences.

Methodological Prospectus

No one method of exploring the causes of nonverbal gender differences is perfect, and no study can be definitive. This is the situation we face whenever we wish to explain psychologically and culturally complex behavior patterns, the ultimate origins of which may be shrouded in the mists of the past. But a difficult task is not the same as a hopeless one, and there is much work to be done.

Theorists can draw more on existing research, both to test its compatibility with various explanations and inductively to develop new hypotheses. Theorists can also make a major contribution by articulating the differences between alternatives, for example between personality-trait and social-situational explanations and between proximal and distal explanations.

Investigators can pursue the problem of explanation by designing new research with theoretical goals in mind. Some directions I perceive to be important are as follows:

- to study developmental trends more fully;
- to document not only the overall frequencies of male and female behaviors but also the distributions of male and female behavior over situations and roles;
- to study nonverbal behavior in naturally occurring settings and relationships;
- to study more than one nonverbal behavior or skill at a time;
- to include more than one theoretically relevant variable at a time, in order to pit one explanation against another, to develop converging evidence for one explanation, and to allow the possibility of controlling for one variable while assessing the effects of another;
- to study nonverbal gender differences via cross-cultural comparisons, and in various subcultural groups and contexts whose norms and requirements may differ;
- to study better the correlates of nonverbal behavior and skill within gender, in order to understand the consequences and meanings of these variables for males versus females.

ISSUES IN THE EVALUATION OF
NONVERBAL GENDER DIFFERENCES

Nonverbal gender differences are hard to interpret partly because nonverbal behavior itself is hard to interpret. Not only are we unsure of why one gender displays more of a particular behavior, we are also unsure of what that behavior means to either gender. In addition, psychologists bring their own ideological views to bear on the data. It is no surprise that at this stage in the development of the field, psychologists' views on the causes of the differences sometimes seem as much a Rorschach response as a distillation of truth. But this is also an exciting time, for there remain many ideas and empirical issues in need of exploration.

With gender differences as robust as some of these are, there arises the inevitable question of what we should do about them. One position is that women should aspire to act more like men, because women's skills and styles reflect and help perpetuate their low status. Henley and LaFrance (1984) and Hall (1984) point to perils in this advice, such as the sacrifice of worthwhile nonverbal behaviors and skills, and the poor reception that may be given to women who deviate from their "proper" female role. On the other hand, one can argue that "female" behaviors and skills are a precious commodity in a world of competition, violence, alienation, and mistrust. Such an argument leads to the suggestion that men should change instead of women.

Another point raised by Henley and LaFrance (1984) and by Hall (1984) is that adopting a more "male" nonverbal style may not accomplish anything useful because the real problem is that men and women have unequal status, not that they use nonverbal communication differently. As long as society makes sexist judgments of women, it will derogate their behavior no matter what it is. And as long as gender stereotypes reflect this inequality, men and women will be perceived differently no matter what they are doing nonverbally, as in Henley and Harmon (1985), where men were rated as more dominant than women even when they used identical body movements intended to convey dominance. Perhaps our recipe for social change should be to change stereotypes to reflect the real potentialities of men and women, to educate people about the difference between display rules and underlying traits (for example, that women's greater expressivity may not indicate more underlying emotionality; Henley & LaFrance, 1984), and to caution ourselves and others about the hazards of assuming that women's nonverbal behavior reflects weakness and subordination.

One important matter to study, in order to resolve whether female nonverbal behavior is "bad" or "good," is the effect of male versus female nonverbal behavior on others' impressions and on real-life outcomes. For example, more smiling in women could be perceived as weakness, whereas more smiling in men could be perceived as self-confidence. Some studies have experimentally manipulated nonverbal behaviors in canned stimuli and elicited subjects' impressions (e.g., Summerhayes & Suchner, 1978). Although not without merit, such studies probably elicit gender stereotypes in the minds of subjects and therefore have limited generalizability. Nonverbal behavior should be conceptualized as an independent variable, but in ecologically sound designs. One would like to know whether males' and females' perceived status is lowered when others approach them closely; whether speech errors affect perceived competence, and if so, if the effect is the same for both men and women; whether smiling in anxious situations eases people's discomfort and whether smiles from a woman work better or worse in this regard; what the interpersonal consequences of possessing decoding or face-recognition skill are; and whether a "male" or "female" nonverbal package works best in various situations and for various goals—in collaboration, negotiation, persuasion, conflict, supervision, teaching, therapy, making and keeping friends, and so on. Only when we know much more about the consequences of nonverbal skill and behavior can we state with any confidence whether men or women have received a raw deal in the nonverbal repertoires imposed on them by society.

In the meantime, psychologists seem to experience serious ambivalence over how to interpret nonverbal gender differences. To illustrate this point, first consider a gender difference that inspires little or no ambivalence: math achievement. When females score lower on an attribute as valuable as this (Linn & Petersen, 1986), it is quite reasonable to argue that society has produced this deficit via subtle or blatant forms of discrimination. Now consider nonverbal variables. Females, the socially subjugated group, score higher than males on behaviors and skills that many would agree are also valuable. This is contradictory. How could the subjugated group have achieved a superior repertoire of social behaviors? One way to resolve this contradiction is to redefine these nonverbal behaviors and skills in a negative light, such that they are now seen as a confirmation of, and contributor to, women's subjugation. As an example of such reasoning, females' greater nonverbal sensitivity has often been viewed as an adaptive skill that enables them to function better in their subordinate role (e.g., Weitz, 1974).

This kind of redefinition has led, in my view, to some contorted interpretations. As one example, Wittig and Skolnick (1978), in the study described earlier, predicted that higher status individuals would be accorded more space, thus putting an interpretation of social value on greater space. But when they observed this exact phenomenon for a female confederate, they suggested that the high-status female was not perceived as high status or that the high-status female was perceived as having "something negative" about her (p. 501). After the fact, Wittig and Skolnick were unwilling to admit that a high-status woman might be treated just as they predicted a high-status man would be; instead they reinterpreted people's behavior toward her as reflecting a stigma. It seems investigators may have the same tendency as society at large to maintain a double standard of interpretation for male versus female behavior.

The difficulty that social psychologists have in deciding what to make of nonverbal gender differences makes for an interesting chapter in the history of our discipline and makes the task of explaining them even more complex. The best we can hope for in future research is open-mindedness and an effort to achieve insight both into our individual ambivalence and into the role that ideology plays in the progress of this field.

REFERENCES

Aiello, J. R. (1972). A test of equilibrium theory: Visual interaction in relation to orientation, distance and sex of interactants. *Psychonomic Science, 27*, 335-336.

Beckwith, J., & Woodruff, M. (1984). Letter in *Science, 223*, 1247.

Benbow, C. P., & Stanley, J. C. (1983). Sex differences in mathematical reasoning ability: More facts. *Science, 222*, 1029-1031.

Bleier, R. (1984). *Science and gender: A critique of biology and its theories on women.* New York: Pergamon.

Buck, R. (1977). Nonverbal communication of affect in preschool children: Relationships with personality and skin conductance. *Journal of Personality and Social Psychology, 35*, 225-236.

Cohen, J. (1977). *Statistical power analysis for the behavioral sciences.* New York: Academic Press.

Cunningham, M. R. (1977). Personality and the structure of the nonverbal communication of emotion. *Journal of Personality, 45*, 564-584.

Dovidio, J. F., & Ellyson, S. L. (1985). Patterns of visual dominance behavior in humans. In S. L. Ellyson & J. F. Dovidio (Eds.), *Power, dominance, and nonverbal behavior.* New York: Springer-Verlag.

Eagly, A. H. (1986). Some meta-analytic approaches to examining the validity of gender-difference research. In J. S. Hyde & M. C. Linn (Eds.), *The psychology of gender: Advances through meta-analysis.* Baltimore, MD: Johns Hopkins University Press.

Eagly, A. H., & Carli, L. L. (1981). Sex of researchers and sex-typed communications as determinants of sex differences in influenceability. *Psychological Bulletin, 90,* 1-20.

Eagly, A. H., Wood, W., & Fishbaugh, L. (1981). Sex differences in conformity: Surveillance by the group as a determinant of male nonconformity. *Journal of Personality and Social Psychology, 40,* 384-394.

Ellyson, S. L., Dovidio, J. F., & Fehr, B. J. (1981). Visual behavior and dominance in women and men. In C. Mayo & N. M. Henley (Eds.), *Gender and nonverbal behavior.* New York: Springer-Verlag.

Halberstadt, A. G. (1986). Family socialization of emotional expression and nonverbal communication styles and skills. *Journal of Personality and Social Psychology, 51,* 827-836.

Halberstadt, A. G., & Baird, U. N. (in press). Gender, nonverbal behavior, and perceived dominance: A test of the theory. *Journal of Personality and Social Psychology.*

Hall, J. A. (1984). *Nonverbal sex differences: Communication accuracy and expressive style.* Baltimore, MD: Johns Hopkins University Press.

Hall, J. A., & Halberstadt, A. G. (1981). Sex roles and nonverbal communication skills, *Sex Roles, 7,* 273-287.

Hall, J. A., & Halberstadt, A. G. (1986). Smiling and gazing. In J. S. Hyde & M. C. Linn (Eds.), *The psychology of gender: Advances through meta-analysis.* Baltimore, MD: Johns Hopkins University Press.

Henley, N. M. (1973). Status and sex: Some touching observations. *Bulletin of the Psychonomic Society, 2,* 91-93.

Henley, N. M. (1977). *Body politics: Power, sex, and nonverbal communication.* Englewood Cliffs, NJ: Prentice-Hall.

Henley, N. M., & Harmon, S. (1985). The nonverbal semantics of power and gender: A perceptual study. In S. L. Ellyson & J. F. Dovidio (Eds.), *Power, dominance, and nonverbal behavior.* New York: Springer-Verlag.

Henley, N. M., & LaFrance, M. (1984). Gender as culture: Difference and dominance in nonverbal behavior. In A. Wolfgang (Ed.), *Nonverbal behavior: Perspectives, applications, intercultural insights.* Lewiston, NY: C. J. Hogrefe.

Hyde, J. S., & Linn, M. C. (Eds.). (1986). *The psychology of gender: Advances through meta-analysis.* Baltimore, MD: Johns Hopkins University Press.

Kimble, C. E., & Musgrove, J. I. (1985). *Dominance in arguing mixed-sex dyads: Visual dominance patterns, talking time, and speech loudness.* Manuscript submitted for publication.

Linn, M. C., & Petersen, A. C. (1986). A meta-analysis of gender differences in spatial ability: Implications for mathematics and science achievement. In J. S. Hyde & M. C. Linn (Eds.), *The psychology of gender: Advances through meta-analysis.* Baltimore, MD: Johns Hopkins University Press.

Maccoby, E. E., & Jacklin, C. N. (1974). *The psychology of sex differences.* Stanford, CA: Stanford University Press.

Maccoby, E. E., & Jacklin, C. N. (1980). Sex differences in aggression: A rejoinder and reprise. *Child Development, 51,* 964-980.

Mackey, W. C. (1976). Parameters of the smile as a social signal. *Journal of Genetic Psychology*, *129*, 125-130.

Maltz, D. N., & Borker, R. A. (1982). A cultural approach to male-female miscommunication. In J. J. Gumperz (Ed.), *Language and social identity*. Cambridge: Cambridge University Press.

Reis, H. T. (1982). An introduction to the use of structural equations: Prospects and problems. In L. Wheeler (Ed.), *Review of personality and social psychology* (Vol. 3, pp. 255-287). Beverly Hills, CA: Sage.

Rosenthal, R. (1976). *Experimenter effects in behavioral research* (enlarged ed.). New York: Irvington.

Rosenthal, R. (1984). *Meta-analysis in summarizing social research*. Beverly Hills, CA: Sage.

Rosenthal, R., & DePaulo, B. M. (1979). Sex differences in eavesdropping on nonverbal cues. *Journal of Personality and Social Psychology*, *37*, 273-285.

Rosenthal, R., Hall, J. A., DiMatteo, M. R., Rogers, P. L., & Archer, D. (1979). *Sensitivity to nonverbal communication: The PONS test*. Baltimore, MD: Johns Hopkins University Press.

Safer, M. A. (1981). Sex and hemisphere differences in access to codes for processing emotional expressions and faces. *Journal of Experimental Psychology: General*, *110*, 86-100.

Sarason, B. R., Sarason, I. G., Hacker, T. A., & Basham, R. B. (1985). Concomitants of social support: Social skills, physical attractiveness, and gender. *Journal of Personality and Social Psychology*, *49*, 469-480.

Snodgrass, S. E. (1985). Women's intuition: The effect of subordinate role on interpersonal sensitivity. *Journal of Personality and Social Psychology*, *49*, 146-155.

Stier, D. S., & Hall, J. A. (1984). Gender differences in touch: An empirical and theoretical review. *Journal of Personality and Social Psychology*, *47*, 440-459.

Summerhayes, D. L., & Suchner, R. W. (1978). Power implications of touch in male-female relationships. *Sex Roles*, *4*, 103-110.

Tieger, T. (1980). On the biological basis of sex differences in aggression. *Child Development*, *51*, 943-963.

Verbrugge, L. M., & Steiner, R. P. (1981). Physician treatment of men and women patients: Sex bias or appropriate care? *Medical Care*, *19*, 609-632.

Vrugt, A., & Kerkstra, A. (1984). Sex differences in nonverbal communication. *Semiotica*, *50*, 1-41.

Weitz, S. (Ed.). (1974). *Nonverbal communication: Readings with commentary*. New York: Oxford University Press.

Wittig, M. A., & Skolnick, P. (1978). Status versus warmth as determinants of sex differences in personal space. *Sex Roles*, *4*, 493-503.

Zuckerman, M., DeFrank, R. S., Spiegel, N. H., & Larrance, D. T. (1982). Masculinity-femininity and encoding of nonverbal cues. *Journal of Personality and Social Psychology*, *42*, 548-556.

8

Women's Ways of Knowing

ON GAINING A VOICE

NANCY RULE GOLDBERGER
BLYTHE McVICKER CLINCHY
MARY FIELD BELENKY
JILL MATTUCK TARULE

Nancy Rule Goldberger is currently a Visiting Scholar at the Research Center for Mental Health at New York University. She coauthored the book *Women's Ways of Knowing: The Development of Self, Voice, and Mind,* with Belenky, Clinchy, and Tarule (Basic Books, 1986). She has been a Research Associate and Psychotherapist at the Austen Riggs Center in Stockbridge, MA. Her interest in developmental epistemology began during her years as Director of Research on Adolescent Development at Simon's Rock of Bard College, an innovative B.A. program for high school-age students.

Blythe McVicker Clinchy is Professor of Psychology at Wellesley College. Her research concerns the development of "natural epistemologies"—conceptions of knowledge, truth, and value—in children and adults, and the implications of epistemological development for education from the preschool through college years.

Mary Field Belenky is an Associate Professor of Psychology at the University of Vermont, where she directs Listening Partners, a program designed to promote the epistemological development of isolated rural women who are raising children alone. She conducted a study of abortion decisions with Carol Gilligan and wrote a doctoral dissertation on the role of conflict in development.

Jill Mattuck Tarule is an Associate Professor at the Lesley College Graduate School and is Director of the Weekend Learning Community. She has devoted her career to faculty development and educational programs designed to sponsor the development of adult students. She is a former dean of the graduate program at Goddard College.

We do not think of the average person as preoccupied with such difficult and profound questions as, "What is truth?" "What is authority?" "What counts for me as evidence?" "How do I know what I know?" Yet, to ask ourselves these questions and to reflect on our answers is more than an intellectual exercise, for our basic assumptions about the nature of truth and the origins of knowledge shape the way we see the world and ourselves as participants in it. In this chapter we describe five different perspectives from which women view reality and draw conclusions about truth, knowledge, and authority. Our description is based on extensive interviews with rural and urban American women of different ages, class and ethnic backgrounds, and educational histories. We examine how women's self-concepts and ways of knowing are intertwined. We describe how women struggle to gain a voice and claim the power of their own minds.[1]

In the course of our prior work on student development (Belenky, Tarule, & Landa, 1979; Clinchy, Lief, & Young, 1977; Clinchy & Zimmerman, 1975, 1982, 1985a, 1985b; Goldberger, 1978, 1981, 1985; Tarule & Weathersby, 1979), we became concerned about why women students spoke so frequently of problems and gaps in their learning and so often expressed doubts about their intellectual competence. We observed that women often felt alienated in academic settings and experienced formal education as peripheral or irrelevant to their central interests and development. Although men, particularly members of minority groups, may also find the educational process alienating, anecdotal reports as well as research on sex differences point to special factors in the alienation of women. Girls and women tend to have more difficulty than boys and men in asserting their authority or considering themselves as authorities (Clance & Imes, 1978; Clinchy & Zimmerman, 1982; Cross, 1968; Maccoby & Jacklin, 1974; Piliavin, 1976; West & Zimmerman, 1983), in expressing themselves in public so that others will listen (Aries, 1976; Eakins & Eakins, 1976; Piliavin, 1976; Sadker & Sadker, 1982, 1985; Swacker, 1976; Thorne, 1979), in gaining respect of others for their minds and their ideas (Hagen & Kahn, 1975; Hall & Sandler, 1982; Serbin, O'Leary, Kent, & Tonick, 1973) and in fully utilizing their capabilities and training in the world of work (Gallese, 1985; Kanter, 1977; Ruddick & Daniels, 1977; Sassen, 1980; Treichler & Kramarae, 1983).

In private and professional life, as well as in the classroom, women often feel unheard even when they believe that they have something important to say. Most women can recall incidents in which they or their female friends were discouraged from pursuing some line of intellectual work on the grounds that it was unwomanly or incompatible with female capabilities. Many female students and working women are painfully aware that men succeed better than they in getting and holding the attention of others for their ideas and opinions. All women, like it or not, grow up having to deal with historically and culturally engrained definitions of femininity and womanhood—one common theme being that women, like children, should be seen, not heard.

We believe that education, as it is traditionally defined and practiced, does not adequately serve the needs of women students and is unresponsive to women's doubts about their competence and worth. Most of our major educational institutions were originally founded by men for the education of men. Even girls' schools and women's colleges have been modeled after male institutions to give women an education "equivalent" to men's (Horowitz, 1984). In spite of the increase in the number of women students in higher education and professional schools, faculties, usually predominantly male, have argued against a special focus on women students and resisted open debate on whether women's educational needs are different from men's. Even when the content of coursework includes issues of concern to women, strategies of teaching and methods of evaluation are rarely examined by faculty to see if they are compatible with women's preferred styles of learning. Usually faculty assume that pedagogical techniques developed by and for men are suitable for women.

Conceptions of knowledge and truth that are accepted and articulated today have been shaped throughout history by the male-dominated majority culture. Up until recently women have played a relatively minor role as theorists in philosophy, the sciences, and social sciences. Indeed, recent feminist writers have convincingly argued that there is a masculine bias at the very heart of most academic disciplines, methodologies, and theories (Bernard, 1973; Gilligan, 1979, 1982; Harding & Hintikka, 1983; Jansen-Jurreit, 1980; Keller, 1978, 1985; Langland & Grove, 1981; Sherman & Beck, 1979). Yet, our accepted concepts of truth, knowledge, and the nature of proof have been left unexamined by most social scientists and educators and have had consequences for how we all, male and female alike, learn, establish criteria and methods for unearthing "truth," and evaluate those who claim to know. It is likely that the commonly accepted stereotype of women's thinking as emotional, intuitive, and personalized has contributed to the devaluation of women's minds and contributions, particularly in Western, technologically oriented cultures that value rationalism and objectivity (Sampson, 1978). It is generally assumed that intuitive knowledge is more primitive, therefore less valuable, than so-called objective modes of knowing. In general, both men and women are taught to value what is assumed to be the objective "male mind" and to devalue "female intuition."

Even after the onset of the women's movement, research studies and critical essays on gender and intelligence have tended to focus more on the demonstration of women's intellectual comparability to men and have minimized gender differences. By and large, these studies have shown that women are the equals of men in intellectual aptitude and academic performance (for reviews of this literature, see Maccoby & Jacklin, 1974; Rosenberg, 1982). However, relatively little attention has been given to modes of learning, knowing, and valuing that may be especially common among women. As Gilligan has pointed out (1979), women have been missing even as research subjects at the formative stages of our psychological theories. If and when scientists turn to the study of women, they typically look for ways in which women conform to or diverge from patterns found in the study of men. Thus psychological theory has established men's experience and competence as a baseline against which both men's and women's development is judged, often to the detriment or misreading of women. From past research, we have learned a great deal about the development of autonomy and independence, abstract critical thought, and the unfolding of a morality of rights and justice in both men and women. We have learned less about the development of attributes typically associated with the female: interdependence, intimacy, nurturance, and contextual thought (Bakan, 1966; Chodorow, 1978; Gilligan, 1979, 1982; McMillan, 1982).

When the woman's voice is included in the study of human development, women's lives and qualities are revealed and the maps that chart the life cycle can be redrawn. Once these qualities are observed and acknowledged, we are more likely to observe their unfolding in the lives of men as well. The power of the woman's voice in expanding our conceptions of epistemology and development is amply illustrated in Gilligan's (1982) work, which influenced our own thinking. By listening to girls and women resolve serious moral dilemmas in their lives, Gilligan has traced the development of a morality organized around notions of responsibility and care. This conception of morality contrasts sharply with the morality of rights described by Piaget (1965) and Kohlberg (1984), which is based on the study of the evolution of moral reasoning in boys and men. In recent work, Gilligan and Lyons (Lyons, 1983) have extended their study of gender-related differences in moral perspectives to the area of identity development. They have shown that a responsibility orientation tends to be more central to those whose conceptions of self are rooted in a sense of connection and a caring concern for others whereas a rights orientation is more common to those who experience relationships in terms of objective fairness between separate individuals. Lyons found that many more women than men define themselves in terms of their connected relationships to others, a point that has also been made by Chodorow (1978) and Miller (1976).

In addition to Gilligan's work, the work of Perry (1970, 1981) on developmental epistemology influenced our thinking. Based on interviews gathered each spring from male students as they moved through their undergraduate years at Harvard, Perry describes how students' conceptions of the nature and origins of knowledge evolve and how their understanding of themselves as knowers changes over time. Perry depicts a passage through a sequence of epistemological perspectives that he calls "positions." It is through these coherent interpretive frameworks that students give meaning to their educational experience. Perry traces a progression from an initial position, which he calls *basic dualism*— where the student views the world in polarities of right/wrong, black/white, we/they, and good/bad—through a position called *multiplicity*—in which the student perceives multiple perspectives on truth— to a position at which the *relativism* of all knowledge is recognized. Perry does not claim that his positions represent an invariant developmental sequence or stages; however, he does believe that each position "both includes and transcends the earlier ones" (1981, p. 78).

The Perry scheme stimulated our interest in modes of knowing and provided us with our first images of the paths women might take as they develop an understanding of their intellectual potential, as well as providing a description of the routes most often taken by men. Our work uncovers themes, epistemological perspectives, and catalysts for development that are prominent among women, but sketchy or missing in Perry's version of male development.

In summary, two major concerns led us to our current research on women's epistemology: (1) women appear to have difficulties in assuming authority and valuing their own minds, and (2) women's modes of thought and experience as knowers have been inadequately investigated. We believe that, until there is a better understanding of how women think and experience themselves as developing beings, families, educators, employers, and others who live and work with women will continue to be ill-informed about what women know and need to know.

THE ANALYSIS OF THE WOMEN'S INTERVIEWS

Our data consist of extensive interviews with 135 women of varied class and ethnic backgrounds drawn from three private liberal arts colleges, an inner-city community college, an urban public high school, a B.A. program for adults, and three rural human service agencies. The women ranged in age from 16 to 65; some were single or divorced, others married; many had borne and raised children.

Our open-ended interview was designed to investigate the respondent's structure of thought as well as her attitudes. The interview is similar in form to the Piagetian clinical interview that has been adopted in the research of many cognitive-developmentalists such as Perry (1970), Kohlberg (1984; Colby et al., 1983), and Gilligan (1977, 1982). Interviews were tape-recorded and transcribed; they ran from two to five hours in length. Because of our prior research at some of the sites, we had more than one interview with 40 women in our sample, obtained anywhere from one to five years apart.

We told each participant that we were interested in her experience—and in women's experience—because it had been so often excluded as people sought to understand human development. We told her that we wanted to hear what was important about life and learning from her point of view. Each interview began with a question adapted from Perry's research—"Looking back, what stands out for you over the past few years?"—and proceeded gradually at the woman's own pace to questions concerning self-image, relationships of importance, education and learning, real-life decision making and moral dilemmas, accounts of personal change and growth, perceived catalysts for change and impediments to growth, and visions of the future. Embedded in the interview were also standard questions adapted from Kohlberg and Gilligan to elicit moral reasoning and concepts of self, and questions we developed for eliciting epistemological assumptions.

We used two approaches in analyzing the interviews. First, we separated out the section of the interview that was designed to yield information on epistemology. This section was scored by coders who were unaware of the woman's age, ethnicity, social class, institutional base, and other factors. We found that the women's thinking did not fit so neatly into Perry's positions. After much discussion about disagreements in scoring, and then about Perry's classification system itself, we decided to regroup and rename the epistemological perspectives to capture more adequately women's ways of knowing. We identified, in our group of women, five major epistemological perspectives or positions that are built upon Perry's, but also diverge from them. They are (1) Silence, (2) Received Knowledge, (3) Subjective Knowledge, (4) Procedural Knowledge, and (5) Constructed Knowledge. These will be described in the next section.

The question of why and when women shift from one mode of knowing to another, as many of our women evidently did at points in their life, is an important one, but is not answered conclusively with our data, which are, for the most part, limited to single interviews with individuals. Nevertheless, based on the repeated interviews available to us and the retrospective accounts of the women, it appears that, when context is held constant (for example, women of similar backgrounds studying at similar institutions), there is a developmental progression across the last four positions in the order we describe them. We believe, however, that it is premature to consider our five positions as stages, particularly as our data suggest that many women do not seem to follow this developmental sequence.

Our second approach to data analysis was what we called the *contextual analysis*. After coding the interviews for epistemological perspective, we reassembled the interviews and read and reread them in their entirety. Gradually we developed a number of additional coding categories (see Belenky et al., 1986, for a description), designed to capture the ways in which women construe their experience of themselves as developing beings and experience their learning environment. During this part of the interview analysis, we stayed alert to the socioeconomic realities of each woman's life. We tried to enter the woman's world so that we might get close to her experience. We asked ourselves, "What problems is this woman trying to solve? What is adaptive about the way she is trying to accommodate to the world as she sees it? What are the forces—psychological or social—that expand or limit her horizons? What are the growth metaphors that she uses to depict her experience of development?"

One growth metaphor in particular reverberated throughout the women's stories of their intellectual and ethical development. Again and again the women spoke of "gaining a voice," by which they meant gaining a sense of having something worthwhile to say and feeling the security within themselves to say it. As these women described their struggle to gain a voice, they also told us much about silence and listening, often using phrases such as "being silenced," "not being heard," "really listening," "words as weapons," "feeling deaf and dumb," "having no words," "saying what you mean," "listening to be heard," and so on in an endless variety of connotations all having to do with sense of authority and self-worth and feelings of isolation from or connection to others.

The tendency we observed for women to ground their epistemo-logical premises in metaphors suggesting speaking and listening is at odds with the visual metaphors—such as equating knowledge with illumination, knowing with seeing, and truth with light—that scientists and philosophers most often use to express their sense of mind. Keller and Grontkowski (1983), tracing the metaphorical uses of vision in the history of Western intellectual thought, argue that such analogies have led to a favored cultural model for truth and the quest for mind. Visual metaphors, such as "the mind's eye," suggest a camera passively recording a static reality and promote the illusion that disengagement and objectification are central to the construction of knowledge. Visual metaphors encourage standing at a distance to get a proper view, removing—it is believed—subject and object from a sphere of possible intercourse.

By holding close to women's experience of voice, we have come to understand conceptions of the mind that are different from those held by individuals who find "the mind's eye" a more appropriate metaphor for expressing their experience with the intellect. For women, a sense of voice and a sense of mind appear to be intricately intertwined.

THE EPISTEMOLOGICAL POSITIONS: WOMEN'S WAYS OF KNOWING

Silence

Only a few women fell into this category at the time of the interview. None of these women was currently in school; all were minimally educated. Although the designation "silence" is not parallel to the terms we have chosen for other epistemological positions, we selected it because the absence of voice in these women is so salient. This position, though rare, at least in our sample, is an important anchoring point for our epistemological scheme, representing an extreme in denial of self and dependence on external authority for direction.

Women at this position are utterly subject to the power and aggression of others. They are dwarfed by authority. Whereas they experience themselves in the world as passive, reactive, and dependent, they see all authorities as being powerful, if not omnipotent. Blind obedience to authorities is seen as being of utmost importance for "keeping out of trouble" and ensuring one's survival. One woman, who grew up in a family with a physically and sexually abusive father, said, "I spent my life, until recently, keeping quiet and looking for a safe place to hide."

Although these women view authorities, generally male, as omnipotent, the power that they see authorities as holding is not communicated through words imbued with shared meanings. Authorities seldom tell you what they want you to do. They apparently expect you to know in advance. If authorities do tell you what is right, they never tell you why it is right.

The references these women make to language suggest that words are not perceived as a means of communication, but as weapons. Authorities have used words to attack them, to denigrate, or to keep them in place. Using words to protest the actions of others—that is, "speaking out"—is to court danger and retaliation. Silence is the best policy. There is little evidence that these silent women actively listen to the content of authorities' voices. It is as if command and action are undifferentiated: to hear is to obey. One woman explained why her abusive husband ruled the roost: "You know, I used to hear his words, and his words kept coming out of my mouth. He had me thinking that I didn't know anything."

These women are not preverbal. Each has developed language. Yet their experience using language has been so limited they have not explored the power that words have for expressing or developing thought. To look for meaning in the words of others or to share one's experience with words seems impossible. Trying to talk to others typically leaves them feeling "deaf and dumb." They may sense that truth is passed from one person to another in the form of words, but they feel left out of the process and incapable of understanding what others know. Seeing themselves as incapable of receiving and retaining truths from others' words, or of having ideas of their own, they are dependent on the continual presence of authorities to guide their actions if they are not to be ruled by impulse. New situations evoke paralysis and the need to cling to others, too often to violent and deprecatory men. Some women speak of clinging to other women—mothers, aunts, friends—whom they feel have lived through similar experiences and share their plight.

Learning in traditional educational settings has been traumatic for them and only reinforced their image of themselves as stupid. They claim that only demonstration helps them to learn: "Someone has to show me—not tell me—or I can't get it." Their thought is utterly dependent on concrete everyday actions and experience. Even their self-definition is embedded in concrete action. In response to our question, "How would you describe yourself to yourself?" they tended to describe themselves in terms of geographic space (if they could answer at all): "I am a person who likes to stay home. Before I got pregnant, I used to describe myself as not being home."

The world of the silent or silenced seems a static and unchangeable place to those within it. With language and thought so limited to the immediate and concrete, they have little ability to anticipate a different future. That anyone should emerge from their childhood years, into a modern society, with so little confidence in their meaning-making and meaning-sharing abilities signals the failure of the community to nurture all those entrusted to its care. To us, the situation of these women seemed to be in part the result of a cultural stereotype of femininity gone awry and at its most pernicious. These are women living in the worst imaginable social conditions as victims of physical abuse, incest, and neglect. Although the silent are by no means the only women in our sample who have experienced sexual and physical abuse, they are notable for their inability to speak out in protest.

Received Knowledge: Learning
Through Listening to Others

At this position women are also oriented to authority outside themselves but believe that close attention to the words and wisdom of others is central to the knowing process. They conceive of themselves as capable of receiving, but not of creating, knowledge. The origins of knowledge lie outside the self. Because these women are subject to the standards, directions, and authority of others, they are conventional in the sense that they adhere to the prevailing cultural stereotypes and expectations of women. They rely on the words of others for self-knowledge; thus self-concept is organized around social expectations and roles. Approximately 9% of our sample are in this category. This perspective was held by some of the youngest women in the sample; many of the older women, in particular those who had returned to school after spending years as homemakers, retrospectively describe themselves in these terms, even though their epistemological outlook may have recently shifted.

When striving to comprehend new ideas, the person at this position discounts the importance of her own experience and actions in the process of knowing. Truth is sought and found in the words of authorities. The woman does not really try to understand or evaluate new ideas. She has little notion of understanding as a process taking place over time. She collects facts, but does not develop opinions. Receiving, retaining, and returning the words of authorities are seen as synonymous with learning. Teachers are always right because ultimately "they can always look up the right answer in a book." Thus even authorities lack the capacity for constructing knowledge. Authorities must receive Truths from the words of even higher authorities.

These women (like Perry's dualists) divide the world into distinctive, polarized categories: true and false, good and evil, black and white, right and wrong. They assume that there is only one right answer to any question. All other answers and all contrary views are automatically wrong. There are no gradations of truth—no grey areas. When faced with controversy, there is for them a category of good authorities who have the right answers and bad ones who are either confused or misled (Perry, 1970, p. 68). Paradox is inconceivable as several contradictory ideas are never imagined to be simultaneously in accordance with fact. Ambiguity is intolerable. To impose oneself in the process of learning is improper: One reads the lines and follows the plot, but one should not read between the lines. People who see things between the lines are making them up. By dichotomizing the world, women at this position appear to value the objective over the subjective. Truth is thought to have a concrete, tangible existence independent of the mind.

From other studies we know that there are males who also see the world from this dichotomized, authority-oriented perspective (Knefel-kamp, Widick, & Parker, 1978; Perry, 1970). However, we believe that there may be a major difference in the way men and women think about authority at this position. Men are taught that they can expect ultimately to join the authorities by virtue of their gender, whereas women do not identify with authority or anticipate being included. Even today it is still relatively rare for women to find authorities of their own sex to serve as models. Leadership in public life still rests predominantly on male shoulders. The schools that these women attend have often ignored the works and achievements of women in developing the curriculum. Their male classmates are more likely to have gotten and held the floor in the classroom. In fact, as Hall and Sandler (1982) have pointed out, the classroom may be experienced as a "chilly" place to women who sense that many teachers do not welcome their words or ideas.

The belief that there is a single right answer and that one can hear it in the words of others encourages women to become aware of and appreciative of their own listening skills. Wanting to do the right thing, but having no opinions of their own to give guidance, they listen to others and shape their behavior to fulfill the expectations and exhortations of others. They come to believe that a good woman listens and lets others do the talking. They listen closely and react to authorities and peers in their immediate community more readily than remote authority. We heard in the stories of our women a theme identified by Gilligan (1982) as characteristic of conventional female morality: that women should devote themselves to the care and empowerment of others while remaining selfless. Many of the women we interviewed had devoted a large part of their lives listening to others, stilling their voices so that others could be heard. Most felt a sense of pride in their response to the needs of others and indeed seemed quite attuned to the nuances and demands of human relationships.

Subjective Knowledge: The Inner Voice

At this position there is an emphasis on the authority within the self, on listening to the inner voice. The words, directives, and admonitions of external authorities fade and lose their power. Truth is defined as personal, private, and subjectively known or intuited.

Most women at this position have a difficult time identifying the source of their knowing, other than that it is within. It is like an inner conviction, a process that bypasses awareness. As one woman said, "I just know. I try not to think because if you trust yourself, you just know the answer." It is clear that these women do not see thought as central to the process of knowing. They do not experience themselves as constructors of truth, but as conduits through which truth emerges. The criterion for truth most often referred to is "what satisfies me" or "what feels right to me." Occasionally women distinguish between truth as feelings that come from within versus ideas that come from without. This differentiation between thinking and feeling may be a consequence of their belief that thinking is not womanly or that thought will destroy the capacity for feeling. Ideas are thus relegated to male authority and as such may or may not have relevance to one's life.

Truth, then, is not universal. Women at this position claim that each person's experience makes her see a different reality from that of any other person. What is more, truth is necessarily a private matter, known only to oneself, and should not be imposed on others. Convergence of truths is possible; however, in the case of disagreement, one's own experience and inner voice are the final arbiters. Another person's opinion may be misguided or disagreeable but there is a tolerance for differences because others "must obviously believe in their opinion." These women recognize that others may disagree with them but seem less concerned than men in persuading others to their point of view, in part because they want to avoid battles that threaten to disrupt relationships. Whereas men claim they "have a right to their opinion" (Perry, 1970), women tend to state more cautiously, "It's just my opinion."

Many women at this position distrust logic, analysis, abstraction, and even language itself, perceiving these as alien territory belonging to men. They tend to argue against and stereotype those experts and remote authorities whom society promotes as holding the keys to truth— teachers, doctors, scientists, men in general. It is as if, after turning inward, they deny strategies for knowing that they perceive as belonging to the masculine world. Some seem never to have learned to use logic and theory as tools for knowing; others imply that they have and have rejected it. Generally they have vague and untested prejudices against a mode of thought that they believe is impersonal, inhuman, or unfeminine and possibly detrimental to their capacity for feeling. They prefer to rely on direct sensory experience and on real interactions and connections with real people—and ultimately on gut response—as a way of informing themselves about the world. Some of these women express a distrust of books and the written word, calling them instruments of oppression that are too often used against women. They prefer to express themselves nonverbally or artistically so as to bypass the categorizing and labeling that language implies.

In our sample, there were a large number of women who viewed reality from the position of subjectivism—46% of all we interviewed. They appeared in every educational and agency setting included in this study and cut across class, ethnic, age, and educational boundaries. What is most remarkable in the stories of our women is that the shift in perspective from adhering to external authority to knowing from the inside is not tied to any specific age or phase. We found that it was the predominant perspective on knowing in women as young as 16 and as old as 60, many of whom claimed that they had only come to this way of knowing very recently.

Women's discovery of the power of inner knowing is experienced as a liberation, and greatly affects changing definitions of the self. Openness to change and novelty is the fulcrum around which their new identity revolves. Many women use the imagery of birth or rebirth to describe their experience of a nascent self.

We believe that a shift into subjectivism is a particularly significant reconceptualization of knowledge for women when and if it occurs. Women's emergent reliance on their intuitive processes is an important move in the service of self-protection, self-assertion, and self-definition. Over half of our large group of subjectivists had recently taken steps to end relationships with lovers or husbands, to reject further obligations to family members, and to move out and away on their own. For these women, subjectivism is a way of knowing that is safe from the dictates of others. It provides the space for a birth of the self without the constraints of social convention and it provides them with a reassuring sense of personal power and authority.

One woman in her 30s described her recent liberation this way:

> Now I only know with my gut. It helps me and protects me. It is perceptive and astute. My gut is my best friend—the one thing in the world that won't let me down or lie to me or back away from me.

Procedural Knowledge: The Voice of Reason

Most of the women in this category—24% of the sample—were attending or had recently graduated from prestigious colleges. Most were privileged, bright, white, and young, ranging in age from late teens to mid-twenties. One can hear in the stories of women in this category how they acquire the tools of reason and attitudes about knowledge that are valued in most of our esteemed institutions of higher education. These are women striving to join the academic elite and the professional public world of men.

All of the women at this position are absorbed in the business of acquiring and applying procedures for obtaining and communicating knowledge. Some seem passionately involved in the process, whereas others seem to treat it as a "game," but the emphasis on procedures, skills, and techniques is common to all. Developing procedures for knowing—such as critical thinking, textual analysis, and scientific method—becomes paramount, as does an emphasis on "learning the way they want you to think" (Perry, 1970, p. 100).

The woman at this position recognizes that some events are open to interpretation, and that some interpretations make better sense than others. Because one's ideas must "measure up" to certain objective standards, one must speak in measured tones, or not speak at all. It is not sufficient to parrot the authorities' words or to blurt out the first thing that comes to mind. One should systematically muster support for one's opinions and be careful not to jump to conclusions.

For most of the women at this position, form predominates over content. It matters less what you think than that you have thought it through thoroughly. The women pride themselves on the skills they acquire. Asked what she valued most about her college education, one woman named her philosophy course.

> I couldn't tell you right now the philosophies of most of the people we studied, but I can tell you how I would set about criticizing their arguments and what types of things you should look for.

Most women in this category retain or regain some trust in authority; authorities are perceived as relatively benign, neither dictatorial nor attacking. Authorities do not offer answers, only techniques for constructing answers. And, most important to the women, they judge, not opinions per se, but the procedures one uses to substantiate opinions. Authorities apparently do not seek to silence but to teach a new language.

However, some of these women, even as they go about developing their intellectual competence and authority, begin to express a deep ambivalence about the institutionalized pressure to conform to normative ideals about the right ways to learn and think. In the process of learning the new academic language, women do come to understand that we can know things that we have never seen or touched, that truth can be shared, and that expertise can be respected. They learn, too, that intuition can deceive and that gut reactions can be irresponsible. They are often told that first-hand experience has no place in the classroom. They are taught to look for general laws, for universal trends, and to avoid personalizing. They are taught that they isolate events and people from contexts in order to arrive at objective evaluations. They are taught to pay attention to objects in the external world, that is, for instance, to the painting itself rather than the feelings a painting arouses in oneself. Most of the women in our sample of procedural knowers have learned these lessons well and have demonstrated that they can excel in academic circles and adversarial debate. Some pride themselves, as the philosopher Sara Ruddick once did, on their "male minds" (Ruddick, 1984, p. 143).

But others speak of a sense of fraudulence about their proven academic abilities and success, feeling that, although they can perform adequately, they have lost a sense of their true selves. They talk about feeling like imposters who no longer aspire to having a male mind. Truth, for them, seems to lie somewhere outside the academy. The voice of reason that they have acquired, though it serves them well, is not necessarily their voice. Nor are the questions asked in academic circles necessarily their questions.

Some of these women have begun to experiment with more "feminine" procedures for knowing, procedures that are more personal and empathic. They speak of learning how to "open oneself up to ideas." The women in the next section have developed these procedures more fully.

Constructed Knowledge: Integrating the Voices

The women in this final category (18% of our sample) are all articulate and reflective people, some quite young, others among the oldest in our sample. All of them were attending or had graduated from college. At some time in their past, they said, they had felt deadened to their inner experience and inner selves; thinking and feeling were split asunder. They told us that their current way of knowing and viewing the world—the way of knowing we call *constructed knowledge*—began as an effort to reclaim the self by attempting to integrate knowledge that they felt intuitively was important with knowledge and methods of knowing that they had learned during their formal education. They had "moved outside the givens" of their social and intellectual world by removing themselves psychologically, and at times even geographically. Their stated intention was to take time out to get to know the self and to reflect on the contexts that confined and defined them. They described the development of a new way of thinking that emphasized not the extrication of the self in the process of knowing but a "letting the inside out and the outside in."

The central insight that distinguishes this position is that all knowledge is constructed and the knower is an intimate part of the known. The woman comes to see that the knowledge one acquires depends on the context or frame of reference of the knower who is seeking answers and on the context in which events to be understood have occurred. One woman put it this way:

> We can assume that something exists out there—but "something" is thinking that something exists. Our consciousness is part of the world. We are creating the world at the time.

Recognizing that everything is relative, these women concern themselves with the basic assumptions that govern the kinds of questions being asked and the methods being used for getting answers. They are aware that even personal truths are a matter of history, circumstance, and timing, and are subject to change. Theories are seen not as truth but as models for approximating experience; theories are "educated guesswork."

Women at this position overcome the notion that there is One Right Answer or a Right Procedure in the search for truth. They see that there are various ways of knowing and methods of analysis. They feel responsibility for examining, choosing, questioning, and developing the systems that they will use for constructing knowledge. Question-posing and problem-posing become prominent methods of inquiry, strategies that some researchers have identified with the "fifth" stage of thought beyond formal-operational or logical thought (Arlin, 1975; Kitchener, 1983; Labouvie-Vief, 1980). The woman tends not to rely as readily or exclusively on hypothetico-deductive inquiry, which posits an answer (the hypothesis) prior to data collection. She prefers to examine the basic assumptions and the conditions in which a problem is cast. She can take, and often insists upon taking, a position outside a particular context or frame of reference and looks back on "who" is asking the question, "why" the question is asked at all, and "how" answers are arrived at.

The way of knowing prized by most constructivist women is anything but detached. For these women, intimate knowledge of the self not only precedes but always accompanies understanding. They are intensely aware of how perceptions are processed through the complex web of personal meaning and values; they resist excluding the self from the process of knowing for the sake of simplicity or "objectivity." They strive to find a way of weaving their passions and their intellectual life into some meaningful whole. All the old polarities—self and others, thought and feeling, subjective and objective, public and private, personal and impersonal, love and work—lose their saliency. The constructivist mode of thought, in women at least, stresses integration and balance and inclusion rather than exclusion and parsimony.

As we noted in the last section, "opening oneself up to ideas" (or people or poems) is stressed by some women as a procedure for knowing, but the relative lack of self-knowledge prevents the procedural knower from finding points of connection between that which she is trying to understand and her own experience. At the position of constructed knowledge, women often describe themselves in terms that denote passionate or "connected knowing"—a union of the knower with that which is to be known. Empathic seeing and feeling with the other is a central feature in the development of connected knowing. The empathic potential—the capacity for what Weil (1951) calls "attentive love" and Ruddick (1980) identifies with "maternal thinking"—is particularly characteristic of constructivist women. They use the language of intimacy and care to describe relationships with ideas as well as with people. Communion and communication are established with that which one is trying to understand. Women use such images as "conversing with nature," "getting closer to ideas," "having rapport with my reading matter," and "communicating with an author" in order to understand, rather than more masculine images such "pinning an idea down," "getting on top of ideas," or "seeing through an argument."

Dialogue is at the center of this way of knowing. A balance is found between speaking and listening. The women here are able to listen to others without silencing their own voice, whereas at other positions they attend to only one or the other. They make a distinction between conversing and what they call "really talking" by which they mean a reciprocal drawing out of each other's ideas and meanings. "Really talking" requires careful listening; it implies a mutually shared agreement that together you are creating the optimum setting so that emergent ideas can grow. This mode of talk is something similar to what Habermas (1973) has called "the ideal speech situation." "Real talk" reaches deep into the experience of each; it also draws on the analytical abilities of each. It is as important in the public as the private sharing of knowledge. To this end, the women strive for an exploration of assumptions and intersubjective reality rather than a one-way didactic stating of views. Domination is absent; reciprocity and cooperation predominate.

These women strive to gain a public as well as a private voice. They want to communicate to others the complexities of the world as they experience it. However, even among women who have found a voice, problems of voice abound. In a society such as ours that values the words of male authority and often dismisses the woman's voice as soft or misguided, constructivist women are no more immune to the experience of feeling silenced than any other group of women.

Needless to say, the women at this position set themselves a difficult task. They want always to be sensitive to context, to include rather than exclude, to listen as often as to speak, to stay open to the ideas of others, to engage in "real talk," and to reevaluate continually their basic assumptions as they acquire knowledge. They do not claim that they always succeed at this task. Most of the women learn to live with compromise and to soften ideals that they find are unworkable. Nevertheless, they set an example of a refreshing mixture of idealism and realism. More than any other group of women, they are seriously preoccupied with the moral or spiritual dimension in their lives. They actively reflect on how their judgments, attitudes, and behavior coalesce into some internal experience of moral consistency. For most of these women, the moral response is a caring response; an opinion is a commitment, something to live by. Further, they strive to translate their moral commitments into action, both out of a conviction that "one must act" and out of a feeling of responsibility to the larger community in which they live.

IMPLICATIONS FOR HUMAN DEVELOPMENT

The epistemological taxonomy that we describe is, at this point in our work, a beginning attempt to understand the variety of perspectives from which women know and view the world. Our descriptive scheme provides a framework for further research on gender similarities and differences in ways of knowing and on life experiences that shape thought. Our study, based on interviews with women, represents both an extension and modification of Perry's scheme of developmental epistemology, which was derived primarily from interviews with Harvard men. We recognize that the five ways of knowing we identify are not necessarily fixed or exhaustive categories; that they are abstract categories that will not always capture the complexities and uniqueness of an individual woman's thought and life; that other people might organize their observations differently; and that the scheme itself awaits further study and validation. The addition of new populations of women might extend the number of categories or lead to their modification. And it will only be with the study of men and women from equally mixed class, ethnic, and educational backgrounds that comparisons between the sexes can be made.

In spite of these cautions, we believe that our study does allow us to raise important questions about women's development and thought and to draw some conclusions. It also provides a firmer grounding than existed before for speculation about when and why women's concepts of self and ways of knowing change.

Because we approached this study with questions about women's sense of competence and authority, we paid particular attention to that part of their stories that dealt with their experience in two of the major social institutions that affect human development: families and schools. In their struggle to develop their voices and minds and hold onto their values in a society that tends to devalue women and their ideas, many women falter, deny their potential and values, accommodate to the views and expectations of others, and suffer from feelings of inauthenticity and/or powerlessness. Some women find their way out of the morass of accommodations, retreat, and self-denial largely on their own initiative, but sometimes with the help of perceptive, responsive families and schools or social agencies.

The women's interviews were, of course, quite diverse, but as we read and reread their accounts of what they had learned and failed to learn, of how they liked to learn and were forced to learn, some common themes emerged, themes that may be distinctly, although surely not exclusively, feminine. We shall touch briefly on some of these themes here; we develop them more fully elsewhere (Belenky et al., 1986).

Confirmation of the Self as a Knower

Our interviews have convinced us that every woman, regardless of age, social class, ethnicity, and academic achievement, needs to know that she is capable of intelligent thought, and needs to know it sooner rather than later. Many women told us of personal incidents of being doubted, overlooked, and teased for their intellectual efforts even in well-intentioned families and schools. Several women spoke of the ambiguity inherent in male professors' praise for women students, of the "games" into which male professors and female students fall. They wonder, "Am I a student or a flirtation? Am I smart or does he want something else from me?"

Women who attended the more prestigious colleges in the sample and who had a history of privilege and achievement were still uncertain of their abilities. Achievement did not protect them from self-doubt. The need for confirmation was even more prominent among the less privileged women, many of whom had grown up being told they were stupid. Their views of themselves began to change when they came across "maternal" social agencies that refused to treat them as dumb. What these women needed and what the agencies provided—perhaps more clearly, consistently, and sincerely than any other institutions we sampled—was confirmation that they could be trusted to know, to learn, and to share this knowledge with others. For these women to discover that they had opinions and experience of value to others was a lesson that they had missed during all their years of formal education. Most of the women we interviewed, rich and poor, educated or not, made it clear that they did not wish to be told merely that they had the "capacity" or the "potential" to become knowledgeable or wise. They needed to know that they already knew something (though by no means everything), that there was something good inside. They worried that there wasn't.

In the masculine myth, confirmation comes not at the beginning of education but at the end. Confirmation as a thinker and membership in a community of thinkers come as the climax of Perry's (1970) story of intellectual development in the college years. The student learns, according to Perry, that "we must all stand judgment" and must earn "the privilege of having [our] ideas respected" (p. 33). Having proved beyond reasonable doubt that he has learned to think in complex, contextual ways, the young man is admitted to the fraternity of powerful knowers. Certified as a thinker, he becomes one of Them (now dethroned to lower-case them). This scenario may capture the "natural" course of men's development in traditional, hierarchical institutions, but it does not work for women. For women, confirmation and community are prerequisites rather than consequences of development.

Collaboration, Community, and Trust

Most women say they learn best in groups and prefer collaborative work. When they are isolated from those who know by a wall of silence or status, their talents for learning through the drawing out of others are left untapped. Opportunities to match experiences, reveal insecurities and obtain reassurance, and try out ideas without fear of ridicule are possible where trust exists. And trust exists in classrooms and groups in which the "believing" rather than "doubting" game is played (Elbow, 1973). As Elbow says, the doubting game involves "putting something on trial to see whether it is wanting or not" (p. 173). The teacher or student playing the doubting game looks for something wrong—a loophole, a factual error, a logical contradiction, an omission of contrary evidence. Good teachers and good parents, according to women, are believers. They trust their students' or children's thinking and encourage them to expand it.

But in the psychological literature concerning the factors promoting cognitive development, doubt has played a more prominent role than belief. People are said to be precipitated into states of cognitive conflict when, for example, their ideas are challenged by some external event, and the effort to resolve conflict leads to cognitive growth. We do not deny that cognitive conflict can act as an impetus to growth; all of us can attest to such experiences in our own lives. But in our interviews only a handful of women described a powerful and positive learning experience in which the teacher aggressively challenged their notions. Because so many women are already consumed with self-doubt, doubts imposed from outside seem at best redundant ("I'm always reprimanding myself") and at worst destructive, confirming women's own sense of themselves as inadequate knowers. The doubting model of teaching, then, may be particularly inappropriate for women, although we are not convinced that it is appropriate for men either.

Firsthand Experience

In considering how to design an education appropriate for women, suppose we were to begin by asking, simply: What does a woman know? Traditional courses do not begin there. They begin not with the student's knowledge but with the teacher's knowledge. Most of the women we interviewed, however, were drawn to the sort of knowledge that comes from firsthand observation, whereas most of the institutions they attended emphasized abstract out-of-context learning. The women spoke as often of the way students interacted in classes as of the course content; they were often more concerned about another's pride or shame than whether he or she supplied good answers; they were relieved when they could find some connection between the course material and their own experience.

For many women, the most powerful learning experiences took place out of school. The mothers usually named childbearing or child-rearing. The kind of knowledge that is gained in child-rearing is typical of the kind of knowledge that women value and schools do not. Ruddick (1980) has argued that "maternal thought" has rules of evidence and criteria for truth, just as do more esteemed modes of thought accepted within academic disciplines. The knowledge of mothers comes not from words but from action and observation, and much of it has never been translated into words, only into actions. As the philosopher Carol McMillan (1982) has noted, this kind of knowledge does not necessarily lead to general propositions. Good mothering, for instance, requires adaptive responding to changing phenomena; it is tuned to the concrete and particular. Mothers are understandably hesitant about "concocting theories about how other people should bring up their children" (McMillan, 1982). Most women are not opposed to abstraction per se. They find concepts useful as ways of making sense of their experiences, but they balk when the abstractions precede the experiences or push them out entirely. Even the women who were extraordinarily adept at abstract reasoning preferred to start with personal experience.

It should come as no surprise that the courses most often mentioned by women as powerful learning experiences were those that helped them translate private experience into a shared public language (for instance, courses on feminist theory or courses requiring the sharing of journals) and courses that provided experiential opportunities (for instance, collecting interviews from old-timers in the study of small-town life or comanaging a student theatrical group).

Models for Learning: Sharing and Listening

There is considerable evidence that parents who enter into a dialogue with their children, who draw out and respect their children's opinions, are more likely to have children whose intellectual and ethical development proceeds rapidly and surely (Baumrind, 1971; Haan, Smith, & Block, 1968; Hauser et al., 1984; Lickona, 1983). Among our women, only the constructivists and a few procedural knowers described both parents as good listeners. Most women at the other positions came from families in which relationships among family members were hierarchical, with talking and listening unevenly divided between the members. Typically the husband spoke, the women and children listened. In these conventionally ordered families, fathers were depicted as being more like conventional teachers—bent on handing out truths; mothers were more like students—listening and trying to understand. The daughters from such families described themselves as students in much the same terms—obediently attentive students before all-wise lecturers. Constructivists, however, painted a different picture of their families and had a different vision of what makes a good teacher. They noticed and valued mothers who had gained a voice and fathers who had developed a listening ear. So, too, these women valued teachers who showed that they could both think and feel, that they could both speak and listen, that they could both teach and learn.

It can be argued, of course, that students need models of impeccable reasoning, that it is through imitating such models that students learn to reason. Perhaps. But none of the women we interviewed named this sort of learning as a powerful experience in their own lives. They did mention deflation of authority as a powerful learning experience. Women have been taught by generations of men that males have greater powers of rationality than females have. When a male professor presents only the impeccable products of his thinking, it is especially difficult for a woman student to believe that she could have produced such a thought. And it must be remembered that in spite of the women's movement, most of the teachers are still male, although more than half of the students are now female. Female students need opportunities to watch how female professors solve (and fail to solve) problems and male professors fail to solve (and succeed in solving) problems. They need role models of thinking as a human activity—as imperfect, yet attainable.

GROWTH AND CHANGE

Based on our research, it appears that women's intellectual growth and shifts in self-concept and worldview are often tied to events beyond classroom and parental teaching—events such as child-bearing and child-rearing, crises of self-doubt and feelings of inauthenticity, value conflicts in relationships, and the failure of male authority on whom the woman has depended. The fact that even well-intentioned families and teachers can hinder, as well as support, women's development has led us to question conventional assumptions about the education of women. In this chapter, we have touched on some correctives to educational practice that would benefit women, and perhaps men as well.

Significant developmental change, according to women's retrospective accounts, often occurs in middle adulthood. These transition points are accompanied by major shifts in the woman's assessment of her value, options, goals, and responsibilities. Most women experience a tremendous sense of growth as they begin to move away from silence and social stereotypes and rely on inner resources for knowing. For some, subjective knowing may be a stopping point and the predominant epistemology for much of their lives because reliance on inner authority provides a security that they need and hold on to. Other women, who have also come to value the power of rational and objective thought, gain a new sense of internal cohesion when they can find ways to balance subjective/intuitive and objective/rational knowledge. It is clear from our data that women's sense of self and voice flourish when they become what we call connected and passionate knowers. We argue that educators can help women develop their minds and authentic voices if they emphasize connection over separation, understanding and acceptance over assessment, collaboration over competition, and discussion over debate, and if they accord respect to and allow time for the knowledge that emerges from first-hand experience. We have learned these things by listening to the woman's voice.

NOTE

1. This chapter is adapted from our book, *Women's Ways of Knowing: The Development of Self, Voice, and Mind* (Basic Books, 1986). An earlier version of the chapter was presented in July 1985 at the Eighth Biennial Meeting of the International Society of Behavioral Development in Tours, France. The research was supported by a grant (#G008005071) from the Fund for the Improvement of Post Secondary Education, Department of Education.

REFERENCES

Aries, E. (1976). Interaction patterns and themes of male, female, and mixed groups. *Small Group Behavior, 7*, 7-14.

Arlin, P. (1975). Cognitive development in adulthood. *Developmental Psychology, 11*, 602-606.

Bakan, D. (1966). *The duality of human existence.* Boston: Beacon Press.

Baumrind, D. (1971). Current patterns and parental authority. *Developmental Psychology Monographs, 4*, (1, Pt. 2).

Belenky, M., Clinchy, B., Goldberger, N., & Tarule, J. (1986). *Women's ways of knowing: The development of self, voice, and mind.* New York: Basic Books.

Belenky, M., Tarule, J., & Landa, A. (Eds.). (1979). *Education and development.* Washington, DC: National Teachers Corp.

Bernard, J. (1973). My four revolutions: An autobiographical history of the American Sociological Society. *American Journal of Sociology, 78*, 773-791.

Chodorow, N. (1978). *The reproduction of mothering.* Berkeley: University of California Press.

Clance, P. R., & Imes, S. A. (1978). The imposter phenomenon in high achieving women: Dynamics and therapeutic intervention. *Psychotherapy: Theory, Research, and Practice, 15*, 241-247.

Clinchy, B., Lief, J., & Young, P. (1977). Epistemological and moral development in girls from a traditional and a progressive high school. *Journal of Educational Psychology, 69*, 337-343.

Clinchy, B., & Zimmerman, C. (1975). *Cognitive development in college.* Unpublished manuscript, Wellesley College.

Clinchy, B., & Zimmerman, C. (1982). Epistemology and agency in the development of undergraduate women. In P. Perum (Ed.), *The undergraduate woman: Issues in educational equity.* Lexington, MA: D. C. Heath.

Clinchy, B., & Zimmerman, C. (1985a). *Connected and separate knowing.* Paper presented at the Eighth Biennial Meeting of the International Society of Behavioral Development, July, Tours, France.

Clinchy, B., & Zimmerman, C. (1985b). Growing up intellectually: Issues for college women. *Work in Progress,* #19. Wellesley, MA: Stone Center for Developmental Services and Studies.

Colby, A., Kohlberg, L., Candee, D., Gibbs, J. C., Hewer, R., Kaufman, K., Power, C., & Speicher-Dubin, B. (1983). *Assessing moral judgments: A manual.* New York: Cambridge University Press.

Cross, P. (1968). College women: A research description. *Journal of the National Association of Women Deans and Counselors, 32,* 12-21.

Eakins, B., & Eakins, G. (1976). Verbal turn-taking and exchanges in faculty dialogue. In B. L. Dubois & I. Crouch (Eds.), *The sociology of the language of American women.* San Antonio, TX: Trinity University.

Elbow, P. (1973). *Writing without teachers.* London: Oxford University Press.

Gallese, L. R. (1985). *Women like us.* New York: Morrow.

Gilligan, C. (1977). In a different voice: Women's conceptions of self and of morality. *Harvard Educational Review, 47,* 431-446.

Gilligan, C. (1979). Woman's place in man's life cycle. *Harvard Educational Review, 49,* 431-446.

Gilligan, C. (1982). *In a different voice: Psychological theory and women's development.* Cambridge, MA: Harvard University Press.

Goldberger, N. (1978). Breaking the educational lockstep: The Simon's Rock experience. In P. E. Kaylor (Ed.). *The early college in theory and practice.* Great Barrington, MA: Simon's Rock.

Goldberger, N. (1981). *Meeting the developmental needs of college students.* Final report to The Fund For the Improvement of Post Secondary Education (FIPSE). Great Barrington, MA: Simon's Rock of Bard College.

Goldberger, N. (1985). *Women's epistemology: An empirical scheme.* Paper presented at the Eighth Biennial Meeting of the International Society of Behavioral Development, July, Tours, France.

Haan, N., Smith, M. B., & Block, J. (1968). The moral reasoning of young adults: Political-social behavior, family background, and personality correlates. *Journal of Personality and Social Psychology, 10,* 183-201.

Habermas, J. (1973). *Legitimation crisis.* Boston: Beacon Press.

Hagen, R. I., & Kahn, A. (1975). Discrimination against competent women. *Journal of Applied Social Psychology, 5,* 362-376.

Hall, R., & Sandler, B. R. (1982). *The classroom climate: A chilly one for women?* Project on the Status and Education of Women. Washington, DC: Association of American Colleges.

Harding, S., & Hintikka, M. B. (Eds.). (1983). *Discovering reality: Feminist perspectives on epistemology, metaphysics, methodology, and philosophy of science.* Dordrecht, Holland: Reidel.

Hauser, S., Powers, S. I., Noam, G., Jacobsen, A. M., Weiss, B., & Follansbee, D. J. (1984). Familial contexts of adolescent ego development. *Child Development, 55,* 195-213.

Horowitz, H. L. (1984). *Alma mater.* New York: Knopf.

Janssen-Jurreit, M. (1980). *Sexism: The male monopoly on history and thought.* New York: Farrar, Straus, & Giroux.

Kanter, R. M. (1977). *Men and women of the corporation.* New York: Basic Books.

Keller, E. (1978). Gender and science. *Psychoanalysis and Contemporary Thought, 1,* 409-433.

Keller, E. (1985). *Reflections on gender and science.* New Haven, CT: Yale University Press.

Keller, E., & Grontkowski, C. R. (1983). The mind's eye. In S. Harding & M. Hintikka (Eds.), *Discovering reality.* Dordrecht, Holland: Reidel.

Kitchener, K. (1983). Cognition, metacognition, and epistemic cognition: A three-level model of cognitive processing. *Human Development, 26,* 222-232.

Knefelkamp, L. L., Widick, C., & Parker, C. A. (Eds.). (1978). *New directions for student services: Applying new developmental findings* (no. 4). San Francisco: Jossey-Bass.

Kohlberg, L. (1984). *The psychology of moral development.* New York: Harper & Row.

Labouvie-Vief, G. (1980). Beyond formal operations: Uses and limits of pure logic in life-span development. *Human Development, 3,* 141-161.

Langland, E., & Gove, W. (Eds.). (1981). *A feminist perspective in the academy.* Chicago: University of Chicago Press.

Lickona, T. (1983). *Raising good children: Helping your children through the stages of moral development.* New York: Bantam.

Lyons, N. (1983). Two perspectives on self, relationships and morality. *Harvard Educational Review, 53,* 125-145.

Maccoby, E., & Jacklin, C. (1974). *The psychology of sex differences.* Stanford, CA: Stanford University Press.

McMillan, C. (1982). *Women, reason, and nature.* Princeton, NJ: Princeton University Press.

Miller, J. B. (1976). *Towards a new psychology of women.* Boston: Beacon Press.

Perry, W. G. (1970). *Forms of intellectual and ethical development in the college years.* New York: Holt, Rinehart & Winston.

Perry, W. G. (1981). Cognitive and ethical growth: The making of meaning. In A. Chickering (Ed.), *The modern American college.* San Francisco: Jossey-Bass.

Piaget, J. (1965). *The moral judgment of the child.* New York: Free Press. (Original work published 1932)

Piliavin, J. A. (1976). On feminine self-presentation in groups. In J. I. Roberts (Ed.), *Beyond intellectual sexism.* New York: McKay.

Rosenberg, R. (1982). *Beyond separate spheres: Intellectual roots of modern feminism.* New Haven, CT: Yale University Press.

Ruddick, S. (1980). Maternal thinking. *Feminist Studies, 6,* 70-96.

Ruddick, S. (1984). New combinations: Learning from Virginia Woolf. In C. Asher, L. DeSalvor, & S. Ruddick, *Between women.* Boston: Beacon Press.

Ruddick, S., & Daniels, P. (Eds.). (1977). *Working it out.* New York: Pantheon Books.

Sadker, M. P., & Sadker, D. M. (1982). *Sex equity handbook for schools.* New York: Longman.

Sadker, M. P., & Sadker, D. M. (1985, March). Sexism in the schoolroom of the 80's. *Psychology Today,* 54-57.

Sampson, E. E. (1978). Scientific paradigm and social value: Wanted—a scientific revolution. *Journal of Personality and Social Psychology, 36,* 1332-1343.

Sassen, G. (1980). Success anxiety in women: A constructivist interpretation of its source and its significance. *Harvard Educational Review, 50* (1), 13-24.

Serbin, L. A., O'Leary, K. D., Kent, R. N., & Tonick, I. J. (1973). A comparison of teacher response to pre-academic and problem behavior of boys and girls. *Child Development, 44,* 796-804.

Sherman, J., & Beck, E. (Eds.). (1979). *The prism of sex.* Madison: University of Wisconsin Press.

Swacker, M. (1976). Women's verbal behavior at learned and professional conferences. In B. L. Dubois & I. Crouch (Eds.), *The sociology of the languages of American women.* San Antonio, TX: Trinity University.

Tarule, J., & Weathersby, R. (1979, Fall). Adult development and adult learning styles: The message for non-traditional graduate programs. *Alternative Graduate Education: The Journal of Non-Traditional Studies, 4.*

Thorne, B. (1979). *Claiming verbal space: Women, speech, and language in college classrooms.* Paper presented at the Research Conference on Educational Environments and the Undergraduate Woman, Wellesley College, Wellesley, MA.

Treichler, P., & Kramarae, C. (1983). Women's talk in the ivory tower. *Communication Quarterly, 31,* 118-132.

Weil, S. (1951). Reflections on the right use of school studies with a view to the love of god. In S. Weil, *Waiting for God.* New York: Harper Colophon Books.

West, C., & Zimmerman, D. H. (1983). Small insults: A study of interruptions in cross-sex conversations between unacquainted persons. In B. Thorne, C. Kramarae, & N. Henley, *Language, gender and society.* Rowley, MA: Newbury House.

9

Women, Men, and the Dilemma of Emotion

STEPHANIE A. SHIELDS

Stephanie A. Shields is an Associate Professor in the Psychology Department at the University of California, Davis. Her research is concerned with identifying the processes through which socialization has an impact on felt emotion.

> Supporting a presidential candidate for his views on feminine issues shows a lack of political maturity and an overabundance of emotionalism. Most women are more intelligent than that. (Letter to editor, *Time Magazine,* August 15, 1983)

The equation of immaturity and lack of intellect with emotion, made here by an indignant letter writer, is neither unique culturally nor novel historically. Nor is it unique to equate femaleness, in this case the "feminine," with emotion. In fact, the letter stands as a succinct illustration of the pervasive belief in a natural link between the biological fact of femaleness and the irrational presence of emotion.

The stereotype is immediately recognizable, and in an important way it has hindered responsible investigation of how gender and emotion may be related. The stereotype suggests the existence of an essential and inevitable difference between the sexes: Women experience more emotion, more frequently, with less capacity for self-control. Too often the stereotype is not also recognized as a statement about the value of

AUTHOR'S NOTE: Partial support for the original research reported here was provided by a Faculty Research Grant from the University of California, Davis. This chapter was completed while I was sponsored by NSF Visiting Professorships for Women in Science and Engineering grant #R11-8503872. Some of the material on feminist psychology and the dilemma of emotion was originally presented at the meeting of the Association for Women in Psychology, March 1983, Seattle. Special thanks go to Phyllis W. Berman, Beth A. Koster, and Karen (Paige) Erickson for their comments on some of the ideas presented here. I'd also like to thank Scott Brown for his exceptionally able assistance in collecting, coding, and interpreting the "most emotional person" data.

females and the value of emotion. The stereotype is regarded as a literal representation, albeit exaggerated, of some substantive difference in the felt emotion of women and men. Although such a sex-related difference may actually exist, the relationship between gender and emotion is not limited to the domain of experience.

Quite distinct from emotional experience and the processes that explain it is the meaning of "emotion" as a social construct. Most research on emotion, as well as lay understanding of emotion, is based on the tacit assumption that the public meaning of emotion is simply a reflection of the individual's private experience. Explicit references to one's own or another's emotion are fundamentally evaluative, however, and are not necessarily a direct reading of the "true" experienced emotion. An adequate description of the relationship between gender and emotion requires some appreciation of the connection between the subjective "felt" emotion and emotion's social meaning. That is, research must distinguish between emotion as a quality of consciousness and emotion as a cultural construct.

This chapter will examine how the construct of emotion is applied to each sex. The focus is not whether the subjective feeling of emotion or the expression of emotion is different for women and men. Instead, I will consider emotion as a concept and the way that concept is applied differentially by women and men to women and men. The first section considers how and why emotion has been problematic for feminist psychology. In the following sections the dimensions of an emotional double standard are considered in more detail.

FEMINIST PSYCHOLOGY AND
THE DILEMMA OF EMOTION

For the past 15 years feminist psychologists have examined an ever-widening range of topics related to sex and gender. Much effort has gone into developing descriptions and explanations of sex-related differences in cognition, socialization, and sexuality: whether they occur, when they occur, and the processes that might mediate differences. Substantial research attention has been paid to the relationship between gender and various cognitive abilities and social behaviors, in terms of both specific research questions and the broad theoretical problems that frame them (e.g., Wittig & Petersen, 1979).

Despite science's long history of identifying emotion with femaleness (Shields, 1980), feminist psychologists have dealt with emotion only tangentially. In her recently published comprehensive review essay on the psychology of gender, Nancy Henley (1985) discussed all of the research topics currently of importance to the area. Although a number of emotion-related issues (e.g., relationships, fear of success) have received attention, core problems in emotion have been ignored. In a sample of a dozen psychology of gender textbooks published in the last eight years, we found only one that included a section on emotion or emotionality, and it simply summarized popular myths. Books do include a variety of topics with obvious connections to emotion: sex-related differences in depression and anxiety, children's fearfulness and exploratory behavior, and the currently fashionable topic, menstrual cycle effects and Premenstrual Syndrome; but direct examinations of the substance of the emotionality stereotype are missing. A cursory overview of research literature from the past ten years in psychology (excluding clinical practices) shows a similar pattern.

Despite the public's acceptance of the belief that "women are emotional, men are rational," the issue has not been studied empirically by contemporary feminist psychologists. In everyday life the statement is recognized as Natural Law; scientifically it remains untested. Emotion's absence from feminist psychology is noteworthy. It is all the more surprising because emotion is historically important in the field of psychology and is an abiding concern in everyday life.

At least some of the reason for overlooking emotion is the questionable value it is believed to have in human affairs. The prevailing American conception of emotion identifies it with the irrational, primitive, and immature (Averill, 1980; de Sousa, 1980). Emotion is believed to be everything that reason is not. At the same time, however, emotion or specific emotions are sometimes considered highly desirable qualities, for example, when the presence of emotion is interpreted as an indicator of one's sincerity. Feminist researchers are not the only ones unsure about emotion; as a culture we are ambivalent about emotion's value.[1] Another impediment to feminist investigation of emotion until recently has been the state of emotion theory itself. First out of favor with behaviorists, later scorned by the cognitive revolution, the psychology of emotion has only recently begun to enjoy a renascence (see, for example, Shaver, 1984). Even given these liabilities, the major impediment to effective feminist research on emotion is the manner in which we have construed the problem. Feminist psychology has not yet developed an adequate theoretical framework for addressing the fundamental problems of emotion. The classic sex-differences approach, by limiting the questions that can be asked, limits the type of answers that can be obtained. One reason that feminist psychologists have avoided emotion research is the obvious inadequacy of our own questions.

"Who's More Emotional, Men or Women?"

In gender research, the standard way to address the relationship between gender and any particular behavior or quality of personality is to measure how much males and females differ on that particular dimension. Often the identification of a difference is presumed to reflect the presence of some fixed attribute of maleness and femaleness, and efforts to explain the difference are directed exclusively at describing its origin. With the focus on whether differences exist, issues regarding how those differences are moderated fall into the background. Rarely are social behaviors so fixed; instead, they are influenced by a variety of factors—for example, age, social setting—throughout the individual's life span. (See, for example, Berman, 1986, on the effects of parental status on care-giving and attraction to the young.)

There is a long tradition of research employing the sex-differences model, but dissatisfaction with its limitations has been growing (Caplan, MacPherson, & Tobin, 1985; Deaux, 1984; Sherif, 1982) and alternative strategies for recasting gender studies in psychology have been offered (Wittig, 1985). Deaux's analysis of research on gender in psychology came to the conclusion that "sex differences" rarely turn out to be durable, replicable main effects, and those that do may be statistically significant but not important. Deaux cites as an example Hall's (1978) finding that sex-related differences in decoding facial expressions, though pervasive, account for less than 4% of the variance in decoding accuracy. (See also Westbrook, 1974.)

The sex-differences model is particularly unproductive if applied to emotion. It limits us to asking about the quantity of emotion expressed and experienced, thereby implying that psychologically relevant emotional phenomena should be viewed exclusively as capacities of the individual, not as functions of the circumstances in which the individual is behaving. In the case of emotion, the sex-differences model suggests that emotionality is a characteristic of the emotional person, not a function of the meaning of behavior in a particular situation. This model ultimately implies that one sex or the other must be the "more emotional." The dilemma for feminist psychologists is that, by virtue of such quantitative comparison of the sexes, they must choose between the unhappy alternatives of denying the significance of sex-related differences in emotion or defending the value of emotion, an undervalued human capacity historically associated with irrationality, immaturity, and extreme subjectivity. We may not know what a feminist theory of emotion is, but we know what it isn't.

How can the dilemma created by the sex-differences model be overcome? How can we create a feminist psychology of emotion? Clearly the question of gender cannot be limited to the issue of how much women and men differ, but must be recast in more constructive terms. One method of achieving a new view is to reexamine what it is about emotion that we wish to explain. Although some attention has been given to experience and expression of emotion, feminist psychologists have yet to consider what it means to identify a person's experience or behavior as "emotion." That is, instead of developing explanations of emotion/emotionality as a trait—that is, a stable attribute of the individual that exists in some quantity—perhaps we should examine the variables that influence how and when emotion, or explicit acknowledgment of emotion, occurs.

The Social Meaning of Emotion

Another person's interpretation of one's emotion may not coincide with private experience. I can know that you are experiencing emotion only if you tell me about it or I see you express it. But you are not consistently able or willing to tell, and my ability to see emotion in another is not infallibly present; nor is emotion's presence perfectly registered in your behavior. To what extent can men and women truly differ in the quality and quantity of emotion they will experience in identical situations? Does the stereotype of female emotionality actually extend to a difference in what, when, and how much emotion is experienced? These questions regarding felt emotion are legitimate concerns if a complete picture of the emotion-gender link is to be obtained, but they are very difficult to answer. Reports or displays of emotion are invariably affected by socially sanctioned display rules and individual expectations of gender-appropriate experience.

In everyday life, overt acknowledgment of one's own or someone else's emotion does not necessarily correspond to an actual emotion episode. There is incomplete correspondence between an individual's private emotional experience and public reference to that experience. In everyday social situations, explicit labeling of emotions does not always occur as a response to the display of emotion. For example, the employee doesn't remark on the boss's anger as the boss irritably demands that a lost file be located. Likewise, explicit acknowledgment of another's emotion may take place whether or not the emotion is felt or displayed, for example, being told "don't take it so hard" when you really don't care one way or another.

Explicit labeling of emotion is fairly infrequent in normal conversation (Shimanoff, 1985). Furthermore, emotion labels often include an assessment of an emotion's appropriateness or desirability in the situation. Application of an emotion label or overt acknowledgment of emotion is rarely value-neutral. The choice of labels can connote an evaluation of the legitimacy of the state (e.g., "whiny" versus "dissatisfied"; "calm" versus "subdued"). Or the context in which the label is embedded can indicate an evaluation; to point out a colleague's anger publicly at a faculty meeting, for example, is a fairly direct way of questioning his or her degree of self-control.

The evaluative aspect of explicit acknowledgment of emotion is further exemplified by the variety of meanings attached to the vocabulary of emotion. "Emotion" and "emotional" are ambiguous concepts lacking clearly defined boundaries (Shields, 1984). Nevertheless, researchers and lay persons alike presume that there is both consensus and consistency in definition. Even though we may agree that being called "emotional" is rarely a compliment, to what aspect of behavior does the term refer? Is the best definition of emotionality one based on response characteristics (e.g., latency to respond emotionally, magnitude of response, frequency of response, duration of response, rise time, time to return to pre-emotion levels)? Is it a judgment based on situational characteristics (e.g., appropriateness of response to the situation, magnitude of eliciting situation in comparison to response, likelihood that the situation will evoke a response from others)? Or is it based on the quality of the individual's emotional repertoire (e.g., expressiveness, number of distinct emotions expressed, extent to which the individual is concerned with own or others' emotional state, sensitivity to emotional responses of others, accuracy of reading others' emotional responses, tendency to express negative rather than positive emotion)?

IS THERE AN EMOTIONAL DOUBLE STANDARD?

The popular wisdom among feminists is that women's emotions are held against them, particularly in the world of work. At the same time there is agreement that women, by and large, are more free than men to express their feelings, with the possible exception of anger. Is there, in fact, an emotional double standard? That is, given the same circumstances for experiencing and expressing emotion, are those displays of emotionality evaluated differently for men and women? The following sections consider three questions bearing on the extent and impact of an emotional double standard:

(1) What is the emotional person believed to be like? What is it about that person that defines him or her as emotional? Is the emotional man viewed differently from the emotional woman?

(2) What defines the socially acceptable display of emotion? Are the criteria different for women and men? Are women's emotions, in fact, more likely to be construed negatively than positively?

(3) What difference does the stereotype make? Does information concerning gender-related beliefs about emotionality have any wider application in the study of human emotion?

Before turning to these questions I will briefly consider one anomaly in the equation of emotionality with femaleness. Anger is unique among the constellation of common emotions in its identification with males rather than females. The case of anger highlights the cultural basis for perceptions of women and men's emotionality.

Anger, the Not-So-Prototypic Emotion

Sing, Muse, of the anger of Achilles, son of Peleus, that brought countless ills upon the Archaeans. Many a brave soul did it send hurrying down to Hades, and many a hero did it yield a prey to dogs and vultures. (Homer, first line of the *Iliad*)

Treating emotionality as a global tendency overlooks the fact that not all types of emotion are invariably associated with girls and women. The kind of emotionality that psychological research attributes to females is fairly restricted. Whereas dependency, passivity, and sensitivity are emphasized, other affect-related qualities such as sense of humor (Sheppard, 1983), feeling self-confident or feeling superior (Deaux & Lewis, 1983), and creativity are not. For example, the emotional female is not the angry female. Anger or aggressiveness, in contrast to nearly all other specific emotions, is considered a typically male response. The association between anger and maleness, and between other common emotions (e.g., happiness, sadness, fear) and femaleness, has been well learned by preschool age (Birnbaum, Nosanchuck, & Croll, 1980). Another part of the stereotype is the expectation that females will typically find it more difficult than males to give voice to their anger and are more inclined to direct that anger inward, self-destructively (e.g., Doyle & Biaggio, 1981).[2]

The little available information on experiences of anger suggests that the emotion is quite similar for women and men. Averill (1982) found few sex-related differences in people's reports of their everyday experiences of anger. The results of his research suggest that "women become angry as frequently and as intensely as men, for much the same reasons, and with about the same effectiveness" (p. 311). Women did report a greater tendency to feel hurt or cry as a result of anger, but it is not clear whether this was a function of women's tendency to redirect the anger toward themselves or the complexities of the contexts in which they experienced anger. Perhaps subtle or overt responses to the perceived justifiability of anger are responsible for the direction in which women aim their wrath. Perhaps women feel, more often than men, that their legitimate complaints will not result in rectification of injustice.

How is it that emotion in general is associated with femaleness, whereas anger, considered by many a fundamental emotion, is associated with maleness? We can point to many things that could influence the likelihood that anger will be expressed by each sex. For example, it has been suggested that women's apparent lesser willingness to express anger is a function of subordinate status (Tavris, 1984). It is true, in fact, that anger is an emotion of entitlement: To be victim to an injustice is rightly to be incited to anger. The peculiar relationship between power and anger makes it unique. Though an emotion, it has at least one attribute of power that other emotions lack: energy directed outward.

Even if expressive differences are accounted for, anger is still an emotion. Why is male anger not popularly regarded as an indicator of the emotionality of males? What accounts for the different evaluation of the out-of-control male? For example, Achilles' anger is the motivating force in Homer's story of the Trojan War, and despite the destruction and pain it causes, Achilles remains the hero of the story. Anger is distinguished not only by energy level but also by self-justification, which works to legitimize angry feelings and displays. When Agamemnon, who had unjustly taken a female slave from Achilles and thus sparked his anger, finally makes amends, Achilles refuses to accept any responsibility for his own pique (even though it had nearly cost the war) because Agamemnon had wounded his pride as a warrior.

The peculiar relationship of gender to anger (as contrasted with other emotions) aptly illustrates that the concept of emotionality and of specific emotions, as publicly acknowledged phenomena, may have social meanings distinct from subjective experience. If this is the case, we would expect some discrepancy between the emotion the observer describes and the emotions reported by the observed. In the case of anger we would expect to see different criteria applied to evaluating anger displays in each sex. There is, in fact, a large body of anecdotal literature suggesting that occurrences of women's anger in particular kinds of situations are less likely to be deemed appropriate than men's (Tavris, 1982). Some have even suggested that a different vocabulary is used to describe women's anger: for example, petulant, bitchy, out of control, overreacting.[3]

Who Is Emotional?

What do we mean by emotional? According to the dictionary, "emotional" is the condition of showing emotion or being "easily aroused to emotion." Many studies have found that, compared to men, women more readily report that they experience a variety of emotions, value emotional expressiveness in themselves and others, and are emotional (Allen & Haccoun, 1976; Fitzpatrick & Indvik, 1982; Lewis, 1978; Warren & Gilner, 1978). Other research suggests that women are more open on self-report instruments and more willing to admit weaknesses on questionnaires, and this difference in response set may account for some of the reported differences in emotionality. Another factor that may account for differences in men's and women's reports is the different standards used to determine emotionality. When women and men talk about emotion, do they mean the same thing? Do they apply the same criteria when assessing emotionality in persons of each sex?

We asked college undergraduates to think of the most emotional person they knew, and then to answer three questions about that individual. The students were drawn from two courses: an introductory level psychology course (n = 30 men and 58 women) and an upper division course on human emotion (n = 12 men and 64 women). The questions were as follows: (1) What is this person like? What about this person makes you see them as emotional? (2) Describe a particular incident in which this person was very emotional. (3) How well do you know this person? The questions were phrased to eliminate any cues about sex or suggestion that sex of target was a pertinent variable (e.g., deliberate use of "them," the third-person plural pronoun). After completing the questions for this individual, students were asked to think of the most emotional person of the sex opposite to the one originally described. The classes polled contained a much higher proportion of female than male students and this is reflected in the number of subjects of each sex for which information was complete.[4]

One indication of whether females are, in fact, perceived as more emotional can be derived from the sex of the person respondents named first. A large proportion of both men and women named a female first ($p < .0001$, two-tailed binomial test), suggesting that the question of emotion more readily brings females than males to mind (see Table 9.1).

Examination of the relationship between respondents and targets showed that respondents named individuals they currently know or once knew very well. Nearly 80% of all targets were close friends or relatives of the respondent; no respondent named a target who was not known personally. Four people named themselves as "most emotional." A summary of relationships between respondents and targets is contained in Table 9.2. We defined "close relationship" as involving a member of the immediate family, a current or former lover, or anyone else specifically identified as a close or best friend. "Acquaintance" included all others personally known by the subject, but not included in the close relationship category.

The close relationship between target and respondent definitely suggests intimacy between the two individuals, but to what extent can the respondent exert choice in such relationships? It may be that individuals with whom the respondent hasn't maintained a relationship or is coerced into a relationship are labeled as emotional. This would certainly be consistent with the popular idea that emotion is an undesirable quality. We separated targets into those with whom the respondent has some obligatory relationship (family members and roommates) or with whom a relationship was terminated (ex-spouses and -lovers) and those with whom the respondent ostensibly has chosen to continue an association (current friends and lovers and family members defined as friends). There was no difference between the proportion of "most emotional" targets nominated from obligatory relationships and the proportion from chosen relationships.

What is it about the emotional person that caused our respondents to see him or her as emotional? We were particularly interested in comparing references to qualitative versus quantitative aspects of

TABLE 9.1

Sex of Target Named First by Male and Female Respondents
(in percentages)

| | Sex of Target | |
	Male	Female
Sex of respondent		
Male (N = 42)	15.6	84.4
Female (N = 122)	19.0	81.0

TABLE 9.2

Relationship between Respondent and Target
(in percentages)

Targets Described	Female	Male
Self	3.4	1.3
Close relationship		
Mother	3.0	8.1
Father	1.3	—
Other close relative	12.0	8.2
Close friend	51.3	42.5
Roommate	4.3	4.1
Current date/spouse	5.6	5.3
Ex-date/spouse	3.8	2.6
Close unspecified	6.0	8.2
	87.2	79.1
Acquaintance	9.4	19.6
Total	100.0	100.0

NOTE: There were 241 responses from females and 84 responses from males. Numbers are percentages of codable responses.

emotion and descriptions of emotion as appropriate versus inappropriate. Mutually exclusive and exhaustive coding categories were developed from a sample of the responses to Question 1. There were nine final categories used to complete a content analysis of the entire set of responses to this question (see Table 9.3). Interrater reliability was 85%. A summary of the qualities defining the target as a emotional are listed in Table 9.4.

As Table 9.4 shows, magnitude of response was most frequently invoked as the defining quality of emotional persons. Together, "extremity of reaction" and "too big for stimulus" accounted for about half of the descriptions. In our respondents' view, the emotional person

TABLE 9.3
Features Identifying the Target as Emotional:
Coding Categories

Qualitative Features:

Variety of emotions. Emphasis is on the many kinds of emotions occurring in the individual and/or the unpredictability of these. (Emphasis on speed with which emotion changes is coded as Latency.)

Appropriate emotions. Emphasis is on how healthy or socially desirable the individual's emotions are. The target is evaluated positively because of his or her emotional authenticity.

Inappropriate emotions. Emphasis is on negative evaluation of the target because his or her emotions are not appropriate for the situation.

Quantitative Features:

Latency. Emphasis is on the speed with which emotion occurs or changes.

Response is too great for stimulus. Emphasis is on the imbalance between the magnitude of the reaction and the size or gravity of what evokes it. The response must describe the emotion as a reaction to something. (If the emotion is judged to be inappropriate, it is coded under Inappropriate Emotions.)

Extreme reactions. The target's emotional responses are described as strong, but not described as too strong or inappropriate.

Acts Emotional:

Emphasis is on the target's propensity to show off emotionally. Descriptions coded in all other categories assume a positive relationship between expression and experience; descriptions coded here do not make that assumption and may suggest that the emotion is dissembled.

Other:

Insufficient information to identify primary reason for judging the target to be emotional.

---

is likely to be a person who reacts strongly or overreacts (i.e., reacts more strongly than the observer believes is warranted). This is consistent with Sommers's (1981) finding that when people are asked to define emotionality, they do so in terms of the magnitude of response.

The "acts emotional" category was included to reflect references to inauthentic emotion, that is, emotionality primarily defined as display. The small number of responses ultimately coded in this category suggests that our respondents view emotionality as reflecting genuine feelings, even if those feelings are thought to be too extreme or inappropriate.

Emotional men and emotional women were assessed fairly similarly by male and female respondents. The only noteworthy difference was in the frequency with which the target was described as manifesting

TABLE 9.4
Features that Identify the Target as Emotional:
Percentage of Responses for Male and Female Targets

	Female Target		Male Target	
Sex of Respondent:	Male	Female	Male	Female
Qualitative features				
Variety of emotions	9.5	11.5	7.1	5.7
Appropriate/healthy emotions	14.3	8.2	9.5	23.8
Inappropriate emotions	2.4	4.1	4.8	4.1
Quantitative features				
Latency to respond	9.5	9.0	2.4	1.6
Response too big for stimulus	28.6	30.3	28.6	26.2
Extremity of reaction	16.7	27.0	21.4	19.7
Acts emotional	4.8	4.1	2.4	0.8
Other/uncodable	11.9	5.7	4.8	13.1
No response	2.4	–	19.0	4.9

NOTE: There were 122 responses from females and 42 responses from males describing each target. Due to rounding error, columns may not sum to 100.0. The relatively high number of missing responses for men's descriptions of a male target is due to the fact that men were less likely to complete the entire questionnaire and most had described a male target second.

healthy emotionality. Close to a quarter of the female responses described a male target in these positive terms, but only 8% described a female target that way. For male respondents the relationship was reversed; more males described female targets as expressing healthy emotionality than described male targets in those terms. Emotionality is therefore not judged to be an exclusively negative quality, but each sex, especially women, tends to see it as a more positive quality in the other sex.[5]

Question 2 asked the respondent to describe a particular situation in which the target had been emotional. Responses were coded for the emotion described. If more than a single emotion situation was described, all mentions of distinct individual emotions were coded for the target. Of the codable responses, the vast majority for both male and female targets referred to either sadness/depression (41.2% of all codable responses) or anger (36.8%). Fewer than 10% of codable responses referred to some other negative emotion, anxious being the most frequent of these (5.8% of codable responses). References to love or happiness made up just 12.7% of codable responses.

Sadness/depression was described for a greater proportion of female than male targets by both men and women (44.4% of all female targets and 35.1% of all male targets); the opposite was true for anger. Anger was named for 41.2% of all male targets and 30.0% of all female targets.

A closer look at the descriptions of the emotion episode revealed that the components of the emotional behavior differed depending on whether a female or a male target was being described and whether a male or a female was giving the description. Of the female respondents who described an angry situation, 16.3% mentioned weeping by the target person, whereas only 11.1% of the male respondents did so. The difference between male and female respondents was even greater in the descriptions of sadness. Over 60% of the descriptions given by female respondents mentioned weeping, but just over 42% given by males did so. The difference in men's and women's descriptions was not due to a greater tendency of female respondents to provide details of the emotion episode. For male respondents, 59.2% of the anger descriptions and 9.5% of the sadness descriptions included reference to emotion behaviors other than weeping. Women mentioned these other behaviors less frequently (37.5% of the anger descriptions, 4.0% of the sadness descriptions).

A similar sex difference was observed for sex of target. Both male and female respondents mentioned weeping much more frequently in their descriptions of female targets. For anger situations, weeping was mentioned in connection with 26.1% of the female targets and 6.6% of the male targets. For sadness situations, the sex difference was also great; weeping was mentioned for 63.2% of the female targets and 42.3% of the male targets. Not surprisingly, both men and women associate weeping more with female than with male expressions of emotion. Women were also readier to include weeping in their descriptions of the emotional target, perhaps because weeping is something that women associate with emotional responses (Lombardo, Crester, Lombardo, & Mathis, 1983).

In summary, both men and women describe people close to them when asked to name a "most emotional" individual, and emotional women come to mind before emotional men. Even though the emotional person may be a close friend, the emotionality is viewed in a negative light, the only exception being the noteworthy minority of males whose emotionality is described (by women) in terms of sensi- tivity. The emotional person is most frequently identified by the magnitude of his or her reactions, particularly what respondents deem to be reactions out of proportion to the eliciting context. Our respondents' willingness to judge what would constitute a "more correct" amount of reaction suggests that people are very willing to presume sufficient knowledge of a situation to make inferences about the causes and appropriateness of others' emotional responses.

"Appropriate" Emotion

Standards of appropriate emotion are rarely explicit, though beliefs about seemly and unseemly emotion are fundamental. The example of anger illustrates this point. Anger is not always construed as a reflection of immature irrationality, and in fact in some circumstances is viewed as not only justifiable but necessary. Nor are "appropriate" displays of anger invariably associated with male displays, though there may be a narrower latitude of acceptable anger for females.

People's emotional displays are a significant determinant of the way they are evaluated socially. Emotion that deviates too much in quality or quantity from the socially appropriate meets with disapproval from others and stimulates efforts to modulate the display (Saarni, 1984), and even to change the quality of felt emotion to conform to social expectations (Hochschild, 1983). What accounts for the difference between an "appropriate" and an "inappropriate" emotion?

Common wisdom suggests that it is the speaker and the situation that alone determine an emotion's perceived appropriateness. That is, something about the expressive content and form of the statements being made, and the social context in which they occur, determine the appropriateness of an emotional display. Such an analysis, however, overlooks the active role played by the observer in assessing the situation.

In our laboratory we have begun to study the relationship between sex and judgments about emotion. In one case study, we examined the relationship between observers' political affiliation and their explicit references to candidates' emotional behavior (Shields & MacDowell, 1986). The importance of emotional displays in political life is well known, and many examples of the disastrous or beneficial effects of emotion can be cited. It is also in the political arena that women politicians' emotions seem a notable liability. To investigate one possible basis for the evaluation of emotion as appropriate or inappropriate, we examined references to emotion made during the course of television news commentary immediately following the 1984 debate between vice-presidential candidates Geraldine Ferraro (D) and George Bush (R) and one of the debates between presidential candidates Ronald Reagan and

Walter Mondale. Each of the networks followed the debates with a brief program of analysis and commentary provided by network employees, journalists, and a range of partisan observers, from members of Congress to campaign workers. We extracted all references to emotion from transcripts of the analysis and commentary provided by the three commercial networks and the Public Broadcasting System. We predicted that an observer's inference of appropriate or inappropriate display of emotion (or appropriate or inappropriate lack of emotion) would be consistent with the value the observer placed on the events and actors in a given situation. In the case of the debates, observers' party affiliation and political orientation should be reliably connected to the kind of assessment made of each politician's emotional displays.

On all networks, political preference was consistently associated with the observer's judgment of the appropriateness of a debater's emotion: If the observer made reference to the presence or absence of emotion in his or her own candidate, the reference was positive—that is, the candidate's reactions were considered appropriate. If the observer made reference to the presence or absence of emotion in the opposing candidate, it was negative. For example, Bush was praised by one Republican politician as "relaxed" and "firm," and by another as "authoritative" and as speaking "with confidence." Democratic observers, however, offered a different evaluation. One "thought that the Vice President was a little whiny and a little bit defensive"; another called Bush "shrill and hysterical."

Of particular relevance to this chapter is the fact that Ferraro's emotions were not more likely to be evaluated negatively than those of the male candidates. Observers' partisanship was as predictive of comments on her emotional displays as it was of comments made about the other candidates. One difference did set the female candidate apart. Ferraro's emotion-related behavior (both absence of emotion and presence of emotion) was mentioned significantly more frequently than Bush's or either of the presidential candidates'. There were nearly twice as many references to Ferraro's emotion as to Bush's. We could not determine whether Ferraro's emotion was noteworthy because she is female, because she was, on account of her sex, a novelty among national candidates, or because of observers' expectations regarding her performance. Women politicians have suggested that male displays of anger are publicly judged as manifestations of deeply held convictions, whereas female anger implies personal instability (Hochschild, 1983). In our study, however, evaluation of the meaning of emotion was a function of observer values and not solely a function of sex of speaker. The apparent double standard among politicians may ultimately be due to the greater likelihood with which females' emotions are commented upon rather than an invariant negative evaluation of females' emotions or a greater tendency for females to display emotion. Our results suggest that it is neither femaleness nor emotion that inspires negative evaluation, but an a priori negative evaluation of the female politician.

The Stereotype as a Belief System

We have also been approaching the question of appropriateness within a historical framework. The issues of emotional display and emotion management, although of everyday concern to adults, come sharply into focus when developmental concerns are addressed. Analysis of the culture's beliefs about emotion as it pertains to child-rearing should thus provide the most comprehensive and most detailed picture of the culture's concept of emotion. In a study of values in emotional child-rearing we extracted all of the references to emotion from a sample of over 50 advice-to-parents books published since 1915 (Shields & Koster, 1985). If we can assume that the parent advice manuals are as much intended to make a profit for the author as they are intended to be an exposition of the author's child-rearing philosophies, and can assume that the author will be as influenced by the culture's view of emotion as by his or her own theory of development, examination of a broad sample of child-rearing manuals should bring into focus the dominant themes within this culture's definition of emotion. Child-rearing manuals thus give a clear picture of the commonly held values and beliefs about emotion, even though they cannot reveal actual parenting practices.

The portion of that project that bears directly on the question of gender and emotion is a comparison of references to emotions of mothers, fathers, sons, and daughters. Given the strength of the emotional female stereotype, we expected that there would be many references to sex differences in both childhood and adulthood. But sex differences in emotion were explicitly mentioned in only 40% of the books sampled, and that proportion remained constant over the eras sampled. Only 4% of the passages included in the full sample made any reference to gender in the context of emotion, and in most books with such passages, there were only one or two statements. Furthermore, few references were made to boys' and girls' emotions; when statements were made about the link between gender and emotion, they focused on the parents. Distinct differences in the purported emotionality of mothers and fathers were apparent even with the small sample.

Across all eras the father was characterized as controlled and controlling. Although his children may fear him, they love him, and, although he should cultivate self-control, he was exhorted to express the full range of emotions toward his children—with the understanding that he would do so appropriately. The father's role in parenting was exclusively cast in terms of his role as disciplinarian. Only one book (published in the mid-1970s) discussed the potentially positive contribution of the man's emotional relationship with his wife. Overall, fathers were noted to have a tendency to respond with less feeling toward their children, a fact that allows fathers to be more objective than mothers about their children's needs and behavior.

Mothers' emotions, both positive and negative, were, in all eras, viewed as potentially damaging if they should somehow get out of control. Mothers were seen as having the tendency to overreact emotionally, which would have deleterious effects on both daughters and sons. Maternal emotion was identified as the source of a number of filial defects: sons' homosexual tendencies, sons' aggressiveness, children's overdependence, and so on. Apparently, one enduring belief about the impact of emotion on children's development in the United States is the potential for negative consequences of mothers' lack of emotional control. A mother's feminine tendency to be emotional is construed as a threat to the child's achievement of rational maturity, especially if the child is a male.

The mother-blaming tone of the child-rearing manuals was not confined to those with a pronounced psychodynamic orientation. It may be that the influence of Freudian theory on child-rearing values occurred as early as the first era we sampled (1915 to 1922). It may also be that the notion of deleterious maternal emotion originates from other traditional American value systems. It is also true that mother is different from father on more than the single dimension of sex, and these other systematic differences may account for the differential treatment of each parent's emotion. All of the manuals included in the sample presumed that the mother served as the child's primary caregiver. It may be that the caregiving aspect of the mother's relationship with the child (e.g., time spent with the child, familiarity with the child, responsibilities for mundane matters in child care) creates a suspect emotional tone.

Apparently, U.S. middle-class culture has for some time credited mothers with extraordinary powers over the well-being of their developing children. Our research suggests that the imputed power has tremendous potential for damage: A woman's emotions are believed to threaten to interfere with her conduct as a parent and, ultimately, the health of her child. The emphasis on female emotion in this archival study is quite consistent with our other research. It is particularly consistent with the idea that a woman's emotions are a very salient component of her own and others' evaluations of her. The power of the stereotype of the emotional female suggests the importance of investigating how the adoption of these beliefs sets up expectations for women's and men's behavior, and affects evaluations of it, from the positive sanctioning of female expressiveness to the denigration of authentic feelings (i.e., viewing emotion as a liability).

CONCLUSION

Preliminary research on social evaluations of women's and men's emotions has yielded three major conclusions. (1) Women's emotion is not invariably viewed as negative, nor are emotional displays by men invariably viewed as positive. (2) Women's emotions are probably more salient in social evaluations than men's. That is, observers may be more likely to look for and explicitly note the presence or absence of emotional qualities in women's behavior than in men's behavior. (3) Even in identical situations there may be different standards for what constitutes "appropriate" emotional experience and display for men and women. We suspect that standards of emotional "appropriateness" are differentially applied to men and women at least in part because of a status/power difference and not simply because of sex. Our current research is aimed at investigating more fully the factors that determine when and how emotion is explicitly acknowledged in others, particularly the basis for the emotional double standard.

Although feminists in sociology have made some advances in the study of emotion (e.g., Cancian, 1985; Hochschild, 1983), psychologists have lagged behind. The sex-differences model is quite limited in its capacity to explain the relationship between gender and emotion. To be successful, feminist research on emotion will require innovations not only in the conceptualization of gender but in approaches to emotion. An understanding of the social meaning of emotion, and of the way the concept of emotionality and assessments of specific emotions are applied differentially to women and men, is essential to explaining the processes that may create different experiences of emotion for each sex. This significant aspect of social perception remains almost wholly unstudied, and promises to be a fruitful area for feminist psychological inquiry during the coming years.

NOTES

1. There is, of course, a popular literature that encourages us to express our feelings, and much of it is written from a feminist, or at least a nonsexist, perspective. Although much of it purports to celebrate emotion, the covert message is to regularize emotion. The reader is admonished to express emotion because it is authentic, natural, and healthy. The implied effect of emotional expression is to prevent it from interrupting "normal" rational functioning. The idea behind "getting in touch with your feelings" is to know them in order to control them, or at least not let them get the best of reason.

2. See Averill (1982, pp. 286-288) for an analysis of the feminist position that women's anger has been socially repressed. Averill's data suggest no such repression of women's anger. He suggests that the feminist argument is "less concerned with women's anger *per se* than with the condition of women within society." Thus, from the feminist perspective, it is not an inability to express anger that is problematic, but rather the misdirection of anger.

3. Some of the practical implications of the observer-observed discrepancy are explored in Shields (1986).

4. For each of the analyses described below we first compared the responses of the two classes from whom participants had been drawn. No statistically reliable differences were found for any analysis. The only noteworthy difference between the classes was that students in the human emotions class were a little more likely to describe only a positive emotion for the target (15.8% versus 7.4% in the introductory class).

An order effect had introduced itself into the data simply because a female target was much more likely to be described first. We examined each analysis for order effects and found none to be statistically reliable. It appears that the differences between descriptions of the emotional female and the emotional male are, in fact, a function of target sex and not order in which the sexes were described.

5. A finer-grained picture of the value placed on emotion can be gained from looking at how the target's emotions were described. There are occasions when particular emotions, even ones typically judged as negative, may be valued or considered desirable. We examined each description of an emotional person and determined whether it emphasized the positive dimension of emotionality or the negative dimension, or described emotion neutrally or in uncodable terms. For both male and female respondents, negative descriptions outnumbered the combination of positive, neutral, and uncodable descriptions for both male and female targets.

REFERENCES

Allen, J. G., & Haccoun, D. M. (1976). Sex differences in emotionality: Multidimensional approach. *Human Relations, 29*(8), 711-722.

Averill, J. R. (1980). Emotion and anxiety: Sociocultural, biological and psychological determinants. In A. O. Rorty (Ed.), *Explaining emotions*. Berkeley: University of California Press.

Averill, J. R. (1982). *Anger and aggression*. New York: Springer-Verlag.

Berman, P. W. (1986). Children caring for babies: Age and sex differences in response to infant signals and to the social context. In N. Eisenberg (Ed.), *Contemporary topics in developmental psychology*. New York: John Wiley.

Birnbaum, D. A., Nosanchuck, T. A., & Croll, W. L. (1980). Children's stereotypes about sex differences in emotionality. *Sex Roles, 6*, 435-443.

Cancian, F. M. (1985). Gender politics: Love and power in the private and public spheres. In A. S. Rossi (Ed.), *Gender and life course* (pp. 253-264). New York: Aldine.

Caplan, P. J., MacPherson, G. M., & Tobin, P. (1985). Do sex-related differences in spatial ability exist? *American Psychologist, 40*, 786-799.

Deaux, K. (1984). From individual differences to social categories: Analysis of a decade's research on gender. *American Psychologist, 39*, 105-116.

Deaux, K., & Lewis, L. L. (1983). Assessment of gender stereotypes: Methodology and components. *Psychological Documents, 13*(25). (Ms. No. 2583)

de Sousa, R. (1980). The rationality of emotions. In A. O. Rorty (Ed.), *Explaining emotions*. Berkeley: University of California Press.

Doyle, M. A., & Biaggio, M. K. (1981). Expression of anger as a function of assertiveness and sex. *Journal of Clinical Psychology, 37*, 154-157.

Fitzpatrick, M. A., & Indvik, J. (1982). The instrumental and expressive domains of marital communication. *Human Communication Research, 8*, 195-213.

Hall, J. A. (1978). Gender effects in decoding nonverbal cues. *Psychological Bulletin, 85*, 845-875.

Henley, N. M. (1985). Psychology and gender. *Signs, 11*, 101-119.

Hochschild, A. R. (1983). *The managed heart*. Berkeley: University of California Press.

Lewis, R. A. (1978). Emotional intimacy among men. *Journal of Social Issues, 34*, 108-121.

Lombardo, W. K., Crester, G. A., Lombardo, B., & Mathis, S. L. (1983). For cryin' out loud—There is a sex difference. *Sex Roles, 9*, 987-995.

Saarni, C. (1984). An observational study of children's attempts to monitor their expressive behavior. *Child Development, 55*, 1504-1513.

Shaver, P. (Ed.). (1984). *Review of personality and social psychology: Vol. 5. Emotions, relationships, and health*. Beverly Hills, CA: Sage.

Sheppard, A. (1983). *Why psychologists should study history: One hundred years of the women's humor debate*. Paper presented at the meeting of the Association for Women in Psychology, Seattle, WA.

Sherif, C. W. (1982). Needed concepts in the study of gender identity. *Psychology of Women Quarterly, 6*, 375-398.

Shields, S. A. (1980). Nineteenth-century evolutionary theory and male scientific bias. In G. W. Barlow & J. Siverberg (Eds.), *Sociobiology: Beyond nature/nurture?* AAAS Selected Symposium #35. Boulder, CO: Westview.

Shields, S. A. (1984). Distinguishing between emotion and nonemotion: Judgments about experience. *Motivation and Emotion, 8*, 355-369.

Shields, S. A. (1986). Are women "emotional"? In C. Tavris (Ed.), *Every woman's emotional well-being*. Garden City, NY: Doubleday.

Shields, S. A., & Koster, B. A. (1985). *Managing emotional development: Advice from childrearing manuals, 1915-1980*. Paper presented at the meeting of the International Society for the Study of Behavioural Development, Tours, France.

Shields, S. A., & MacDowell, K. A. (1986). *Judging "appropriate" emotion in politicians: A study of the vice-presidential candidates debate in 1984* (Under review.)

Shimanoff, S. B. (1985). Expressing emotions in words: Verbal patterns of interaction. *Journal of Communication, 35*, 16-31.

Sommers, S. (1981). Emotionality reconsidered: The role of cognition in emotional responsiveness. *Journal of Personality and Social Psychology, 41*, 553-561.

Tavris, C. (1982). *Anger: The misunderstood emotion*. New York: Simon & Schuster.

Tavris, C. (1984). On the wisdom of counting to ten: Personal and social dangers of anger expression. In P. Shaver (Ed.), *Review of personality and social psychology: Emotions, relationships, and health*. Beverly Hills, CA: Sage.

Warren, N. J. & Gilner, F. H. (1978). Measurement of positive assertive behavior: Behavioral test of tenderness expression. *Behavior Therapy, 9*, 178-184.

Westbrook, M. (1974). Sex differences in the perception of emotion. *Australian Journal of Psychology, 26*, 139-146.

Wittig, M. A. (1985). Metatheoretical dilemmas in the psychology of gender. *American Psychologist, 40*, 800-811.

Wittig, M. A., & Petersen, A. C. (Eds.). (1979). *Sex-related differences in cognitive functioning: Developmental issues*. New York: Academic Press.

10

Gender Schema Theory and the Romantic Tradition

SANDRA LIPSITZ BEM

Sandra Lipsitz Bem is Professor of Psychology and Women's Studies at Cornell University. From 1978 to 1985, she was Director of Cornell's Women's Studies Program. Before moving to Cornell, she was on the faculty of Carnegie-Mellon and Stanford Universities. She received her Ph.D. in developmental psychology at the University of Michigan in 1968. For her research on sex typing and androgyny, she received APA's Early Career Award in 1976 and the Young Scholar Award of the American Association of University Women in 1980.

Sex typing is the process through which the developing child comes to match the template of preferences, skills, personality attributes, behaviors, and self-concepts prescribed by the culture as appropriate for his or her sex. It is the process through which a culture transforms male and female children into masculine and feminine adults.

Gender schema theory (Bem, 1981b, 1985) asserts that children become sex typed, in part, because they come to perceive, evaluate, and regulate their own behavior in terms of these gender templates; that is, they come to construe and organize reality in terms of gender. Moreover, the theory asserts that gender comes to have such priority over alternative conceptual classifications because the culture communicates to the developing child both implicitly and explicitly that sex is one of the most important categories—if not the most important category—in human social life; that unlike other social categories with more limited reach, the dichotomy between male and female has and ought to have intensive and extensive relevance to virtually every domain of human experience.

Because of its emphasis on the individual's use of cognitive schemas in social and self-perception, gender schema theory appears to swim

AUTHOR'S NOTE: My debt to Richard Shweder's brilliant essay on the romantic tradition in anthropology will be apparent to the reader. I would also like to express my gratitude to him and to Lee Ross for their insightful comments on an earlier draft of this chapter and to Daryl Bem, whose attempts to move my prose a step closer to poetry are always appreciated—ultimately, if not at the time.

within the current mainstream of cognitive social psychology, especially that dealing with schematic information-processing. I do not believe it does, however. Indeed, my goal in this chapter is to argue that gender schema theory fits more comfortably into an alternative tradition within psychology and to explicate at a more general level than heretofore the theoretical and metatheoretical assumptions of the theory.

To do so, I shall use a recent distinction made by Shweder (1984) in the context of cognitive anthropology between "enlightenment" and "romantic" views of mind. Specifically, I shall argue that whereas the dominant concerns of most theories in contemporary cognitive-social and cognitive-developmental psychology are more closely linked to an enlightenment view of mind, the concerns of gender schema theory are more closely linked to a romantic view of mind.

THE ENLIGHTENMENT AND ROMANTIC TRADITIONS

In his essay on anthropology's romantic rebellion against the enlightenment, Shweder (1984) argues that cognitive anthropologists—and indeed all social theorists—can be seen as falling into one or the other of two opposing camps, the one advancing an image of mind as intendedly rational, the other advancing an image of mind not as irrational but as nonrational or arbitrary. The first camp—into which he places Socrates, Spinoza, Hobbes, Voltaire, Diderot, Condorcet, Frazer, Tylor, the early Wittgenstein, Chomsky, Kay, Levi-Strauss, and Piaget—he labels the "enlightenment" tradition. The second camp—into which he places the Sophists, Hume, Leibnitz, Goethe, Schiller, Schleiermacher, Levy-Bruhl, the later Wittgenstein, Whorf, Kuhn, Schneider, Sahlins, Feyerabend, and Geertz—he labels the "romantic" tradition.

According to Shweder, the enlightenment tradition views the human mind as striving to be rational and scientific, as destined by its nature to respect universal canons of reason and evidence. The enlightenment tradition does not assume that all human minds or human cultures achieve such rationality, only that they strive to do so. This assumption operates at both the normative and the descriptive levels, and it applies both to how people think and what they think.

At the normative level, it is assumed that there exists a single standard of judgment for all thought and action, a universal criterion based on the canons of reason and evidence. Persons and cultures should gather data and evidence in a rational way and their substantive conclusions should be "true" beliefs rather than "false" superstitions. Within anthropology, the distinction between "primitive" and "modern" cultures is predicated on this normative assumption.

At the descriptive level, it is assumed that there exists not only a rational way of acquiring knowledge and reaching substantive conclusions toward which all human minds naturally strive, but a universal body of knowledge and a way of representing that knowledge that all minds will ultimately discover. Within anthropology, the search for cross-cultural universals in the structure of human knowledge—for example, in dimensions for classifying stimuli or in patterns of lexical development within particular domains such as color, kinship, or botany—is driven by this assumption.

It should be noted that a particular view of the child and of child development fits snugly into the enlightenment tradition, namely, the child as an independent and autonomous mind searching for the universal structure inherent in the world and gradually discovering for him- or herself a valid body of "true" knowledge and an understanding of the scientific and logical canons of thought. This is, of course, the prototypical Piagetian child.

In an epilogue to his article, Shweder expands the enlightenment tradition to include theorists who subscribe to rationality at a normative level, but who are concerned—at a descriptive level—with the ways in which human minds systematically and universally depart from that normative ideal. Although Shweder does not mention him explicitly, Freud would seem to belong in this category. For Freud, the normative ideal of rationality is embodied in the reality principle of the ego. That ideal is rarely achieved, however, because of universal irrational processes in the unconscious—including the ego's own mechanisms of defense.

In contrast to the enlightenment tradition, the romantic tradition emphasizes that there are many domains in which the canons of reason and evidence are irrelevant, many contexts in which questions of truth and falsity are beside the point. "Should the group have authority over the individual?" "To what categories of individuals should 'rights' be granted?" Logic and science cannot provide "correct" answers to questions such as these. Similarly, they cannot provide individuals with the "right" classification system through which to perceive and comprehend the world because there is no inherent universal structure in the world waiting to be discovered, no "ideal or unitary pattern of relative likeness and difference frozen into reality" (Shweder, 1984, p. 44). In these domains, thought and action are neither rational nor irrational, but nonrational and arbitrary.

But if logic and science are inherently unable to provide right answers to questions such as these, where do the necessary answers come from? They come, for the romantic, from culture. Indeed, they are culture: a shared classification system through which reality is perceived, a shared arbitrary and nonrational partitioning of the world into equivalence classes. This so-called symbols-and-meaning conception of culture was formally defined by Clifford Geertz in 1973 as "an historically transmitted pattern of meanings embodied in symbols, a system of inherited conceptions expressed in symbolic form by means of which . . . [humans] communicate, perpetuate and develop their knowledge about and attitudes toward life" (p. 89). From this view, fundamentally different ideas and practices are all seen as having equal validity. Each culture is thus seen as having its own self-contained and valid framework for understanding experience.

Those who share a culture are not typically aware, of course, that they perceive reality through some arbitrary set of lenses; for them, the reality they perceive and the category system through which they perceive are "indissoluble" (Geertz, 1984, p. 125). Accordingly, the intergenerational transmission of culture is most frequently implicit, not explicit or didactic. That is, through the particular patterning of their words and actions, adults nonconsciously communicate to the child a whole package of metamessages about what is of importance, what is of value, which differences between people and other entities should be emphasized, which should be overlooked, and so forth. They do not do this with the explicit intention of letting the child in on their code. But because the structure of their words and actions necessarily embodies their code, it is there for the child to learn incidentally even when no explicit transmission of the code is intended.

The romantic tradition thus yields a view of the child not as a lone seeker of absolute truth but as a newcomer whose task it is discover the particular lenses through which his or her culture perceives reality. Like the enlightenment child, the romantic child is also an active seeker and discoverer of patterns. But the patterns to be discovered are arbitrary cultural codes, not universal truth structures; and to pick up these codes, the child must be wholly immersed and enmeshed in a cultural and linguistic community. The prototypical romantic child is thus a Whorfian child, whose learning of a particular language—and culture— is simultaneously the learning of a particular classification system through which to perceive reality.

THE ENLIGHTENMENT ORIENTATION IN PSYCHOLOGY

Among the several differences between the enlightenment and romantic orientations listed by Shweder, the one that best maps onto the recent history of psychology is the distinction between the enlightenment emphasis on the abstract, universal processes of mind versus the romantic emphasis on the arbitrary content of mind and the socio-cultural processes that implant that content. When cast in these terms, moreover, it becomes clear that the zeitgeist in psychology these past thirty years has been dominated by an enlightenment perspective.

Piaget, of course, is the prototype here. The only psychologist listed on Shweder's original list of enlightenment thinkers, Piaget is concerned not at all with the culturally derived content in mind, but with the abstract structures and processes of mind that are presumed to characterize all minds at all times in all places and across all content domains.

It is not only Piaget—and hence much of cognitive-developmental psychology—that has focused on structure and process rather than content. Until quite recently, cognitive psychology had focused almost exclusively on "information processing" with virtually no attention to the content of the information being processed. Similarly, under the influence of Chomsky (who is surely one of the purest enlightenment figures on Shweder's list), psycholinguistics focused for a time on universal syntactic structures with virtually no attention to either semantics or pragmatics.

The area of psychology that ought to be most concerned with sociocultural process, of course, is social psychology. And in an earlier period, social psychologists did study the acquisition, content, and consequences of socially significant beliefs, attitudes, and cultural ideologies—such as authoritarianism—in a sociocultural context. Since the late 1950s, however, social psychology too has been dominated by an enlightenment perspective. In this latter period, social psychologists studying beliefs and attitudes have treated both the content and the context of those beliefs and attitudes as irrelevant, emphasizing instead such things as their abstract structure, the degree to which they obey principles of consistency, and the cognitive processes by which they are changed or maintained.

In the last ten or so years, the mainstream of social psychology has been fascinated by the question of selective perception; in particular, whether there is something about the nature of mind itself—independent of affect and motivation—that universally leads humans to perceive social reality (and perhaps all reality) selectively. Social psychologists have approached this question with two assumptions. First, that there are cognitive structures in the mind representing both the individual's social knowledge and the individual's subjective theories about the world. These cognitive structures are often referred to generically as "schemas." Second, that once activated, these schemas guide information processing selectively, making some information more likely to be encoded, stored, and retrieved than other information, providing default values for missing information, and so on (this research is reviewed in detail by Markus & Zajonc, 1985).

At first glance, social psychology's interest in selective perception might seem to signify a return to a more romantic perspective. After all, it does presuppose that perception is at least partially determined by mind rather than being wholly determined by external reality and, in principle at least, it thereby leaves room for the subjectivity and the arbitrariness of content that—for the romantic—are the very essence of both mind and culture. In fact, however, the approach taken by most contemporary schema researchers is decidedly nonromantic. That is, it virtually eliminates all those degrees of freedom in mind where subjectivity and arbitrariness might play a role and thereby transforms the question of selective perception into a purely enlightenment focus on the universal intellectual processes and structures involved in the representation of social knowledge.[1]

The subjectivity that can be read into the selective perception question is eliminated in two ways. First, most schema researchers experimentally activate a schema of interest to them (which they presume is also present in the subject's mind) and then examine the effects that activation has on the subject's subsequent information processing. Does the activation of a schema enhance perception by allowing the individual to respond more quickly? Can the selective influence of an experimentally activated schema be observed at every stage of information processing (e.g., encoding, storage, retrieval), at all levels of processing (e.g., conscious, preconscious), and on all parameters (e.g., speed, confidence, accuracy)? Given the particular ways in which the activation of a schema does influence information processing, what, if anything, can be inferred about the abstract nature of cognitive representation? These are all legitimate questions, but they bypass both theoretically and empirically what—for the romantic—is the critical issue in selective perception: the question of how and why one schema gets constructed and selected for activation rather than another.

Subjectivity is eliminated in a second way as well. Although schema researchers describe schemas as representing both the individual's social knowledge and his or her subjective theories, in fact, their research focuses almost exclusively on small, isolated knowledge packages (such as what an extrovert is) without reference even to the larger conceptual structures into which these knowledge packages fit. This focus virtually guarantees that the only important difference between minds is that which derives from having more (or more organized) knowledge rather than less (or less organized) knowledge.

But clearly this is not the only—or even the most important— difference between minds. For one thing, the very same knowledge packages can be embedded into different conceptual structures and thereby have different meanings. Also, individuals have more than knowledge; they even have more than subjectively organized knowledge. They also have theories, beliefs, presuppositions, and classification systems; that is, they have conceptual schemes for construing reality that make some things seem alike and other things seem different, some things seem good and other things seem bad. But none of these profound differences in the content of one's conceptual lenses are emphasized or even made visible when one's theory and method focus only on those aspects of mind that are derived from the experimental activation of isolated knowledge packages. Accordingly, the contemporary research on schemas in social psychology has little to offer the analysis of how different perspectives of reality emerge; it also has little in common with the romantic tradition.

THE ROMANTIC ORIENTATION IN PSYCHOLOGY

Although the focus on abstract, universal processes of mind has clearly been the dominant orientation in psychology for the past several decades, it is possible to discern—or to construct—a romantic tradition quietly flowing beside the mainstream, a tradition concerned with the content of mind and/or the sociocultural processes that create that content.

As we shall see, some of the psychologists I place in this tradition have been concerned primarily with the mind's classification systems, the substantive dimensions or categories that individuals or cultures use for partitioning reality into equivalence classes and imposing meaning on a multidimensional world. These are the transparent lenses through which the person or culture perceives reality. Others have been primarily concerned with specific, implicit beliefs or theories that persons or cultures bring to the task of perceiving and interpreting the world. Similarly, some have been interested in the content of individual minds and the personal or idiographic histories that produce individual differences; others have also been interested in the contents of mind that are shared by all the members of a given culture. These shared contents are the "arbitrary codes," the "master metaphors," the "self-contained frameworks for understanding experience" that actually define culture for the romantic anthropologist.

These subtle differences notwithstanding, the critical issue for all these "romantic" psychologists—and the aspect of mind they all agree must be elucidated if the individual's behavior is ever to be fully understood—is how the individual construes reality, that is, which conceptual schemes the individual spontaneously imposes on reality, which conceptual lenses the individual looks at reality through.

Out of the many psychologists who can legitimately claim membership in this new club I have organized, I have chosen four theorists (or sets of theorists) who, collectively, best illustrate the several facets of the romantic tradition: George Kelly, Richard Nisbett and Lee Ross, the authors of *The Authoritarian Personality,* and David McClelland. (Some other psychologists whose work would also seem to place them in the romantic tradition include Gordon Allport, Jerome Bruner, Daryl Bem, Robert Rosenthal, Milton Rokeach, Richard Christie and Florence Geis, Mark Snyder, Carol Dweck, and Lawrence Wrightsman.)

George Kelly

Despite the fact that he begins with an enlightenment-sounding emphasis on "man-as-scientist," Kelly is the theorist in personality and social psychology most closely identified with the romantic notion that each individual perceives social reality through an arbitrary set of meaning-giving lenses. (Kelly called them "goggles.")

According to Kelly's theory, what is in each individual's mind that shapes both perception and behavior is "a personal construct system," a hierarchically ordered structure of bipolar contrasts or dichotomies. All aspects of the hierarchy's content, including the particular contrasts that are incorporated within it and the status of each contrast relative to the others, are assumed to differ from individual to individual. The content of the hierarchy is thus seen as subjective and arbitrary, invented by mind and imposed upon reality rather than emerging from the true or objective nature of reality. Of particular interest to Kelly is which constructs or contrasts the person uses when perceiving or describing the self or anyone else; of far less interest is which pole of that bipolar contrast the person sees as especially descriptive: "Whether [a person] sees himself as powerful or weak is of interest . . . but secondary to the fact that [he] . . . has ordered his world and himself with respect to the powerful-weak dimension" (Bannister & Mair, 1968, pp. 27-28).

An important implication of Kelly's theory is that the same behavior can have a different meaning for different individuals. Hence, if one wants to understand (or even to perceive) the consistency across a given individual's whole set of behaviors, one must first discover what constructs are subjectively meaningful for that particular individual and then analyze his or her behavior in those terms. Put somewhat differently, one simply must accept a priori that there is no single set of constructs or trait dimensions that can meaningfully be applied to all individuals. This is also the point made by both Gordon Allport and Daryl Bem, who argue that personality psychology has failed to find cross-situational consistency in behavior because "nearly all of the research is based on some variant of the nomothetic assumption that a particular trait dimension or set of trait dimensions is universally applicable to all persons and that individual differences are to be identified with different locations on those dimensions" (Bem & Allen, 1974, p. 509).

Richard Nisbett and Lee Ross

Like Kelly, social psychologists Nisbett and Ross (1980) begin their analysis of human inference with an enlightenment-sounding emphasis on "man-as-scientist." They are even categorized by Shweder as enlightenment thinkers because they explicitly reject the notion that all theories or presuppositions are equally valid; and, somewhat like Freud, they are concerned with the universal processes of mind that produce systematic departures from normative rationality.

These enlightenment considerations notwithstanding, the Nisbett-Ross view of human inference makes two critical assumptions that place it squarely within the romantic tradition: (a) that the world is sufficiently ambiguous and multidimensional as to permit a variety of different theories or presuppositions to be imposed upon it at any given moment; and (b) that an individual's perceptions and judgments are shaped not by any objective features inherent in reality itself but by the particular a priori theories, beliefs, and presuppositions that he or she brings to bear on a given situation at a given moment in time. Like truly good romantics, moreover, the kinds of "a prioris" Nisbett and Ross consider important vary enormously from the relatively narrow generalizations that people make about particular individuals or groups to the broadest conceptions of human nature and the determinants of human behavior. The critical issue for Nisbett and Ross, as for Kelly, is thus which particular a priori content in the individual's mind is serving as his or her subjective lens on reality, which particular theory or presupposition is serving as the basis for the individual's judgments and inferences.

Like Kelly, Nisbett and Ross focus primarily on how the a priori content in an individual's mind subjectively shapes his or her perception of reality. But there is also a cultural dimension to the Nisbett-Ross view, an assumption that in addition to whatever theories and presuppositions are uniquely present in a given individual's mind, there is also a set of theories and presuppositions present within the minds of all the individuals living within a given culture or subculture, and these shared theories in turn are what provide the members of that culture with a common cultural outlook, a common perception of reality. This, of course, is precisely the view articulated by the romantic anthropologists discussed earlier.

This cultural dimension is best illustrated by Nisbett and Ross's discussion of why it is that people in our culture disproportionately attribute behavior to an actor's dispositions, thereby ignoring powerful situational determinants—a pattern known as the "fundamental attribution error." According to Nisbett and Ross, this readiness to attribute behavior to persons rather than to situations exists because of an overarching "dispositionalist theory" that is thoroughly woven into the fabric of our culture and shared by almost everyone socialized in our culture, a theory that says that although "good or bad luck, accidents of birth and situational adversities may forestall matters . . . one's fate will eventually mirror one's character, and one's personal traits and abilities will ultimately prevail over circumstances" (Nisbett & Ross, 1980, p. 31). A romantic anthropologist couldn't have said it better.

In fact, this dispositionalist theory is itself embedded within an even more profound cultural theory that we (and other Westerners) hold about the nature of the person, a theory that says that a person is an autonomous individual with a stable character structure that exists independently of the social roles that the person plays and independently of the social situations in which the person behaves. But, says anthropologist Clifford Geertz (1984, p. 126), this "Western concept of the person as a bounded, unique, more or less integrated motivational and cognitive universe, a dynamic center of awareness, emotion, judgment, and action organized into a distinctive whole and set contrastively both against other such wholes and against its social and natural background is, however incorrigible it may seem to us, a rather peculiar idea within the context of the world's cultures." Far more common, according to anthropologists Geertz (1984), Rosaldo (1984), and Shweder and Bourne (1984), is a holistic sociocentric theory that focuses on the context-dependent relationship of part to part and part to whole—and hence does not differentiate the person either from the social context in which he or she lives or from the roles that he or she plays.

In both our theories and our empirical studies, we Western psychologists have already begun to recognize that different individuals in our culture organize their self-concepts around different constructs. But we have not yet begun to recognize that the self we study is itself merely one more conceptual scheme that our subjects impose on a kaleidoscopic reality.[2]

The Authoritarian Personality

Kelly, Nisbett, and Ross all make the same general point that the a priori content in mind shapes both perception and behavior. By and large, however, they do not focus in depth on any particular conceptual scheme that the individual or the culture imposes on reality. Two early research programs in social psychology do precisely this. They are McClelland's theory and research on achievement motivation—which will be discussed shortly—and the theory and research on the authoritarian personality by Adorno, Frenkel-Brunswik, Levinson, and Sanford.

These two programs of theory and research are well known; they are also, in 1986, quite unfashionable. I highlight them here for two reasons. First, they both predate the moment in psychology's history when process and structure came to be seen as more important than content, and hence they deal with profoundly important aspects of human experience. Second, they illustrate how a romantic perspective can encompass both the individual and the culture within the same theoretical and empirical analysis.

The research on the authoritarian personality (Adorno, Frenkel-Brunswik, Levinson, & Sanford, 1950) was initiated in 1943, during the latter days of Hitler's reign in Nazi Germany. Some of the psychologists working on that research were themselves Jewish refugees from Germany, and they and their colleagues were all deeply committed to trying to understand how anti-Semitism and Fascism could have become such powerful political forces not only in Germany but in other parts of Europe as well. Their research agenda, briefly stated, was to demonstrate the existence of an authoritarian or antidemocratic personality, a personality with a susceptibility or readiness to respond positively to fascist propaganda.

This susceptibility was thought to derive from the particular way the authoritarian conceptualizes social reality. People are conceptualized by the authoritarian either as members of high-status in-groups or as members of low-status out-groups. Those in low-status out-groups are derogated and treated with contempt. Those in high-status in-groups are endowed with moral authority; hence their right to their high status is never questioned and their views are submissively and uncritically accepted. In the spirit of the romantic tradition, the authoritarian is thus conceptualized as someone who views social reality through the lens of status and power.

And where does this particular way of conceptualizing reality come from? According to the original theory, the authoritarian's lifelong pattern of displacing negative affect and projecting negative characteristics onto low-status groups has its origins in the psychodynamics of the parent-child relationship. More specifically, the pattern derives from having parents who are rigid disciplinarians, who allow the child no avenue for ever challenging parental authority. Such parents, it is argued, arouse a great deal of hostility in their children, but because that hostility cannot safely be directed toward the parents, the fact that the parents are both the source and the legitimate target of the hostility is repressed, and the hostility is displaced onto some safer target.

Because of its emphasis on the Freudian defense mechanisms, this intrafamilial account would seem to reflect an enlightenment concern with universal irrational processes. But there are at least two aspects of the account that allow for a more romantic reading of it. First, the parents of the authoritarian are seen as conceptualizing the parent-child relationship in terms of dominance and submission. Second, they are seen as insecure about their own status in the social community. The parents of the authoritarian can thus be seen as implicitly conveying a set of metamessages to the child about the importance of status and power as conceptual schemes for organizing the social world. To the extent that these metamessages are affectively charged—whether through the parents' status anxiety or the child's hostility or both—they are all that much more likely to be assimilated by the child.

There is a wealth of empirical evidence supporting the intrafamilial account of authoritarianism. But there is also compelling evidence that authoritarianism is particularly high in groups with low levels of education and/or lesser socioeconomic status. On the basis of this sociocultural evidence, critics of the theory have argued that it is inappropriate to conceptualize authoritarianism as a personality variable derived from an individual's family dynamics and thereby to ignore the larger sociocultural context in which both individuals and families are embedded. Instead, they argue, authoritarianism should be conceptualized as a set of cultural or subcultural norms to which the individual conforms. (See Brown, 1965, for a discussion of both the theory and its critics.)

From a romantic perspective, of course, there is no sharp distinction to be made between an account of authoritarianism based on "personality" and an account based on "culture." Authoritarianism is a way of construing reality and, as such, it is derived from the metamessages that the individual picks up—either from the family or from the larger social community or from both—about what differences between people are especially important and what differences are to be overlooked. Like any other way of construing reality, moreover, it can be shared—or not shared—by all the members of a social community. If a whole community has a readiness to divide people into in-groups and out-groups on the basis of status and power, then that classification system will be picked up and used as a lens by virtually all of the children in the community—which will give authoritarianism the appearance of a sociocultural phenomenon. On the other hand, if the whole community does not have such a readiness, then only the children from authoritarian homes will develop an authoritarian outlook—which will give authoritarianism the appearance of a personality phenomenon. The underlying sociocultural process is the same in both cases, however.

David McClelland

Like the authors of *The Authoritarian Personality*, McClelland was also interested in a psychological question with great cultural and historical significance; in particular, the role that motivational variables play in economic history. His major thesis: that both individuals and cultures can be said to have characteristic levels of achievement motivation, which, in turn, determine their levels of entrepreneurial and other achievement-oriented activity (McClelland, 1961; McClelland, Atkinson, Clark, & Lowell, 1953).

Although McClelland himself typically described individuals in terms of their "motives," "needs," and "concerns," his basic theoretical assumption was a romantic one: To predict an individual's behavior, one must know how he or she spontaneously construes reality. Some individuals have a readiness to perceive the world in terms of its achievement possibilities; others have a readiness to perceive its affiliative possibilities; still others, its possibilities for power.

McClelland's use of the Thematic Apperception Test, or TAT, followed directly from this romantic assumption. By asking subjects to write down whatever story happened to come into their minds while looking at a photograph of some relatively ambiguous interpersonal scene, McClelland was not merely "simulating" in the laboratory what happens in the "real" world, nor was he trying to delve deep into his subjects' unconscious minds. Rather, he was getting a behavior sample that was theoretically defined as highly diagnostic, that is, a sample of what conceptual scheme the individual has a spontaneous readiness to use in the context of an ambiguous stimulus array.

McClelland tried not only to characterize individuals on the basis of how they construed reality, but also to characterize whole cultures—and to predict a given culture's economic rise and fall—on the basis of how that culture construed reality. This attempt to encompass both individuals and cultures within the same theoretical and empirical analysis is unique, and it highlights McClelland's implicit assumption that mind is simultaneously an individual and a cultural entity.

GENDER SCHEMA THEORY

As noted in the introduction to this chapter, gender schema theory is a theory of how and why male and female children become masculine and feminine, respectively; how and why virtually every child in our culture comes to match the template defined by our culture as sex-appropriate.

Gender schema theory argues that because our culture communicates both explicitly and implicitly that sex is one of the most important categories in human social life, children develop a spontaneous readiness to impose a gender-based classification system on social reality, a spontaneous readiness to see reality as carved naturally into gender categories. This readiness, in turn, is what leads to the child's becoming sex typed. As one aspect of their imposing a gender-based classification system on reality, children evaluate different ways of behaving in terms of the culture's definitions of gender-appropriateness, and then reject any way of behaving that does not match their sex.

This account of sex typing is based on three romantic presuppositions: (a) Social reality is sufficiently ambiguous as to afford the imposition on it of many different conceptual schemes; (b) perception and behavior are shaped in large part by the particular conceptual schemes that are prominent in one's mind; and, (c) which conceptual schemes are prominent in one's mind is itself largely determined by which differences between people one's culture emphasizes.

This third presupposition highlights an important but previously unarticulated aspect of gender schema theory: namely, that it is as much a theory about our culture and its lenses as it is a theory about personality or individual differences. Similarly, the empirical research derived from the theory was designed as much to reveal the readiness of our culture to perceive reality through gender lenses as it was to reveal the readiness of particular individuals within our culture to do so. Like the theory of the authoritarian personality and the theory of achievement motivation, gender schema theory thus fuses the psychologist's interest in the individual with the anthropologist's interest in the culture. It also encompasses both the individual and the culture within the same theoretical and empirical analysis.

Gender schema theory's special interest in the culture was never obvious before because of the particular way the theory was articulated. What was described as the theory's first proposition—and what was tested empirically—was that individuals become sex-typed by virtue of their acquiring a spontaneous readiness to perceive reality through gender lenses. No mention of the culture here. What was then described as the theory's second proposition—and what was not tested empirically in any direct way—was that individuals develop this readiness because of messages from the culture about which differences between people are important.

But consider the following question: Why the focus on gender? If the theory were primarily interested in the different conceptual schemes that are prominent in the minds of different individuals, then, as a romantic theory, it should have proceeded more idiographically to discover what those conceptual schemes might be. Certainly it should not have begun with some a priori category that just happened to be of interest to its feminist creator.

But it is not its creator's pet category that gender schema theory begins with; it is our culture's pet category. Of special interest to the theory is thus the part of mind that reflects the "master metaphors" of the culture as a whole, not the part of mind that is uniquely derived from the individual's personal biography. Yes, gender schema theory does focus on individual differences within our culture, but its larger purpose is to illuminate one of the dominant lenses of our entire culture.

Anthropologists frequently try to illuminate the lenses of a particular culture by contrasting that culture's way of construing reality with some other culture's. Similarly, gender schema theory tries to illuminate the lenses of a culture by contrasting how highly enculturated individuals construe reality with how less enculturated individuals construe reality. Both of these strategies make the culture's lenses visible—that is, they enable us to look at the lenses rather than through them—because they show us previously unimagined alternatives and thereby teach us that the culture's dominant way of construing reality is not the only way of construing reality.

In previous discussions of gender schema theory, subjects have been described as sex-typed and non-sex-typed. But both conceptually and methodologically, the theory defines sex typing in a way that makes it just as appropriate to describe subjects as more enculturated and less enculturated.

Thus, at the conceptual level, sex-typed and non-sex-typed individuals are seen as differing from one another in the extent to which they utilize cultural definitions of masculinity and femininity as idealized standards against which their own personality and behavior are to be evaluated. Sex-typed individuals are seen as highly attuned to these cultural definitions and as highly motivated to regulate their behavior in accordance with them; non-sex-typed individuals are seen as less attuned to these cultural definitions and as less motivated to regulate their behavior in accordance with them.

At the methodological level, this cultural conception of sex typing is embedded in the Bem Sex Role Inventory (BSRI), the 60-item self-report instrument used to assess both sex typing and androgyny (Bem, 1974, 1981a). What distinguishes the BSRI—apart from the methodological independence of its masculinity and femininity scales—is the way in which the masculine and feminine items were selected. Judges who prescreened the initial pool of items were treated as "native informants" about the culture, rating each item's desirability in American society generally either for a man or for a woman. Items were then defined as masculine or feminine if, and only if, they were judged to be significantly more desirable for males or females in American society generally by four independent samples of native informants. This procedure was designed to ensure that the masculine and feminine items on the BSRI would constitute cultural definitions of gender appropriateness. It was also designed to be consistent with a conception of the sex-typed individual as someone whose self-concept has incorporated cultural definitions of masculinity and femininity.

This item selection procedure taps not what particular individual members of a given culture themselves define as masculine or feminine but what they collectively believe to be the prevailing definitions of masculinity and femininity in the culture at large. And, according to gender schema theory, it is these collective cultural definitions that the sex-typed individual uses as the criteria for his or her gender conformity.

Because gender schema theory proposes that it is the process of construing reality in terms of gender that is critical to the process of sex typing, the empirical research designed to test the theory all focuses on the question of whether sex-typed individuals have a greater readiness than other individuals to impose a gender-based classification system on reality, a greater readiness to see reality as carved naturally into gender categories.

In one study (Bem, 1981b), for example, subjects were shown a series of 61 words in random order, and they were then asked to recall as many of those words as they could, in whatever order they happened to come to mind. The words included animals, articles of clothing, verbs, and people's first names. Half of the names were male and half were female. One-third of the items within each of the other categories were masculine (e.g., gorilla, hurling, trousers), one-third were feminine (e.g., butterfly, twirling, nylons), and one-third were neutral (e.g., ant, stepping, sweater). Of interest in this study was not the number of words recalled but the number of times the subject recalled two feminine words or two masculine words in a row. The existence of many such clusters in the subject's sequence of recall constitutes evidence that he or she has spontaneously imposed a gender-based classification system on the stimulus array.

Several aspects of this procedure are worth noting. First, other categories besides gender were incorporated into the structure of the list.

This multidimensionality not only ensured that gender was but one of many possible ways to organize the available information; it also enabled us to examine the use of other conceptual schemes besides gender and thereby to determine whether sex-typed individuals have a greater readiness than other individuals to use gender in particular, as postulated by the theory, or merely a greater readiness to use whatever conceptual schemes are available in the stimulus array. Second, nothing about the experimental situation elicited or reinforced the use of gender in particular as a conceptual scheme. Its presence within the structure of the list was masked by virtue of its being embedded within other, more obvious categories. No explicit mention was ever made of it. Optimal task performance was in no way dependent on it. In a situation that has these features, any systematic relationship between any aspect of a subject's response and the latent gender structure of the stimulus array—indeed, anything that suggests that a gender-based classification system is embodied in the subject's response—constitutes evidence that he or she has a readiness to use gender in particular as a conceptual scheme, a readiness to look at reality through gender lenses.

These same features were present in a quite different study by Frable and Bem (1985). Subjects listened to a group discussion and were then asked to recall "who said what." Of interest in this study was not how many errors the subject made overall but how much the subject erroneously attributed male statements to other males rather than to females and female statements to other females rather than to males. Such "within-sex" errors indicate that the subject is confusing the members of a given sex with one another, that is, that he or she is sorting people into equivalence classes on the basis of gender in particular rather than on the basis of some other dimension. The "other dimension" included in this study was race.

In yet another study (Bem, 1981b), the sixty masculine, feminine, and neutral attributes from the BSRI were all projected on a screen one at a time, and the subject was requested to push one of two buttons, "ME" or "NOT ME," to indicate whether the attribute was self-descriptive. Of interest in this study was the relationship between the subject's response latency and the gender of the attributes, in particular, whether sex-typed subjects would respond quickly when endorsing sex-appropriate attributes or rejecting sex-inappropriate attributes and slowly when admitting either to having some sex-inappropriate attributes or to lacking some sex-appropriate attributes. Such a pattern would suggest that sex-typed individuals have a readiness to decide on the basis of gender which attributes are to be associated with their self-concepts and which are to be dissociated from their self-concepts. It would further suggest that when filling out the BSRI, what sex-typed individuals are doing—in addition to trying to describe themselves—is sorting the attributes into equivalence classes on the basis of gender.[3]

These and other related studies are described at length in Bem (1985). Taken as a whole, they provide evidence that sex-typed individuals do, in fact, have a greater readiness than many other individuals to impose a gender-based classification system on reality.

Process Versus Content

Because sex-typed individuals are seen as processing information and regulating their behavior according to whatever definitions of femininity and masculinity their culture happens to provide, I have argued in previous articles that gender schema theory is "a theory of process, not content"; in other words, that "it is the process of dividing the world into feminine and masculine categories—and not the contents of the categories—that is central to the theory." On the face of it, this characterization of gender schema theory as a theory of process would seem to contradict the current argument that, like all good romantic theories, gender schema theory is primarily concerned with the culturally derived content of mind that is presumed to shape both perception and behavior.

There is no real contradiction here, however, because the kind of content that is of interest to a romantic theory itself constitutes a particular way of processing information. It is not knowledge or information per se that is the essential romantic content of mind; it is the conceptual schemes used to organize knowledge and information. To borrow a library metaphor for a moment, it is not how full the file drawers in one's mind are nor what particular items of information are contained within them; it is what the labels on those file drawers say and what classification system generated those particular labels.

So I still agree with the spirit of my earlier characterization. The way I would put it now, however, is that neither the process nor the content of mind by itself is critical to gender schema theory—or to any romantic theory. What is critical is the process of construing reality in terms of one kind of content rather than another. What is also critical are the sociocultural processes that implant that content.

NOTES

1. Two bodies of theory and research that do not bring an enlightenment approach to the study of selective perception are Nisbett and Ross's work on human inference and my own work on gender schema theory. Although this work is often assimilated with the schema research described here, I shall argue below that it is more appropriately placed within the romantic tradition.

2. One psychologist who has recently begun to explore the different theories of the self that different individuals can have is Mark Snyder (in press). And interestingly, the two theories of the self that he has discovered in his research on self-monitoring are analogous to the context-independent and context-dependent theories described above as Western and non-Western.

3. A study virtually identical to this one was carried out by Markus, Crane, Bernstein, and Siladi (1982) as part of Markus's research on self-schemas. The empirical focus of that study, however, was whether sex-typed individuals process masculine and/or feminine items rapidly, not whether a gender-based classification system is embodied in the overall pattern of their latencies. In contrast to the research derived from gender schema theory, Markus's research seems poised on the fence between the romantic and enlightenment traditions. Because of its concern with individual differences in spontaneous schema selection, it has more in common with the romantic tradition than any of the schema research described earlier in this chapter. Like that research, however, it focuses on the knowledge structures in mind, not on the mind's classification systems. Like that research, it also presupposes that a schema necessarily produces rapid responding. This focus on rapid responding is consistent with the definition of a schema as a knowledge structure. It is also quite common in studies that experimentally activate a particular schema and then examine the effects that activation has on subsequent information processing. It is not consistent, however, with the romantic goal of discovering what classification systems the individual spontaneously imposes on reality.

REFERENCES

Adorno, T. W., Frenkel-Brunswik, E., Levinson, D. J., & Sanford, R. N. (1950). *The authoritarian personality*. New York: Harper & Row.

Bannister, D., & Mair, J.M.M. (1968). *The evaluation of personal constructs*. New York: Academic Press.

Bem, D. J., & Allen, A. (1974). On predicting some of the people some of the time: The search for cross-situational consistencies in behavior. *Psychological Review, 81*, 506-520.

Bem, S. L. (1981a). *Bem Sex Role Inventory Professional Manual*. Palo Alto, CA: Consulting Psychologists Press.

Bem, S. L. (1981b). Gender schema theory: A cognitive account of sex typing. *Psychological Review, 88*, 354-364.

Bem, S. L. (1985). Androgyny and gender schema theory: A conceptual and empirical integration. In T. B. Sonderegger (Ed.), *Nebraska symposium on motivation 1984: Psychology and gender*. Lincoln: University of Nebraska Press.

Brown, R. (1965). *Social psychology*. New York: Free Press.

Frable, D.E.S., & Bem, S. L. (1985). If you're gender-schematic,, all members of the opposite sex look alike. *Journal of Personality and Social Psychology, 49*, 459-468.

Geertz, C. (1973). *The interpretation of cultures*. New York: Basic Books.

Geertz, C. (1984). "From the native's point of view": On the the nature of anthropological understanding. In R. R. Shweder & R. A. LeVine (Eds.), *Culture theory: Essays on mind, self, and emotion*. Cambridge: Cambridge University Press.

Kelly, G. A. (1955). *The psychology of personal constructs*. New York: W. W. Norton.

Markus, H., Crane, M., Bernstein, S., & Siladi, M. (1982). Self-schemas and gender. *Journal of Personality and Social Psychology, 42*, 38-50.

Markus, H., & Zajonc, R. B. (1985). The cognitive perspective in social psychology. In G. Lindzey & E. Aronson (Eds.), *The handbook of social psychology: Vol. 1. Theory and method*. New York: Random House.

McClelland, D. C. (1961). *The achieving society*. New York: Van Nostrand Reinhold.

McClelland, D. C., Atkinson, J. W., Clark, R. A., & Lowell, E. L. (1953). *The achievement motive*. New York: Appleton-Century-Crofts.

Nisbett, R., & Ross, L. (1980). *Human inference: Strategies and shortcomings of human judgment*. Englewood Cliffs, NJ: Prentice-Hall.

Rosaldo, M. Z. (1984). Toward an anthropology of self and feeling. In R. A. Shweder & R. S. LeVine (Eds.), *Culture theory: Essays on mind, self, and emotion*. Cambridge: Cambridge University Press.

Shweder, R. A. (1984). Anthropology's romantic rebellion against the enlightenment, or there's more to thinking than reason and evidence. In R. A. Shweder & R. A. LeVine (Eds.), *Culture theory: Essays on mind, self, and emotion*. Cambridge: Cambridge University Press.

Shweder, R. A., & Bourne, E. J. (1984). Does the concept of the person vary cross-culturally? In R. A. Shweder & R. A. LeVine (eds.), *Culture theory: Essays on mind, self, and emotion*. Cambridge: Cambridge University Press.

Synder, M. (in press). *Public appearances/private realities: The psychology of self-monitoring*. New York: Freeman.

11

Children's Sex-Role Stereotypes

A CROSS-CULTURAL ANALYSIS

VANDA LUCIA ZAMMUNER

Vanda Lucia Zammuner is a Research Associate in the Department of Developmental Psychology at the University of Padova, Italy. Besides the topics dealt with in this chapter, her research interests include cognitive and social antecedents of emotions in children and adults, and ways of coping with negative emotions (especially embarrassment); attitudes concerning abortion, pregnancy, and motherhood; and various aspects of language processing, including perception of pauses in speech, children's understandi..ᵦ and production of discourse, and, especially, cognitive strategies of discourse production.

Several years ago, Rosenberg and Sutton-Smith (1972) answered the question of whether psychological sex differences are desirable by suggesting that "though some of today's sex differences may disappear, others may arise, for men and women may well invent new techniques for polarization[;] it may be that a society without sex stereotypes is much less interesting and productive than societies with definitions of sex role behavior" (p. 90). Katz (in press), in contrast, concludes her paper on the development and consequences of gender identity with the proposal that "vive la similitude" might be a more appropriate attitude toward maleness and femaleness than "vive la difference." These two value orientations can be found not only among present-day psychologists and laypersons but also throughout the history of research on masculinity, femininity, and other sex differences (Morawski, 1985, and this volume).

Research on sex differences is thriving today, and the range of values held by investigators is as great as ever. Nevertheless, the field is more complex today than before, as evidenced by (1) the number of dimensions under investigation and the use of multivariate measurement strategies; (2) the distinction between sex and gender, which suggests that sex-role related psychological differences may be somewhat

AUTHOR'S NOTE: I am grateful to Phillip Shaver for comments on an earlier draft of this chapter, and for his help with matters of English style in the present version.

independent of biological sex; (3) the emphasis on contextual variation, including differences across cultures, subcultures, concrete life experiences, and so on; and (4) the drawing of connections between sex-role stereotyping and other forms of social-cognitive schematization and discrimination. The approach I have been using in my own cross-national studies of children's sex-role stereotyping is informed by these contemporary trends.

Sex and gender constitute perhaps the single most important grounds for discrimination between types of human individuals. Katz (in press) defines gender as a "life script," Bem (1984) as a "sprawling associative network" that functions as a powerful schema in the processing of social information. Spence (1984) suggests that masculinity and femininity, although clearly influential aspects of personality and social life, are "amorphous concepts, rich in their connotations, but left undefined and unanalyzed." All of these characterizations remind us of the pervasive and complex role of gender in our lives—regardless of where we live, I might add—and of the importance of studying how males and females are imagined and perceived.

The social world in which children grow up is everywhere pervasively gender typed. Starting with linguistic labels—including, usually, the child's own name—and continuing with toys, clothes, hairstyles, parents' socialization practices, the content of children's books, television programs, advertisements, school teachings and socialization efforts, and peer socialization, gender differentation is everywhere imposed from "outside," so to speak. In addition, as soon as gender identity is rudimentarily established, it begins functioning as a processing schema, which allows for the encoding and organization of new information actively sought by the child (Bem, 1984). Presumably, sex and gender are used as organizing principles because the social world in which the child develops is structured along sex-differentiated lines. To the extent that local social worlds vary in ways related to sexual differentiation, children's perceptions and conceptions of sex differences should also differ. That possibility has been the focus of my recent work.

ITALIAN AND DUTCH CHILDREN'S
SEX-ROLE KNOWLEDGE AND PREFERENCES

The research projects I will summarize here concern ways in which children of different ages, living in different European countries, perceive males and females in terms of (1) toy and play preferences, (2) personality and behavioral characteristics, and (3) aggression and dependency. The data were collected during the late 1970s in Italy and Holland, two countries that can be taken as fairly representative of Mediterranean and northern European societies. As anyone familiar with these societies will agree, sex-role norms and behaviors are generally more traditional in the former than in the latter, which is my main reason for comparing them. It has also been possible, mainly within Holland, to compare children from progressive and traditional schools, thereby adding a "cultural" contrast not based on nationality.

Play Activities: Judgments and Preferences

Children's preferences for certain toys, games, and play activities have been interpreted as indications of internalization of local norms concerning sex-role appropriateness (e.g., Brown & Tolar, 1957; Flerk, Fidler, & Rogers, 1976; Frueh & McGhee, 1975; Perloff, 1977; Sears, 1953; Sutton-Smith, Rosenberg, & Morgan, 1963). Although the methodology of these studies varies, children are usually assigned a sex-role identity score based on the number of "correct" preferences they exhibit, where correct means in line with established norms for children of each sex. For children between 4 and 10 years old, the most common results are that "correct" choices increase with age and that, at every age, girls make more "incorrect" choices than boys. These findings have been interpreted as indicating that acceptance of one's sex role is more stable with age and less conflicted for boys than for girls. The same methodologies have been used to measure sex-role stereotyping rather than gender-identity formation (e.g., Hartley & Hardesty, 1964). In general, it has been difficult, based on the published literature, to separate what children know about local norms from what they apply to themselves.

Studies of toy and play preferences have been based on more or less implicit acceptance of a single-dimensional model of masculinity and femininity; a child is placed somewhere along the continuum depending on the number of "correct" preferences expressed. Not only is this procedure questionable, because masculinity and femininity may be independent rather than opposite (e.g., Constantinople, 1973; Spence, 1984), but investigators have often used very heterogeneous options without equating them for intrinsic attractiveness and associated play styles and without inquiring about what children have in mind when they make "incorrect" choices. I have tried to overcome some of these problems in my work.

The main ideas behind my initial studies (Zammuner, 1980, 1981) were as follows: (1) Children's preferences would vary not just as a function of age and sex, but also as a function of social context. In particular, I expected toy preferences to vary as a function of country (Italy versus Holland) and school setting (progressive versus traditional). (2) Children's knowledge and preferences might differ from those of the surrounding adult community because children are not just passive absorbers of adult values and norms; they may alter or elaborate the norms based on their own needs and experiences. (3) There may be a discrepancy between children's own preferences and their knowledge of appropriate norms. Previous tests involving preference have tended to confuse these potentially different phenomena (especially the studies that have made girls look conflicted or slow to learn what is appropriate for their sex). (4) Children's preferences for and judgments about toys might be influenced by general processes of intra- and intergroup stereotyping; that is, children of a particular sex might conceptualize appropriateness in ways that maximize their own, and their own group's, pleasures and prerogatives.

I chose 20 toys based on previous research (Brown, 1956, 1957; De Lucia, 1963; Rosenberg & Sutton-Smith, 1959; Sutton-Smith et al., 1963), personal observations, and pilot testing. These toys had to be familiar and attractive to 5- to 10-year-olds and similar in their intrinsic value. Both stereotypically masculine and stereotypically feminine toys were included, as well as toys that were presumed not to be sex-typed. To control somewhat for attractiveness response bias, similar black and white drawings of the toys were used, each presented on a 20cm × 30cm card. Male, female, and neutral child figures, to be used as response options in the toy judgment task, were also drawn in black and white.

There were two tests administered to independent samples, a toy judgment test (TJT) and a toy preference test (TPT), the idea being that judgment and preference might not be the same. The TJT was administered to 57 Italian and 68 Dutch men and women, with or without children, married or single, and with either more or less than 12 years of schooling. It was also administered to 31 Italian children (5-9 years old) and 170 Dutch children (7-10 years old), the latter from schools classified as either progressive or traditional based on atmosphere, teachers' sex-role attitudes, kinds of reading materials assigned, and so on. The TPT was administered to 118 Italian children (7.7, 8.5, and 10.7 years old, on the average) and to 194 Dutch children (4.8, 7.9, and 10.6 years old, on the average). The children came from predominantly middle-class backgrounds, and in both countries most of their mothers were housewives.

Toy Judgments

Dutch men and women were more homogeneous in their judgments than Italian men and women, and Italian adults did more sex-role stereotyping. For example, the Italians rated about five toys as sex-neutral, whereas the Dutch rated 11 in this way. On the other hand, both groups of adults categorized most of the toys in the same direction—as masculine (M) or feminine (F)—although the Dutch subjects' judgments were less extreme. (Unlike the children, who indicated M, F, or N via the drawings of male, female, and sex-neutral child figures, adults also gave quantitative ratings of degree of M or F.)

More than half of the Italian children judged 10 or more of the 20 toys to be appropriate for either males or females, but there was considerable variability on the remaining toys. The toys judged M or F were the same ones classified in that way by the Italian adults—namely, the football, airplane, race car, train, and construction bricks were viewed as M, and the telephone, jump rope, sewing machine, kitchen utensils, and doll as F. The similarity between children's and adults' judgments suggests that considerable sex-role socialization has occurred by 8 years of age. For the supposedly intermediate (i.e., non-sex-typed) toys, M and F judgments were frequent but different for boys and girls. For example, the guitar was categorized as M by 80% of the boys but by only 37% of the girls. Toys were rarely categorized in opposite directions (i.e., as M by one sex and F by the other), but girls more often judged a given toy—including the most stereotyped M and F ones—as N. This is one of several indications I will be mentioning that girls are more motivated than boys to redefine sex-role boundaries.

Dutch children, like Italian children, judged about half of the toys as M or F. Unlike the Italian children, however, both boys and girls in the Dutch sample defined a higher number of toys as appropriate for their own sex. Children attending a progressive school were less inclined to categorize toys as M or F, especially at younger ages. Once again, toys that were categorized as M or F tended to be the same ones that adults categorized that way. Dutch children, like Dutch adults, were more homogeneous in their judgments than the Italian children despite the progressive-traditional school distinction in the Dutch sample.

In both countries, adult-like judgments tended to increase with age, suggesting that between 5 and 10 years of age children learn a great deal about local conceptions of sex roles.

Toy Preferences

For this test I used a score based on "correct" choices, that is, choices that were, by adult consensus, sex-appropriate. Children were asked to choose the toy that they preferred from each of 22 pictured toy pairs. The "correct" score was based on preferences expressed for the 11 most discriminating pairs, according to adult judgments. On the average, Italian children chose a sex-appropriate toy more often than the Dutch children, and in both countries boys more often than girls made "correct" choices. These findings are compatible with published results from English-speaking countries. The number of "correct" choices actually decreased with age, however, indicating that preferences depend on more than the kind of age-related knowledge discussed in the previous section. Knowledge does not necessarily dictate preference. Looking at the preference results as a whole, it was clear that boys did not differ as much across cultures or age levels as girls did. It seems, therefore, either that girls are more sensitive to socialization pressures and opportunities or that the pressures are more uniform for boys.

Additional Findings

Because one of my goals is to familiarize English-speaking audiences with work that they may not see otherwise, I will briefly mention some related Italian data from other studies I have conducted (Zammuner, 1983). On the basis of toy judgments provided by a new sample of adults—which, incidentally, confirmed the previous results—I selected toys to be presented in all possible pairs: football and race car as M, skittles as slightly M, roller skates as N, jump rope as slightly F, and doll carriage and kitchen utensils as F. The preferences expressed by 5- to 6-year-olds and 7- to 8-year-olds (analyzed in terms of Thurstone's case V method of paired comparisons) formed a perfectly ordered continuum, with boys least often selecting the feminine toys and most often selecting the masculine toys, and girls doing the reverse. Girls more often than boys chose sex-inappropriate toys, but both groups' "incorrect" choices tended to involve the less extremely sex-typed toys. In other words, both girls and boys acknowledged the continuum, both made more sex-appropriate than sex-inappropriate choices, but girls defined their part of the continuum more broadly than males did.

Another study involved kindergarten children who judged the 20 toys used in my previous research as M, F, or N. On the average, only 4-5 toys were consistently judged by boys and girls as appropriate for their sex. The number of toys that children thought were sex-neutral was higher for 6-year-old than for 4-year-old children, and was higher for girls than for boys. Finally, in a third study, 10-year-old children listed toy and play activities preferred by and appropriate for members of each sex. Of the 245 items listed, 17% were categorized by both boys and girls as F, and 24% were categorized as M; also, boys provided more masculine items than girls did. Of all the listed activities, 46% involved motor behavior (e.g., hide and seek, skating); boys defined more of such activities as appropriate for their sex, whereas girls did not. Of the listed activities, 13% were table or social games (e.g., chess); girls attributed these equally to boys and girls, but boys characterized most of them as appropriate for girls only. On the average, boys characterized 6.4 activities as feminine and 9.2 as masculine; girls assigned about 10 activities to each sex.

Taken together, the results indicate that both boys and girls tend to enlarge the pool of activities available to themselves, but girls do this differently than boys. Girls more often make "incorrect" choices and judge more items as appropriate for both sexes. Rather than interpreting these results as evidence for sex-role identity confusion in girls, as has been done in much of the American literature, I interpret them as signs that girls would like to engage in a greater range of activities than sex-role norms have traditionally allowed them. An egocentric bias is present in both boys and girls, but boys do not generally have to make "incorrect" choices in order to engage in the activities that both they and girls like. Moreover, I get the sense from talking with the children that boys feel that the "unmarked" activities are rightfully theirs, in addition to the masculine activities. As in the case of language ("man" for people, "he" for he and she, and so on), whatever is "neutral" seems to have male rather than female as a default value. The burden therefore rests on girls to appropriate actively what is supposedly neutral.

Personality Attributes and Behaviors of Men and Women

Sex-role stereotypes have been studied not only in terms of judgments and preferences but also in terms of personality traits, occupational roles, and so on, using, again, a variety of methodological and theoretical approaches (e.g., Best et al., 1977; Broverman, Vogel, Broverman, Clarkson, & Rosenkrantz, 1972; Nadelman, 1974; Rosenkrantz, Vogel, Broverman, & Broverman, 1968; Scheresky, 1976). In my own research, I have focused especially on qualitative and structural differences in children's perceptions of personality and behavioral characteristics of men and women (Zammuner, 1982; Zammuner & Heiser, 1983).

My hypotheses were as follows: (1) Children's perceptions of sex-related attributes are influenced by general processes of self-enhancement (i.e., children tend to attribute positive but not negative characteristics to themselves and to members of their sex). (2) This process, however, interacts with the child's perception of judgments made by other people concerning characteristics of the two sexes. Therefore, to the extent possible given their sex-role knowledge, children should express judgments that deemphasize links between positive traits and the opposite sex (by claiming these traits for their own sex or for both sexes), and deemphasize links between negative traits and their own sex (by attributing them to the opposite sex or both sexes). (3) Age, nationality, and school atmosphere may influence attributions. (4) Personality traits may be more stereotyped than behavioral characteristics, because traits are perceived as basic and inherently stable whereas behaviors are more variable and situationally specific.

Based on pilot testing, two sets of 28 words or phrases were chosen for use in the study. The first set referred to personality attributes (traits) such as *generous, intelligent,* and *shy* (see Figure 11.1); the second set to behavioral dispositions (actions) such as *to help, to give advice,* and *to quarrel* (see Figure 11.2). Except for a few stimuli that were expected to be sex-neutral, the selected characteristics were related to important aspects of masculine and feminine sex roles. In a "game" that they enjoyed a great deal, children were asked whether each word or phrase better described men or women, or described both sexes to the same degree. The study included 84 Italian children (10.1 years old, on average) and 220 Dutch children (10.2 and 12.4 years old, on average).

Italian children defined personality traits as descriptive of men or women more often than Dutch children did, a trend that also characterized their judgments concerning behavioral dispositions; and both groups attributed more characteristics to their own sex. In both countries, boys made sex-differential attributions more often than girls did. Italian children categorized about eight traits as F or M; Dutch children did so with six traits. In general, women were stereotyped more than men, although Italian children attributed more characteristics to men than Dutch children did (e.g., eight versus five personality traits). Indeed, the two national samples differed mainly in their perceptions of men. The older Dutch children, especially those from a traditional school, categorized more stimuli as masculine or feminine than their younger counterparts did, again suggesting that learning the sex-role definitions and stereotypes of one's local culture continues well into childhood. In this particular study, I included Italian children from both progressive and traditional schools (as I had with Dutch children in all of the studies reported here). There were fewer indications in the Italian data for the lessening of stereotyping due to progressive education. There were, however, some clear interschool differences on the contents of the sex stereotypes, indicating that schooling has an influence.

The traits *patient, shy, sensitive, chatter-box, gossipy, vain,* and *weak* and the actions *to comfort, to cure, to spend, to cry, to be curious, to serve,* and *to obey* were, on average, viewed as feminine by children in both countries. Therefore, although I have been emphasizing differences between Italy and Holland, there is no shortage of stereotyping in either country. *Lazy, superficial, clever, absent-minded, loud, violent,* and *strong,* and *to yell, to protect, to make jokes, to construct, to repair, to break,* and *to punish* were viewed as masculine characteristics in both countries. There were interesting differences, however, both within and across national samples, and I would like to turn to those next.

A Structural Account

The qualitative aspects of sex-role stereotypes were investigated via multidimensional scaling analyses (ALSCAL-3; Carroll & Chang, 1970; Takane, Young, & de Leew, 1977). Children's perceptions of personality traits and behaviors were described in terms of two-dimensional spatial configurations of the stimuli (for examples from the Dutch analyses, see Figures 11.1 and 11.2). These diagrams, each containing three vectors (masculine, feminine, sex-neutral), allow one to see both the relationships between stimuli and (by comparing diagrams for different samples) the differences between samples. (Unfortunately, there is space here to show only two illustrative diagrams.)

The Italian children's configuration of personality traits included a compact sex-neutral cluster formed by such stimuli as *altruistic, sincere, generous,* and *loyal.* Many traits, however, clustered in between the M and N axes, and the F and N axes. Some of these had been categorized as

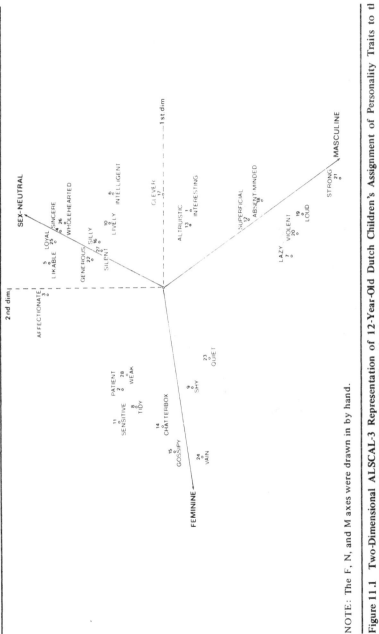

NOTE: The F, N, and M axes were drawn in by hand.

Figure 11.1   Two-Dimensional ALSCAL-3 Representation of 12-Year-Old Dutch Children's Assignment of Personality Traits to the Categories Masculine, Feminine, and Sex-Neutral

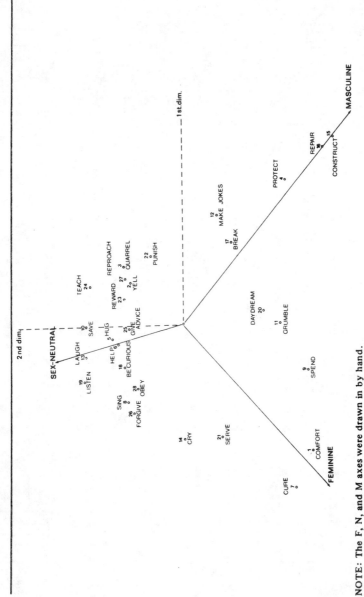

NOTE: The F, N, and M axes were drawn in by hand.

Figure 11.2 Two-Dimensional ALSCAL-3 Representation of 10- and 12-Year-Old Dutch Boys' Assignment of Behavioral Dispositions (actions) to the Categories Masculine, Feminine, and Sex-Neutral

282

descriptive of either one or both sexes (e.g., *lazy, clever,* and *lively* as M or N; *quiet, sensitive, shy,* and *patient* as F or N). Other stimuli, such as *vain, superficial,* and *absent-minded,* were perceived by some children as descriptive of men and by other children as descriptive of women, and these therefore fell between the M and F axes. In general, traits indicating interpersonal qualities were judged as descriptive of women or of both sexes, whereas those referring to intellectual characteristics were attributed to men or to both sexes. The positions of boys' and girls' stimulus judgments indicated that boys stereotyped men more than women, whereas girls stereotyped both sexes to the same extent. The configuration obtained for actions was characterized by larger distances—interpretable as measures of differentiation—between extreme M and F stimuli, whereas distances among the remaining traits were much smaller. This reflected extreme homogeneity of judgment regarding a few actions perceived as very characteristic of one sex or the other, and extreme variability in the gender-related categorization of the remaining behaviors. The three main clusters can be designated M-N, F-N, and M-F. The M-N cluster included *to quarrel, to give advice, to break, to yell, to reproach, to make jokes, to grumble,* and *to reward.* The F-N cluster included *to hug, to listen, to laugh, to teach, to forgive, to obey,* and *to sing.* The M-F cluster included *to help, to save, to daydream, to spend, to punish,* and *to protect.*

The separate configurations obtained for each sex revealed that it was mainly boys who associated the same personality traits with both men and women. However, both sexes failed to differentiate clearly between sex-neutral traits and the traits associated with their own sex, indicating either greater ambivalence and uncertainty in attributing traits to the same-sex than to the opposite-sex group or greater motivation to claim neutral traits for one's own group. Both boys and girls placed more actions in the same-sex and sex-neutral categories than in the other-sex category. Both sexes seemed to feel more comfortable characterizing the other sex in terms of personality traits than in terms of behaviors.

In the Dutch sample, recall, there were two age groups—roughly 10 and 12 years old. Results for the older group were more homogeneous than for the younger group, especially where personality traits were involved. The younger children characterized only a few extreme masculine and feminine traits as clearly applying to only one sex or the other. There were few effects of progressive versus traditional school. Girls, as a group, categorized stimuli as masculine or feminine less often than boys, but all of their categorizations tended to be more homogeneous. For girls, there were three large M, F, and N clusters and no assignment of stimuli to categories opposite to what was expected; for boys, personality traits were less consistently differentiated and formed looser clusters. Examples of the diversity in categorization follow: (1) The traits *patient, sensitive, shy,* and *quiet,* which were seen by girls as typical of women, were judged largely as sex-neutral by boys. (2) For girls, most actions fell into one of two large clusters, which were located near the extreme sex-neutral point but in either the M or the F region; for boys there were several small, loose clusters, only one of which was clearly sex-neutral, and some stimuli fell in a category opposite to what was expected. In short, boys' perceptions of sex-role related attributes were not nearly as coherent as girls'.

Among the Dutch girls, there was a very clear age effect. The younger group's configuration was like a loose horseshoe, evidencing little differentiation. The older group's judgments formed three compact M, F, and N clusters. Even then, the 10-year-old girls' results were more clearly patterned than the results for 10-year-old boys.

Overall, the results support my hypothesis that assignment of sex-related characteristics to males and females is constrained by knowledge, which is in turn related to age, sex, and sociocultural context. It is also related to egocentric bias, as girls assign traits such as *patient* and *sensitive* to themselves, whereas boys see these traits as sex-neutral and hence as potentially self-descriptive. Boys claim that *interesting* and *clever* are masculine traits, whereas girls place them in the sex-neutral category, leaving open the possibility that girls as well as boys can exhibit these desirable characteristics.

There were some unexpected results. Personality traits elicited sex-differential attributions more frequently than behavioral characteristics, which contradicts previous hypotheses to the effect that overt behavioral patterns are easier than traits to associate with social categories (e.g., Williams, Bennett, & Best, 1975). Researchers need to look more closely at the possibility that books, television, and adults' comments convey accessible information concerning gender-related traits: "What a strong man!" "What an intelligent boy!" "What a shy, sweet little girl!" Perhaps children learn these linguistic tags more readily than developmental theories would suggest.

Another unexpected result was that women were generally stereotyped more (i.e., described more often in stereotyped terms) than men. This finding was also obtained in a study of Brazilian children, for whom, the authors claim, female models may have been more frequently available (Tarrier & Gomes, 1981). The results from that study and from my own are at variance with data reported by Best et al. (1977), who found that male traits were better known by children of both sexes. Their subjects were from England, North America, and Ireland. There may thus be some cross-cultural differences in this regard, although it would be important to compare details of methodology before drawing that conclusion.

It is my impression that sex-role stereotyping is influenced by so many different variables that we may find it more useful to focus on details of the specific contents and processes involved than to try to compare samples on global indices of amount of stereotyping. The different groups I have tested vary not only in how much they distinguish between the sexes, but in the way they organize sex-relevant descriptive information. It may be important to understand why the constructs are what they are for different groups of children—in other words, to take a functional approach to the study of sex-role stereotyping.

Attribution of Dependent and Aggressive Behaviors to Males and Females

Among the personality characteristics considered masculine or feminine are independence/aggressiveness and dependence/passivity. A review of the literature on adult aggression (Frodi & Macaulay, 1977) indicates that stereotyped differences between males and females occur mainly on self-report measures of general hostility and aggressiveness, rather than in the sex-related forms of anger and aggression. (Averill, 1982, has shown, for example, that there are few differences between males and females in anger experiences or angry behavior, one exception being the prevalence of crying when angry.) Males and females seem to react somewhat differently to provocations to aggression, females more often becoming anxious, males more often becoming angry. And males more often than females engage in physical aggression. Both males and females behave less aggressively toward females, and both males and females are more likely to be aggressive when aggression is viewed as socially acceptable. In fact, when aggression is viewed as acceptable for both sexes, there are few sex differences.

There are wildly conflicting interpretations of the available data concerning the role of socialization in creating sex differences in aggression (Maccoby & Jacklin, 1980; Tieger, 1980). We know that children associate aggressiveness and independence with males, and dependency and passivity with females. For instance, they see women as more emotional, weak, forgiving and so on, and men as strong, violent, and quarrelsome, as I have shown earlier in this chapter (see also Williams et al., 1975). A study by Marantz Connor, Serbin, and Ender (1978), with children of 8, 10, and 12 years of age, showed that the degree of approval for aggressive, assertive, and passive behavior depends on the sex of the character engaging in the behavior, and on the age and sex of the child making the judgment.

In my own work (Zammuner & Grego, 1985) I have focused on aggressive and dependent behaviors thought by children to be typical of boys and girls. Two simple stories were presented to children, both referring to a play situation that becomes frustrating for the protagonist (Paul or Mary) because of the actions of another child (John or Liza). (The action was either breaking Paul or Mary's toy, or excluding Paul or Mary from a group game.) Children were asked to rank how likely it was that Paul or Mary would react in certain ways (crying, being verbally aggressive, calling mother, calling father, breaking or taking the other child's toy, pushing, helping to repair the broken toy, finding another group to play with, and so on). The stories were presented to 343 Italian children (8.0 and 10.4 years old, on average) and 827 Dutch children (5.1, 8.0, and 10.2 years old, on average). The stories were also presented to several different groups of Italian adults.

Analysis of the data from Italian children revealed that age was an important predictor of reaction. Eight-year-old children most often chose crying and breaking or taking away the play partner's toy and least often chose calling the father for help and pushing the partner. The action preferred most by older children, especially boys, was more socially desirable: repairing the broken toy with the partner or, for the group situation, finding another group of children with whom to play. Their least preferred choices were calling the father and verbal aggression. The younger children differentiated their choices more according to sex, and girls were more homogeneous in their choices across age than boys.

The choices made by the Dutch children similarly changed mainly according to age. Both 8- and 10-year-olds rejected calling the father and crying; however, older children frequently chose object aggression (breaking the other's toy) and rejected the cooperative behavior, whereas the younger ones frequently chose the latter, in addition to calling the mother for help. Only the youngest Dutch children exhibited notable sex differences in their choices, girls preferring to call an adult or break the partner's toy and rejecting verbal aggression, boys differentiating little between the behaviors although preferring crying above the others. Dutch girls chose aggressive behaviors much more frequently than Italian girls, who seemed to prefer a cooperative attitude or adult intervention.

As in previous studies, the protagonist's sex influenced which actions children—especially the Italians—saw as most and least likely. Mary, as the story protagonist, was more often associated with crying and calling mother for help; Paul, in contrast, was associated with calling father. However, the choice of other behaviors varied according to age. Calling father, for example, was the least chosen behavior for Paul among 10-year-old boys and girls, who instead said that he would push the other child; these same children ranked all forms of aggression low for Mary, the female protagonist.

This result fit my hypothesis nicely but contrasted sharply with the results for Dutch children, who saw aggression as more likely for Mary than for Paul. In general, the Dutch children's choices did not seem to be based on sex-role appropriateness, at least as defined by adults. If the protagonist was Paul, he was expected to be aggressive toward the partner Liza but cooperative toward the partner John. If the protagonist was Mary and the partner was Liza, Mary would call her mother; if the partner was John, Mary would break or take away his toy. In other words, the Dutch children predicted cross-sex aggression.

The judgments by Italian adults were especially interesting to me, because they revealed the probable source of my own culturally biased expectations. Although crying was the most likely action predicted by adults for Paul and Mary, they next said that Paul would be aggressive and Mary would call mother. Men more often than women attributed aggressive reactions to both Paul and Mary, whereas women chose crying more often for both characters. In general, Italian men and women, my peers, ranked the alternatives the way I thought that both adults and older children would.

In summary, there were significant effects of children's age and sex of story protagonist, but the main differences were due to nationality. Dutch children, on average, seemed to base their judgments less on stereotypes than Italian children did, and the two national groups revealed different behavioral expectations. There were more effects of protagonist's sex than of subject's sex, suggesting that children based their judgments more on sex-role stereotypes than on what they themselves might do. As with the difference mentioned earlier, between toy judgments and toy preferences, there may be a difference between behaviors predicted for others and those chosen by oneself. That potential difference—and, if it exists, its determinants—remains to be explored in future studies.

SEX-ROLE STEREOTYPES: A DISCUSSION

The research I have summarized in this chapter indicates that, generally speaking, Dutch children differentiate between the sexes less than Italian children do. This conclusion is congruent with my personal impression that adult sex roles in Holland—including division of labor in the family, amount and kinds of employment, and leisure activities— are less sharply differentiated than in Italy. This, in turn, affects the models available to children and the socialization pressures applied to them. The generally lower intragroup variability exhibited by Dutch children, and by Dutch adults, probably reflects the greater homogeneity of Dutch culture. By comparison, Italian culture is, for well-known historical reasons (e.g., long-standing differences between regions that were once distinct city-states, differences between north and south), not very homogeneous. Heterogeneity is especially great regarding social values, such as those related to sex roles; it appears even among people of the same education and SES levels.

Elsewhere in this volume, Bem draws a distinction between schemas (knowledge structures) based on encounters with reality and schemas that are culturally invented and taught to children. If the goal of this distinction is to indicate that what Bem calls "gender schemas" are not concerned with a static reality, I would agree. My results show that children's conceptions of sex differences vary between Italy and Holland, and between different kinds of schools, clearly indicating that conceptions of sex roles are not cross-culturally invariant. However, if Bem is saying that gender schemas have to be taught and are not derivable from children's observations of local social reality, I would disagree. Because sex roles themselves really do differ between Italy and Holland, children in those two countries can form schemas largely by observing what men and women are actually like and what they actually do. To the children, sex differences are part of reality, just as much as differences between other kinds of creatures (e.g., cats and dogs) and phenomena (e.g., weather patterns). True, sex-role stereotypes are also directly taught by parents, teachers, media figures, and other children, so gender schemas are probably a joint function of observation and tuition.

The fact that sex-role related norms and behaviors include so many different aspects of personal and public life helps explain why children's conceptions are complex. This is especially likely in a historical period characterized by rapid mobility and social change, and by a complex pattern of information flow within and between sociocultural groups. (I am myself an example, working simultaneously with colleagues in Italy, Holland, and England, and writing for an American publication.) Moreover, prescriptive sex-role norms have undergone many changes in recent decades due to socioeconomic forces—changes in family structure, birthrates, job opportunities, and so on—and to widely publicized feminist thinking. The extent and impact of these changes are not homogeneous, across cultures or within cultural groups. Thus it is not surprising that different cultures and subcultures, and different individuals within them, fail to share all of the same values and norms at any particular time.

In comparison with studies conducted in other countries, the results I have discussed indicate less sex-role stereotyping. This difference may be due in part to my provision of a sex-neutral response category in most of my studies. It may also be due to the relative recency of my studies compared to many of those I relied on for methodological precedents. I would not want to dismiss too quickly, however, the possibility that there really are cultural differences that would show up even if the same measures were used across cultural boundaries at the same time. The detection of cross-cultural similarities is clearly important, both for theorizing about the causes of sex differentiation in roles and personal styles and for adjusting to practically and politically significant social change; but if we are to comprehend the interplay of social-cognitive development and culture, more attention should be paid to genuine cultural variations. There certainly seem to be cross-cultural similarities in male and female roles, and in the corresponding stereotypes and ideologies, but there are important differences as well, as I hope I have shown in my comparison between two European societies that are, after all, not nearly as dissimilar as some other pairs of societies in the world.

The methods I employed enabled me, to some extent, to focus on the contents of children's sex-role stereotypes. The results show that there are differences in the kinds of sex-role knowledge children acquire and exhibit related to nationality, age, and sex, and to the tasks in which they are engaged. Nevertheless, the interaction among all of these variables is such that variations in stereotypes (e.g., in the simple amount of stereotyping, the stereotyping of one sex more than the other, or the contents of specific groups' stereotypes) cannot easily be explained in terms of the predictable effects of those variables. Factors besides the sex-role knowledge imparted to children of a certain age in a certain setting—for example, more general social-cognitive developmental processes and cognitive and affective processes involved in in-group versus out-group discrimination—contribute to children's conceptions of the sexes. An example is the young child's tendency to use an "inflexible and evaluative mode of thinking about group differences," discussed by Katz (in press), or the child's disposition to describe others in overly simple stereotypic terms, especially while initially attempting to grasp new social categories. Better insights about the genesis, purpose, structure, and salience of sex-role stereotypes might result from an approach that is more qualitative, functionalist, and dynamic rather than quantitative and dimensional in traditional psychometric ways.

The developmental trend that generally emerged in my studies was such that children differentiated less between the sexes at younger ages, but this pattern changed considerably depending on whether children were judging or choosing toys, categorizing personality traits or actions, or attributing dependent and aggressive responses to hypo- thetical children. Moreover, the developmental trend is clear only if we consider the extreme age groups—5-year-olds versus 10- to 12-year- olds. If these trends were due only to changes in cognitive processes and capacities, it seems unlikely that they would show as much variability as they do with respect to task, stimuli, and nationality and sex of subject. We may conclude instead that, though a child's age definitely places certain constraints on the categorization process (e.g., flexibility versus rigidity, amount and kind of social knowledge available), other more idiosyncratic factors will also influence which aspects related to sex roles will be differentiated stereotypically, and to what extent.

Sex of child is obviously an important variable. In general, girls stereotype less than boys, but within certain age-by-task categories boys sometimes stereotype less. Sometimes both sexes stereotype the charac- teristics or preferences of the opposite (or same) sex more, but under other conditions they stereotype both groups equally. Sometimes girls are the more homogeneous group (across cultures or age levels), but at other times boys are. There are no simple generalizations about sex of child, just as there are none concerning age. One of the most interesting sex effects, which appeared in more than one context, had to do with boys' and girls'—especially girls'—tendency to expand the range of options available to their sex. This suggests, I think, that children would like sex roles to be less constraining than they are at present. Fortunately, there were signs in my data, different from what I expected based on previous studies in the literature, that older children do not always base their personal preferences on sex-role stereotypes even when they know quite well what the stereotypes are. If this trend can be maintained into adolescence and adulthood, life choices may be made despite knowledge of traditional stereotypes.

Sex, nationality, age, and local socialization environment are all important determinants of children's sex-role knowledge and preferences, but they interact in very complex ways. In order to understand what children think and feel about sex roles, we need to consider what they see around them, their level of social-cognitive development, their egocentric biases (both personal biases and biases related to group membership), and probably other factors as well. Studying sex-role stereotyping within a cross-cultural framework helps to reveal its complexity and at the same time suggests that the definitions of masculinity and femininity need not be static—and need not constrain the members of either gender to the point where they resent each other's socially defined activities and prerogatives.

REFERENCES

Averill, J. R. (1982). *Anger and aggression: An essay on emotion.* New York: Springer-Verlag.

Bem, S. L. (1984). Androgyny and gender schema theory: A conceptual and empirical integration. In T. B. Sonderegger (Ed.), *Nebraska symposium on motivation: Psychology and gender* (pp. 170-226). Lincoln: University of Nebraska Press.

Best, D. L., Williams, J. E., Cloud, J. M., Davis, S. W., Robertson, L. S., Edwards, J. R., Giles, H., & Fowles, J. (1977). Development of sex-trait stereotypes among young children in the United States, England, and Ireland. *Child Development, 48,* 1375-1384.

Broverman, I. K., Vogel, S. R., Broverman, D. M., Clarkson, F. E., & Rosenkrantz, P. S. (1972). Sex role stereotypes: A current appraisal. *Journal of Social Issues, 28*(2), 59-78.

Brown, D. G. (1956). Sex-role preference in young children. *Psychological Monographs, 70,* No. 14.

Brown, D. C. (1957). Masculinity and femininity development in children. *Journal of Consulting and Clinical Psychology, 21,* 197-202.

Brown, D. G., & Tolar, A. (1957). Human figure drawings as indicators of sexual identification and inversion. *Perceptual and Motor Skills, 7,* 199-211.

Carroll, J. D., & Chang, J. J. (1970). Analysis of individual differences in multidimensional

Constantinople, A. (1973). Masculinity-femininity: An exception to a famous dictum? *Psychological Bulletin, 80,* 389-407.

De Lucia, L. (1963). The toy preference test: A measure of sex-role identification. *Child Development, 34,* 107-117.

Etaugh, C., & Hughes, V. (1975). Teachers' evaluations of sex-typed behaviors in children: The role of teacher sex and school setting. *Developmental Psychology, 11,* 394-395.

Fagot, B. I. (1977). Teacher's reinforcement of sex-preferred behaviors in Dutch preschools. *Psychological Reports, 41,* 1249-1250.

Flerk, V. C., Fidler, D. S., & Rogers, R. W. (1976). Sex role stereotypes: Developmental aspects and early intervention. *Child Development, 47,* 998-1007.

Frodi, A., Macaulay, J., & Thome, P. R. (1977). Are women always less aggressive than men? A review of the experimental literature. *Psychological Bulletin, 84,* 634-660.

Frueh, T., & McGhee, P. (1975). Traditional sex-role development and amount of time spent watching television. *Developmental Psychology, 11,* 109.

Hartley, R. E., & Hardesty, F. P. (1964). Children's perception of sex roles in childhood. *Journal of Genetic Psychology, 105,* 43-51.

Hoffman, M. L. (1977). Personality and social development. *Annual Review of Psychology, 28,* 295-321.

Katz, P. A. (in press). Gender identity: Development and consequences. In R. D. Ashmore & F. K. Del Boca (Eds.), *The social psychology of female-male relations.* New York: Academic Press.

Maccoby, E. E., & Jacklin, C. N. (1980). Sex differences in aggression: A rejoinder and reprise. *Child Development, 51,* 964-980.

Marantz Connor, J., Serbin, L. A., & Ender, R. A. (1978). Responses of boys and girls to aggressive, assertive, and passive behaviors of male and female characters. *Journal of Genetic Psychology, 133,* 59-69.

McGurk, H., & Glachan, M. (1985). Como piensan y las creeccias de los ninos y los adultos. In E. Enesco & J. Enaza (Eds.), *Como Piensan y Actuan los Social.* Madrid: Alianza Universidad.

Miller, S. M. (1975). Effects of maternal employment on sex-role perception, interests, and self-esteem in kindergarten girls. *Developmental Psychology, 11,* 405-406.

Morawski, J. G. (1985). The measurement of masculinity and femininity: Engendering categorical realities. *Journal of Personality, 53,* 196-223.

Nadelman, L. (1974). Sex identity in American children: Memory, knowledge, and preference tests. *Developmental Psychology, 10,* 413-417.

Perloff, R. M. (1977). Some antecedents of children's sex-role stereotypes. *Psychological Reports, 40,* 463-466.

Rosenberg, B. G., & Sutton-Smith, B. (1959). The measurement of masculinity and femininity in children. *Child Development, 30,* 373-380.

Rosenberg, B. G., & Sutton-Smith, B. (1972). *Sex and identity.* New York: Holt, Rinehart & Winston.

Rosenkrantz, P., Vogel, S., Broverman, I., & Broverman, D. M. (1968). Sex role stereotypes and self-concepts in college students. *Journal of Consulting and Clinical Psychology, 32,* 287-295.

Scheresky, R. (1976). The gender factor in six- to ten-year-old children's views of occupational roles. *Psychological Reports, 38,* 1207-1210.

Sears, R.R., Whiting, J.W.M., Nowlis, V., & Sears, P.S. (1953). Some childrearing antecedents of aggression and dependency in young children. *Genetic Psychology Monographs, 47,* 135-236.

Spence, J. T. (1984). Gender identity and its implications for the concepts of masculinity and femininity. In T. B. Sonderegger (Ed.), *Nebraska symposium on motivation: Psychology and gender* (pp. 59-95). Lincoln: University of Nebraska Press.

Sutton-Smith, B., Rosenberg, B. G., & Morgan, E. F. (1963). Development of sex differences in play choices during preadolescence. *Child Development, 34,* 119-126.

Takane, Y., Young, F. W., & de Leew, L. (1977). Nonmetric individual differences multidimensional scaling: An alternating least squares method with optimal scaling features. *Psychometrika, 42,* 7-67.

Tarrier, N., & Gomes, L. F. (1981). Knowledge of sex-trait stereotypes: Effects of age, sex, and social class on Brazilian children. *Journal of Cross-Cultural Psychology, 12,* 81-93.

Tieger, T. (1980). On the biological basis of sex differences in aggression. *Child Development, 51,* 943-963.

Williams, J. E., Best, D. N., Tilquin, C., Keller, H., Voss, H. G., Byerke, T., & Baarda, B. (1979). Traits associated with men and women: Attribution by young children in France, Germany, Norway, the Netherlands and Italy. *Journal of Cross-Cultural Psychology, 12,* 327-346.

Williams, J. M., Bennett, S. M., & Best, D. L. (1975). Awareness and expression of sex stereotypes in young children. *Developmental Psychology, 11,* 635-642.

Zammuner, V. L. (1980). *Dutch children's judgment of, and preference for, sex-stereotyped toys.* Unpublished manuscript., University of Padova.

Zammuner, V. L. (1981). Le preferenze dei bambini rispetto ai ruoli sessuali. *Eta' Evolutiva, 9,* 38-52.

Zammuner, V. L. (1982). Sex role stereotypes in Italian children. *International Journal of Psychology, 17,* 43-63.

Zammuner, V. L. (1983). *Tra i 4 e i 10 anni: Alcuni dati sulla percezione dei ruoli sessuali.* Unpublished manuscript, University of Padova.

Zammuner, V. L., & Grego, M. (1985). The attribution of behaviors to male and female agents by Italian and Dutch children. *Cahiers de Psychologie Cognitive, 5,* 421-422.

Zammuner, V. L., & Heiser, W. (1983). *Dutch children's perception of the two sexes in terms of actions and qualifiers: The influence of age, sex, and school setting.* Unpublished manuscript, University of Padova.

12

Parents' Beliefs and Values About Sex Roles, Sex Differences, and Sexuality

THEIR SOURCES AND IMPLICATIONS

JOHN K. ANTILL

John K. Antill is a Senior Lecturer in Psychology at Macquarie University in Sydney, Australia. In 1973, he returned to Australia as a lecturer at Macquarie University after completing his Ph.D. at the University of Michigan. He also holds a B.Sc. in mathematical statistics from Sydney University and an M.A. in psychology and philosophy from Oxford, where he studied as a Rhodes Scholar. His current interests are the measurement and implications of aspects of adult sex roles (attitudes, personality, and behavior), parents' theories about sex-role development and their implications for children, psychometrics, and survey methodology.

Recent child development literature has shown a considerable rise in interest in the ideas, beliefs, knowledge, and lay theories possessed by parents regarding developmental processes in their children (Bell, 1979; Parke, 1978; Sigel, 1985). These ideas may include notions about developmental timetables (i.e., what a child should be able to do by a certain age); the causes of behavior (e.g., socialization versus an emphasis on biological/hereditary factors); the major sources of influence on children (e.g., parents, media, peers, school); how children learn, and so on.

This attention to parents' ideas rather than an exclusive focus on their behavior reflects part of a general trend in psychology over the past decade. Mahoney (1977) refers to it as the "cognitive revolution." Within social psychology, for example, Harré and Secord (1972) have

AUTHOR'S NOTE: The research reported here was supported by several grants from Macquarie University and Grant No. A2 84/15694 from the Australian Research Grants Scheme. I would like to acknowledge the critical part played by the writings and ideas of several of my colleagues at Macquarie University. They are Professor Jacqueline Goodnow, and Drs. Graeme Russell and Rosemary Knight. These colleagues together with Sandra Cotton, Pauline Presland, and Drs. Kay Bussey and John Cunningham offered very helpful suggestions on earlier drafts of the chapter.

argued that we need to know more about people's naive theories or "subjective reality" and about the everyday or commonsense knowledge with which people operate. They claim that people behave according to their interpretations of the meaning of situations, their beliefs, plans, and purposes, and that it is therefore critical to examine these phenomena.

Such reasoning provides *part* of the rationale for studying parents' ideas about child development. What parents believe about the capabilities and limitations of children at various stages of development, and what they see as the major causes or influences on behavior, could have considerable bearing on how they raise their own children, and in turn on their children's interests, personality, performance, and general behavior. Indeed, it may prove in time that parents' ideas provide more efficient predictors of child outcomes, and a better means of understanding them, than do the parental behaviors themselves (McGill-icuddy-DeLisi, 1985). Besides the *impact* that parental ideas have, they represent an interesting study in their own right as a form of adult cognition, with questions to be asked about their content and sources (Goodnow, 1984). Are the ideas derived from experiences such as being a parent, and how do they vary as a function of various family patterns? Do they vary with age, education, sex, religion, and social status? If they are related to both background characteristics and parental behaviors, they may provide an important explanatory link between the two sets of variables. They may help explain why, for example, parents of different educational backgrounds or religious orientations treat their children differently. Finally, as Goodnow (1984) points out, parents' ideas offer a possible avenue for education regarding appropriate child-rearing practices; the ideas may provide a point of leverage for constructive intervention.

Within the broad category of ideas, it is important to contrast beliefs on the one hand with attitudes and values on the other (Sigel, 1985). It is proposed here that beliefs represent ideas about facts—ideas that could, in principle, be proved or disproved. Attitudes, on the other hand, represent an individual's reaction to, or evaluation of, the supposed facts. Finally, values reflect abstract goals or coherent sets of attitudes to a class of stimuli. For example, one may believe that men's and women's roles in the home are still very segregated. One may then react positively or negatively to this situation. Finally, this attitude may be seen as a consequence of or related to a value representing positive (traditional) or negative (egalitarian) reactions to differentiated roles for men and women in the home and the workforce, and in terms of acceptable behaviors, interests, and characteristics. In these terms, then, variables such as parents' goals (Knight, 1983) and ideas about desired states (Goodnow, 1985) represent values rather than beliefs. Both types of cognitions (beliefs and values) may be important in understanding or predicting a parent's behavior toward a child, but it seems worthwhile maintaining the distinction because the two types of variables may serve different functions and have quite different impacts.

The area of sex-role development provides a fertile testing ground for studying the content, sources, and outcomes of parents' beliefs and values. During the last 10 to 15 years, there have been many changes resulting in considerable variation in the behavior of men and women and, more particularly, in the attitudes people hold regarding the range of behaviors, characteristics, and interests that are deemed appropriate for each sex. Recent studies have documented clear shifts in attitudes and values regarding the work and family roles of men and women from earlier traditional views to more recent egalitarian ones. In the United States, Mason, Czajka, and Arber (1976) documented these changes in women during the period 1964-1974, and Helmreich, Spence, and Gibson (1982) found similar changes in both male and female college students and their parents during the 1970s. In Australia, Rowland (1977) reported a liberalization of attitudes among university students in the space of a year (1975-1976), as well as a convergence in attitudes between males and females. In a more recent study, Glezer (1983) reported attitude changes toward egalitarianism over a 10-year period, 1971-1981.

Changes in attitudes have to some extent been paralleled by shifts in behavior. For example, women have substantially increased their participation in the paid workforce—traditionally the domain of men. This increase has been particularly dramatic among married women, especially those with young children (Van Dusen & Sheldon, 1976). In 1980, 41% of married women were in the Australian workforce (Bagnall, 1981). At the same time Bryson (1974) draws attention to a tendency for some men to become disenchanted with their work and more committed to their families, suggesting that, with the continued movement of women into the workforce, a convergence of roles may be taking place. Bryson (1983) provides further evidence of increasing involvement of fathers in housework and child care in particular, but suggests that this change is not of great magnitude.

Consistent with the trend toward more egalitarian social roles has been a change in the views of many psychologists who have, until recently, long held that the acquisition of a masculine identity for males and a feminine identity for females is the foundation of a healthy personality (Terman & Miles, 1936). Some 10 years ago, Sandra Bem (1974) proposed a new model of mental health based on the concept of psychological androgyny. She claimed that it was both possible and desirable for each individual to develop both masculine _and_ feminine behaviors, interests, and personality characteristics. Androgynous individuals, having at their disposal both sets of characteristics, are seen as more flexible in their approach to situations. Not only are they able to call forth whatever behaviors are appropriate, but they are assumed to feel quite comfortable carrying them out. On the other hand, the strongly sex-typed person is seen as behaviorally restricted—bound by the thought that certain behaviors or responses are inappropriate. An implication of androgyny theory is that rather than psychological health being equated with sex-typing, it is androgyny that represents healthy personality development. That is, the development of masculine and feminine characteristics is seen as desirable for both sexes (Bem, 1976).

Within this environment of changing sex-role attitudes, values, beliefs, and behavior, it is of considerable interest to assess the range of ideas that parents hold regarding sex differences, sex-role development, and sexuality, as well as the sources of these ideas and their implications for child-rearing practices and for children themselves.

THE MODEL

Figure 12.1 provides an outline of what follows. The depicted model suggests that parents' beliefs and values about sex roles derive from their general background characteristics, their experiences, and their personalities. Then, their beliefs, values, personalities, and background characteristics feed into the way they raise their children in terms of sex typing. Finally, the degree of sex typing of their children in terms of their personalities, preferences, values, and so on is partly derived from parental child-rearing practices, and partly from parents' beliefs and values. Feedback loops suggest that the children themselves affect the way their parents treat them and also play some part in developing their parents' beliefs and values. This general model will be elaborated in what follows and the various links reviewed in light of a study of 94 couples reporting on their oldest child. As the study did not include collection of data from the children, some aspects of the model will be discussed only briefly.

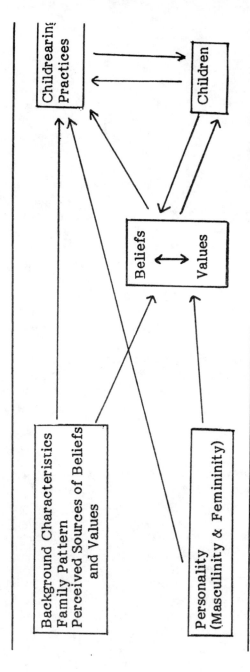

Figure 12.1   The Model

I will begin with a discussion of sex-role beliefs, explaining what they are and how they are measured. These will be distinguished from sex-role values, but the relationship between them will be assessed. I will then show how these beliefs and values vary as a function of various background characteristics such as sex, education, and religion, and examine whether they differ as a function of the sex of the children in the family. I will also consider what parents feel are the sources of their beliefs, and whether their beliefs and values vary with their personalities in terms of masculinity and femininity. I then compare the impacts of background, personality, sex-role beliefs, and values on sex-typed child-rearing practices to determine whether they affect the extent of encouragement or discouragement of masculine and feminine personality traits and interests. I then look to future studies and introduce sex-typed characteristics of the children as the end product in the model. How well are these predicted from parental behaviors on the one hand and parental beliefs and values on the other? Do the beliefs and values provide predictive utility beyond parental behaviors? Conversely, how do children affect their parents' beliefs, values, and child-rearing practices?

DESCRIPTION OF THE STUDY

Twelve interviewers trained in survey methodology and I developed an extensive questionnaire/interview schedule in line with the aims of the study. Each interviewer then recruited couples by approaching principals of primary schools in their areas of residence. A note indicating that we were interested in finding out what sorts of things parents think are important in raising their children was distributed to parents with two children, whose oldest child was aged between 6 and 12. Parents willing to participate arranged a mutually convenient time for the interviewer to go their home. There, questionnaires were given to the husband and wife, and they were asked to complete them separately. The interviewer's task was to ensure that this was done and that neither spouse knew his or her partner's responses, thus ensuring that confidentiality was maintained. Answers to open-ended questions were obtained by interview rather than questionnaire.

The subjects for the study were 94 married couples living in the Metropolitan Area of Sydney, Australia. SES figures as estimated by status of suburb of residence (Congalton, 1969) reflect a higher-status sample than the general Sydney population. In terms of education, 33%

had completed or partially completed university degrees. A further 22% were either working toward or had completed a certificate or diploma, whereas 18% were in a similar position with regard to a trade or technical qualification. The remainder had not continued their education beyond high school, with 11% having completed five or six years and 16%, four years or less. A total of 96% of the males and 57% of the females were in paid employment.

The age range of the sample was 26-51 years with means of 37.8 years for males and 35.4 years for females. Most were born in Australia (74%), with the majority of those born overseas being from English-speaking countries (16%). Five percent of the sample had been married before.

The oldest child in each family was the focus for this study. Of these children, 45 were boys and 49 were girls; their ages ranged between 6 and 12, with an average of 9.2 years. The second children ranged in age from 1 to 10 with an average of 6.2 years; 44 were boys and 50 were girls. There were 29 families with a third child who ranged in age from 1 to 8 with an average of 3.6 years; 17 were boys and 12 were girls. In order to study the effects of family pattern, we tried to obtain comparable numbers of families having each of the four possible sex-of-child combinations: oldest child a boy-second child a boy (BB), girl-girl (GG), boy-girl (BG), girl-boy (GB).[1] In this we were reasonably successful—BB (n = 23), GG (n = 28), BG (n = 22), GB (n = 21).

BELIEFS AND VALUES

The content of parents' beliefs regarding sex differences and sex-role development was initially explored in some preliminary testing for the present study by means of two open-ended questions. These dealt with what parents saw as the major differences between boys and girls (e.g., in areas such as behavior, personality, interests, abilities, attitudes, and thought processes) and why they thought boys and girls are different (e.g., whether they are born that way and naturally develop differently, or whether the differences are caused mainly by socialization practices). Partly from the responses to these two questions, a series of structured questions was developed. These were broader in scope, covering, in addition to the issues above, the major socializing influences on children (e.g., parents, siblings, media, teachers, peers), the causes of homosexuality (e.g., biological versus social), and parents' views on cross-sex behavior (e.g., whether, if persistent, they thought it an indication of later homosexuality). The interest in contrasting biological with social causes comes from extracting common themes from answers given to the open-ended questions in the preliminary phase of the present study and also from answers given by children to similar questions in a study conducted by Smith and Russell (1984).

Presented below are the various questions regarding parents' beliefs and a summary of the responses given to them.

(1) In what ways, if any, do you think boys and girls differ from one another? Altogether, there were 654 responses coded into 50 different categories. The most frequently occurring response was "physical make-up" (given by 32% of the total of 188 mothers and fathers), with the only other response mentioned to any extent without specifying the direction of the difference being "think differently" (10%). Other popular responses that were thought to be more applicable to boys than girls were as follows: aggressive, dominant, rough (20%); strength (16%); noisy and loud-mouthed (16%); outgoing, friendly (13%); playing rough games (12%); active, energetic (11%); honest, open, frank (7%); liking outside sports (7%); liking team sports (7%); masculine (6%); athletic (6%); cheeky, mischievous (6%). The most popular responses thought to be more applicable to girls than boys were as follows: IQ level and schoolwork performance (18%); temperamental, emotional (16%); liking housework such as sewing and cooking (9%); feminine (8%); an interest in the opposite sex (7%); devious, cunning (7%); liking clothes and dressing up (7%); gentle (7%); sensitive to others (6%); neat (6%); responsible (6%). For certain qualities there were thought to be differences, but there was disagreement as to the direction of the difference. For example, 10% of parents thought there were differences in terms of how affectionate boys and girls were, but fathers saw girls as more affectionate whereas mothers saw boys this way. Similarly, 7% of parents saw differences in terms of independence and self-reliance, but fathers saw boys as independent whereas mothers saw girls being so.

(2) Why do you think boys and girls are different from one another, in terms of the things they like to do and the way they behave? Altogether, 390 responses were coded into eleven categories. Of these, two categories referred to biological, genetic, or hormonal reasons mentioning the way a person is born or naturally develops, whereas nine categories referred to socialization or upbringing, or mentioned a variety of specific socializing agents.

On the biological side, 22% of parents said that children were born that way or that differences were genetic; 6% indicated that children naturally develop differently or that hormones are responsible. On the other hand, 25% indicated that general socialization and upbringing are responsible for the differences, with a further 10% referring to societal or historical reasons. Others mentioned specific socializing agents such as parents (16%), school teachers/school (5%), peers (5%), and TV/radio (4%); newspapers, magazines, books, siblings, and grandparents were mentioned by 1% each. Finally, 2% said they disagreed that boys and girls are different.

(3) Structured questions concerned with biological versus social-ization influences on sex differences. The responses to the above question, as well as previous studies (e.g., Knight, 1983; Smith & Russell, 1984), indicate the importance of both biological and social factors in the minds of nonpsychologists for explaining the differences between people. To explore this notion further, a number of structured questions were developed. The most general of these asked, "Do you think any differences that exist between boys and girls are because they're born that way and naturally develop differently, or because they learn to be different due to the way we bring them up?" Subjects favored the socialization position, although almost a third saw both factors as equally important (almost all biology, 12%, more biology than social-ization, 8%, biology and socialization equally, 32%, more socialization than biology, 18%, almost all socialization, 30%).

This same scale (with the option of saying "there are no differences between boys and girls") was then applied to a series of 32 characteristics and interests that can be grouped as follows: 10 masculine personality characteristics (e.g., adventurous, aggressive, competitive); 6 masculine interests (e.g., rough and tumble play, playing competitive sports, playing with trucks and cars); 10 feminine personality characteristics (e.g., gentle, affectionate, sensitive to others); 6 feminine interests (e.g., playing with dolls, playing dressing up, learning to cook). The answers in each group were summed to form an index.

The results showed that the interests were generally seen as more socially determined than the personality characteristics, but there were large variations in this regard. While for all items, social factors were seen as more important than biological factors, the items where biological factors were seen as most relevant were as follows: athletic, mischievous, noisy, an interest in rough and tumble play, adventurous, aggressive, gentle, shy, and affectionate. Items viewed as most dependent on social factors were as follows: an interest in learning to cook, learning to do minor repairs around the house, courteous, learning to play a musical instrument, ambitious, self-reliant, playing competitive sports, science, independent, and writing stories and poetry. It would be interesting to explore whether those qualities seen as more socially determined were also perceived as the most open to change.

Four additional indices were formed to reflect the number of "no difference" responses to (1) masculine personality characteristics, (2) masculine interests, (3) feminine personality characteristics, and (4) feminine interests. For each of these indices, approximately 70% of subjects felt there were at least some items for which there were no differences. Overall, differences were more readily acknowledged for the interests than for the personality traits.

(4) Biological versus socialization influences on homosexuality. Parents' beliefs regarding homosexuality were tapped in several ways. As with sex differences generally, parents were first asked to indicate whether they thought people turned out to be homosexual because of the way they are born and naturally develop, *or* because of what they learn from particular experiences during their formative years. The results indicate that opinion is very evenly divided between the two positions, with more than a third viewing both factors as equally important (almost all biology, 23%, more biology than socialization, 11%, biology and socialization equally, 36%, more socialization than biology, 10%, almost all socialization, 20%). A comparison between these results and those for the same question asked regarding general sex differences (see Section 3 above) indicates that for mothers and fathers, a biological stance is far more likely for homosexuality than it is for sex differences. It could be that one's sexuality is seen as less changeable than one's interests and personality characteristics.

Another question explored the perceived causes of homosexuality more extensively. There were 18 possible causes listed: 4 broadly concerned with biochemical/genetic problems (e.g., unusual sex hormone levels, a fault in the sex chromosome), 8 concerned with experiences of boys[2] (e.g., an overbearing mother, absence of father, being allowed to have feminine interests), and 8 concerned with experiences of girls (e.g., a failure to relate to men, a seductive mother, being sexually interfered with by a female homosexual). Each item was rated in terms of its importance, and the groups of items were summed to form the three scales indicated. One noteworthy feature of the results is the importance attached to biochemical/genetic problems; these were all regarded as far more important than any of the social factors. Items indicated as most important were, in order: fault in the sex chromosome, genetic problem, unusual sex hormone levels, chemical imbalance, failure to relate to the opposite sex, a weak or rejecting mother or father, being sexually interfered with by a homosexual, having an overbearing opposite-sex parent.

The relationship between homosexuality and cross-sex behavior was assessed in a question that proposed that "a boy's persistent interest in *feminine* things (such as playing with dolls and playing dressing up) *rather than masculine* things (such as playing with trucks and cars and rough and tumble play) is an indication that he may turn out to be homosexual." A similar question applied to girls with masculine interests. Although the connection was not rated particularly highly, an interesting difference emerged. For both mothers and fathers, an interest in cross-sex activities was seen as more likely to be connected to homosexuality for boys than girls, thus providing one rationale for the fact that in this age range, girls are given more latitude than boys to engage in cross-sex activities (Block, 1983).

An interesting extension of these findings was provided when parents were asked how they would react if their oldest child showed more of an interest in activities of the opposite sex than in those of their own sex. The majority of parents responded in a fairly neutral way whereas others reacted very negatively with considerable concern. The responses in order of popularity were as follows: wouldn't worry, should grow out of it, treat as a passing phase, as part of growing up (38% of all responses, given for girls more often than for boys); some concern if child was older (36%); it wouldn't worry me even if it continued, ignore it, it's up to them (30%, more in reference to girls); upset, disappointed, worried, concerned (19%, given more often by fathers of boys than other combinations); concern about homosexuality (16%, more regarding boys); encourage appropriate-sex activities (14%); try to reason with child (12%); it's healthy sign, well-balanced personality, it's normal, I'd encourage whatever interests are present (11%, said more by mothers); discourage these behaviors (9%, for boys); seek professional help (8%, boys); feel it's unnatural (7%, boys); problem with values, sense of identity (6%, fathers of boys); concern about ridicule from peers or society generally (6%, fathers of boys); don't know, hard to imagine (6%).

Although the most frequently occurring responses were either positive or neutral, there were many different kinds of negative reactions, and these almost balanced the positive responses. The most interesting finding was that the ratio of positive to negative responses varied greatly across the four (sex of parent $\times$ sex of oldest child) groups. The proportion of positive/neutral responses in each group was as follows: fathers of first-born sons (34%), mothers of first-born sons (47%), fathers of first-born daughters (68%), mothers of first-born daughters (77%). The results clearly show fathers' greater concern than mothers' and greater concern expressed regarding sons than daughters. Almost three times as many fathers expressed concern regarding their sons (66%) than did mothers regarding their daughters (23%).

Reducing the Set of Parental Belief Variables

In order to study the relationship between parents' beliefs and other variables, it was decided to reduce the set of structured belief questions to a more manageable set of variables. Thus, 15 variables were subjected to separate factor analyses for males and females. These comprised nine variables from section 3 and six from section 4 above. The factor analyses (SPSS principal axis, oblique rotation of factors with eigenvalues > 1) provided five factors for fathers and four for mothers accounting for 76.7% and 72.7% of the variance, respectively. For both sexes, extremely clear factor structures emerged. The female factor analysis was then repeated specifying five factors to be rotated; these were identical to the original five male factors. As these factors were relatively independent of one another (average $|r| = .15$), it was decided to construct five new belief indices based on the following sets of items: (1) *Social influence*—the general question regarding sex differences as biologically or socially based and the four specific indices concerning this issue: masculine personality, masculine interests, feminine personality, feminine interests; (2) *No difference*—the four "no difference" indices; (3) *Homobiological*—the index concerning the biological influences on homosexuality, the general question regarding homosexuality as due to biological or social causes; (4) *Homosocial*—the two indices concerning the social influences on homosexuality in boys and girls; (5) *Homo-cross-sex*—the two items concerning the connection between cross-sex behavior and homosexuality in boys and girls.

The Relationship Between Sex-Role Beliefs and Values

As already indicated, beliefs and values can be distinguished from one another—beliefs representing ideas about facts, values reflecting one's reaction to or evaluation of the facts. The present study used the 15-item version of the Attitudes Toward Women Scale (Spence, Helmreich, & Stapp, 1973). According to proposals in the introduction, this scale measures attitudes or values rather than beliefs (i.e., views as to what *should* be the case, rather than what *is* the case). Of the 15 items, 11 use the word "should" (e.g., "Women should be given equal opportunity with men for apprenticeship in the various trades"). The 4 items that do not contain "should" use words such as insulting, repulsive, and ridiculous, resulting in statements that are not, in principle, provable or disprovable and hence do not represent beliefs. Overall, the scale assesses whether the subject's ideal world would have men and women in separate roles (traditionalism) or have no distinctions drawn between the opportunities and roles of men and women (egalitarianism).

Despite the theoretical distinction that has been drawn between beliefs and values, statistical relationships between them were expected. The results suggest that parents with egalitarian or nontraditional views concerning the roles of men and women also believe that sex differences are due to social rather than biological factors, and that there are fewer differences between boys and girls. Concurrently, these parents (particularly the fathers) are less willing to speculate on the probable causes of homosexuality—either biological or social—or on the possibility of cross-sex behaviors being a precursor.

If the distinction between beliefs and values is worth maintaining, then some speculation as to how one kind of cognition leads to the other must be made. Logically, one forms one's values on the basis of what one believes; for example, a belief that sex differences are biologically based and fundamental is more likely to result in the view that the roles of men and women should be kept separate rather than the view that there should be no such distinctions. However, such values may also derive from a basic philosophy of life (e.g., regarding equal opportunity for all people) or from what one's parents or friends have communicated. Nevertheless, if challenged about beliefs, then logically consistent ones may be stated as a form of rationalization for values. Certainly, in the present instance, one may have general values about the way society should be structured well before one has specific beliefs about the differences between boys and girls, the source of these differences, or the link between cross-sex behavior and homosexuality. These latter issues may arise only as one observes children, most probably one's own, and consequently has an investment in forming a view. It would appear, then, that only through extensive interviews could the causal links between these cognitions be sorted out, and it may well be that the processes involved vary considerably from one individual to the next.

The next section looks at the issue of where the beliefs and values come from: Are different beliefs and values associated with different experiences dictated by one's sex, education, religious upbringing, and contact with children of different sexes?

SOURCES OF BELIEFS AND VALUES

Perceived Sources and Family Structure

As a direct means of determining where their sex-role beliefs and values came from, parents were asked to indicate how influential various people or experiences were in forming their ideas about how the similarities and differences between boys and girls develop. Subjects were provided with a list of 14 items and asked to rate how influential each was. The most important sources of information were, in order: observing children, general upbringing, education, and spouse. Rather less important were friends, mother, books, and father. Finally, of very little importance were various media (newspapers and magazines, television, and radio), workmates, doctors, and grandparents.

As expected, observing children was a particularly prominent source of information and not unexpectedly this was particularly true for mothers. To study this issue further, the belief variables were assessed as a function of the age and sex of the children in the family. It was thought, in particular, that beliefs might vary across families with all boys, all girls, or a mixture of boys and girls. For instance, having children of the one sex may lead to stereotyping the other sex, and an assumption that boys and girls are very different. Direct experience may negate this point of view. From another perspective, having children of different sexes may lead one to assume that any differences between them are fundamental (i.e., biologically based). Perhaps parents are less likely to assume a biological basis for differences between children of the same sex. In terms of values, having girls may raise one's consciousness regarding feminist issues through an increased awareness of barriers that exist for them. Higher egalitarianism may thus be expected.

In order to assess whether there was any impact of age and sex of children on the belief variables, a 3-way analysis of variance was conducted for each of the 10 (5 male, 5 female) belief variables. The 3 factors were age of oldest child (young versus old) and sex of oldest and second child. Of the 70 main effects and interactions studied, the only significant effect was a 3-way interaction, which may well have been due to chance. It was therefore concluded that family composition has no impact on parental beliefs. Similar analyses were carried out for mothers' and fathers' sex-role values, and once again no significant results emerged. It would seem, then, that if one's children do have an impact on one's beliefs and values, this impact is based on more than just their sexes. Having a more extensive data base in terms of how parents view their children's personalities and interests in comparison to one another, and whether they view their behavior as consistent or inconsistent with sex-role stereotypes, may provide a more reliable basis on which to predict or understand parents' views.

Background Characteristics

An important variable to consider here is the sex of the parent. Do the sex-role beliefs and values of mothers and fathers differ? Results show that they differ only for the homo-cross-sex belief and the sex-role values. Fathers more strongly agreed with the connection between homosexuality and cross-sex behavior than did mothers, and mothers' sex-role values were more egalitarian than fathers'. At the same time, the relationships between husbands' and wives' beliefs and values were all significantly positive. Given that the information was obtained independently from husbands and wives, these figures back up the comments obtained from direct questioning that an important source of information regarding ideas about sex roles, sex differences, and their causes may be from one's spouse. However, this correspondence may simply represent one basis on which couples select one another or reflect the likelihood that both members of a couple are exposed to similar social environments. Nevertheless, it is of interest to note that ideas between husbands and wives closely correspond on specific issues that may not have had an extensive airing—for example, the causes of homosexuality.

The relationships between other background characteristics and beliefs were fairly weak and sparse, whereas those for values were somewhat stronger. Egalitarianism, an emphasis on the social causes of sex differences, and a belief that there are few sex differences were generally associated with a less conservative profile (e.g., lower suburb status, more education, less religious commitment, voting for the Australian Labor Party, though higher occupational status). At the same time, a willingness to commit oneself regarding any possible causes of homosexuality (i.e., social, biological or the possible link between cross-sex behavior and personality) was associated with conservative background characteristics. Caution should be exercised in interpreting these results, as the sample is generally a higher-status, well-educated one, and hence the views of the people at the lower ends of these scales are not represented (i.e., comparisons are generally between high- versus medium-status individuals). Furthermore, as with many variables, simple notions rarely do justice to the complexities involved. For example, the *amount* of education is not a perfect reflection of the range of ideas one encounters. In a semester of behavioral sciences one may be exposed to more egalitarian values and liberal beliefs than one would encounter while obtaining a doctorate in some of the sciences. Similarly, high status in job or suburb may result from very different experiences in terms of providing opportunities to develop beliefs and values.

There were two further background variables investigated, but they were generally found not to be related to people's beliefs. These both concern religious affiliation: upbringing and present preference. The general conclusion from the results is that beliefs in the social rather than biological causes of sex differences, or beliefs that there are in fact no differences between boys and girls, are more strongly held by people with no religious preference.[3] Among those with a preference, Protestants hold these views more strongly than Catholics. Views about homosexuality appear not to differ as a function of religious upbringing or religious preference. Consistent with these findings are those for sex-role values, which show that religious upbringing has no association with egalitarianism. In terms of present religious preference, however, those claiming no religion have significantly higher egalitarian scores than Protestants and Catholics, who do not differ from one another.

Masculinity and Femininity

The notion of gender schema (Bem, 1981)—that is, sex-typed and androgynous individuals' views of the world are fundamentally different—provides a link between sex-typing and parental belief systems. Essentially, sex-typed individuals, with their strong gender schemas, have a greater investment than androgynous people in seeing the world in terms of two sharply defined and distinct categories—male and female. Thus it is proposed here that they will see a greater number of differences between boys and girls, believe such sex differences to be biologically based rather than due to social forces, and see it as inappropriate that children should exhibit cross-sex behaviors and interests. Unfortunately, none of these hypotheses was supported— neither masculinity nor femininity (as measured by an Australian sex-role scale, the Personal Description Questionnaire [PDQ]; Antill, Cunningham, Russell, & Thompson, 1981) had any systematic associations with any of the belief variables. At the same time, some significant associations occurred between masculinity and femininity and sex-role values. Based on previous research (Antill, Cotton, & Tindale, 1983), egalitarianism was expected to be positively related to masculinity and negatively to femininity for females, with the reverse pattern for males. All results were in the directions expected, but only the findings for females were significant.

Overall, then, none of the variables examined has given any indication that there is a single main source of beliefs or values. "Observing children" appears to be an important source, but there is clearly a need to know more about the parents' own children beyond their ages and sexes. Although no single background variable has any fully consistent associations with the beliefs or values, patterns of associations emerged. These led to a distinction between more or less conservative background profiles and their associated clusters of beliefs and values.

BELIEFS AND VALUES AS PREDICTORS
OF CHILD-REARING PRACTICES

Despite recent changes in sex-role orientations and attitudes toward sexual equality, surprisingly little attention has been given to questions about the impact that these may be having on parenting and child development (Baumrind, 1982; Spence & Helmreich, 1978). For example, do parents who are androgynous rather than sex-typed, or egalitarian rather than traditional, adopt child-rearing practices that differentiate less between boys and girls? Do they produce children who have egalitarian values and/or are androgynous? It is proposed here that an important set of predictors for parents' child-rearing practices in the sex-role domain are their beliefs regarding the nature of sex differences, sex-role development, and sexuality.

The Child-Rearing Variables

A section of the questionnaire given to parents explored the sex-typed personality characteristics, interests, and activities parents claimed to encourage in their eldest child. The first question listed a set of 20 personality characteristics (10 masculine, 10 feminine) taken from the Bem Sex-Role Inventory (BSRI; Bem, 1974) and the Australian equivalent (PDQ; Antill et al., 1981) that were applicable to primary-school-aged children. Parents were asked to indicate to what extent they encouraged (high score) or discouraged (low score) each of the characteristics. Two indices, formed by summing the 10 masculine (e.g., independent, ambitious, aggressive) and the 10 feminine (e.g., considerate, gentle, affectionate) items, reflected the extent to which parents encouraged masculine and feminine personality characteristics, respectively.

In another question, a set of 12 activities was listed and the parents were asked to indicate the extent to which they encouraged or discouraged an interest in them. On the basis of previous research and research-group consensus, six of the activities were viewed as masculine (e.g., learning to do minor repairs around the house, playing competitive sports, number work/math) and six as feminine (e.g., playing with dolls, learning to cook, writing stories and poetry). Masculine and feminine indices were formed by summing each set of items.

In the final questions in this section, parents were directly asked to indicate the extent to which they encouraged or discouraged their eldest child (if a boy) "to be like other boys and have typically masculine interests and behaviors," and to what extent they encouraged or discouraged him "to have interests and behaviors traditionally thought to be more typical of girls"; there were equivalent items for girls. Parents were also asked to indicate the extent to which they thought they would treat their eldest child differently if he or she were of the opposite sex. Answers could range from very differently (low score) to exactly the same (high score).

There are thus seven child-rearing variables, three concerned with encouraging/discouraging masculinity, and three with femininity. The seventh variable asked whether the child would be treated very differently or exactly the same if he or she were of the opposite sex. In what follows, results are reported for four separate groups of subjects: fathers of first-born boys (n = 45), fathers of first-born girls (n = 49), mothers of first-born boys (n = 45), and mothers of first-born girls (n = 49).

Before proceeding, it is worth commenting on the relationships among the various child-rearing measures. For both the masculinity and femininity variables, encouraging the personality characteristics and the interests are highly correlated. However, the direct questions about encouraging masculinity and femininity generally share little with their corresponding characteristics and interest variables. In exploring these direct measures further, they seem to be of a different character from the other variables. Whereas the distribution of all variables may range from discouraging a characteristic, through neither encouraging nor discouraging it (neutral), to encouraging it, the distributions of the personality characteristics and interest variables range essentially from neutral through to strong encouragement. The direct questions regarding masculinity and femininity are rather different. Briefly, a large number of people say they neither encourage nor discourage masculinity and femininity. When they take a stand, they tend to encourage same-sex characteristics, discourage femininity in their sons and both encourage and discourage masculinity in their daughters, although in this latter case the neutral response is heavily favored. The distributions of these questions clearly have an impact on some of the relationships among the child-rearing variables, and they should be kept in mind when interpreting relationships between these variables and the beliefs and values.

With regard to the question concerning the same or different treatment if the child were of the opposite sex, we might expect that parents who strongly claim they would treat the child in the same way would be more likely to encourage opposite-sex characteristics and less likely to encourage same-sex characteristics. Conversely, those who say they would treat the child differently are more likely to encourage same-sex characteristics and discourage opposite-sex ones. Although not all of the results are consistent with this line of reasoning, all of the significant ones are in the hypothesized direction.

Sex-Role Values as Predictors of Child-Rearing Practices

Egalitarian values were expected to be associated with the encouragement of opposite-sex traits, and, to a lesser extent, the discouragement of same-sex traits. In addition, it was expected that parents expressing egalitarian views would tend to claim that they would treat their child similarly rather than differently if he or she were of the opposite sex.

The results show egalitarianism to be a strong predictor of whether a parent claims to encourage or discourage sex-typed or cross-sex-typed characteristics and interests. All significant results (16/28) are in the expected directions and many of these represent strong relationships (see Table 12.2). Thus, as anticipated, egalitarian relative to traditional parents encourage cross-sex characteristics and interests and discourage same-sex characteristics and interests. In addition, egalitarian parents generally claim that they would treat a child similarly if he or she were of the opposite sex. The child-rearing variables showing the highest associations with egalitarianism are the two that ask the direct question regarding the encouragement or discouragement of masculine and feminine characteristics; all eight associations involving these variables are highly significant in the expected direction.

An important cautionary note here is to recall that many of the distributions of the child-rearing variables run from neutral through to strong encouragement, and hence being relatively discouraging often implies being neutral. Thus, in absolute terms, egalitarian parents are generally neutral with regard to same-sex characteristics. However, in absolute terms, traditional parents sometimes discourage cross-sex characteristics. There seems little doubt, though, that the expression of egalitarian or traditional values is a major predictor of whether parents claim to encourage or discourage same- or opposite-sex characteristics and interests. Those who claim that opportunities for both sexes should be equal and that traditional sex roles are outmoded are more likely to report that they encourage opposite-sex characteristics than those parents who are advocates of separate roles for men and women. Similarly, those who believe in men and women having separate roles in society are more likely to report that they encourage traditional sex-typed characteristics and interests. As expected, egalitarian parents who believe in equal opportunities with no separate roles for men and women are more likely than parents holding traditional values to say they would treat their child similarly if he or she were of the opposite sex.

Belief Variables as Predictors of Child-Rearing Practices

The predicted relationships between the belief variables and the child-rearing measures are more complex than those for the sex-role values, so each belief variable will be considered in turn.

(1) Social influence (sex differences are caused by socialization rather than biology). Logic suggests that a belief in the importance of socialization is more likely to result in the encouragement *or* discouragement of sex-linked characteristics than is a belief in the importance of inherited characteristics and biological determinants, which may result in a more neutral stance. However, the sort of impact would seem to depend on one's egalitarian versus traditional values. For example, parents having egalitarian values would be more likely to encourage

cross-sex and discourage same-sex characteristics if they believed that social rather than biological influences were important in determining sex differences. Conversely, if they held traditional values, we would expect them to encourage same-sex and discourage cross-sex characteristics if they believed that social rather than biological influences were important in determining sex differences. Thus it was predicted that a belief in social influences rather than biological/genetic influences in causing sex differences would lead to a more active participation by parents in encouraging or discouraging sex-linked behavior; the direction this encouragement/discouragement takes, however, would depend on the parents' views regarding an ideal society in terms of segregated roles versus a lack of such differentiation.

To test these predictions, the four samples of parents were each divided into traditional and egalitarian subsamples. The major finding consistent with the predictions is that among the parents valuing an egalitarian society, those who believe in social causes of sex differences encourage cross-sex characteristics more strongly than those who believe in biological determinants. However, these parents do not more strongly discourage same-sex characteristics as was expected. There is also little support for the proposition that for traditional parents a social versus biological orientation to sex differences would be associated with the encouragement of same-sex and discouragement of cross-sex characteristics.

(2) No difference (there are no differences between boys and girls regarding many characteristics). In discussions with parents who had large "no difference" scores, it was apparent that this view also reflected the further point that there *shouldn't* be any sex differences. It was thus expected that parents indicating that boys and girls are similar (or should be) would be more likely to encourage cross-sex and discourage same-sex characteristics and treat their child similarly if he or she were of the opposite sex, when compared to parents who believe that large sex differences exist or should exist.

The results are not consistently in the predicted direction, but significant results tend to be. Interestingly, a claim to treat a child of the opposite sex similarly is significantly positively correlated with a belief in no sex differences in all groups except fathers reporting on their sons. However, it is this group that shows the results most in line with the predictions for the other six variables—that is, masculinity tends to be discouraged and femininity encouraged in their sons by fathers who believe there are no sex differences between boys and girls.

(3) Homosocial (homosexuality is caused by social factors). Assuming that parents in general wish to guide their children toward a heterosexual lifestyle, and that there is some association in their minds between homosexuality and cross-sex behavior, the following predictions were made. A strong belief in social causes of homosexuality will result in the encouragement of same-sex characteristics and discouragement of cross-sex characteristics and different treatment of one's child if he or she were of the opposite sex. A number of results are significant and in the expected direction. In particular, all results for "same treatment of child if opposite sex" are in the expected direction and three are significant. As with the "no difference" variable, the results are strongest for the fathers reporting on their sons. Another interesting finding is that the results are generally stronger for the encouragement of same-sex characteristics rather than the discouragement of cross-sex characteristics, although the results for mothers reporting on their daughters is an exception. As indicated earlier, many of the child-rearing measures tend to range from neutral through to strongly encourage. Thus, when making predictions involving discouraging characteristics, some inconsistencies may occur.

(4) Homobiological (there is a biological basis to homosexuality). Interestingly this does not imply a belief that social factors are not important. A belief in biological causes is not likely to have any systematic impact on whether parents encourage or discourage sex-typed characteristics. The results generally support this prediction, although four of five significant results are in a direction that reflects that biological beliefs are related to the encouragement of same-sex characteristics and the discouragement of cross-sex characteristics. The implications of these results, which are not strong, are that parents tend to reinforce social stereotypes even though they view biology as an important determinant of homosexuality.

(5) Homo-cross-sex (cross-sex behavior is a precursor to homosexuality). It was predicted that a strong affinity with this point of view would result in the encouragement of same-sex and discouragement of cross-sex characteristics, and different treatment of one's child if he or she were of the opposite sex. The results are particularly strong for fathers—especially those reporting on their sons. However, for mothers the results are weak and in three instances run contrary to prediction. A partial explanation of these results is that such views were held far less strongly by mothers than fathers, and less strongly in relation to daughters than sons. Perhaps in the case of mothers and daughters, the views are not held strongly enough to have much impact.

In many instances the belief variables are related to the treatment of children by parents in terms of encouraging or discouraging same-sex and cross-sex behaviors and interests, but the results are somewhat scattered and clearly require further in-depth investigation. None of the belief variables was as strong a predictor as egalitarian versus traditional values.

BACKGROUND AND PERSONALITY AS PREDICTORS OF SEX-ROLE CHILD-REARING PRACTICES

It was expected that traditional/conservative parents, such as those who are older, live in higher-status suburbs, are less educated, more religious, and vote for the Liberal (more conservative) Party, would be more likely to encourage same-sex characteristics in their children. Conversely, less traditional/conservative parents as defined by the reverse of these characteristics may be more inclined to encourage cross-sex characteristics. However, very few consistently significant results emerged among the relationships between background variables and the encouragement of masculine and feminine personality traits and interests, and hence there is little support for these hypotheses.

Another background variable is the parent's sex; to what extent do mothers and fathers differ in their child-rearing practices? Table 12.1 provides the mean values for each of the seven child-rearing variables for each parent-sex by child-sex combination. Of particular interest is the comparison between mothers and fathers of oldest boys (columns 1 and 2) and between mothers and fathers of oldest girls (columns 3 and 4). Ignoring the "same treatment" variable, all of the results except one suggest that fathers are more inclined to encourage masculine qualities than mothers, whereas mothers are more likely to encourage feminine qualities; four of the twelve results are significant.

The sex of the parent has the most consistent impact of all background characteristics on what is encouraged or discouraged in the children. Parents seem to encourage the qualities and interests that are most typical of their own sex. Before leaving Table 12.1, another important result should be noted—the impact of the child's sex. As can be seen by comparing columns 1 and 3 (fathers' treatment of boys and girls) and columns 2 and 4 (mothers' treatment of boys and girls) both mothers and fathers are more likely to encourage masculine traits and interests in sons than daughters and feminine traits and interests in daughters than sons. That is, both sets of parents significantly dis-

TABLE 12.1
Means of Child-Rearing Variables for Each Sex of Child
by Sex of Parent Combination

	Parent × Oldest Child Combination			
Quality Encouraged	Fathers (Boys)	Mothers (Boys)	Fathers (Girls)	Mothers (Girls)
Masculine personality	36.07	35.20	35.04	34.80
Masculine interests	22.33[a]	22.13[a]	21.18[b]	20.88[b]
Masculinity	3.91[a]	3.78[a]	3.04[b]	2.80[c]
Feminine personalty	36.62[a]	38.71[b]	38.49[b]	38.73[b]
Feminine interests	19.69[a]	21.13[b]	21.49[b]	22.53[c]
Femininity	2.51[a]	2.44[a]	3.45[b]	3.51[b]
Same treatment	3.29[a]	3.67[ab]	3.71[ab]	3.90[b]

NOTE: Different superscripts on means in the same line imply a significant difference between them ($p < .05$).

tinguish between the sexes and enforce sex-role stereotypes (see Johnson, 1977).

Turning to the sex-role personality characteristics of parents, the general prediction was that high scores on masculinity and femininity would be associated with the encouragement of similar traits in one's children. The predictions for masculinity are partially borne out. This is most clearly true for mothers and fathers with their daughters; parents with high masculine scores encourage masculine traits and interests in their daughters. There is some inconsistency for the mothers of sons, but on balance, mothers with high masculine scores encourage masculine traits and interests in their sons. For fathers with sons, no relationships with masculinity are apparent. Unexpectedly, there is some indication that mothers with high masculine scores encourage feminine interests in their children. Perhaps masculine characteristics in women serve as a driving force to encourage activities generally, irrespective of their sex-typedness. For femininity, the results are generally in the expected direction and often significantly so. Thus fathers with high feminine scores encourage feminine characteristics and interests in their sons and daughters and mothers with high feminine scores do likewise for their daughters. However, contrary to the predictions, mothers with high feminine scores tend to discourage feminine characteristics and interests in their sons. Why this group should be an exception is not clear, although there may be a competing tendency for strongly sex-typed parents to encourage "appropriate," and discourage "inappropriate," sex-typing in their children.

IMPACT ON CHILD-REARING PRACTICES:
THE PREDICTORS COMPARED

Having studied a variety of predictors of parental child-rearing practices, the question arises as to which ones make a unique contribution—that is, which predictors still make a significant contribution after the contributions of others have been removed.

Sex-role values in the form of egalitarianism were found to be the strongest predictor of reported child-rearing practices (significant as predicted in 16 of 28 cases). However, many of the belief variables made a contribution, and indeed they continue to do so after partialing out egalitarianism scores. Specifically, in 5 of the 16 cases where egalitarian scores were significant, one or more belief variables have significant ($p <$ .05) partial correlations with the child-rearing variables after the egalitarian scores are partialed out. On the other hand, in 9 of 12 cases where egalitarian scores were not significant, at least one belief variable has a significant partial correlation with the child-rearing variable after the egalitarian scores are partialed out. It would thus seem that the beliefs make independent contributions to the child-rearing variables, over and above those made due to their associations with sex-role values.

A related question of interest is whether egalitarianism as a predictor can survive the partialing out of the belief variables. As would be expected, the partial correlations between the egalitarian scores and the child-rearing variables are reduced considerably, indicating that beliefs and values share a good deal in common in predicting child-rearing practices (see Table 12.2). However, 7 of the 16 significant correlations between egalitarianism and child-rearing practices are still significant ($p < .05$) after partialing out the beliefs. Thus, as with the beliefs, we see the values making an independent contribution to child-rearing practices.

The overlap between beliefs and values in predicting child-rearing practices allows some speculation as to parental rationales for action. For example, part of the reason why people with traditional values encourage same-sex characteristics and discourage cross-sex characteristics may be that they believe that doing the reverse could result in later homosexuality. They also believe that homosexuality is influenced by socialization and that there are many differences between boys and girls and indeed that this is the way society should be. Parents with egalitarian values, on the other hand, tend to encourage cross-sex and discourage (or are neutral to) same-sex characteristics, when compared

TABLE 12.2
Correlations between Child-Rearing Variables and (i) Egalitarianism, and (ii) Egalitarianism with the Belief Variables Partialed Out

	Parent × Oldest Child Combination							
	Fathers (Boys)		Mothers (Boys)		Fathers (Girls)		Mothers (Girls)	
Quality Encouraged	(i)	(ii)	(i)	(ii)	(i)	(ii)	(i)	(ii)
Masculine personality	−.24*	−.14	.05	−.04	−.19	−.15	.16	.01
Masculine interests	−.49***	−.19	.14	.21	.22	.28	.12	.0:
Masculinity	−.45***	−.19	−.56***	−.51***	.41**	.25	.47***	.3{
Feminine personality	.13	.03	.29*	.26	−.11	−.08	−.11	−.3(
Feminine interests	.42**	.19	.44***	.37*	.03	−.04	.16	−.0
Femininity	.51***	.32*	.43**	.49**	−.59***	−.49**	−.37**	−.2(
Same treatment	.56***	.29	.38**	.20	.42***	.33*	.11	−.0!

*p < .05; **p < .01; ***p < .001.

319

to parents with traditional values. Part of their reasoning may be that there are fewer sex differences between boys and girls, which they see as appropriate, and that sex differences can be manipulated by socialization practices. They also disagree with the proposition that cross-sexed behavior and homosexuality may be linked.

As was seen earlier, the background characteristics (except for parents' sex) offer little in the way of predictive utility for the child-rearing variables. The personality variables, masculinity and femininity, were more predictive, but still, significant relationships were somewhat scattered. It is therefore not surprising to find that when these sets of variables are entered first in regression equations, many significant relationships with both the belief variables and egalitarianism still exist. In other words, both sex-role beliefs and values provide significant predictive power beyond that provided by background and personality variables. Thus the importance of studying the former variables is again firmly established.

DISCUSSION

Summary

The study reported here was conducted on the basis of two assumptions. The first was that parental belief systems and values provide relevant sources of information for trying to understand parental child-rearing practices and child outcomes. An addendum to this assumption was that they may also help to explain links between background and sex-role characteristics on the one hand and parental practices and child outcomes on the other. The second assumption was that the area of sex-role development provides a fertile testing ground for studying beliefs and values and their links to these other variables.

The initial aim of the study was to develop a set of measures of parental beliefs about sex differences, sex-role development, and sexuality. A theoretical distinction was then drawn between these sex-role beliefs and sex-role values. Despite this distinction, beliefs and values were related to one another in a logical way. For example, those who thought that men's and women's roles should have few distinctions (egalitarianism) also thought that there were few differences between boys and girls in terms of their interests and personalities, and that where differences did exist they were a product of socialization rather than biology.

Consideration was next given to the sources of the beliefs and values. Although background characteristics as a whole showed some logically consistent relationships with the beliefs and values (along a liberal-conservative dimension), the relationships with individual variables such as education, religiosity, political orientation, and so on were somewhat scattered. One "source" that showed some consistency was a parent's spouse; husbands' and wives' beliefs and values were all moderately similar even though information was obtained from them separately. However, as indicated earlier, one cannot conclude from the results that one's spouse is a major source of information.

When parents were asked directly about sources of information, "observing children" was acknowledged as the most important. However, beliefs and values were found not to vary as a function of the age of one's oldest child or the sexes of one's children. Either parents are wrong about the sources of their beliefs and values, or knowing only the age and sex of the children fails to capture the complexities of their personalities and interests—the more elaborate information to which parents are exposed.

Turning to the range of variables that were predicted to have an impact on the child-rearing variables, we see first that background characteristics generally afford little in the way of a consistent picture as to who is most likely to encourage or discourage same- or opposite-sex characteristics in their children. The one exception is the sex of the parent. For both boys and girls considered separately, mothers are more likely than fathers to encourage feminine traits and interests, whereas fathers are more likely than mothers to encourage masculine traits and interests. Furthermore, both sets of parents significantly distinguish between the sexes and enforce sex-role stereotypes. A similar finding occurred for the sex-role characteristics. Parents with high scores on either masculinity or femininity tend to encourage that characteristic in their children. Far more consistent, however, are the relationships between egalitarianism/traditionalism and the child-rearing variables. Parents who claim that, within the adult world, opportunities for both sexes should be equal, and that traditional sex roles are outmoded, are more likely to encourage opposite-sex characteristics than are parents who are advocates of separate roles for men and women. Similarly, those who believe in men and women having their separate roles in society are more likely to encourage same-sex characteristics and interests. As expected, egalitarian parents are more likely than parents holding traditional values to say they would treat their child similarly if he or she were of the opposite sex.

In considering the belief variables, we see further evidence that values or goals have an impact on reported behavior. For example, among parents who hold egalitarian values, those who see socialization rather than biology as being responsible for sex differences more strongly encourage cross-sex characteristics. Furthermore, fathers of boys who believe there are few sex differences discourage masculine and encourage feminine interests and characteristics. At the same time, parents in the other three groups who believe that there are few sex differences say they would treat their child similarly if he or she were of the opposite sex.

For the belief variables concerned with homosexuality, it was predicted that strong beliefs in the social causes of homosexuality and the connection between homosexuality and cross-sex behavior would lead to the encouragement of same-sex characteristics, discouragement of cross-sex characteristics, and different treatment if the child were of the opposite sex. These predictions were most strongly borne out for fathers reporting on sons and, to a somewhat lesser extent, for fathers reporting on daughters for the "homo-cross-sex" variable. For mothers, the results were weaker and in some instances inconsistent with the predictions. It seems that beliefs regarding homosexuality have a far less systematic effect for mothers than fathers, and that the effect for fathers is more consistent and stronger in relation to sons.

Despite the emergence of a number of interesting relationships between the belief variables and the behaviors, the egalitarian versus traditional values emerge as the strongest predictor. However, further analyses point to the belief variables playing an important predictive role. First, it was found that in the majority of cases some of the belief variables were significantly related to the child-rearing variables after the effects of egalitarianism were partialed out. These anayses indicate that in many cases the beliefs make a unique contribution to the prediction of child-rearing practices. Second, it was asked whether part of the relationship between values and behavior can be explained by beliefs. Due to the marked reduction in both the strength and significance of the relationships between values and behavior after controlling for beliefs, the answer is a clear "yes." One final point to note here is that the relationships between the belief and value variables on the one hand and the child-rearing behaviors on the other are essentially unaffected by partialing out the background and personality variables. This implies that a good deal of predictive power is gained by considering beliefs and values as predictors of child-rearing behaviors.

Evaluation

In evaluating the present study, various aspects of the methodology need to be examined. For example, it is worth considering whether the methods used here for capturing parental cognitions are the most appropriate, and whether the range of questions asked of parents allowed the full spectrum of ideas to be canvassed. In the present study, open-ended questions with the guidance of some previous research provided the basis for the structured belief questions. Other methods of determining beliefs focus on an action and ask "why?" (Russell & Russell, 1985). For example, actions may be observed or information sought as to which actions are normally carried out, and then parents questioned as to why these particular actions and not others were performed. Russell and Russell (1985) found that at the first line of questioning, beliefs and values rarely emerged, further questioning presumably being required to extract these sorts of abstractions. Most reasons were in terms of parental needs, goals, or rules; the particular child's needs or characteristics; or situational constraints. These results raise a question as to whether abstract ideas, in the form of beliefs and values, or fairly specific notions provide the best understanding for actions. Both levels of abstraction would seem to have their benefits and limitations. The Russell and Russell approach clearly has the advantage of providing understanding and predictability in the context of a particular child and parent. But the generalizability of these findings must be questioned in relation to understanding how this parent might react with other children, in other contexts, or indeed how other parents with different ideas may act. As already indicated, further questioning of parents regarding their actions may lead to an understanding at a more abstract level. However, the particular ideas in relation to a given child are lost in abstractions, and these may be critical for an adequate understanding of what is going on, or in trying to gain any reasonable level of prediction.

Beyond the method by which the beliefs and values are obtained and the level of abstraction deemed most suitable, consideration must be given to the content of these beliefs and values. Have the methods used in the present study covered a wide enough range of beliefs and values? A more extensive open-ended pilot study might have resulted in the canvassing of a wider section of beliefs as a starting point. In the only other study conducted in this particular area of parental beliefs, Brooks-Gunn (1985) used essentially one belief: whether various masculine and feminine characteristics were more likely to occur in one sex or the other, or equally likely to occur in both sexes. Conceptually this variable would appear to be related to the second belief variable in the present study—the extent to which there are seen to be many versus few differences between boys and girls in a number of interests and personality variables. Beliefs to be examined in the future include the following: the relative importance of biological versus social factors in causing cross-sex behavior, the relative importance of mothers and fathers in influencing the sex-typed characteristics and interests of boys and girls at different ages, and the degree of influence parents feel they have with a particular child. Clearly, it would be useful to have a standard set of belief variables that could be used in a range of different studies.

On another methodological note, it was found that when the importance of biological and social factors with regard to homosexuality were evaluated separately, the two were seen as relatively independent of one another. Thus the construction of bipolar scales running from biological to social can be misleading. Among those in the middle of the scale—indicating that both factors are equally important—there are apparently some who see both factors as very important and some who see neither as important. Clearly, independent assessments of the importance of biological and social factors need to be made.

One of the major findings in the present study was that parental values are important predictors of child-rearing practices, both on their own and in combination with beliefs. It is thus important to explore these values in more detail. The scale used here represents a mixture of items concerning work roles, family roles, and acceptable behaviors for men and women in a range of different situations. Many different topics can be tapped in the area of sex-role attitudes and values: division of labor regarding household chores and child-rearing, rights in divorce and family planning, acceptable sexual practices and dating behavior, and stereotypes of men and women. As these may not all function in a similar way with regard to parental child-rearing practices, it is important to make a systematic study of the various components. In the present study no attempt was made to tap parents' values regarding homosexuality, and this would seem to be important considering the content of the belief variables studied.

One limitation of the present study was that no observations of behavior were made. The problem with relying solely on self-reported behaviors is that they may be more reflective of what parents would like to do or think they ought to do than what they actually do. As such, they may to some extent reflect the parents' values and in so doing serve to inflate correlations with measures specifically aimed at capturing these values. As with any psychological variable, there are limitations to every method of measurement and the ideal situation is one in which each variable is measured in a number of different ways. Observations could clearly help give confidence to the present results. Alternatively, the self-reported behaviors could be backed up with reports by either children or spouses.

Looking Ahead

The study reported here did not look at the final outcome in the model, child variables. There was an implicit assumption that parental behaviors are important in that they have a fairly direct and predictable impact on children. This, of course, is an empirical question worthy of study and not necessarily a valid assumption. Indeed, worth examining is the possibility that parental beliefs and values are translated fairly directly to children in the form of their own beliefs and values, and that parents' behaviors do not represent a useful mediating variable (McGill-icuddy-DeLisi, 1985). Both direct and indirect associations between parents' and children's sex-role beliefs and values need to be studied extensively. In order to do this, it is important to use a wide range of child measures. The standard measures, including toy preferences, knowledge of stereotypes, and self-reported masculinity and femininity, may be far from sufficient to capture the complexities of what is transmitted from parents to children (Huston, 1983). Children's own beliefs and particularly their values need prominent consideration. These along with measures tapping the following concepts have been developed for a major study currently being conducted by Antill, Russell, and Goodnow: preferences for and participation in activities, sports, future occupations, and household chores; satisfaction with one's own sex, desire to be the other sex, similarity in interests and behaviors to children of both sexes.

The processes involved in transmitting sex-role information to children are doubtless numerous, subtle, and complex. By substantially widening the range of these final outcome measures, we hope to increase our chances of capturing some of these complexities. Parents will be asked to comment on their perceived effectiveness as transmitters of sex-role information and the methods they use; and how important they see themselves in relation to the school environment, the media, and peers. The new study once again uses children in middle childhood, but in due course we intend to extend the age range of the sample. Choosing a younger age would possibly increase the importance of parents relative to schools, peers, and the media. However, the range of measures that could be used with such children would be substantially reduced. In order to study the possible longer-term effects of parental sex-role messages, subjects will be followed up in 1.5-2 years. We may find, however, that by early adolescence, peer group influences have swamped the messages that parents have attempted to convey.

On the basis of the current research, I feel there is enough evidence to suggest that the two areas of inquiry that have been brought together—parents' ideas and sex-role socialization—are able to enrich one another through their concurrent investigation. Parents' beliefs and values represent a promising addition to understanding sex-role child-rearing practices, and, it is hoped, the acquisition of sex-role characteristics, interests, and attitudes of children. At the same time, the study of parents' beliefs and values about child development has found a fertile domain in the area of sex differences, sex roles, and sexuality.

NOTES

1. To expand our potential population we allowed a number of families with three children to be included. These were classified on the basis of their first two children except that the two combinations boy-boy-girl and girl-girl-boy were not included in the sample. Their first two children would suggest that they are same-sex families, but the third child changes this classification. If this child is very young, the family will have lived for some time as a same-sex family and recently changed its status. If the child is older, the family will have lived as a mixed-sex family for a more extended period of time. Rather than trying to take this time factor into account, it was decided to omit these two types of families from the sample.

2. Of the eight items, two were viewed as pertinent to both boys and girls and hence were included in both sets of eight items.

3. In terms of religious upbringing, the majority of subjects (86 males, 85 females) fell into one of two groups: Protestant (59 males, 66 females) and Catholic (27 males, 19 females). For present religious preference most (88 males, 85 females) were in three groups: Protestant (37 males, 52 females), Catholic (23 males, 18 females) and none (28 males, 15 females). Other groups were too small to be represented in the analyses.

REFERENCES

Antill, J. K., Cotton, S., & Tindale, S. (1983). Egalitarian or traditional: Correlates of the perception of an ideal marriage. *Australian Journal of Psychology, 35*, 245-257.

Antill, J. K., Cunningham, J. D., Russell, G., & Thompson, N. L. (1981). An Australian sex-role scale. *Australian Journal of Psychology, 33*, 169-183.

Bagnall, A. R. (1981). Labour force status and other characteristics of families—Australia, July, 1980. *Australian Bureau of Statistics*. Canberra.

Baumrind, D. (1982). Are androgynous individuals more effective persons and parents? *Child Development, 53*, 44-75.

Bell, R. Q. (1979). Parent, child and reciprocal influences. *American Psychologist, 34*, 821-826.

Bem, S. L. (1974). The measurement of psychological androgyny. *Journal of Consulting and Clinical Psychology, 42*, 155-162.

Bem, S. L. (1976). Probing the promise of androgyny. In A. G. Kaplan & J. P. Bean (Eds.), *Beyond sex role stereotypes: Readings toward a psychology of androgyny*. Boston: Little, Brown.

Bem, S. L. (1981). Gender schema theory: A cognitive account of sex typing. *Psychological Review, 88*, 354-364.

Block, J. H. (1983). Differential premises arising from differential socialization of the sexes: Some conjectures. *Child Development, 54*, 1335-1354.

Brooks-Gunn, J. (1985). Maternal beliefs about children's sex-typed characteristics as they relate to maternal behavior. In I. E. Sigel (Ed.), *Parental belief systems: The psychological consequences for children*. Hillsdale, NJ: Lawrence Erlbaum.

Bryson, L. (1974). Men's work and women's work: Occupation and family orientation. *Search, 5*, 295-299.

Bryson, L. (1983). Thirty years of research on the division of labour in Australian families. *Australian Journal of Sex, Marriage and Family, 4*, 125-132.

Congalton, A. A. (1969). *Status and prestige in Australia: Studies in Australian society*. Melbourne: Cheshire.

Glezer, H. (1983). *Changes in marriage and sex-role attitudes among young married women: 1971-1982*. Paper presented at Australian Family Research Conference, ANU.

Goodnow, J. J. (1984). Parents' ideas about parenting and development: A review of issues and recent research. In M. Lamb, A. Brown, & B. Rogoff (Eds.), *Advances in developmental psychology* (Vol. 3). Hillsdale, NJ: Lawrence Erlbaum.

Goodnow, J. J. (1985). Change and variation in ideas about childhood and parenting. In I. E. Sigel (Ed.), *Parent belief systems: The psychological consequences for children*. Hillsdale, NJ: Lawrence Erlbaum.

Harré, R., & Secord, P. F. (1972). *The explanation of social behaviour*. Oxford: Blackwell.

Helmreich, R. L., Spence, J. T., & Gibson, R. H. (1982). Sex-role attitudes: 1972-1980. *Personality and Social Psychology Bulletin, 8*, 656-663.

Huston, A. (1983). Sex-typing. In E. M. Hetherington (Ed.), P. H. Mussen (Series Editor), *Handbook of child psychology (Vol. IV): Socialization, personality, and social development*. New York: John Wiley.

Johnson, M. M. (1977). Fathers, mothers and sex typing. In E. M. Hetherington & R. D. Parke (Eds.), *Contemporary readings in child psychology*. New York: McGraw-Hill.

Knight, R. A. (1983). *Parents' beliefs about child development*. Unpublished Ph.D. thesis, Macquarie University.

Mahoney, M. J. (1977). Reflections on the cognitive-learning trend in psycho-therapy. *American Psychologist, 32*, 5-13.

Mason, K. O., Czajka, J. L., & Arber, S. (1976). Changes in women's sex-role attitudes, 1964-1974. *American Sociological Review, 41*, 573-596.

McGillicuddy-DeLisi, A. V. (1985). The relationship between parental beliefs and children's cognitive level. In I. E. Sigel (Ed.), *Parental belief systems: The psychological consequences for children*. Hillsdale, NJ: Lawrence Erlbaum.

Parke, R. D. (1978). Parent-infant interaction: Progress, paradigms and problems. In G. P. Sackett (Ed.), *Observing behavior, I: Theory and applications in mental retardation*. Baltimore, MD: University Park Press.

Rowland, R. (1977). Australian data on the Attitudes Toward Women Scale: Norms, sex differences, reliability. *Australian Psychologist, 12*, 327-331.

Russell, A., & Russell, G. (1985). *Parental explanations of their child-rearing behavior*. Paper presented at the International Society for the Study of Behavioral Development Conference, Tours, France.

Sigel, I. E. (1985). *Parental belief systems: The psychological consequences for children*. Hillsdale, NJ: Lawrence Erlbaum.

Smith, J., & Russell, G. (1984). Why do males and female differ? Children's beliefs about sex differences. *Sex Roles, 11*, 1111-1120.

Spence, J. T., & Helmreich, R. L. (1978). *Masculinity and femininity: Their psychological dimensions, correlates, and antecedents*. Austin: University of Texas Press.

Spence, J. T., Helmreich, R. L., & Stapp, J. (1973). A short version of the Attitudes Toward Women Scale (AWS). *Bulletin of the Psychonomic Society, 2*, 219-220.

Terman, L. M., & Miles, C. C. (1936). *Sex and personality*. New York: McGraw-Hill.

Van Dusen, R. A., & Sheldon, E. B. (1976). The changing status of American women. *American Psychologist, 31*, 106-116.